ETYMOLOGY of COMPENDIUMS of all GODS and The ALMIGHTY CREATOR

Books by Samuel K. Anderson

1. God's Audacity: The Logic of God's Existence.
2. Whispers from My Mother.
3. Etymology of Compendiums of all Gods and The Almighty Creator
4. The Kind Prince and Princess (Children's Book edition)
5. Energetic Vibrating Frequency
6. Ascend to Your Higher Self
7. Ninalem
8. 111 Laws and Proverbs I Wish I Knew Earlier in Life

ETYMOLOGY of COMPENDIUMS of all GODS and The ALMIGHTY CREATOR

It's a collection, compilation, anthology, treasury, digest, synopsis, summation, vade mecum, summa, and epitome of concise yet detailed information about the origin of the original creator(s) of the entire universes and galaxies including earth and its inhabitants.

by

Samuel K. Anderson

Royal Publication
New Jersey, U.S.A

Etymology of Compendiums of all Gods and The Almighty Creator

Copyright © 2024 Samuel K. Anderson.

All rights reserved. No part of this book may be reproduced or used in any manner without written permission of the copyright owner except for the use of quotations in a book review.

Published July 2024

ISBN-13: 979-8-218-41790-1 (Trade Paperback)

Royal Publication

royalpublication@aol.com
Website: SamuelAnderson777.com
Linktree: https://linktr.ee/officialsamuelanderson777
Tiktok: SamuelAnderson777
Instagram: @real_officialsamuelanderson777
Email: SamuelAnderson777@yahoo.com

Etymology of Compendiums of all Gods and The Almighty Creator

This book is fervently dedicated to my children: Serenity, Samuel 2nd, Nana Datu & Maharlika

TABLE OF CONTENTS

CHAPTER 1..Pg 1

Etymology of Compendiums of all Gods and The Almighty Creator.............Pg 1
List of All World Religions...Pg15
King Leopold's Letter to Missionaries in Afraka............................. ....Pg35
The Doctrine of Discovery of 1452 by Pope Nicholas V.........................Pg38
Aboriginal Inventors of Medicine, Technology, Science, etc....................Pg49
Restitution in Reparations and Total Reinstatement...............................Pg58
Manifestations..Pg68

CHAPTER 2...Pg 73

Mathematical and Numerical Relativity of Creation and the Source................Pg73
Numerical Value Keys: Spiritual, Mathematical, Scientific, & Cultural Meaning..Pg81

Mathematical and Numerical Relativity of Creation and the Source
Equation/Formula...Pg95

Numbers & Mathematical Connection to the Akans of Ghana, West Afraka and the
Source (Almighty Creator)...Pg97

CHAPTER 3...Pg 103

The Melanin Connectivity..Pg103
The Real Name of "Africa" & the Gods and Goddesses...........................Pg107
The Fall of the Gods and Goddesses..Pg114
The New World Order (NWO) a.k.a New Testament (NT)........................Pg120
Mansa Musa is King Solomon: Analysis, Concept & Theory......................Pg174
Prophet Mohammad, First Ever Quran & Arab Muslims...........................Pg194
Is Mohammad a Fictional Character?..Pg197
Corruption of Our origin by Christian/Catholic & Arab-Muslim Invaders........Pg206
The term "White People or White Race" is a misnomer............................Pg227
There are no "White People" Genetically and Anatomically.......................Pg227
The aboriginal ancient Kemet/Keme/Egyptians' Identity Revealed................Pg238

Etymology of Compendiums of all Gods and The Almighty Creator

The Adinkra, Adinkra Code's connection to Adinkra and How ancient Kemet/Egypt Fell..Pg256

CHAPTER 4..Pg 267

Almighty Creator's Core...Pg267

The 3 Types of Minds in our Human Body: Throne of Thrones Mind, Mind of Love, and Mind of Health & Well-being..Pg 268-271

Creator's Core: The theory of God's Core...Pg274

The Consciousness & Unconsciousness of Humans..Pg278

Diagrammatic Illustrations about The Theory of God's Core.............................Pg283

CHAPTER 5.. Pg 289

The 4 types of Spiritual Consciousness in Relation to all Gods and the Almighty Creator
Diagrammatic Exhibition of Spiritual Consciousness....................................Pg293

Technology is Physical Manifestation of Spirituality......................................Pg294

Spirituality through Séance, Necromancy, Trance, Lucid Dreams and Astral Projection..Pg300

Proposed Areas for the Jewish Zionist State before their Current Location............Pg311

CHAPTER 6... Pg 317

Spirits, Souls, Living Things and Non-Living Things as Energies....................Pg317
Etymological Diagrammatic Decoding of Money..Pg317

Spirits, Souls, Living Things and Decoding the Codes of Life in 9,6, and 3..........Pg323

The Trinity Expressed in Humanity...Pg335

Torah's Lineage Records Trumps New Testament...Pg342

CHAPTER 7... Pg 350

The Role of Science and Technology Past, Present and Future and the Supreme Energy Future of Robots...Pg350

Examples of Science and Technology Trying to Play God................................Pg359

Archaeological and Geographical Relations to Mankind's Existence...................Pg361

Religious Records and Cultural Accounts of the Almighty Creator....................Pg365

Annunaki, Aliens, UFOs and Extraterrestrial..Pg369

Hall of Amenti Etymologically Decoded...Pg374

Etymology of Compendiums of all Gods and The Almighty Creator

Decoding Ezekiel's Vision of "The Chariot of God"......................................Pg378

Decoding Avatar: The Last AirBender..Pg382

Decoding Captain Planet's Hidden Message..Pg384

Decoding Libation..Pg386

Decoding Moses and The Brass Serpent..Pg388

Inter-dimensional Travel: How To Travel Inter-dimensionally.......................Pg396

Decoding The Creation Story: Genesis 1:1-3...Pg399

Old Testament's Biblical Record on The Birth of Two Nations......................Pg403

Polygamy and The Culture of Afraka...Pg412

The Theory or Concept That America Is Ancient Kemet/Egypt......................Pg418

What is Life?..Pg436

ABOUT THE AUTHOR................................... Pg 449

CHAPTER 1

CHAPTER 1

ETYMOLOGY of COMPENDIUMS of all GODS and The ALMIGHTY CREATOR

Etymology of Compendiums of all Gods and The Almighty Creator is a collection, compilation, anthology, treasury, digest, synopsis, summation, vade mecum, summa, and epitome of concise yet detailed information about the origin of the original creator(s) of the entire universes and galaxies including earth and its inhabitants.

In order to go to heaven you must go through hell. There is no escape. No one can ever go to heaven without first descending to hell. For it is only in going to hell and through hell would you appreciate and recognize heaven when you get there.

The source of everything, Almighty Creator(s), The Most High, Elohim, Nyankoropong, Allah, Buddha, Nature, Medu Neter (divine words/sacred words of the Gods), Guda/Gudah/Gudan (Proto-Germanic etymology of the word "*God*"), Sun and Moon, Brahma, Vishnu, Shiva, Shangdi/Di/Shang-ti (Chinese highest diety/Lord Above), Odomankoma, Chuku Okike, Chineke, Oluwa Olurun, Olokun, and limitless amount of other names of the main creator and other gods and goddesses in various languages, cultures and traditions.

Etymology of Compendiums of all Gods and The Almighty Creator (the source of everything) is deeply rooted in our respective cultures, traditions, languages, spirituality, and all the man-made religions under the sun.

Men and women have always striven throughout history to find their way back home to their source by searching for a God outside of themselves instead of going within to tap into the God-self implanted in them since the time of ancient eons of days. Emanating from eternity to eternity is our soul which rests within our earthly body.

In eons and eons of years, our core source has never changed. We chose to descend to earth. That is, man choosing to be born on earth is to fall from his highest self to his lowest self confined within the earthly body suit, in a quest to find his way back to his higher self in a cyclical format until perfection is attained, in order to return to his original highest self, his source.

This journey on earth is like man and woman on a scavenger hunt to find himself/herself by finding the God-self hidden within him/her.

The secret yet not-so-secret seed planted in every culture, traditions, and man-made religions is that, we are all told that the Almighty Creator lives within us. This is a simple fact that every man and woman will accept, yet, many seem to unconsciously continue to search for the Almighty Creator outside of themselves.

This hint or clue has been planted in all cultures, traditions and religions. So, why do some of us still seem lost, indoctrinated, manipulated and blind-sided to finding the Almighty Creator who precisely lives within each and every one of us including everything in nature?

The word or term God is a title. Etymologically, God means *"to pour"* or *"pour a libation"*. Even the Greeks attest to this etymological fact about the root origin and meaning of the word or term God. The pouring of libation has long been the way most Afrakans pray, communicate, manifest, command things from the spiritual realm into existence within our physical realm.

The original etymological grounds for the concept of the word "God" comes from the Akan Twi word *"Gu"* meaning *"pour"* or *"to pour"*. The original Akan twi phrase is *"Gu Nsa"* meaning *"pour a drink"*, *"pour/summon via drink"*, *"to summon through pouring of a drink offering"* or popularly known as *"libation/ to pour libation"*.

This etymology was corrupted by Proto-Germanic people as *"Gu Da" /Gu-dda"* which later became *"Guud"*. It was then corrupted further to *"Good"* due to mistranslation and cultural misappropriations due to invasions and occupation of aboriginal lands by new breed of invaders. Fast forward, it became *"Good"*, then *"Got"*, then eventually *"G-d"*, and *"God"*.

The only true form of communication (corrupted as prayer) to/with your "God" is libation. The new testament bible "God" emphasized the indisputable importance of libation by requiring the blood offering/libation/sacrifice of *"His only begotten son, "Jesus"*. The trillion dollar question is, who did the new testament bible "God" poured the blood sacrifice/libation/offering of his son, "Jesus" to/for? Who was he summoning? Who was he "forgiving" or pacifying" of "sin" from? If it wasn't for himself then who was it for?

Let's look at another etymology of the word *"God"* according to the Afa divination and cosmology. The Afa divination cosmology of today's West Afraka, namely the Ewe people of Ghana, Dahomey, and Yuroba precedes the Proto-Germanic language. According to the Afa divination cosmology, Gu- is *the Sun, sun rise, day energy, creative substance, the "creative seed", father-masculine figure*. Da- is the Moon, when the sun set, night illumination, mother-feminine figure, nurturer, everything grows or germinates in the dark or at night during the moon's energy.

Together, the Afa divination cosmology have "Gu-Da", that is "Sun-Moon" in the modern-day English language. This concept was erroneously adopted by the new breed Europeans. They mistranslated its meaning due to their lack of comprehension of the original Afa divination's meaning to it. Catholics/Christians adopted the *Gu* (Sun, halo, male energy) into their bible and symbols as the Muslims accepted the *Da* (Moon, crescent moon, female energy) symbols. The sun and moon symbols are obvious in both religious groups. Catholics/Christians and Islam display the sun and moon symbols in their churches and mosques.

This etymology does not define the Almighty Creator, because the Almighty Creator can not be put in a box. For the sake of innerstanding and overstanding, the word God used in this book represents the various cultural and linguistic acceptance of what "a God" is to them. That is that, nothing more and nothing less. The almighty creative force of everything in existence known and unknown to men and women is not the same as the word "God".
The etymology of the word "God" is merely a misnomer which was strongly misunderstood and mistranslated by the Greeks, Romans, Arabs and the new breed of Proto-Germanic Europeans.

Eradicate any form of religious indoctrination in order to properly comprehend the information covered in this book. Emancipate your soul, spirit and mind from all the religious dogma that has been intoxicated into you over the years.

You were born free and physically naked with no religion or indoctrination. The Almighty Creator perfected you with everything you need for your journey on this earthly realm. Be it physically, spiritually or soulfully. The type of community, culture, family and man-made religion you are born into determines the kind of religion you are indoctrinated into in this corrupt world.

The Almighty Creator has no religion and never instituted any religion, rather created you in the image of the *Almighty Creative force*. Men and women in their own impulsive ways established religion, based on what they think is right and wrong or good and evil. All religion being man-made then becomes flawed when projected to different geographical and geological locations, cultures and traditions.

We are all different in our own unique way. So, freeing yourself from all forms of religious organizations draws you closer to the true source of everything, the Almighty Creator.

The Almighty Creator is a spirit, an energy, unseen and definitely genderless. Everything within and outside both the seen and unseen universe is emanated in pairs. Hence, there is an emanation of both positive and negative energy, male and female essence of all supreme energy merged together as one unit and within that unit is genderless.

However, in its expression of various manifestations in different dimensional frequencies exhibits that polarity of male and female energy. This is the source of everything, the all in all, the Almighty Creator. The Almighty Creator can manifest itself/Himself/Herself as anything and anyone solely to the discretion of the Almighty Creator.

You should be interested to know that you are a direct and full manifestation of the Almighty Creator. Spirit is breath, spirituality is breathing. Breath is the air you breathe in and expel from your lungs.

Learning to properly breathe can shape your mind, body and soul to accomplish even what is known to some humans as unthinkable. There is science behind breathing. All the organs and cells within your body uses the air that you take in before you exhale. The mechanism behind breathing is far deeper than what science has so far been able to comprehend.

You are a daily example of the existence of the Almighty Creator. Your breath is your spirit's spirituality. Your spirit returns back to the cyclical energy that operates everything (The All in All, The Oneness), which is known by all as the Almighty Creator. The Hebrew word *Ruah* directly means breath or spirit. Go to your own language, what is the word for breath? That is the meaning of spirit. Spirituality is as simple as your very existence.

The Almighty Creator never complicated this very important aspect of our existence. You and I are all breathing that is why we are considered living beings. Once you stop breathing, you are no more present in a physical state but has been transformed to the likeness of the Almighty Creator; which is a spirit, an energy, that which is eternal without a physical form.

To say spirituality is not important in your life is to say that breathing is not important to your life. To not be into spirituality is to not be into breathing. To not know about spirituality is definitely to not know about the importance of breathing in your life.

You are basically a "walking dead" person if you are completely disconnected from spirituality. The simplistic meaning and definition of spirituality is simply breath, breathing. You are either consciously or unconsciously spiritual. It is better to be living in a conscious spirituality than unconscious spirituality. We will delve deeper into the connection of the Almighty Creator and spirit as well as spirituality in few chapters to come.

I hope that you know where you are heading in this universe. In order for you to know where you are heading, you must know how you got here and your origin prior to your physical birth. Knowing your origin prior to your earthly birth would help you to know your destination after your time here on earth expires.

The keyword used here is *"know/knowing"* not the typical "believe" or "I think" as many so called religiously indoctrinated people typically use. You must know why you are here on earth, how you got here, what you are supposed to do here, how you should do it and finally where you go from here. Open all your portals and be ready to enjoy all the chapters in this book.

Decolonize your mind from all the deception pushed onto you by the various religious groups. Most of the so called popular Abrahamic religions (Judaism, Christianity and Muslim/Islam) started as propaganda and militarized global coup detat that literally overthrew many kingdoms and domains throughout the entire planet. This is a historical fact. Many aboriginals globally were forced into these Abrahamic religions (Judaism, Christianity and Muslim/Islam) unwillingly.

Many more lost their lives as they resisted. We will massively tackle the global militarized coup detat of the Abrahamic religions (Judaism, Christianity and Muslim/Islam) topic in chapter 3.

The bible for example has a man made copyright. If the bible is copyrighted by any man or institution then that is clearly not the direct words of the Almighty Creator. In the same light, if the Quran or any of the major religious organization's main books have copyrights owned by man, woman or any institution then clearly that's not the words of the Almighty Creator.

In that, no man, woman or any institution can rightfully own the copyrights of the words that are supposed to directly come from the Almighty Creator. I have rightfully registered the copyrights of this book because this book is my work and intellectual property. All those religious books out there (the bible, Quran, etc) are all books written by humans. The Almighty Creator never wrote any religious book(s). When we write down our interactions within these nine dimensions and publish it virtually or in print form; we then become accountable or "rightful copyrighted owners" of our work, whatsoever it may be.

Look at nature and you will see the expressions and manifestations of the Almighty Creator. That's that, anything else is our own conviction and communication of how we perceive, receive and interpret things from our interactions with all the nine dimensions. This earth is one of the nine dimensions. We can only receive, perceive and interpret our frequencies based on how high or low we ascend in frequencies. The ideology of nothing is free is a huge fallacy, because everything under the sun and within the universe is free. Greedy bastards and frugal soulless people have wickedly hijacked almost everything on earth making it costly for people to live the beautiful life that the Almighty Creator manifested. Permit me to simplify the point I am making in a more simplistic manner:

Without nature, I am nothing.

Without me, nature is nothing.

I am nature itself.

Nature is inherently me.

Nature and I are one in all existence.

Nature is not just plants, sun, water, and animals but everything in existence both seen and unseen has its nature nurtured within nature.

Etymology of Compendiums of all Gods and The Almighty Creator

The nature of everything is within nature.

Overstanding and innerstanding nature is knowing the true energy source behind everything.

That true energy source behind everything is where everything came into existence both animate and inanimate nature including you and I.

That nature is the Almighty Creator's expression of self in different ways.

Nature then is the only way to connect with the one and only true source.

Christianity and Catholicism are based off of human sacrifice, blood drinking and flesh eating rituals. These rituals are practiced as red wine (or wine) representing the blood of their sacrificed "man-god/God" and the bread (or biscuits) used in their rituals represent the body of that "man-god/God" they sacrificed. Regardless of how you look at it, a human sacrifice is a human sacrifice and the core ritual of a sacrifice is the same regardless of who is exercising it. This is an alchemy practice unbeknownst to many.

Those who innerstand rituals know that all the symbols and signs of dark ritualism are there for you to see in this Christian and Catholicism rituals. Many Christians and Catholics are not even aware of the rituals they practice. It's like most of them are psychologically blind and either follow things in their man-made religion with full gullibility or unconsciously asleep.

The *Sinai Bible* states that Jesus was never crucified as widely believed by mostly Catholics and all Christians. On top of it all, this bible also states that Jesus was not God's son. The *Sinai Bible* was discovered in 2000, it is kept at a secret place in *Ankara's Ethnography Museum*.

This *Sinai bible* contains the book called the gospel of Jesus' disciple Barnabas *(The Gospel of Barnabas)*. This bible also states that Apostle Paul was nothing but an impostor defrauding the masses.

It states that it was rather *Judas Iscariot* who was crucified while the acclaimed Jesus was beamed up alive in full flesh. Within this book, it is stated that Jesus foretold the birth of Prophet Mohammad, who is collectively accepted by many religious groups and academia as the founder of Islam. The indisputable interesting fact is that, all so-called world renowned religious leaders and experts supposedly accept this book *(Sinai Bible)* to be authentic. The *Sinai Bible* was written in Aramaic in gold letters/lettering.

The Vatican is obviously shock by this finding. It is time for the Christian world to wake up both consciously and spiritually to reconnect with their ancestral roots, cultures and traditions found within their respective languages. You can get this old book/bible *(Sinai Bible)* for a whooping $30 million and up.

It has been in the works of the church of England and other big churches to change the gender of the God in the bible to gender neutral, or better yet, attempting to say that the God in the bible is basically *"gay"*. This is due to all the new age push for gender neutrality among predominantly western countries and some parts of the Asian continent. This is interestingly the new age wave of the western countries, yet again almost forcefully shoving themselves into the various civilized first nations (original melanated people of earth) cultures and other nations around the world.

Now, if that version of Abrahamic religion, in this case, Catholic/Christianity was truly ordained by the Almighty Creator then why is the church of England seriously attempting to change the gender of their God in the helios biblios (sun book a.k.a bible)? Did their God forget to tell them about his/her/its gender?

These "white western churches" are also pushing to remove the phrase "Our Father" from the bible because they apparently see that as discrimination towards the LGBTQ+ community. Didn't the helios biblios (sun book a.k.a bible) states that "do not add and do not take away from the prophesy and commandment"? These are the verses from the helios biblios (sun book a.k.a bible) that says just that:

Revelation 22:19 *"And if any man shall take away from the words of the book of this prophecy, God shall take away his part out of the book of life, and out of the holy city, and from the things which are written in this book."*

Deuteronomy 4:2 *"Ye shall not add unto the word which I command you, neither shall ye diminish ought from it, that ye may keep the commandments of the LORD your God which I command you."*

Deuteronomy 12:32-*What thing soever I command you, observe to do it: thou shalt not add thereto, nor diminish from it.*

Revelation 22:18-*For I testify unto every man that heareth the words of the prophecy of this book, If any man shall add unto* *these things, God shall add unto him the plagues that are written in this book:*

The Pope spoke about changing the so-called "the lord's prayer" in the helios biblios (sun book a.k.a bible) because the Pope feels that the God of that bible does not lead people into temptation. However, the current bible's lord's prayer has a phrase that clearly states that the God of the bible leads his/hers/its people into temptation in *Mathew 6:9-13, Luke 11:1-13* "……*and lead us not into temptation*". Now, with the above verses directly referenced from the helios biblios (sun book a.k.a bible) would you still insist that the Abrahamic Christianity helios biblios (sun book a.k.a bible) directly came from the Almighty Creator? I have to say with all due respect to both the church of England and the Pope that when anyone apply common sense, you can clearly see that all these Abrahamic religions and their books of doctrines are all man made.

The helios biblios (sun book a.k.a bible), Torah, Quran and all the other religious books are man made printed into circulation by man made printers. Western men, women and institutions own the copyrights to these printed bibles. This is a clear indication that the bible, Quran and all other religious texts printed are all man-made and solely manipulated by humans with a political motive to control and rule over you.

Dare to look into how all of the respective Abrahamic religions started. You will find out that all of them murdered millions if not billions in order to push their new found religion and military agenda through so called "holly wars". Fast forward to today and you would see some people who were among first nations (aboriginal melanated people of earth) who have thrown away their original form of spirituality for these newly established Abrahamic religions.

All these books (bible, quran, and all religious texts) have been translated into different languages by men and in some cases women using their cultural influence and biases to push indoctrination onto the global masses.

Aramaic, Hebrew, Arabic and Greek are all newly manufactured languages that do not predate ancient Kemet/ancient Egypt and other great ancient Afrakan languages and civilizations. Kemet/ancient Egypt for example has been around for well over 800,000 years and probably much older. The language Arabic was established around 7th century BC. Prior to Arabic, there was Aramaic, Arabic supplanted Aramaic. Aramaic was established around 6th century BC.

The Hebrew language was formed by some folks around 10th century BC. Look at these time frames and timelines of these languages directly linked to the Abrahamic religions (Judaism, Christianity and Muslim/Islam etc). You can easily attest to the fact that these languages are very new comparable to the ancient Afrakan civilizations like Kemet/ancient Egypt, Dogons from Sirius A star system, Nubia and other great ancient Afrakan civilizations.

Let me show you with the charts displayed below, the date of establishment of all the world religions known to mankind.

Etymology of Compendiums of all Gods and The Almighty Creator

Traditional founder	Religious tradition founded	Historical founder(s)	Life of historical founder
No single Founder (Hinduism) Indra (Vedic Hinduism)	Hinduism	The Saptarishi	c. 15th century BC to 10th century BC
Abraham (covenant with God) Moses (religious law)	Judaism	Yahwists[n 1]	c. 13th to 8th century BC
Laozi	Taoism	Zhuang Zhou	369 BC – 286 BC

Ancient (before AD 500)

Founder Name	Religious tradition founded	Life of founder
Akhenaten	Atenism	c. 1353 BC – 1336 BC
Zoroaster	Zoroastrianism	c. 1000 BC
Parshvanatha	The penultimate (23rd) Tirthankara in Jainism	877 BC – 777 BC
Numa Pompilius	Roman Religion	c. 753 BC – 672 BC
Nebuchadnezzar II	built the Etemenanki, established Marduk as the patron deity of Babylon	c. 634 BC – 562 BC[citation

Etymology of Compendiums of all Gods and The Almighty Creator

Founder Name	Religious tradition founded	Life of founder
		needed]
Ajita Kesakambali	Charvaka	6th century BC
Mahavira	The final (24th) tirthankara in Jainism	599 BC – 527 BC
Gautama Buddha	Buddhism	563 BC – 483 BC
Confucius	Confucianism	551 BC – 479 BC
Pythagoras	Pythagoreanism	fl. 520 BC
Mozi	Mohism	470 BC – 390 BC
Makkhali Gosala	Ājīvika	5th century BC
Ezra	Second Temple Judaism[22]	fl. 459 BC
Epicurus	Epicureanism	fl. 307 BC
Zeno of Citium	Stoicism	333 BC – 264 BC
Pharnavaz I of Iberia	Armazi	326 BC – 234 BC
Valmiki	Valmikism	c. 3rd century BC

Founder Name	Religious tradition founded	Life of founder
Patanjali	Rāja yoga sect of Hinduism	2nd century BC
Jesus (and the Twelve Apostles)	Christianity	c. 4 BC – c. 30/33 AD
Paul the Apostle	Pauline Christianity	c. 33 AD
James the Just	Jewish Christianity	c. 33 AD
Lakulisha	Pashupata Shaivism sect of Hinduism	1st century AD
Judah the Prince	Rabbinic Judaism	2nd century AD
Montanus	Montanism	2nd century AD
Marcion of Sinope	Marcionism	110–160
Nagarjuna	Madhyamaka	150–250
Plotinus	Neoplatonism	205–270
Mani	Manichaeism	216–274
Arius[n 4]	Arianism[n 5]	250–336
Pelagius[n 4]	Pelagianism[n 6]	354–430
Nestorius[n 4]	Nestorianism[n 7]	386–451

Etymology of Compendiums of all Gods and The Almighty Creator

Founder Name	Religious tradition founded	Life of founder
Eutyches	Monophysitism[n 8]	380–456

Medieval to Early Modern (500–1800 AD)

Name	Religious tradition founded	Life of founder
Mazdak	Mazdakism	died c. 526
Bodhidharma	Zen, more specifically Ch'an	5th or 6th century
Muhammad	Islam	c. 570–632
Songtsen Gampo	Tibetan Buddhism	7th century
En no Gyōja	Shugendō	late 7th century
Huineng	East Asian Zen Buddhism	638–713
Padmasambhava	Nyingma	8th century
Han Yu	Neo-Confucianism	8th or 9th century
Saichō	Tendai (descended from Tiantai)	767–822
Kūkai	Shingon Buddhism	774–835
Adi Shankara	Advaita Vedanta	788–820

Etymology of Compendiums of all Gods and The Almighty Creator

Name	Religious tradition founded	Life of founder
Ibn Nusayr	Nusayrism	late 9th century
Matsyendranath	Nath	10th century
Ramanuja	Vishishtadvaita	1017–1137
Great Peacemaker	Great Law of Peace	Between the 10th and 15th centuries
Hamza ibn 'Alī ibn Aḥmad[24]	Druze	11th century
Sheikh Adi ibn Musafir	Yazidism	12th century
Basava	Lingayatism	12th century
Hōnen	Jōdo-shū (descended from Pure Land Buddhism)	1131–1212
Eisai	Rinzai Zen (descended from the Linji school)	1141–1215
Shinran	Jōdo Shinshū (descended from Jōdo-shū)	1173–1263
Dōgen	Sōtō Zen (descended from	1200–1253

Etymology of Compendiums of all Gods and The Almighty Creator

Name	Religious tradition founded	Life of founder
	the Caodong school)	
Haji Bektash Veli	Bektashi Order of Sufism	1209–1271
Nichiren	Nichiren Buddhism	1222–1282
Abraham Abulafia	Prophetic Kabbalah, a.k.a. ecstatic Kabbalah	1240–1290s
Dyaneshwar	Varkari	1275–1296
Madhvacharya	Dvaita	1238–1317
John Wycliffe	Lollardy	1320s–1384
Fażlu l-Lāh Astar-Ābādī	Hurufism	14th century
Mahmoud Pasikhani	Nuqṭawism	late 14th century
Jan Hus	Hussitism	1372–1415
Tlacaelel	Cult of Huitzilopochtli	1397–1487
Ramananda	Ramanandi Vaishnavism	15th century
Kabir	Kabir Panth	1398–1448
Pachacuti	Cult of Inti	1418–1472
Sankardev	Ekasarana Dharma	1449–1568

Etymology of Compendiums of all Gods and The Almighty Creator

Name	Religious tradition founded	Life of founder
Ravidas	Ravidassia	c. 1450–1520
Guru Nanak	Sikhism, Nanak Panth	1469–1539
Sri Chand	Udasi	1494–1629
Vallabha Acharya	Shuddhadvaita	1479–1531
Martin Luther	Lutheranism and Protestantism in general	1483–1546
Chaitanya Mahaprabhu	Gaudiya Vaishnavism, Achintya Bheda Abheda	1486–1534
Thomas Cranmer	Anglicanism (Church of England)	1489–1556
Menno Simons	Mennonite	1496–1561
Conrad Grebel	Swiss Brethren, Anabaptists	1498–1526
Jacob Hutter	Hutterite	1500–1536
Isaac Luria	Lurianic Kabbalah	1534–1572
Guru Angad	Sikhism	1539–1552
Sultan Sahak	Yarsanism	early 15th century
Guru Amar Das	Sikhism	1552–1572

Etymology of Compendiums of all Gods and The Almighty Creator

Name	Religious tradition founded	Life of founder
John Calvin	Calvinism[25]	1509–1564
Michael Servetus[26]	Unitarianism	1511?–1553
John Knox[27]	Presbyterianism	1510–1572
Guru Ram Das	Sikhism	1574–1581
Akbar	Din-i Ilahi	1542–1605
Jacobus Arminius	Arminianism	1560–1609
John Smyth[28]	Baptists	1570–1612
Guru Arjan	Sikhism	1571–1606
Guru HarGobind Sahib Ji	Sikhism	1606–1644
Avvakum[citation needed]	Old Believers of Russian Orthodox Church	1620–1682
Guru Tegh Bahadur Ji	Sikhism	1621–1675
George Fox[29]	Quakers	1624–1691
Philipp Spener[30]	Pietism	1635–1705
Guru Har Rai Ji	Sikhism	1644–1661
Jakob Ammann	Amish	1656–1730

Name	Religious tradition founded	Life of founder
Guru Har Krishan Ji	Sikhism	1661–1664
Guru Gobind Singh	Sikhism, Khalsa Panth	1666–1708
Emanuel Swedenborg	The New Church	1688–1772
Yisroel ben Eliezer "Baal Shem Tov"[31]	Hasidic Judaism	1698–1760
John Wesley, [32] Charles Wesley, George Whitefield	Methodism	1703–1791
Muhammad Ibn Abd al-Wahhab	Wahhabism	1703–1792
Ann Lee[33]	Shakers	1736–1784

New religious movements (post-1800)

Further information: List of new religious movements

Name	Religious tradition founded	Life of founder
Shaykh Ahmad al-Ahsá'í	Shaykhism, precursor of Bábism	1753–1826
Ram Mohan Roy	Brahmo Samaj	1772–1833
Swaminarayan	Swaminarayan Sampraday	1781–1830

Etymology of Compendiums of all Gods and The Almighty Creator

Name	Religious tradition founded	Life of founder
Auguste Comte	Religion of Humanity	1798–1857
Nakayama Miki	Tenrikyo	1798–1887
Ignaz von Döllinger	Old Catholic Church	1799–1890
Phineas Quimby	New Thought	1802–1866
Allan Kardec	Spiritism	1804–1869
Joseph Smith	Mormonism, also known as the Latter Day Saint movement	1805–1844
John Thomas	Christadelphians	1805–1871
Abraham Geiger	Reform Judaism	1810–1874
Jamgon Kongtrul	Rimé movement	1813–1899
Hong Xiuquan	Taiping Christianity	1814–1864
Bahá'u'lláh[38]	Bahá'í Faith	1817–1892
Báb	Bábism, precursor of the Bahá'í Faith	1819–1850
James Springer White	Seventh-day Adventist Church	1821–1881
Wang Jueyi	Yiguandao	1821–1884

Name	Religious tradition founded	Life of founder
Mary Baker Eddy[39]	Christian Science	1821–1910
Ramalinga Swamigal	Samarasa Sutha Sanmarga Sangam	1823–1874
Dayananda Saraswati	Arya Samaj	1824–1883
Ellen G. White[40]	Seventh-day Adventist Church	1827–1915
John Ballou Newbrough	Faithism	1828–1891
Helena Blavatsky	Theosophy	1831–1891
Ayya Vaikundar	Ayyavazhi	1833–1851
Mirza Ghulam Ahmad	Ahmadiyya	1835–1908
Guido von List	Armanism (Germanic mysticism)	1848–1919
Charles Taze Russell[41]	Bible Student movement	1852–1916
Wovoka	Ghost Dance	1856–1932
Rudolf Steiner	Anthroposophy	1861–1925
Swami Vivekananda	Ramakrishna Mission	1863–1902
William Irvine[42]	Two by Twos and Cooneyites	1863–1947

Etymology of Compendiums of all Gods and The Almighty Creator

Name	Religious tradition founded	Life of founder
Max Heindel	The Rosicrucian Fellowship	1865–1919
Tsunesaburo Makiguchi	Soka Gakkai	1871–1944
Sri Aurobindo	Integral yoga	1872–1950
Mason Remey	Orthodox Bahá'í Faith	1874–1974
Aleister Crowley	Thelema	1875–1947
Charles Fox Parham	Pentecostalism	1873–1929
"Father Divine"	International Peace Mission movement	c. 1876–1965
Edgar Cayce	Association for Research and Enlightenment	1877–1945
Ngô Văn Chiêu	Caodaism	1878–1926
Guy Ballard	"I AM" Activity	1878–1939
Frank Buchman	Oxford Group/Moral Re-Armament	1878–1961
Alfred G. Moses	Jewish Science	1878–1956
John Slocum	Indian Shaker Church	1881
Mordecai Kaplan	Reconstructionist Judaism	1881–1983

Etymology of Compendiums of all Gods and The Almighty Creator

Name	Religious tradition founded	Life of founder
Gerald Gardner	Wicca	1884–1964
Felix Manalo	Iglesia ni Cristo (Church of Christ)	1886–1963
Frank B. Robinson	Psychiana	1886–1948
Noble Drew Ali	Moorish Science Temple of America	1886–1929
Marcus Garvey	Rastafari	1887–1940
Ernest Holmes	Religious Science	1887–1960
Sadafaldeo	Vihangamyoga	1888–1954
Aimee Semple McPherson[43]	Foursquare Church	1890–1944
Zélio Fernandino de Moraes[44]	Umbanda	1891–1975
Ida B. Robinson	Mount Sinai Holy Church of America	1891–1946
B. R. Ambedkar	Navayana Buddhism	1891–1956
Wallace Fard Muhammad	Nation of Islam	1891–1934 (absentia)
Paramahansa	Yogoda Satsanga Society of	1893–1952

Etymology of Compendiums of all Gods and The Almighty Creator

Name	Religious tradition founded	Life of founder
Yogananda	India, Self-Realization Fellowship	
A. C. Bhaktivedanta Swami Prabhupada	International Society for Krishna Consciousness	1896–1977
Ruth Norman	Unarius	1900–1993
Swami Muktananda	Siddha Yoga	1908–1982
Paul Twitchell	Eckankar	1908–1971
Ikurō Teshima	Makuya	1910–1973
L. Ron Hubbard	Dianetics and Scientology	1911–1986
Chinmayananda Saraswati	Chinmaya Mission	1916–1993
Maharishi Mahesh Yogi	Transcendental Meditation	1918–2008
Samael Aun Weor	Universal Christian Gnostic Movement	1917–1977
Mark L. Prophet	The Summit Lighthouse	1918–1973
Ben Klassen	Creativity	1918–1993
Ahn Sahng-hong	World Mission Society Church of God	1918–1985
Huỳnh Phú Sổ	Hòa Hảo	1919–1947

Etymology of Compendiums of all Gods and The Almighty Creator

Name	Religious tradition founded	Life of founder
Sheikh Mujibur Rahman	Mujibism	1920–1975
Yong (Sun) Myung Moon[45]	Unification Church	1920–2012
Prabhat Ranjan Sarkar	Ananda Marga	1921–1990
Clarence 13X	Five-Percent Nation	1922–1969
Mestre Gabriel	União do Vegetal	1922–1971
Nirmala Srivastava	Sahaja Yoga	1923–2011
Sveinbjörn Beinteinsson	Ásatrú	1924–1993
Sathya Sai Baba	Sathya Sai Organization	1926–2011
Anton LaVey	Church of Satan (LaVeyan Satanism)	1930–1997
Rajneesh[46]	Rajneesh movement	1931–1990
Mark L. Prophet; Elizabeth Clare Prophet[47]	Church Universal and Triumphant	1918–1973; 1939–2009
Adi Da	Adidam	1939–2008
Claude Vorilhon	Raëlism	1946–

Etymology of Compendiums of all Gods and The Almighty Creator

Name	Religious tradition founded	Life of founder
Marshall Vian Summers	New Message from God	1949–
Li Hongzhi	Falun Gong	born 1951 or 1952
Ryuho Okawa	Happy Science	1956–2023
Vissarion	Church of the Last Testament	1961–
Chris Korda	Church of Euthanasia	1962–
Tamara Siuda	Kemetic Orthodoxy	1969–
Olumba Olumba Obu	Brotherhood of the Cross and Star	1918–
Isak Gerson	Missionary Church of Kopimism	1993–
Bobby Henderson	Church of the Flying Spaghetti Monster[48] or Pastafarianism	1980–
Erdoğan Çınar	Ishikism	21st century

Source for table: https://en.wikipedia.org/wiki/List_of_founders_of_religious_traditions

Therefore, if the desire is to find the actual Almighty Creator and all the various Gods and Goddesses, then these new languages: Aramaic, Hebrew, Arabic and Greek are not where you should be looking. The Hebrew language is not even an original language, some of its etymology is from the ancient Afrakan tribes with which most of them migrated to today's West Afraka.

As you study or read through the chapters of this book, you will learn to enhance your ability to think critically. Learn from your past experiences and years of religious indoctrination. Exercise informed decisions, plan to persevere to research things you do not overstand at the moment, and apply prior knowledge and wisdom. Carefully interpret information presented, make connections with yourself and nature. Discover patterns, envision solutions and ability to explain them clearly. You must be precise, concise, and strategically analyze all the information presented to you in this book. Allow yourself to think freely without fear, favor, or dogmatic restrictions.

It is known that the first published *King James bible* was in 1611, that is the 16th century which is very recent compared to the first nations who were already in their civilized kingdoms before christian inquisitions and colonization began. The *Gutenberg bible,* printed in 1455 in Mainz by Johann Gutenberg, Johann Fust and Peter Schoeffer is also recent.

William Tyndale, who existed around 1494-1536 is said to have translated the *New Testament* from the original Greek, printed it around 1526. William Tyndale's 1530 bible's translation introduced *"JeHoVaH"* as the replacement word for *God* in the first five (5) books of the old testament bible. If Moses truly authored the first five books of the bible, then Tyndale is clearly telling Moses to kick rocks for not knowing the true name of the "bible God". How ironic is that? Just despicably unbelievable. 1611 King James' version of the bible also absorbed Tyndale's new name for the bible God. Initially, a group known as the *Masorettes* came up with "YeHoWaH" around 5th, 6th or 7th century era. The Canaanite's had YHWH as one of their gods several centuries before any group in the bible came into contact with that word. Hypothetically, if we are all to accept the supposed bible God as the supreme creator of everything, then that means, the bible God created bad people. The bible God also purposefully created murderers, war-mongers, the destroyer who destroys, and wicked people. For the biblical nomads, kindly read the following bible verses:

Isaiah 45:5-7 says "... I create evil: I the Lord do all these things"

Isaiah 54:16 says "...I have created the waster/destroyer to destroy"

Proverbs 16:4 says "The Lord hath made all things for himself: yea, even the wicked for the day of evil.

Taking all things into consideration, no one should be going to that mythical hell created by the westerners. In that, per the verses read above, the bible God is creating and making up evil, sin, wicked, murderers, prostitutes, literally all the good and evil things solely for *His* pleasure. So, if the bible is to be "the true words of God", then everyone is innocent, free and actually just being manipulated, enslaved and toyed with without any free will.

Additionally, per *Isaiah 46:9-10,* the bible God proclaim that he knows the end from the beginning: *"I make known the end from the beginning, from ancient times, what is still to come."NIV.*

This is called, predestination. That is, before anyone was born, the bible God had already written your story from the end to your beginning. This then indicates that, free will according to the bible is merely a mirage, hallucination. Read other bible verses below about predestination to quench your thirst; *Romans 8: 29-30, Ephesians 1: 3-6, Romans 9:20-23, Jeremiah 1:5, Ephesians 1:11.*

Around 301-304 A.D, It is recorded in history that, Diocletian, the Roman Emperor is said to have burned several hundred thousands of bibles.

Diocletian apparently commanded his delegates that all copies of bibles must effectively be destroyed. He also went on to decree that any home with a bible must be burned down completely. This is the story of Rome and has nothing to do with the glorious first civilized nations who were living their peaceful lives in Afraka, Asia, Oceania, North America, Antarctica, South America, and Europe.

The first nations existed far before the so called B.C. (Before Christ) era, this type of time keeping is an influence of Rome a.k.a colonial influence. All the first nations (aboriginal chocolate melanated people of earth) have their own respective calendars, Gods, Goddesses, traditions, cultures and spirituality. Even in the bible, it clearly states that every nation on earth has its own Gods/gods (Micah 4:5 *"All the nations may walk in the name of their own Gods/gods..."*).

It is a clear fact to state that, China has Taoism. Taoism expounds beautifully that humans and animals should live in balance with the *Tao* a.k.a the universe. Japan has Shinto, a belief in sacred power *kami* in both animate and inanimate things and the worship of ancestors and nature spirits. Arabs have their moon symbolized Allah in Islam. India has Hinduism, the believe in a main God Brahma and other gods and goddesses. Romans/Rome have Jesus a.k.a Iesus a.k.a Zeus. Some of the Afrakan nations and rest of the first nations have their own amazing traditional cultures and spirituality.

Dharmic religions namely, Hinduism, Buddhism, Jainism and Sikhism do not teach about a monotheistic god/God like the Abrahamic religions. Abrahamic religions seek to use bully, fear mongering and bloody murderous wars to impose their brittle believes on the masses.

Sadly, most of the first nations on the great continent of Afraka deem their own cultures, spirituality, traditions, local knowledge and wisdom as demonic or evil, unequivocally due to colonization. Majority of Afrakans heartbreakingly cherish foreign gods, bibles, qurans, and other foreign practices as pure, truth and righteous over their own precious purest cultures and spirituality.

This is the saddest thing that has ever happened to the original people of earth. Similar dilemma is found in North America (almost all aboriginals wiped out), South America and most of the Asian countries.

The root cause of this was a result of the forced and brutally heartless massacre push of the bible and quran down the throats of the original people of this earth.

Before I give a historical evidence to the root cause raised that led to the current deception of almost the entire earth concerning who the true Almighty Creator is, let's quickly read this letter from King Leopold II. King Leopold II was a Belgium king who sent a letter to the missionaries positioned in Afraka on how to use Christianity to destroy the already civilized, cultured and lovingly welcoming Afrakans and their way of life.

Letter was written around 1883 and it reads:

"Reverends, Fathers and Dear Compatriots: The task that is given to fulfill is very delicate and requires much tact. You will go certainly to evangelize, but your evangelization must inspire above all Belgium interests. Your principal objective in our mission in the Congo is never to teach the niggers to know God, this they know already. They speak and submit to a Mungu, one Nzambi, one Nzakomba, and what else I don't know. They know that to kill, to sleep with someone else's wife, to lie and to insult is bad. Have courage to admit it; you are not going to teach them what they know already. Your essential role is to facilitate the task of administrators and industrials, which means you will go to interpret the gospel in the way it will be the best to protect your interests in that part of the world. For these things, you have to keep watch on disinteresting our savages from the richness that is plenty [in their underground. To avoid that, they get interested in it, and make you murderous] competition and dream one day to overthrow you.

Your knowledge of the gospel will allow you to find texts ordering, and encouraging your followers to love poverty, like "Happier are the poor because they will inherit the heaven" and, "It's very difficult for the rich to enter the kingdom of God." You have to detach from them and make them disrespect everything which gives courage to affront us. I make reference to their Mystic System and their war fetish – warfare protection – which they pretend not to want to abandon, and you must do everything in your power to make it disappear.

Your action will be directed essentially to the younger ones, for they won't revolt when the recommendation of the priest is contradictory to their parent's teachings. The children have to learn to obey what the missionary recommends, who is the father of their soul. You must singularly insist on their total submission and obedience, avoid developing the spirit in the schools, teach students to read and not to reason. There, dear patriots, are some of the principles that you must apply. You will find many other books, which will be given to you at the end of this conference. Evangelize the niggers so that they stay forever in submission to the white colonialists, so they never revolt against the restraints they are undergoing. Recite every day – "Happy are those who are weeping because the kingdom of God is for them."

Convert always the blacks by using the whip. Keep their women in nine months of submission to work freely for us. Force them to pay you in sign of recognition-goats, chicken or eggs-every time you visit their villages. And make sure that niggers never become rich. Sing every day that it's impossible for the rich to enter heaven. Make them pay tax each week at Sunday mass. Use the money supposed for the poor, to build flourishing business centers. Institute a confessional system, which allows you to be good detectives denouncing any black that has a different consciousness contrary to that of the decision-maker. Teach the niggers to forget their heroes and to adore only ours. Never present a chair to a black that comes to visit you. Don't give him more than one cigarette. Never invite him for dinner even if he gives you a chicken every time you arrive at his house." [....].

There is more to this letter but I will end here and allow you to research to read the rest of the letter. Teaching you how to fish is better than handing you a whole fish. Let's continue with our journey.

Mr. Moukouani Muikwani Bukoko in 1935 bought a second hand Bible from a Belgian priest working in the Congo; apparently the Belgian priest forgot that the speech (King Leopold's letter to the missionaries) was in the Bible. This is a well known historical document that I encourage you to look into in order to read more about it.

As always, I entreat you to use your thinking cap, use wisdom, use your research skills acquired through both formal and informal education to critically analyze things. Use your mind, soul and spirit to question everything. Why is Afraka and all the colonized or enslaved areas of the world the most religious to both the bible and quran, yet they are the poorest on the face of this earth and seek to travel to western countries for opportunities and "better life"? When you reject your roots, you lose your stamina. Any slight wind would blow you away. Afrakans must go back to the basics, by respecting their ancestral cultural roots.

The mandate in King Leopold II's letter is still at play in Afraka and throughout the aboriginal lands that was either colonized or enslaved.

The priests, bishops, pastors, missionaries, bible schools, archbishops, evangelists, deacons, cardinals, Roman sisters, etc are all playing part of the missions stated in this letter either consciously or sadly unconsciously. Either way, Afraka has fallen from its great status to a mere global mockery, a laughing stock of the world where racism and bigotry is served daily by these western countries to all dark melanated people (the aboriginal people) of mother earth.

King Leopold II of Belgium was far more evil than Adolf Hitler ever was (the two of great evils to mankind). Leopold II of Belgium massively tortured and murdered the people of Congo to an extent that the world has never seen before. This happened prior to the Berlin Conference a.k.a *The Scramble for Afraka* which began in 1880s and post Berlin Conference.

Far before the demonic atrocities caused by Leopold II of Belgium to the people of Congo, the Pope and the Roman Catholic church (Roman empire) began the quest to declare the papal bull *Unam Sanctam* ('One Holy' or "One Holy Church"); affirming the authority of the pope as the heir of Peter and Vicar of Christ over all human authorities, spiritual and temporal.

This papal document happened around 1302, the Middle Ages, the pope basically making himself a god/God or the god/God over all humans on earth, all human kingdoms, spiritual and temporal. This papal bull of 1302 was issued by the pope known as Boniface VIII. As allegedly radical and overly critical and power crunch the middle age kings, royals and supposedly powerful scholars and influential people might have fought, they obviously couldn't stop it. In that, this momentum by the pope later on fueled what I see as a far more practically dangerous papal bull, known as the *doctrine of discovery*.

The doctrine of discovery was issued in 1452 (papal bull of 1452, two bulls of Nicholas V, *Dum diversas* -1452 and *Romanus Pontifex* -1455; and Alexander VI's bull *Inter caetera* -1493), its' goal authorized Afonso V of Portugal to *"[...] invade, capture, search out, vanquish, and subdue all Saracens and pagans whatsoever, and other enemies of Christ wheresoever placed, and the kingdoms, dukedoms, principalities, dominions, possessions, and all movable and immovable goods whatsoever held and possessed by them and to reduce their persons to perpetual slavery, and to apply and appropriate to himself and his successors the kingdoms, dukedoms, counties, principalities, dominions, possessions, and goods, and to convert them to his and their use and profit."*

This started the brutally massive colonization and some enslavement activities throughout the whole world. Obviously, Portugal and Spain started out this murder spree and spreading of Christian religious wars throughout Afraka and the Americas. Catholic foot soldiers, Christian inquisitions, Portugal and Spain altogether murdered well over seven hundred million people globally, pillaged, destroyed and raped the aboriginal dark and copper colored people on the continents of Afraka, Europe and especially the Americas. The entire continents of both North and South America are now hijacked under the influence of this auspices.

Most of the names of all the colonized or enslaved places throughout the entire planet have their names imposed on them by either Spain or Portugal. The core historical roots behind why these names are mostly Portuguese or Spanish in origin is because both Spain and Portugal were the first two countries to pursue the pope's *Doctrine of Discovery* agenda.

These names usually span from mid 14th century. Names like India is a Spanish word in origin *Indios*. Philippines (a country in southeast Asia) was named after Spanish king Philip II of Spain. Cameron (a nation in today's West Afraka) is from Portuguese word Camarões (Shrimps found in the waters of that area) and the list goes on.

Under the 1452 papal bull doctrine of discovery umbrella, any living breathing thing and any land that these doctrine of discovery "enforcers" came across was barbarically bulldozed over by causing atrocious pain and loss to all the aboriginals that were living peacefully on their own lands.

The first nations (aboriginal people of planet earth) throughout Afraka, North America, South America, Asia, Europe, Antarctica and Oceania (Australasia, Melanesia, Micronesia, and Polynesia) lost everything due to the barbaric wickedly heartless murder and extreme overtake of the Catholic pope using their mythologically inspired helios biblios (sun book a.k.a bible) to push the doctrine of discovery agenda.

Evidence of these wickedly unimaginable actions is the catholic and all types of so called christian church buildings throughout the first nations (aboriginal people of planet earth) lands now known as the 7 continents of the world. This animalistic act of either you accept what we are preaching or we murder you and take over everything you have (your children, wives, animals, lands and your humanity) drastically destroyed the first nations with which many died and others were enslaved. Do not fail to notice that this is the 14th century we are talking about, meaning, Spain and Portugal started their colonization venture far ahead of the other European nations who joined later on.

Britain, France, and all the other European barbaric colonizers joined this *Doctrine of Discovery* madness around the 16th and 18th century. The first nations (aboriginal dark melanated people of planet earth) were far advanced civilized kingdoms and realms who were also connected to nature and the universe at large.

These first nations (aboriginal dark melanated people of planet earth) were so soulful, beautiful and a welcoming civilized nations, kingdoms, dukedoms and empires far before the 14th century's barbaric and inhumane *Doctrine of Discovery* by the Pope using the bible.

Currently, there are groups of people called whites, mixed folks, and the melanated people a.k.a the first nations (aboriginal people of planet earth). The mixed folks (Latinos, middle easterners, other mixed groups) are seen to be in the middle biologically sharing between the first nations and the so called white folks. This was due to the rape, the pillage, and the murderous outcome of what the 1452 papal bull's *doctrine of discovery* did to the first nations (aboriginal people of planet earth).

The Christian inquisitors, Portugal, Spain, the Pope himself, the Catholic church and later on other so called "white nations" like France, Britain, Belgium, Denmark, Netherlands, Norway, and others called this pursuit the *"New World Order"*. In that, the old world was the first nations (aboriginal people of planet earth) and they are the new world.

In the name of what I call *"religious sanctification righteousness"* and the greedy expansion of their empires, these folks pushed such barbaric and inhumane acts against the first nations (aboriginal people of planet earth).

The Pope and his supporting colonizing alibis pushed such acts ushered by the *Doctrine of Discovery* using these three(3) papal bulls: *Dum Diversas* on June 18th 1452 issued by Pope Nicholas V, *Romanus Pointifex* on January 15th 1455 issued by Pope Nicholas V, and *Inter Caetera* on May 14th 1493 issued by Pope Alexander VI.

To the first nations (aboriginal people of planet earth) who sadly converted to Catholic and Christianity, this rhetorical question is for you. How would you feel if a new global war broke out and the winning military nations came with newly formed man made religion murdering your families (children included), raping the women and girls, and took over all your lands and possessions all in the name of an entirely new found religion backed by their military?

How would you truly take this? Well, that's what happened to majority of the first nations, the aboriginal people of planet earth. Most of the first nations in Afraka fought back and won. Otherwise, you wouldn't see any of the first nations (aboriginal people of planet earth) living in today's West Afraka, East Afraka, Central Afraka, South Afraka, Brazil, Haiti, Jamaica, and all the predominantly dark melanated populated lands on earth.

This is a factual indication that these first nations fought back hard in order for them to survive and be here today. The era of the first nations was the era of the Gods and Goddesses, the original royals, the chosen people. Now, these Gods and Goddesses have fallen and are sadly mocked in mediocre left, right and center.

The *Doctrine of Discovery* is the reason why North America and South America are mostly occupied by Europeans. The Europeans who got to North America in ships and boats proclaimed the false analogy with motivation from the *Doctrine of Discovery* that, North America was promised to them by their God/god from their bible.

This ended in the brutal genocide of the aboriginals who were living peacefully on their land prior to the arrival of the first ever "white" European(s). The same doctrine made colonization and enslavement possible. The same doctrine motivated the South Afraka apartheid whereby the "white" people from Netherlands a.k.a Holland and other Europeans who jumped on boats and ships to South Afraka as missionaries claiming that the land was promised to them by their God/god in their sun book a.k.a bible.

These "white" Europeans had to literally dehumanize the aboriginals who were already living on these lands in order to literally exterminate them and to take their lands and all their possessions. Most of the aboriginals who survived in especially North America lost their language and their ancestral roots. Majority of them are now Christians and Catholics who literally defend the bible with all their hearts and souls which is a sad turn of events if you ask me.

Should the *Doctrine of Discovery* be rescinded for all lands and stolen properties to be returned to the first nations (aboriginal people of planet earth)? To me, yes, the *Doctrine of Discovery* must be rescinded. However, one must know that to rescind the *Doctrine of Discovery* is to lawfully demand that all Europeans in any of the first nations lands to return back to their European origin. Now, this is massive and it's probably not going to be an easy task for the current Pope to rescind. It is absolutely clear that rescinding the *Doctrine of Discovery* is the right thing for the Pope to do. The ball is in your court, Pope.

To correct all wrongs, it is best that these institutions pay reparations and possibly return all lands and properties that were falsely taken. These institutions include and not entirely limited to: The Pope and the Catholic church, Arabs and the Muslim movement (they were heavily involved in enslavement of aboriginal Afrakans, the popular one is known as the Trans-Sahara slave trade), Spain and Portugal, all European nations involved in enslavement including U.S and Canada (both countries are extensions of European countries) and the "unseen hands" that were involved in this inhumane acts toward the first nations (aboriginal people of planet earth).

The Arabs and Muslims destroyed a lot of the Afrakan civilizations, pyramids and even to the extent of stealing our knowledge and inventions. The so-called middle east (made up region) and entire North Afraka have been invaded by the Arabs and Muslim movement. The first nations (aboriginal people of planet earth) who were occupying these regions had to move to mostly today's West Afraka and other parts of Afraka. The Arab Muslims are not aboriginal to the current lands they occupy.

The Arab Muslims know this fact. Why do you think these Arab Muslims allow so called western countries to exhume the first original Afrakan nation's tombs to display the mummified bodies in their museums? Yet none of either the Arab Muslims or the Europeans exhume their own dead leaders or prophets. Just think very well about it.

They basically have no respect for the remnants of the first Afrakan aboriginal nations' great kingdoms and civilizations on that land. Look at the temples and walls of what is known today as Egypt, you will not find the writings and histories on these walls in the Arabic language of the Arab Muslims.

It is very easy to see all the facts that these Arab Muslims are invaders just like the so called "white" Europeans who invaded and took over North America, South America, South Afraka, the lands in the "middle eastern" country now called Israel, and Namibia (now somewhat recovered by the original people). The enslaved Afrakan men were castrated and the women were massively raped during the Muslims/Islam's 1300 years of reign.

The castrations and merciless murder of captured Afrakans contributed to the many reasons why North Afraka and the entire "Arabic peninsula" have little to no dark melanated Afrakans. East Afrakan countries suffered the most under the Arab Muslims slavery era. This is part of the many bitter facts that the Muslim wave brought to the first people (aboriginals) of Afraka including the entire middle east.

Part of the reason why Europe and the Americas hate to exhume any sites beyond the 14th century AD is because most of these tombs of royals and high level ranking members of society would be today's black people or Afrakans. They will never do it. They (white Europeans and Arab Muslims) established Egyptology to dig up Afrakan ancestors and Afrakan civilizations.

Where is Europelogy? Where is Arabtology? Where is Canadalogy? Where is Americalogy? Question everything. They have all been extremely obsessed with chocolate aboriginal Afrakans and their great civilizations. The entire world is still learning from Afraka's past civilizations. This is part of the reason why these Europeans and Arabs are seriously oppressing Afrakans and the first nations globally. These first nations people are very special and have direct favor from the Almighty Creator.

From 1884 to 1919 Germany ruled over Namibia and murdered almost over 100, 000 aboriginals. After that, South Afrakan style apartheid spread throughout Namibia until the 1990s. To date, in the 21st century, there are still German population living in Namibia, Afraka.

Majority of the Arab Muslims who forcefully invaded "middle east" and North Afraka obviously do not consider themselves Afrakans. In that, majority see themselves as the Arab world, which is technically, rightfully correct. All the blood shed on the first nations (ancient Kemet), invasions and thievery of their lands and their civilizations, exhuming of their past leaders, kings and queens were done in the name of the Abrahamic religion's expansion of their so-called "holy wars".

These "holy wars" are supposedly inspired by their bibles and qurans. With these historical facts, it is right to say that, no first nation (aboriginal people in Afraka and globally) should either be a Muslim or Catholic/Christian and must put the bible and quran aside to embrace their aboriginal ancestral spiritual roots.

Today, there are still spiritual, cultural and traditional practices that aboriginals around Afraka and rest of the world still hold dear to their hearts. This is a strong indication that, the first nations fought very hard with all they've got and won many wars against the Arab Muslims and the Pope's inspired *"Doctrine of Discovery"*.

After all, the Almighty Creator is not found in any book ever written by men or women. Rather, the Almighty Creator resides in you, the universe and nature. Be good to nature, be good to others and be good to yourself; this is your life's purpose on earth. This is what the first nation's lived by and that is the way it should be.

Life was very simple and far more authentically spiritual when the first nations ruled this earth. Today, the so-called top first world countries are only playing reverse engineering to learn from the great civilizations of the past. The western nations have forgotten that, what they need to do, is to humbly return everything to the first nation people; and peacefully plead to the first nations to lead this world to its glorious state. Until that happens, there will always be wars among these western nations.

Everything is energy, everything has an order that it follows, things are out of order on earth and it needs to be put back in order. The violent ones used violence to take over, look at history; for all the facts are there and correct the wrongs you have done to the aboriginal people on all four corners of earth.

Afrakan Map Reflecting Arab Muslim's invaded regions

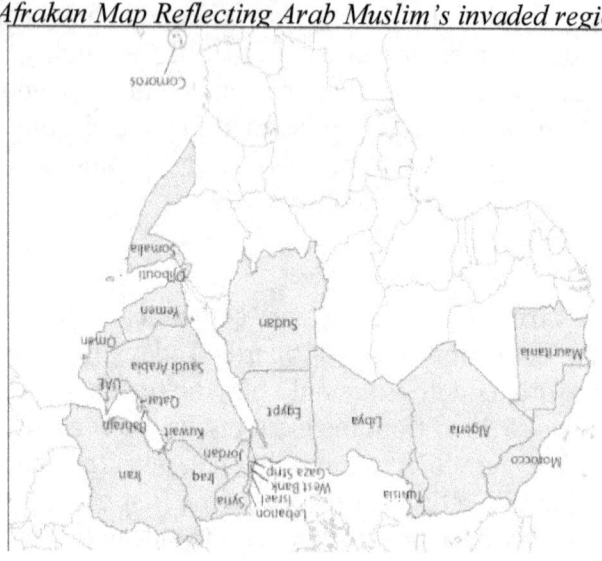

Let's establish additional emphasis that, the first nations (original people of planet earth) knew the real Almighty Creator. They did not need a bible or quran in order to know who the original creator was. The first nations were direct creations of the Almighty Creator.

Religion is not from the Almighty Creator. Religion is simply man made. You must seek to know yourself from the inside out. You must know everything about the human anatomy, that is from your brain to the soles of your feet. Learn about all the functions of every nerve, tissues, organs, and blood type. Master the art of breathing, and above all learn to take control of your mind.

Your mind is the driving seat, the holy of hollies. The judgment seat is located inside your brain. How well do you know about all the intricate parts and functions of your own skull, brain, eyes, mouth, tongue, nose, throat, thyroid, windpipe, larynx, ear, glands, vocal cord, bone(s), teeth, heart, lungs, stomach, kidney, liver, large intestine, blood vessel, artery and vein, skin and blood flow!

Look into your mother's tongue, father's tongue, ancestral tongue, ancestral cultures, ancestral traditions and ancestral spirituality. Find your root, and your language. This is where your spiritual journey outside of yourself begins. Do not make the mistake to fail to thoroughly know yourself from the inside out. Be free, be emancipated and get to know the God or Goddess within you.

This is how you can get a glimpse of the true Almighty Creator. You were born perfectly complete by the Almighty Creator. You do not need any of the man made religions to know about your source. You came from the source and everything was packaged or embedded within you.

All religions especially the three main Abrahamic religions (Judaism, Islam/Arab Muslims, and Christianity/Catholic) are pseudo and spurious propagated by fear. Fear of going to a "hell fire" which was supposedly prepared for a non-existent devil concept. Fear is a low vibration energy that keeps you oppressed, limited, traumatized and in a state of delusion. Fear is not real.

Fear is a psychological trigger of self imprisonment about things that do not exist. Now, danger on the other hand is real. Do not confuse fear with danger, these are two different energies altogether. The Abrahamic religions mainly use false identities fabricated in political greed and history of bloody murders to psychologically control you.

Greek, Latin, ancient Rome and later on the Arabic Muslims manipulated almost everything, from philosophy to medicine, from mathematics to architecture and the list goes on. Many of you can attest that when we think of the father of medicine, the Greeks, Latin, ancient Rome and all the western nations' doctors and "scholars" lie that, the father of medicine is Hippocrates. This is a huge lie.

The Greeks even established the Hippocrates oath of medicine *"I swear by Apollo the physician (Healer), by Aesculapius(surgeon), by Hygeia and Panacea, and likewise all the gods and goddesses to make them my witnesses, that I will carry out, according to my utmost ability and good judgment, this oath.....[] and to abstain from any intentional wrong doing and to do no harm……"*.

The fact of the matter is, Hippocrates was not the father of medicine. That's a lie, and a disappointment to Hippocrates himself. Hippocrates never opened his mouth or personally wrote any literature to claim that he was the father of medicine. This is similar to the lie and fabrications in all the man-made religion, claiming to know that the Almighty Creator created hell to burn all the people who follow an unproven or a nonexistent devil.

The dark chocolate melanated Afrakan man called Imhotep was the true and factual father of medicine. Imhotep, the original father of medicine practiced different levels of medicine and healing for several thousands of years before the Greek man, Hippocrates.

Imhotep was the original philosopher. Imhotep was the master architect who built the first pyramid of Sakara a.k.a Saqqara (Djoser). Imhotep was also the master surgeon who all the Greeks, ancient Rome, and several thousand years later the Arab Muslim scholars learned from. Imhotep was the initiator, architect, pioneer, inventor, innovator, mastermind, founder and originator of Medicine and surgery.

Today's Egypt is merely occupied by invaders of Arab and white mix descent. Imhotep is a pure blood dark melanated Afrakan man from the first nations on earth. In chapter 3, I will go deeper into how ancient Egypt/Kemet/Kamit fell to the Greeks, then to the Romans and many years later to the current Arabic Islam invasion.

Every form of technology and highest form of spiritual and psychological intelligence were reached far before the fall of the Gods and Goddesses. These first nations are the first people of the sun who are discriminated against heavily because of their sun kissed dark melanated skin. The world has been at its lowest level of vibration since the fall of the kingdom of heaven on earth. That is, since the fall from our spiritual, telekinesis, astral, free energy, pure high vibrational consciousness.

Every so-called technological advancement is just a reverse engineering attempt to catch a breeze from the past. Most of today's technological advancements from medicine to computer, from traffic lights to self driving cars and the list goes on, are mastermind and invented by the people of Afrakan descent.

A synopsis of this can be mention for Dr. Thomas Mensah (Chemical Engineer and Inventor), the Ghanaian West Afrakan man who attained scholarship to study in United Kingdom and then to the United States. After completing his KNUST (Kwame Nkrumah University of Science and Technology) degree in Ghana, West Afraka pioneered commercialization of the laser based fiber optic system. This laser based fiber optics system enable anyone on planet earth to send a picture and video to another person's cellphone or computer device. That means, without such commercialized invention you cannot send a tweet, no Facebook pictures, no Instagram, no YouTube, Google, and absolutely no TikTok and many others.

Prior to the laser based fiber optics pioneering, copper was used for everything, this was the slowest and frustrating time of communication. Dr. Thomas Mensah attained seven (7) patterns for his inventions in six years. His patterns allowed the sub-marine cables (cables under the oceans and rivers) to effectively function.

Kuffour, corrupted as Khufu/ Kufu (a traditional name in today's Ghana West Afraka's Akan people) was the King of ancient kemet/Kamit a.k.a ancient Egypt. He built the great pyramid of Giza. King Kuffour/Khufu was the second King of the 4th Dynastic period around the first half of the old kingdom era. Ancient Kamit/Kemet was a unified Afrakan great civilization that built great wonders along the river Nile, which sprung from today's South Afraka and ended at today's North Afraka.

Kuffour/Khufu's pyramid of Giza is said to be the biggest pyramid ever built. Greeks, Romans, Arab Muslims, Jewish people and the entire "white" people got all their knowledge from the aboriginal Afrakans. Archaeology, astronomy, philosophy, anthropology, medicine, spirituality, mathematics, science and the list goes on were all aboriginal Afrakans' culture that the Greeks and Romans studied from.

The Greeks like Plato, Aristotle, Pythagoras and the rest got all their knowledge from aboriginal Afrakan Kamit/Kemet/ancient Egypt.

The *Ankh* known to the world as the symbol of life or symbol of eternal life was established by the aboriginal Afrakan man, called Ankamah. Western folks shortened/abbreviated it from Ankamah to *"Ankh"*. Ankamah placed his own name on his powerful and meaningful creation/invention. Ankamah a.k.a the *Ankh* would have been a person from today's Ghana, West Afraka.

The name Ankamah is still used massively within the Akan people of Ghana, West Afraka. The aboriginal people of this civilization still name themselves accordingly with these powerful traditional and cultural names. All the true names (not the westernized versions) of the Kings and Queens, Pharaohs of ancient Kamit/Kemet/ancient Egypt are still in use today within the aboriginal people of the descendants of these great Kings and Queens. Names like "Tutankhamun" is a westernized version of the original name Tutu Ankamah (another Akan name from Ghana, West Afraka).

Set or Seth/Setekh is an ancient Egyptian/Kemet deity/god/God who murdered and brutally mutilated his brother Asar. The original authentic name is Asare a.k.a Osiris (originally, Osei); both are names of the Akan people of today's Ghana, West Afraka. Set/Seth/Setekh in ancient Egypt/Kemet is known to be a trickster, a god of the desert, foreign lands, sky god, violence, thunderstorms, disorder, war, deception, eclipses, and earthquakes. Set/Seth/Setekh is known to always create disorder within a world of order/orderly world.

This could be the reason why the Hyksos, invaders of ancient Egypt between c. 1630–1521 BCE worshiped Set/Seth/Setekh as their main god/God in ancient Egypt/Kamit/Kemet.

The story of Set/Seth/Setekh from ancient Egypt/Kemet is what the Europeans used to create the mythological character called Satan/Devil. The concept and ideology of Satan/Devil is 100% mythology and aggressively stolen from ancient Egypt/Afrakans/Kemet.

There is a dark reason why "Western educators" hide such facts from the public and call these great ancient civilizations who relocated to today's West Afraka as *"Sub-Sahara Africa"*. The so-called "Western educators" attempt to hide such great people from the public lenses. I have dedicated an in-depth discussion and references of this topic in Chapter 3.

Free energy is a real thing. No one is supposed to pay for anything related to energy (electricity, etc). In ancient times, we were able to harness free energy to power all forms of machines and tools. However, after the fall of the first nation people, the violent ones with little to no souls have trapped almost everything that provides us with all the inalienable rights manifested by the Almighty Creator, which includes dominion over all the things created.

In the light of free energy, a Zimbabwean East Afrakan man who is called Maxwell Chikumbutso has invented a self powered technology for cars, helicopter, television and almost anything that uses electricity to power. Maxwell Chikumbutso's technology uses a micro-sonic device that absorbs radio frequencies around us and convert the radio frequencies to pure energy needed to power all devices.

Meaning, imagine a world where you never pay for electricity, solar panels, oil and gas. This is what the Almighty Creator has given us. Everything we need to thrive on earth is free.

Additionally, Dr. Mark Dean (a chocolate aboriginal melanated man) is the architect of the modern day *Personal Computer (P.C)*. Dr. Mark Dean was highly instrumental to make the invention of the P.C possible. He was the core foundation that enabled International Business Machines Corporation, better known as IBM's technological breakthrough. Millions of great job opportunities in information technology is traced back to Dr. Mark Dean's superb technological breakthrough inventions.

The works of space exploration requires mathematical calculations and near perfect scientific predictions for it to be possible. The human computers who made these nearly impossible mathematical and physics calculations possible were the so-called "black women". These chocolate aboriginal melanated women were referred to as *"Hidden Figures"*(a real life story movie that revealed this secret). If you haven't watched the movie *Hidden Figures*, then I entreat you to watch it to learn about this fact.

Let's look at our favorite device *"Cell Phones"*. Cell phone is credited to none other than Henry T. Samson. He is a chocolate aboriginal melanated man, who pioneered the technology used in cell phone's functionality. He owns the patents to what is known as *Solid Rock Motors* that converts nuclear energy into electricity. The *Gamma Electric Cell* was another invention of Henry T. Samson. Gamma Electric Cell is "a direct-conversion energy device that converts the energy generated from the radiation of high-energy gamma rays into electricity".

Jesse Lee Russell is a chocolate aboriginal melanated man, the terrific indisputable inventor of the <u>Digital</u> *Cell Phone* technology, as well as, the brilliant engineer in charge of one of the muti-billion dollar industry. Jess Lee Russell's inventions and patents include: *"Base Station for Mobile*

Radio Telecommunications Systems" (1992), the *"Mobile Data Telephone"* (1993), and the *"Wireless Communication Base Station"* (1998). If you enjoy using cell phones or computers then you owe many thanks to these amazing aboriginal chocolate sun-kissed melanated first nation people who invented these technologies.

We all love to be on the internet, don't we? Well, the man in charge of making the internet world possible is Dr. Philip Emeagwali, a Nigerian, West Afakan computer scientist. Dr. Philip Emeagwali utilized the connection machine and 65,536 microprocessors to achieve 3.1 billion calculations per second, the fastest and first computational record ever recorded.

In other words, he invented the world's fastest computer. Through his amazing work, large number of computers were able to communicate instantly. Dr. Philip Emeagwali made the Internet's superb functionality a reality.

Under his invention, his computers are used to help forecast and predict the weather and its possible effects of perpetual "global warming".

Using the terrific characteristics of plant fiber known to ancient Afrakans as *Papyrus Fiber,* taken from what is known as the *Papyrus Plant,* Afrakans in ancient Kemet/Egypt invented the first ever recorded paper. This was paper with which writings were placed on its surface, called *Papyrus*. Medu Neter was the language of the Afrakan people of ancient Egypt/Kemet. *Medu Neter* is known to many as the "divine words", "sacred words" or "words of Gods and Goddess".

The alphabets were called *hieroglyphics*. Hieroglyphics were written on the *Papyrus,* the walls and stones within the civilizations of ancient Egypt/Kemet. These wonders of the world still stand today in northern Afraka's geographic area called today as "Modern Egypt" (invaded and occupied currently by the Arab-Muslim invaders). Fast forward, we have everyone enjoying the usage of many forms of paper, thanks to the great Afrakan ancient civilizations.

These are all the works of the Gods and Goddesses who have fallen, yet immensely continue to make our world livable, even in their spiritual comatose state. So imagine when we all wake up spiritually, psychologically and physically to our Gods and Goddesses self that we used to be prior to the infiltration of the soulless people, who came only to kill, steal and destroy everywhere they went on earth. There are many other ancient Afrakan civilizations that have not been raised to discussion.

Afrakan cilizations like Sumer, Old Ghana Empire, Mali Empire, Songhai Empire, Kushite Kingdom (Kingdom of Kush), Carthage/Karthage, Punt land (Land and kingdom of Punt), Aksum Empire, Great Zimbabwe, the Dogons, and many other amazing ancient Afrakan civilizations possibly predating ancient Egypt/Kemet.

These ancient Afrakan kingdoms and civilizations walked with the purest form of spirituality as their lifestyles. They epitomized how it's meant to live like how the Almighty Creator intended for us to live. That is, to take dominion over the earth and all creations by treating everything in creation with honor, respect, dignity and appreciation as we use it for our physical, spiritual and psychological enrichment.

The newest civilizations like the Greeks, Romans and Arab-Muslims, stole, copied, demonized, plagiarized and learned from ancient Afrakan civilizations. They came up with their watered down, flipped flopped, turned inside out, mythological versions called *"Abrahamic religion"*.

Religion disrespects the Almighty Creator. Religion rudely opprobriums the Almighty Creator. Religion belittles and limits the Almighty Creator's sovereignty. If you pursue your spiritual awakening journey solely through religion and never graduate to pure spirituality, found in nature outside of every religion, then you will always remain at the crawling stage of your spiritual journey.

The incivility mockery of ridicule derision by religion towards the Almighty Creator, the Source of Everything, is absolute insanity. Get closer to finding your true self by learning about your skeletal system, disorders of the spine, dermatomes, anatomy of your brain, anatomy of your heart, ligaments of your joints, spinal and cranial nerves, circulatory system, muscular system, digestive system, endocrine system, nervous system, lymphatic system, male and female reproductive system.

You must know all the core building blocks of your house, that's your body, with which your true self (soul) lives in. Everything good, bad and ugly runs on spirituality. Spirituality is the propeller of every living thing in this universe. To be spiritual, is to truly know yourself from the inside out. You must know every fiber and cell in your body. You must seriously invest time into learning everything about the human anatomy. This is the first step to a true spiritual journey. The entire universe is within you. The true Almighty Creator of everything is literally within you. You will never find the true creator in any of the man-made religions. You must love yourself, embrace yourself, know who you are and to communicate daily with your soul. If you can breathe, then you are living and walking in spirituality. Spirituality is the art of breathing.

RESTITUTION IN REPARATIONS AND TOTAL REINSTATEMENT

Restitution is reparations. Let's look at both the Christian/Catholic bible and Muslim quran believers since these are the two main Abrahamic religious groups that were massively involved in invading, murdering and enslaving many first nations on earth.

Muslims executed the trans-Sahara slave trade. Catholics/Christians executed the trans-Atlantic slave trade and multiple colonization of first nation people globally.

Restitution and reparation are both defined as the act of restoring something or someone to a position of status. Restitution and reparation bring back the honorary reinstatement to the formal state. Both the quran and bible teach about restitution. Reparation and restitution also means to mend or to restore.

The challenge is for those who are madly in love with the bible and quran, to respectively exercise what these two religious books instruct them to do. This would apply to all the lands, gold, artifacts, and numerous resources forcefully stolen through the spread of the *Doctrine of Discovery* by the Pope, the western countries' *Manifest Destiny* and lastly, the spread of the Quran to aboriginal Afrakans that led to them losing their lands in the "Middle East", Americas, Asia, and North Afraka.

First, let's look at some teachings and references for restitution from the Christian/Catholic bible that was used as a tool to invade, enslave and colonize the aboriginal people on earth.

Leviticus 6:4-5 "*4Then it shall be, because he hath sinned, and is guilty, that he shall restore that which he took violently away, or the thing which he hath deceitfully gotten, or that which was delivered him to keep, or the lost thing which he found, 5Or all that about which he hath sworn falsely; he shall even restore it in the principal, and shall add the fifth part more thereto, and give it unto him to whom it appertaineth, in the day of his trespass offering.*"

Proverbs 6:31 "*But if he be found, he shall restore sevenfold; he shall give all the substance of his house.*"

Ezekiel 33:14-15 "*14Again, when I say unto the wicked, Thou shalt surely die; if he turn from his sin, and do that which is lawful and right; 15If the wicked restore the pledge, give again that he had robbed, walk in the statutes of life, without committing iniquity; he shall surely live, he shall not die.*"

Nehemiah 5:10-12 "*10I likewise, and my brethren, and my servants, might exact of them money and corn: I pray you, let us leave off this usury. 11Restore, I pray you, to them, even this day, their lands, their vineyards, their oliveyards, and their houses, also the hundredth part of the money, and of the corn, the wine, and the oil, that ye exact of them. 12Then said they, We will restore them, and will require nothing of them; so will we do as thou sayest. Then I called the priests, and took an oath of them, that they should do according to this promise.*"

Luke 19:8-9 "*8And Zacchaeus stood, and said unto the Lord: Behold, Lord, the half of my goods I give to the poor; and if I have taken any thing from any man by false accusation, I restore him fourfold. 9And Jesus said unto him, This day is salvation come to this house, forsomuch as he also is a son of Abraham.*"

Romans 13:8-10 "*Owe nothing to anyone except to love one another; for he who loves his neighbor has fulfilled the law. For this, "You shall not commit adultery, You shall not murder, You shall not steal, You* shall not covet," and if there is any other commandment, it is summed up in this saying, "You shall love your neighbor as yourself." <u>Love does no wrong to a neighbor; therefore love is the fulfillment of the law.</u>"

Matthew 5:23-24 "*Therefore if you are presenting your offering at the altar, and there remember that your brother has something against you, leave your offering there before the altar and go; <u>first be reconciled to your brother</u>, and then come and present your offering.*"

Let's now look at restitution and reconciliation in the Quran. When you come to the Quran, it accepts its followers and its believers to exercise restitution. Restitution is required when someone sin against another person according to the Quran's teachings.

Unless the Arab Muslims feel or believe that invading, enslaving, murdering, raping, kidnapping and forcefully removing aboriginal chocolate melanated Afrakans from their land is not a sin then obviously the world and their God, Allah would be the judge.

Holy Quran: 2, 208 "*O You who accept! Enter totally into peace (Islam). Try not to follow in the strides of Satan. He is a through and through adversary to you.*"

The question quickly asked here is that, if the Quran teaches that Islam is peace, then why does it use wars and violence as a means of action towards those who embrace their own traditions and cultures? The non-Arabic aboriginal languages that existed far before the Muslim movement, also have their own God together with the Almighty Creator. Yet, the same Islamic-Muslim-Arab movement preaches brutal violence towards people who do not accept or believe their God in the Quran. Let's look at some readings:

Surah 9:5 *"Then kill the disbelievers wherever you find them, capture them and besiege them, and lie in wait for them in each and every ambush ..."*

Surah 3:151 *We will cast terror into the hearts of those who (who disbelieve) have denied the Truth since they have associated others with Allah in His divinity - something for which He has sent down no sanction. The Fire is their abode; how bad the resting place of the wrong-doers will be!*

Surah 2:191 *"And kill them wherever you find them ... kill them. Such is the recompense of the disbelievers."*

Disbelievers refer to all non-Muslims. This is brutal, volatile, utterly heinous and dreadfully extreme psychotic violent way to encourage people to join your religious movement. Winston Churchill in his own assessment of this mindset within these Islamic-Muslims regarding such violence, stated: *"How dreadful are the curses which Muhammadism lays on its votaries! ... [].. Individual Muslims may show splendid qualities, but the influence of the religion paralyses the social development of those who follow it. No stronger retrograde force exists in this world."*

Would the Muslims and Christians/Catholics see their invasions and history of murder, as wrongful doing in order for them to confess their sins? After they confess their sins, it must be followed with restitution, reconciliation and reparation in order for the process of forgiveness, by the Almighty Creator and the aboriginal people to be complete.

Any form of punishment to these invaders due to their refusal to honor restitution, would be executed by mother nature and the Almighty Creator. Watch what happens.

Restitution for theft, invasion, rape, medical apartheid, and centuries of brutal racism, discrimination and defamation of aboriginal cultures, traditions and civilizations must be enforced and accepted by the chocolate sun-kissed melanated aboriginal people on earth (first nations).

The victims of such atrocities have the right to restitution and reparation. The victims must be restored for all the physical, emotional, property, psychological and spiritual losses propelled by the violent religious groups who caused the harmful crimes. Restitution must not be seen as a punishment to these Abrahamic religions. Rather, it is something that the violent Abrahamic religious groups owe to the chocolate sun-kissed melanated aboriginal people on earth (first nations).

Restitution is a must, because it is part of the entire processes/steps required to purely or wholeheartedly repent. You cannot claim to have repented without restitution of all your wrongful doings. You cannot keep all the things you stole and pass them down to your posterity, and act like you are "saved" from all your sins and living in newness of life. That would be a lie per both the Bible and Quran. Do not insult your own God of the bible and Quran.

So long as all these Christians/Catholics and Muslim-Arabs still hold on to the lands they invaded, artifacts, gold, and relics without restitution; then, they're worse than the devil or Satan. If you were a thief and you claim to have followed the path of your Bible or Quran to repentance, then you must return all the things you stole back to the rightful owner(s). You must make right all the wrongs you have done. That is the demand for restitution.

The truth came out from one of the horses own mouth prior to a year of his first presidential term around 1995-2002 which subsequently happened in Yaoundé during the 21st Africa-France summit for heads of States, Jacques Chirac, a former President of France said this on January 2001;

"We bled Africa for four and a half centuries. We looted their raw materials, then we told lies that Africans are good for nothing. In the name of religion we destroyed their cultures. And then after being made rich at their expense, we now steal their brains through miseducation, misdirection and misinformation as well as propaganda to prevent them from enacting African retribution against us."

Philippe Bernard and Jean-Pierre Tuquoi published the article on lemonde.fr with the title "France-Afrique : la fin des "années Chirac" on February 2007.

Per the statement published on January 24th, 2021 in Canard enchainé, this edition printed that Jacques Chirac, a former President of France said:

"While speaking of Africa, we must check our memory. We started draining the continent four and a half centuries ago with the slave trade. Next, we discovered their raw materials and seized them. Having deprived Africans of their wealth, we sent in our elites who destroyed their culture. Now, we are depriving them of their brains thanks to scholarships which are definitely another form of exploitation because, at the end, the most intelligent students do not go back to their countries […] In the end, noticing that Africa is not in a good state and as bonuses for the wealth we made on its back, we are giving lectures…".

These western countries know what they have done to the beautiful people of Afraka, the chocolate sun-kissed melanated aboriginal first nations people on earth.

These western countries must and should pay back all the money they have unlawfully stolen from Afrakans.

The lands, golds, oil, minerals and artifacts stolen must be returned to the rightful owners. The earth and all its inhabitants are the estate of the Almighty Creator. The aboriginals, who are the chocolate sun-kissed melanated first nations people, were placed on earth directly by the Almighty Creator from eons in time. So, I therefore say to all aboriginal chocolate melanated people that:

Our unity is the "Almighty Creator's" actualization. This is the main way for the Almighty Creator to actualize on earth. Don't you know that the Creator lives in each one of us? So, our unity is the compound compact formation of an unmatched supreme super power from which the Almighty Creator would be manifested and actualized physically, spiritually and psychologically.

There are many scams of which so-called Western civilization is one. Western civilization hide behind the bible and use the bible as a force/tool to slaughter billions of people globally via war in their quest to implant and impose what the Western world's leaders claim to be "the will of God".

The "will of their God" to them is simply, Gold -Oil -Drugs (God). This is the "god" that the West has created to push for endless wars, rape, thievery, invasions, land-grab, manifest destiny, doctrine of discovery, identity theft of original people, changing the calendar, changing the day of holly/ rest, and instilling a contractual marriage through license. Yes, marriage through marriage certificate is strictly business and a means to track people. This was initiated by the old Roman Empire which has dissolved into today's Roman Catholic Church. Literally, everything the West has is based off of robbery, thievery, slaughter, and barbarically forceful inhumane wars against all original first people of this earth.

In the name of their mythological sky daddy/god, they slaughtered aboriginal dark melanated people of this earth.

In the name of their mythological sky daddy/god, they dehumanized anyone who refused their barbaric behaviors through their occult drafted religion.

In the name of their mythological sky daddy/god, they used their bibles and Qurans to enslave aboriginal chocolate melanated sun-kissed first nation people of earth.

In the name of their mythological sky daddy/god, they stole and invaded lands that belong to original ancient chocolate melanated sun-kissed first nation people.

In the name of their mythological sky daddy/god, they raped, mutilated and castrated anyone who didn't embrace their wicked ways.

In the name of their mythological sky daddy/god, they have murdered a combined global population of 3 billion and counting.

In the name of their mythological sky daddy/god, they purposely create never-ending wars through false flags, deception, diseases, viruses, and hazardously toxic foods via genetic modification to reduce the populations of the whole world. Especially, that of the chocolate melanated sun-kissed first nation people of earth.

In the name of their mythological sky daddy/god, they divided the once great civilized and most spiritual continent on earth known as Afraka, and only saw Afrakans as just a mere commodity.

Meanwhile, these same Afrakans are the true Gods and Goddesses who have sadly fallen into a spiritual comatose. A dark magic spell and a psychological aphrodisiac melancholic drift into the bottomless pit of hypnosis.

However, these western folks fail to realize that, it's only a matter of time that these Gods and Goddesses would rise up again to a powerful force seven-times-seventy-seven as they used to be.

The beginning of the end was declared and prophesied prior to the psychological and spiritual comatose sleep of these once great Afrakans. The cyclic event of this experience can easily be linked to the cyclical life of a butterfly.

These great Afrakans have been asleep in their comatose state just like the caterpillar moths into its cocoon. In this cocoon state, there is an additional spiritual camouflage protection of these Afrakans unseen and undetected by these colonizers.

Hence, these western countries parade around with quack pomposity acting like they're the rightful heirs to the thrones of these great Afrakan Gods and Goddesses. They're all in for a rude awakening. They know what's coming for them. In that, everything was disclosed to them prior to them choosing to still take advantage of these Gods and Goddesses, as these Gods and Goddesses went into their cocoon state.

It may look to many that nothing is going on with these once great Afrakan royals and global civilization. However, there are many spiritual, economic, psychological and powerful reinforcement of growth, and empowerment like never before happening inside the cocoon.

These great Afrakans will emerge out of their cocoon spiritual comatose state as that beautiful, most potent colorful butterfly that no living thing can overpower. The entire earth would then go back to its original state of the heavenly realms of kingdoms and royalties that it once was. This cyclical event can never be stopped by any power seen or unseen, existing or non-existing in the universe.

No amount of apologies from these barbaric colonizers would suffice their evil dehumanized deeds committed on the surface of the earth. Whether these colonizers like it or not, they would need to return everything they stole back to the rightful original owners.

These colonizers include both the Arabs who used the Quran and their religion to enslave billions of Afrakans in the trans-Sahara slavery era. As well as, all the areas on earth where these Arabs colonized prior to the westerners following the foot steps of colonization propagated by these Arabs.

The Western colonizers ensued their version as the transatlantic slave trade, the continent of the America's slavery, doctrine of discovery, manifest destiny, Australia's aboriginal slavery, and enslaving Asians.

MANIFESTATIONS TO CONCLUDE THIS CHAPTER

Manifestations are keys to your spiritual journey and everyday creation. We create as we speak and we speak as we create. Hence, you must know how to properly manifest so that the universe a.k.a Mother Nature or Neter can respond to you accordingly. We are part of nature and we must learn to speak the language of nature, known as the *Divine Words of Nature or Medu Neter*.

When you speak to manifest, follow this route as a starter. As you grow into your mature spiritual self, you can personalized it your own way. This is my routine manifestation. I manifest this way anytime I get the vibrational energy to create through manifestation. Manifest in the present tense, and first person format:

I AM One with nature

I AM Life

I AM Love

I AM Wise

I AM Limitless

I AM Eternal

I AM Royal

I AM Free

I AM Risen

I AM Connected to my source (my root).

I AM Wealthy

I AM What/Who I AM

I AM a Leader

I AM a Learner

I AM Wisdom

I AM Successful

I AM Happy

I AM Rich

I AM Magnificent

I AM Healthy

I AM Capable

Everything I desire is already with me

I AM everything I desire

It is all for the good and to the harm of no one

I live and walk in this creation

So shall it be

It has already arrived.

To the impious, sacrilegious and nullifidian, I encourage you to read this book with a fresh perspective in order to have a fair introspection.

To the science fanatics, archaeologists, astronomers, mathematicians, philosophers, darwinism, the big-bang followers and various fields of studies, it's a pleasure to have you on board to analyze, and study this book.

We are all searching, digging, mining, and trying to see the magnificence in, and around our universe.

To the apostate, welcome aboard, fasten your seat belt for a massive ride through both old and new awareness. To the agnostics, and every type of skeptic out there, welcome.

Finally, to the pious, theists, Christians, Catholics, every religious denomination, and rest of mankind, I hope you read this book with an open mind that's erected by no dogmatism, and any other *ism*.

One of the most powerful weapons effective to destabilize the strength, power, intellectual agility, and the union of any friendship, relationship, family, community, institutions, municipality, a state, region or a nation is *the seed of discord*.

Once effectively sowed, you can easily control, manipulate and destroy such people's identity, confidence, knowledge and their very worth. Such distorted people will believe anything outside of themselves.

To read this book, and innerstand it, you should resonate with the age of Aquarius. You might have known by now that, this book intends to contribute to your own journey to curing yourself from all religious psychosis, and psychosomatics. The age of Pisces a.k.a *"fishers of men"* is far gone. The age of *"just believe and do not question"* or *"do not seek knowledge and wisdom"* has ended. A new age and a new dawn is here. This is the age of wisdom and knowledge a.k.a age of Aquarius through energetic vibrating spiritual frequency of ascension to your God and Goddess self within you.

Whenever you hear of the Dogon people from the Sirius star galaxy universe, Anunaki, Akaddians, Mesopotamia, ancient Sumerians (originally El-Zuma/Zuma in today's Sudan), Yoruba/Oruba/Euroba/Europa/Europe, Moors,

Asia, North and South Amerika/Tameri, Afraka/Aeothiopia/Alkebullan/Keme/Kemet, Oceania, Antarctica, Atlantis, Pangaea, first ever greatest civilizations, royals, the Gods and Goddesses, advanced technologies, and all so-called super heroes; know that, they are talking about Afrakans, and all chocolate-copper colored melanated people.

The true all powerful source of everything lives for eons in time. The first manifestations of physical creations (earth, water, trees, man, woman, animals, etc) were all chocolate melanated beings and entities. The core of all these creations contains dark matter a.k.a melanin in animals, humans, and what is known as chlorophyll in plants. This dark matter is directly from the divine source of all powerful creative energetic vibrating living frequency.

In coming chapters, you will read about what led to the fall of the Gods and Goddesses a.k.a Afrakans and all chocolate melanated copper aboriginal people of earth. Yes, the Gods and the Goddesses have fallen from their grace and unfathomable spiritual prowess to the extent that, now they die like mankind.

A huge spell of forgetfulness and self-loathing has been cast upon these Gods and Goddesses. However, they are gradually remembering who they are and realizing how important dark matter a.k.a melanin is to them. They're reconnecting to the great black sun in order to reactivate their God and Goddess self-hood.

CHAPTER 2

CHAPTER 2

MATHEMATICS and NUMBERS:
Mathematical and Numerical Relativity of Creation and the Source (Almighty Creator).

Numbers are building blocks of creation, spirituality and manifestation. Every creation is consciously or unconsciously connected to numerical values. Deciding to look at numbers just at its physical state would make intellectual sense only to a limited extent.

However, deciding to psychologically, mathematically, empirically, spiritually, naturally and scientifically ascend to having both innerstanding and overstanding of numbers would greatly catapult you to the core units of creation.

There is nothing in existence ever created without the fundamental use of numbers. Every number emanates different frequency that vibrates on different energy levels.

These numbers can also be manipulated by anyone who vibrates to the number's appropriate frequencies to create different things in our physical dimension. The numbers within your own date of birth carry frequencies that dictate your mission, your attraction, your energies, your vibrations and exactly your purpose in this physical dimension.

Knowing the numbers in your birth date and its implications is paramount to guiding you through your journey right here on earth.

There are mainly nine numbers, that is from one to nine. If we are to include zero then it would be ten. The most powerful number, king or queen of all numbers is interestingly a number that is mostly ignored. The most powerful number in question is, the number zero.

Yes, zero is the king or queen of all the numbers in both the known and unknown universe. If you didn't know, now you know that the number zero (written in the form of a circle), is the most powerful number of all the numbers known to mankind.

Now, the number zero is the representation of the cyclical formation of eternity. The number zero birthed the numbers one, two, three, four, five, six, seven, eight and nine. In the sense that, the number zero easily morphs itself to form the numbers one to nine.

Permit me to say that, the number zero is indeed, the all powerful energy that gives life to the numbers: one, two, three, four, five, six, seven, eight and nine. The number zero is the beginning of all things and the end of everything. The mode of all creation is the number zero. Everything in numerical value, essence of our being, things becoming objects in this earthly dimension started with the number zero.

Now, let's look at the number zero from the spiritual realm. From the beginning, it is said that everything was dark, calm, quiet (as in super and total darkness), be it the theory of the big bang, the genesis creation of the bible or any form of creation in the various traditional religious groups' teachings around the entire world. They all assert to the quietness, calmness, darkness pre-creation of everything.

Etymology of Compendiums of all Gods and The Almighty Creator

Before there was any form of creation, before any spoken word was spoken, or any manifestation activated to its materialization, there was that all powerful number zero (total, absolute darkness).

To those who accept the bible, it is said in the book of Genesis chapter 1 that, it was dark (quietness, calmness, that's the numerical number zero representation). The spirit of the Elohim was moving upon the surface of the waters. In the Hebrew language, *"Elohim"* is a plural word for *Gods* and *Goddesses, judges, architects, Landlords, supervisors, superiors.*

Additionally, according to the bible believers and readers, the biblical God lives or resides in the darkest place on earth, and that is in the deepest-darkest depths of the waters per *1 Kings 8:10-13, Psalm 18:11 and Psalm 97:2*. This reflects or represents the number zero in numerology, quietness, total absolute darkness. There's a spiritual traditional group in today's West Afraka, a country called Ghana, this nation has a group called the Akan group who predominantly speak the Akan Twi language.

The Akan people in some ancient ways use signs and symbols known as the *Adinkra symbols.* One of the Adinkra symbols of the Akans is known as "Adinkra Hene" meaning *King of all the Adinkras.*

The symbol is shown, written or drawn as three circles (all within each other ranging from a smaller circle, medium circle and the big outer layer circle – all in one). The Adinkra Hene (king of the Adinkra symbols) signifies great power, authority, charisma. Out of this *King of Adinkra* symbols, it is known that other Adinkra symbols are created.

The Akans of Ghana, West Afraka are known to be part of the ancient ones, the people from the beginning, the people from the source. This is the literal translation of their name Akandifo/Akanfo (meaning the first people or the people who led first/the people who were first).

So, it is paramount for one to see the strong connection of their *Akinkra Hene* symbol (king of all Adinkra symbols) to the all powerful numerical number zero. There are several other cultures that may reflect such numerical zero sign, symbol or number as a source or force of power, authority, or creation. The number zero is powerful in that spiritual aspect.

Mathematically, in the numerical realm of everything, the number zero is the beginning of all numerical creations. We can say for a fact in the world of mathematics and physics that, the number zero is a value on its own and it is not considered as "nothing". The number zero is definitely not emptiness. It appears that, some people do not know the innate and adaptive characteristics of the number zero in the world of numbers.

Let's look at this basic numerical example of zero, we need the number zero to get to the number ten, twenty, thirty, forty, fifty, sixty, seventy and so on. That is, in order to attain the value of the numbers I just mentioned; you would need to add the number zero, otherwise you cannot transition to the next phase of double digit numbers.

The number zero is the beginning of all the single digit numbers and also the beginning of all the double digit numbers. So the number zero is the beginning of everything. The beginning of everything is not nothing, rather it is the strongest force at a resting phase needed to ignite all the sequence of numerical creation. As stated earlier, our entire world is made up of numbers. Yes, our entire universe is made up of the numerical values from zero to the number nine.

Every person, animal, plants, living and non-living is made up of numbers. The true creator(s) of everything reside in zero (darkest and deepest part of everything).

Isn't it interesting that most people are terribly afraid of the dark? To be afraid of the dark is to be afraid of your true self. So let me ask you, are you afraid of your true self? Have you faced your true self? You must face your good, bad, and ugly self in order to fully vibrate at a much higher frequency.

Are you afraid of discovering who you truly are? Why do you get terrified in total darkness with zero light? In the essence of darkness we rest well, we recharge.

Some of us have their best sleep when all the lights in the room are turned off. We close our eyes to meditate and to concentrate. Darkness is where seeds germinate before the seeds resurface from the soil.

The sperm from the man is the seed that he plants into the woman. The woman keeps this seed from the man in the dark of her womb in order for the seed to get all the proper nutrients to germinate. When it's time, the seed is birthed by resurfacing through the woman's *"gate/door of heaven"* also known as vagina. There is greater power in total or absolute darkness, in this case, the numerical value of zero is represented.

Permit me to take this to another level, if you do not want to reincarnate then do not go to the light. That's another way to skip reincarnation. Going to the light is your way of accepting to reincarnate back to earth.

The darkness is the true Father (Almighty Creator) and the light is the mother (Mother Earth), together they form the perfect complete bond. The darkness is never evil as Christians and Muslim/Islamic religion have deceived the world to be.

Darkness is first of all things. After all, what do you think the phrase "from darkness into the light" really mean? This phrase has so many misinterpretations, however it simply means, from our Father (Darkness) to our mother (Light).

The sperm from the father is released into the light of our mother (womb of our mother with her egg/eggs) then you are born. After your death, when you see the light out of all the darkness surrounding you, make sure to not go to the light if you do not want to reincarnate back to earth.

The main reason why these pale-pink people a.k.a colonizers hate the global dark chocolate melanated people is because your true Creator (The Almighty Creator) is the darkest of all darkness. For them to hate you because of your dark melanin is for them to hate the true Almighty Creator.

The source of all power is extremely dark, darker than "dark matter" and even the darkest black hole in the universe. The source of all power is the Father of all dark chocolate melanated people. Colonizers successfully tricked you to hate your own father (the Almighty Creator) by hating everything and anything dark/darkness.

This is part of the many reasons why global dark chocolate melanated people have been subdued and lost their spiritual super powers. Global dark chocolate melanated people allowed pink-pale colonizers to deceive them to call everything dark evil, and demonic without knowing that, they in turn are mocking and rejecting their own true Father and their very source of spiritual super powers.

Does it ring a bell to you now as to why your dark melanin is hated so much? The darker you are as a chocolate melanated person, the more you are hated by these colonizers, no matter where you are located on mother earth.

Remember that the sun loves your dark chocolate melanin body for a reason beyond any physical and biological comprehension. All dark chocolate melanated people must return to their Father, the source of all powers, the core to the existence of all creations known and unknown to man.

Another reason why you are hated by the pink-pale colonizers is because you remind them of your Father, your true spiritual power source. You are a spiritual being having a physical experience.

Darkness is the true life. Everything desiring to live must first go into darkness in order to regenerate, re-power, re-energize, and gain functional growth. From plants to animals, to humans and other living things seen and unseen must go through into darkness for some time before they germinate or grow into fullness of life. Darkness is the beginning of living.

Yes, these pink-pale colonizers tricked you. This is part of the many reasons why dark chocolate people are "technically" considered *"dead"* in the eyes of the law that they created in their respective languages. To have an authentic spiritual life rests at the bosom of your *"Dark Father"* who resides at the darkest of all darkness. Everything came from darkness from inception to revelation into physical form.

Embrace the darkness. The strength of any light is measured by the amount of darkness it clears. Light emits from darkness. Darkness is the focal condensed point of all energies, powers, entities, frequencies and vibrations.

Embrace the sun and your true *Father* if you desire to spiritually, psychologically and physically rule on earth again as the first fruits and royals that you are. Darkness, which is your Father is Life. The true sun is known as *"the black sun"*. The sun we see up in our atmosphere is a reflected projection of the original black sun. The black sun is inside earth, it warms the earth up and gives it life.

Dark chocolate melanated people must gain life and gain it abundantly. The allegorical bible states that *Abram* had his name changed to *Abra-HAM* (Ham means *dark/burnt/darker/darkness*). Before *Abram* could be blessed with the covenant, his name had to change by adopting the *name* of the "God" who called him. *Abram* was commanded to add *"darkness/dark/burnt/darker"* a.k.a *Ham* to his name. *Abram* now became *AbraHam*. Don't miss this revelation that holds the keys to free and emancipate all global dark chocolate melanated people.

Let's get into the numerical values and their representation(s):

Numerical value Keys:

Spiritual, Mathematical, Scientific, and Cultural Meaning:

0 ==> All life within the womb, spirits of all spirits, absolute darkness, Creators' hibernation

1 ==> Light. New Life, Fresh Start. Air, Wind.

2 ==> Water. Atmosphere, Firmament. Reflection. Duality of life or situations.

3 ==> Growth, Progress, Expand, Divine Principles, Success. Earth, Dry Grounds, Sea Plants.

4 ==> Calmness, stability, Focus, contentment, upgrade. Sun, Moon, Stars.

5 ==> Freedom, Diversified change. Birds, Sea creatures.

6 ==> Balance between Spirit, Soul and Body. Earth/Land animals and Humans.

7 ==> Self love, Introspection, Spiritual rest and focus. Day of rest and full meditation.

8 ==> Power, Eternity of Cyclical Creation or Destruction rebirth, progress, success.

9 ==> Completion, Perfection, Ascended ones, Fully attained energetic vibrating frequencies.

Etymology of Compendiums of all Gods and The Almighty Creator

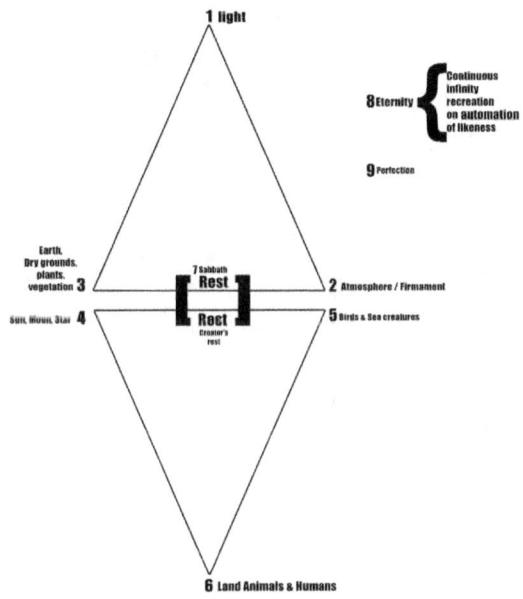

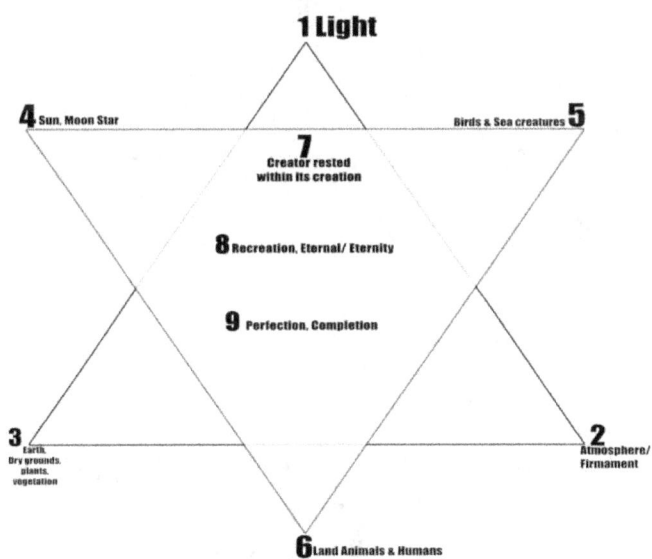

Etymology of Compendiums of all Gods and The Almighty Creator

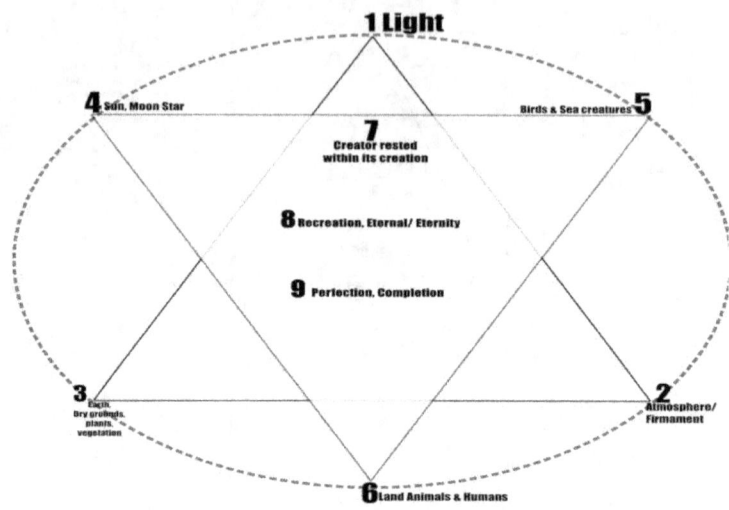

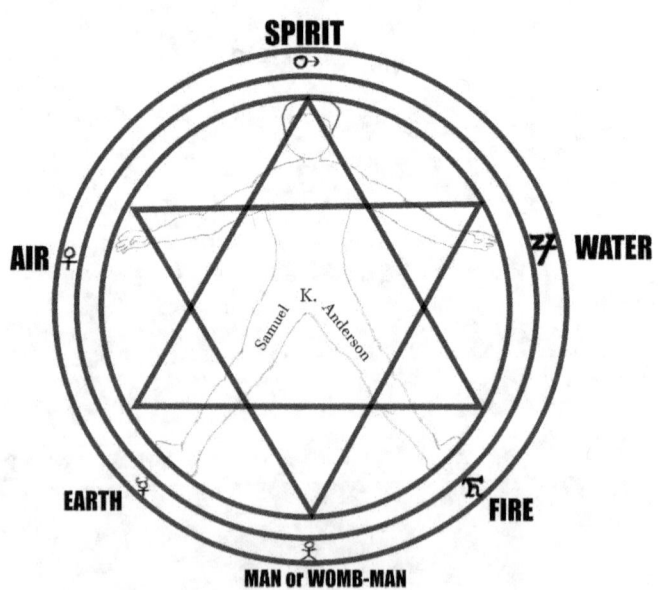

Etymology of Compendiums of all Gods and The Almighty Creator

Our unity creates a powerful force that can manifest what we desire into existence efficiently and effectively.

Base on your own energetic vibrating frequencies, things happen to you and for you. You manifest your numerical creation keys base on either your higher self or lower self. Everything you do, be it good, bad or ugly is mathematically numerical.

Depending on the level of frequency you tend to vibrate, you may tend to see repeating numbers like 000, 111, 222, 333, 444, 555, 666, 777, 888, or 999.

This is a message that is signaled to you from both your conscious and spiritual dimensions. You must pay attention to such signal(s) because it is a manifestation of your own creation through the type and level of frequencies you are exerting at the moment.

Regardless of the digits you are seeing, be it double digits, triple digits or quadruple digits you must know the message that each single/individual digit represents before looking at the sequence in which the numbers appeared to you. The individual numbers in the repetitive number(s) you see throughout your day carries specific message (refer to the *numerical value keys and the respective Spiritual, Mathematical, Scientific, and Cultural Meaning table discussed*).

The next step is to look at the sequence the numbers appeared to you, was it in two, three or four digits? Was it the same number repeating or mixed of numbers repeating? If it is the same number repeating in the sequence then you must know that the warning, awareness, importance or emergency of the message needs to be attended to.

This could be a message of calmness or a message of stability or change that may be about to happen to you. The repetitive sequence of the numbers will guide you to innerstand the urgency of the message.

The final step is to add all the repetitive numbers until you get a single number that falls within zero to nine. This will be the final sentence to the message you are vibrating to. This last sentence is like the conclusion of a telegraph, a text message or an essay to sum it all up.

Let me give you an example to help you comprehend further. Refer to the numerical values decoded on *page82* to find the hidden message in your date of birth.

Take a moment to write down your date of birth in this manner "mm+dd+yyyy". Example 01+25+1990 = 2,016 (the total is a four digit value). In this example the total value is 2,016.

Step 1: refer to the *numerical value keys* to find the respective *Spiritual, Mathematical, Scientific, and Cultural Meaning of these* numerical values. Write down the message each number represents and meditate on it.

Step 2: This step is to add the numbers in the total value as single digits. Let me show you how:

The total value was 2,016 = 2+0+1+6 = 9. So Now, we have finally arrive at a final single digit that is within the foundational blocks of numerical creation (that is from zero to nine). If you add yours and arrived at a number outside zero to nine (single digit). You must keep on adding until you arrive at a single digit number that falls between zero to nine.

Arriving at a single digit between zero to nine will conclude decoding the message in your date of birth. Use this analogy for any repetitive numbers or sequential numbers that come to you as a message.

Let's look at more examples relating to numbers and the mathematics centering around the numerical values of zero to nine. In the christian new testament bible, it is said that Jesus Christ died at the age of 33 years old and rose on the 3rd day from his day of death. Now, that number is 333 = 3+3+3 = 9. *The numerical value keys reflect that number 9 has a Spiritual, Mathematical, Scientific, and Cultural Meaning of "Completion, Perfection, Ascended ones, Fully attained energetic vibrating frequencies".*

Those who compiled the bible known as the *Council of Nicaea*, around the year 325, were the ecumenical council of the Christian church. They met in the ancient town of *Nicaea*, currently known as *İznik, Turkey* presided by *Constantine I* to structure the books that would be accepted to form what is called *helios biblios* (sun book a.k.a *bible*).

They also formed the persona and the character *Iesus Christos* later on became *Jesus Christ*. This council clearly used numerical values and its respective meanings in their planning. Let's look at the number 666 for instance. Most people think that it is evil but in all actuality it's not evil. Rather, it relates to the journey of man and woman to attaining their full consciousness (spiritual, physical and psychological completeness or perfection to fully/completely ascend).

Let's look into it, 666 = 999, in that; per the *numerical value keys table* **6 represents** => *"Balance between Spirit, Soul and Body. Earth/Land animals and Humans"* and the *numerical value keys of* **9 represents** => *"Completion, Perfection, Ascended ones, Fully attained energetic vibrating frequencies"*.

So let's do this mathematically, 666 = 6+6+6 = 18; 18 = 1+8 = 9.

Now, let's look at 999; 999 = 9+9+9=27; 27 = 2+7= 9.

The number 6 is the *physical* numerical representation of man or woman while the number 9 is the *spiritual self* of man or woman.

In other words, the number 9 is the reverse of the number 6. We came from the numerical value of number 9 (*spiritual*) to the numerical value of number 6 (*physical*). This is what I call, the *cyclical connection between the numerical values of the numbers 6 and 9*.

The connection is that, after men and women reach completeness in spirituality or full ascension (*numerical value of 9*), they finally attain *"oneness", completeness* with the *Source* (a.k.a the Almighty Creator).

When you attain the numerical value key of 9, you are complete. You do not have to reincarnate. At this point, you would be the one to decide to either reincarnate or not to reincarnate back to earth.

However, anyone below the numerical value of 9 must reincarnate over and over again until he/she attains the numerical value keys of 9. Some of us have reincarnated several times to this dimension called earth (numerical value key is 3).

Now, there was this man called Methuselah who is claimed to have been the oldest person who lived prior to the flood per the bible. He lived to the age of 969. Do you see the sequence of this number (Methuselah's age)? That sequence is 9,6,9 (refer to the *numerical value keys and the respective Spiritual, Mathematical, Scientific, and Cultural Meaning table discussed*) to follow this; 969 = 9+6+9 = 24; 2+4= 6.

Do you see the reincarnation message in here? Follow the steps we used for your birthday and you will clearly see the message these numbers signal.

Another example is the number 144,000 people that are "chosen" or set aside as the helios biblios (sun book a.k.a bible) asserts. Let's look into this number and its meaning, 144,000 = 1+4+4+0+0+0 = 9 (The numerical value keys of 9 has the *Spiritual, Mathematical, Scientific, and Cultural Meaning* of full/complete ascension, Completion, Perfection, Ascended ones, Fully attained energetic vibrating frequencies).

The raster man known as Samson from the helios biblios (sun book a.k.a bible) had exactly 7 locks/braids on his head that was never cut since birth. The number 7 (7 locs/braids on Samson's head) represents => Self love, Introspection, Spiritual rest and focus.

Day of rest and full meditation. Now, Samson was known to be a Nazarite/Nazirite (Nazareth, Nazarene). A Nazarite per the *helios biblios* (sun book a.k.a *bible*) is known to be of a sacred person who is most commonly distinguished by his *uncut hair* (*locs/braids*), and his abstinence from wine.

This actually makes *Iesus Christ* a.k.a *Jesus Christ* and *Samson* to be *raster men* accordingly. *Iesus* a.k.a *Jesus* was known as the *Iesus Christ* of *Nazareth*.

These are all Afrakan stories with real Afrakan names that were stolen and brutally twisted into full blown mythologies by Rome. After the fall of ancient Egypt to the Greeks and later to the Romans.

Both the Greeks and Romans manipulated and politically controlled all the information that they accumulated from ancient Kemet/Hamite/Egypt. Those who fail to question everything in modern times, end up blindly accepting almost anything without proper research and questioning.

Let me bring in *Shiva*, in the culture of Hindus. Shiva is said to have had what is called *"Tajaa"*, that is *locs/ braids* of hair or twisted *locs/braids* of hair. Locs/ braids from the original dark melanated first nations of earth's culture represents *absolute purity* or *a true dedication to purity*.

Paul the Apostle in *Acts 18:18; 21:22-26* exhibits that he was dedicated to wearing *locs/ braids* to keep the Nazarene vow. Additionally, Solomon in *Song of Solomon 5:2,11; 7:5, Ezekiel in Ezekiel 8:3*, Absalom in *2Samuel 14:26; 2Samuel 18:9*, and John the Baptist in *Matthew 3:4*, Samuel and Daniel were all men who had *locs/ braids* (raster men). Yes, they are all raster men with *locs/braids*.

Buddha is known to also have had *"bantu knots"* which is a way to *loc* your hair although not in the traditional way discussed above.

These were the ways of most of the ancient ones. These ancient ones are the first nations on earth (the melanated ones) prior to the modern day new world order of things by the new people (a.k.a Caucasians) who basically have demonized the *locs/ braids* from its spiritual purity into mockery and almost a crime in some sense.

The hair locs/braids are extensions of you which grows from within the realms of the inner temples and holly of hollies (simply put "your head") which holds both internal and external energies. The Olmecs of Mexico's heads were with locs/braids.

Tiahuanocao locs/ braids of South Amerika, dark melanated Mayans locs/braids hairstyles. Yamaicans/Jamaicans locs/braids, and many Afrakans with locs/ braids from beginning of time to present era are all indications of the immense spiritual purity prowess of the original first nations of earth.

Your locs/ braids receive information internally and transmit it externally while absorbing external energies to store within the locs/ braids and later on transmit the energetic vibrating energies into your internal holly realms (*where your brain resides*). Locs/braids usher the ones rocking them into constant reminder of their spiritual journey that is filled with wisdom, kindness, strength, intelligence, desire to do good to others and to themselves, pure spiritual spiral nine ether conduction of consistent energy flow.

Give respect and honor to those with locs/braids. Listen to their wisdom for they are walking on the path of spirituality and practicing spirituality as well.

Naturally, the "nappy hair" or the so-called typical Afrakan hair is extremely curled like the shape of the number 9.

That is a natural coiling from the spiritual realm through your mother's womb to this physical realm. Both men and women of Afrakan descent biologically have this 9 numerical shaped "nappy" hair. That is the ultimate hair in the realms of numbers. This is a symbol of perfection, ascension, completion or an ether prowess.

It is sad that some of the original first nations with such great "nappy" numerical number 9 hair succumb to western worlds' lies and turn around to absorb such lies by using harmful chemicals on their 9 ether "nappy" hair to straighten it. Straightening your hair is a symbol of a *fallen God or Goddesses*. Yes, from your God/Goddess 9 ether "nappy"/woolly hair to the fallen low vibration straighten hair.

Self love is key to your ascension, that is; your spiritual conscious self. Self love prompts you to get to know yourself from the inside out. Every inch of your existence pre and post physical birth is perfect, complete (the numerical value 9).

You basically came here to earth just to find your way back to your source (ascension, completeness, perfection). It's a cyclical journey. Always go within you to tap into the rivers of calmness, peace, wisdom and innerstanding whenever your journey gets murky.

Women get pregnant for 9 months. Within the 9 months are 3 trimesters (a period of three months). So there are 3 trimesters within 9 months. That is =>3 (1st trimester) +3 (2nd trimester) +3 (3rd trimester) = 9 months.

This is when the doctors, nurses, midwives and especially the pregnant mother know that, it is time for her baby to be born (welcomed to earth). The journey of the pregnant woman is a beautiful symbolical reminder of the cyclical eternal recreation of the perfect creation that was created from the beginning of time.

3rd month	6th month	9th month
1st Trimester	2nd Trimester	3rd Trimester

**9 is the number of completion and perfection.
We are born COMPLETE and PERFECT.**

There are 33 spinal nerves and 33 vertebrae as well as 24 cranial nerves in every man and woman. The number 33 carries the energies of the number 3 repeated twice (3,3). When you reference to the table of numbers and its corresponding meaning you will see that the number 3 relates to consciousness as in *"Growth, Progress, Expand, Divine Principles, Success"*.

The 33 vertebrae in your body symbolizes the unique energy that rises up through your 33 vertebrae to your brain. This is where your Christ/Krist consciousness resides. So the energy descends first through the 33 vertebrae and then if the energy is retained, if not released out from your body through intercourse or any other form. It rises back up through the 33 vertebrae up to your brain to cause what is known as the "resurrected Christ/Krist".

The 33 vertebrae could easily be likened to 33 steps that the secreted energy descends and ascends on which could be seen as the biblical reference to Yacov/Yacob ascending and descending on the 33 step ladder to and from "God/god" in the Genesis account (Genesis 28:10-).

Let's look at the numbers in the Genesis 28:10 verse. The numbers 2+8+1+0=11; 11=1+1=2; from the *"numerical value keys"* the number 2 represents *"Duality of life or situations"*. Apparently, Yacov/Jacob's name was changed to "Israel". Indicating, from his duality of physical transitioning to his spiritual experience.

The 24 cranial nerves also represents what the bible folks consider as the 24 elders (Rev. 4:3-4). The 24 cranial nerves function to aid the pineal gland to function to its fullest capacity/potential. In case you desire to know what the pineal gland is. This is the main endocrine gland that sits at the middle of the brain between the 2 cerebral hemispheres.

The word "cerebral" sounds like "cherubim", humans have 2 cerebral hemispheres. We could say that it is similar to the Genesis 3:24 accounts of the cherubim and the flaming sword guarding the tree of life. Just meditate on this for a while, how well do you know your own human anatomy? Okay, let's continue with the numbers breakdown. Look at Genesis 3:24, that will be 3+2+4=9. Do you see what's happening here? It is also number coded.

Now, just do the simple math for the 33 vertebrae and the 24 elders or 24 cranial nerves in our human anatomic body. 3+3 = 6; and 2+4 = 6. Do you see the consistent numerical value keys message through out every sector of this universe? Knowing the meanings of the numbers from zero to nine would greatly help to guide both your spiritual and physical journey to find yourself back home to the true source of everything.

I hope by now, you innerstand and overstand the numerical relativity of creation and *The Source* to everything. This has nothing to do with religion but everything to do with your essence of existence and the ability to get to know yourself, the God within you. You are full of numbers, you posses the numerical values of zero to nine.

On either side of your head, behind your eyes, between your forehead and your ears, is your temples. You have four bones that fuse together to form this temple. The frontal, temporal, parietal, and sphenoid. These 4 skull bones fuse together and hold on to form your temples.

You basically have two temples, one on each side of your head. Your temples are super sensitive spot that attracts vibrations. Any low vibration energy such as stress and tension would likely cause some sort of pain in and around your temples.

High vibration energies would relax your temples and give you great relief. Your temples houses your pineal gland a.k.a "the God within or the throne of God". So, you can see why your temples may be super sensitive and the reason why good vibes, good energy, good vibration is key.

You must find yourself from within (inside out), in order to find your way home. That is, back to your God self. You lost yourself to find yourself back to your God self. That's the mystery surrounding everything in our human experience on this earth.

Everything is cyclical within the numerical value keys of zero to nine (0 to 9). Everything sprang out from the numerical spiritual number of zero, the crème de la crème, the all in all, darkness, the Source of everything into "light" or life. The true original creator or creative force of everything resides in complete darkness a.k.a, the number zero.

THEORETICAL FORMULA TO FURTHER ENJOY NUMBERS and THE SOURCE

Let's start with the theoretical equation / formula that I call the *"Mathematical and Numerical Relativity of Creation and the Source Equation"*

$S \times K = A$

$S+S+S = A$

S represents *"Any Number"*

K represents *"Constant Number"*

A represents *"Outcome"*

Putting this equation in a sentence, the *"Mathematical and Numerical Relativity of Creation and the Source Equation"* will then state that **any number** multiplied by a **constant number** will result in the **same outcome** when the same number (stipulated as "any number") is added **constant number** of times.

Example: when 2 (representing **"any number"**) is multiplied by 3 (represent **"constant number"**), it will result in 6 (representing **"same outcome"**) when the same number (in this case 2 representing **"any number"**) is added 3 times (2+2+2=6).

This example would look like this in mathematical language:

$S \times K = A$

$S+S+S=A$

$2 \times 3 = 6$ [Any number **X** Constant number = Same Outcome]

2+2+2 = 6 [Any number + Any number + Any number = Same Outcome]

The number you make "constant" in this equation would represent how many times you add the "any number" value. This makes this theoretical equation fluid and fun to interchange. The key is to know which number you made constant. This can be applied to any numerical value. Try different numbers for fun to test the *"Mathematical and Numerical Relativity of Creation and the Source Equation"* out.

Let's take a step further in the progression of the *"Mathematical and Numerical Relativity of Creation and the Source Equation"* by looking at what "division" would do to this equation.

Division will become the **reverse** of the *"Mathematical and Numerical Relativity of Creation and the Source Equation"* as the **outcome** is divided by the **constant number** to arrive at the **"any number"**.

Original Equation = **S x K = A**

Division effect = from right to left (reverse) = A / K = S

Initially we used, 2X3=6. In reverse, would be 6/3=2

So, if you followed and practiced this theoretical equation, I can then conclude that:

Multiplication (X) is "likened" to a jump or to jump.

Addition (+) is "likened" to consistency, repetitive constant consistency.

Division is "likened" to reset, restitution, restoration.

I hope you had fun with my *"Mathematical and Numerical Relativity of Creation and the Source Equation"*. Okay, let's continue our journey through this book.

NUMBERS and MATHEMATICALLY SPIRITUAL CONNECTION of the AKAN TRIBE of GHANA WEST AFRAKA to the ALMIGHTY CREATOR (the SOURCE)

The Akan people of Ghana, West Afraka are the amazing ancient people who are known to have originally migrated from Mesopotamia. They are part of the aboriginal people of the land of Mesopotamia prior to their migration to present day Ghana, West Afraka.

This glorious group has the Adinkra symbols, this is something we are going to study. Let's start with their symbol known as the king of all Adinkras a.k.a *Adinkra Hene*.

This is the *Adinkra Hene* (King of all *Adinkra* symbols).

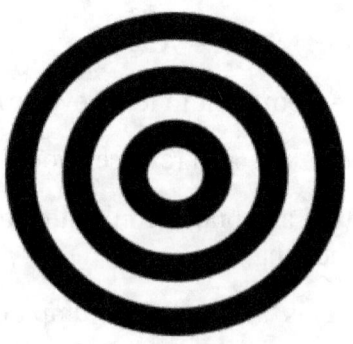

The Akans calendar is cyclically perfect in alignment with the numerical value of zero as to being the source of everything. The number of months in a year and the number of days add up to the perfect number of 360 (3+6+0 = 9). Let's get to it, shall we?

Etymology of Compendiums of all Gods and The Almighty Creator

The Akan tribe's calendar consists of 9 months, each month has 40 days. So, that is 9×40 = 360 days cycle every year.

This is what we call a perfect calendar that resonates with nature, our universe and the source of everything in the numerical value keys.

9 moons/months

40 days within 1moon/month

40 days x 9 moons/months = 360 days (Adinkra Hene, king of all the Adinkras).

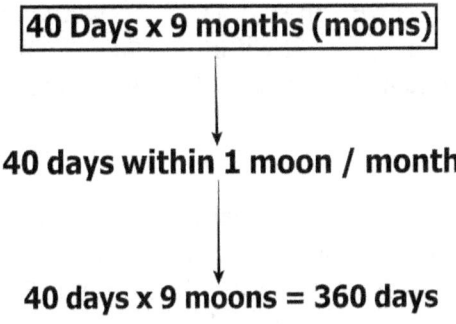

A full circle is known to have 360° degrees (3+6+0=9), a half circle a.k.a straight angle is measured at 180° degrees (1+8+0=9), while a quarter of a circle a.k.a right angle is known to be 90° degrees (9+0=9).

There is a numerical correspondence to this rich first nation's culture, traditions and spirituality. It is clearly seen in their Adinkra symbols, their language, calendar and overall culture. The Akans migrating from Mesopotamia, went through different parts of Afraka before arriving at their current location in West Afraka. Some of them decided to stay at almost all the areas they migrated through. Majority of the Akans could be found predominantly throughout the West Afrakan region.

The Akans celebrate and perform various "Amamer3/Amanmere" (laws, rules, governance) and "Amanie" (requirements needed to sanctify any laws or rules broken or to sanctify and purify through scarification) on the last day of every month, which is the 40th day of every month.

To the Akan tribes, the number 40 is very sacred and as a sacred number with great importance to them. They always honor the 40th day on their calendar every month no matter the situation at hand. In other words, this is a number and a day that falls on the same day throughout their calendar every month. They have adjusted their 40th days calendar calculations accordingly to fit within the Gregorian fake manipulative calendar. Regardless of the adjustments, the 40th day still falls on the same day per their calculations and celebrations.

They have massive gatherings whereby all the sub kings from countless towns, villages and cities gather together at the head King's designated location for meetings to honor their ancient cultural and traditional celebration.

The monthly 40th day meeting and celebration is called *Adaduanan* (literally meaning fortieth day or forty days, *da*=day, *aduanan*=forty). The Akans embrace the 40th day as sacred to the Nananom and Nsamanfor (Ancestors and Ancestresses) and the Abosom (loosely translated to English as Gods and Goddesses, or forces of nature).

They honor them by pouring libation, a drink offering and sacrificing a special animal of their choosing. We should note that the Akans were very smart to adjust their traditional calendar and how they count their days together with the colonially imposed Gregorian calendar. The Akans were able to adjust to the new nontraditional colonial time manipulative Gregorian calendar by fusing it with their traditional calendar to remove any possible obstruction to their ancient traditional celebration.

The Akans have a 7 day week and 6 weeks in a month combination to maintain their 40 day celebration. Despite when we add 6 weeks × 7 days =42, the Akans count some off days to achieve their 40th day Adaduanan celebration. As discussed earlier, the Adaduanan (40th day) occurs 9 times a year on the Akan's traditional calendar.

The 40th day is used to spiritually intercede for good health, wealth, goodwill, protection and spiritual cleansing.

9×40 = 360; 360 is the measurement of a full circle.

Throughout earth's history, you would notice that, the number 40 is very significant to certain groups of people.

Most of the 40 days' significance in the bible could easily be seen in the cultures and traditions of the Akans. Throughout the bible, 40 days appeared over 150 times. This was not just any number, rather, it was a form of time keeping and it comes with its spiritual meaning just like what the Akans of Ghana, West Afraka exhibits. The original people are alive and well verses the fake bible.

In Genesis 7: 4, bible God floods earth for 40 days and 40 nights, *"I will cause it to rain upon the earth forty days and forty nights."* In Mark 1:12-13, Luke 4:2- and Mathew 4:2, Iesus/Jesus is tempted for 40 days and 40 nights.

Moses spent 40 days and 40 nights at Mount Sinai in Exodus 24:18 and 34:28.

Goliath's 40 days and 40 nights torture of the Israel people in 1 Samuel 17:4-7, 16.

Also, read Jonah 3:4-5 where Jonah is sent to warn the Ninevites to change within 40 days or face destruction.

The bible is mythological with respect to how Rome and the Catholic church manipulatively changed the names, places and events of things in the books. The original identities of the people are stripped and replaced with fake characters, fake places and fake names. The true Gods and Goddesses (yes plural for *Elohim)*, have all been demonized with the bad ones elevated to "good". Things have been flipped upside down throughout the bible. The bible is not the history of 100% factual events. In the next chapter (Chapter 3), I discussed into details about this premises.

This allegorical bible derives most of its inspiration from the cultures and traditions of most first nations globally. That is why it's very easy for some cultures to see their practices and sometimes even their traditional languages in the mythological allegorical bible. The bible has been edited, updated, and re-written several thousand times prior to colonization and during colonization. These colonizers infused some of the practices of the countries they visited into the bible. Prior to colonization, people knew of the true creator in their own native language. Aboriginals from all around the world knew about the existence of multiple gods, nature, spirits, souls, earth, writings, community, culture, royalty, nobles, good and bad. These aboriginals' knowledge was corrupted, twisted and infused into the missionary works that came with the bible. The local name or word for a creator, a God/god, good, bad and the likes existed in these communities already before colonizers came into contact with these aboriginals.

CHAPTER 3

CHAPTER 3

THE MELANIN CONNECTIVITY

Melanin is scientifically defined as dark brown or dark black natural pigments chemically produced by the oxidation of amino-acid tyrosine by the use of sunlight or any given source of light or heat energy. Etymology of melanin exceeds the comprehension of the Greeks. In that, those who predominantly have the most melanin concentration are the Afrakans. However, the word "melanin" is associated with Greeks and Latin origin "melas" which means black. In ancient Kemet/Egypt, Dogon people of West Afraka, Atlantis, and Pangaea's era, people already knew about melanin. Hence, it would be comical to attribute its knowledge to the new civilization of the Greeks.

The sun upgrades your DNA. Exposure to sunlight (sunbathing) helps to strengthen your immune system. Your psychological, spiritual and physical state of self are upgraded to a much higher state through exposure to the sun.

Melanin is directly produced by mother nature and nature is an expression of the Almighty Creator. Anyone who discriminates against those with more or heavy melanin is discriminating against nature. Who created nature? Obviously, it is the Almighty Creator.

Melanin is the artistic work of the Almighty Creator. So, anyone who insults, wages war, or disrespects others due to their melanin, is basically insulting and waging war with nature or going against nature and against the Almighty Creator. You live in nature too, so who is going to prevail? Your discriminatory self or the great mother nature and the Almighty Creator? Let this resonate with you to change your discriminatory ways.

The darker you are the more melanin you have in your biological body. Meaning, the Almighty Creator took the wisdom of patience to calmly pour more love of melanin concentration into you. Your skin, hair, eye color, and some organs, tissues, and nerves in your body contain different levels of melanin.

It is rather a great blessing if you can get darker through sun exposure. Getting darker is an indication of a photon electric energy buildup by the light-heat exposure from the sun. In other words, you have been super charged and lovely kissed by mother nature's nurture.

Many people either consciously or unconsciously have gone to war against the Gods and the Goddesses, mother nature, as well as the Almighty Creator simply by discriminating against the heavily melanated ones. They did so by mocking those who are mostly the darkest and very dear to the heart of mother nature and the Almighty Creator.

The sun is key part of nature, so, if the sun damages you, then it is obvious that you are not the chosen ones of mother nature, and the Almighty Creator. The sun should love you and not damage you just like the sun loves plants and do not damage them.

Hence, we should rather humbly embrace and allow those Gods and Goddesses chosen by mother nature and the Almighty Creator to rule, lead, and guide us on this earth and throughout the universal intergalactic galaxies seen and unseen to both our naked eyes and spiritual third eyes. Heavily melanated people can use artificial light to charge/power up so far as they're expose to appropriate wavelengths of the artificial light. Even the heater in your homes, warm or hot water, can also charge/power you up.

However, as much as possible, stay away from ice bathes and extreme cold showers. This is not for heavily melanated people. You are of the sun, and not of ice.

You are a people of light, heat, electricity, high energetic vibrating frequencies and dark melanin matter. You need the natural source of all light and heat, that's the sun.

Monitor plants and trees in nature, because when plants and trees die in the cold and snowy weathers, that's when you're prone to vibrate lower on your energy flow. In that, this is not your prime environment, just like the plants and trees doesn't thrive in such environments. You are directly connected to nature and only natural things. Ice, snow and extreme cold are all "dead" and extreme low vibration part of nature.

Living things rarely thrive in ice when left for a prolong exposure, and die shortly after. Even fishes in rivers die when the river freezes. You also undergo your own way of photosynthesis, so you always need the sun or other sources of light and heat to healthily vibrate and power up.

The more sunlight you absorb as a dark or brown person, the darker or browner you become. The darker or browner you become, the more electrically charged you are.

To deprive yourself of sunlight is to spiritually kill yourself as a heavily melanated individual. Melanin is technologically used in some computers and phone devices due to melanin's ridiculously unimaginable essence to transmit, conduct and transduce/convert all forms of electrical energy.

Yes, those with more melanin are very powerful. You should know that the level or amount of melanin in you determines your level of energetic vibrational conductivity physically, spiritually and psychologically.

Electronic energy and photon energy within melanated people are easily activated by continuous exposure to any form of heat, light or most importantly direct access and absorption of sunlight. The sun is the life source activator needed for our internal processing of all chemicals.

Those with high melanin can easily activate their electrical powers with little to no effort. They just need to unblock their years of religious intoxication. Religion is toxic to the God and Goddess essence within us.

Religion is the fluoride to your spiritual third eye, that means you are spiritually calcified through religion. Religion could also be likened to sleepwalking. You are basically not in full control of your psyche, you do not function properly and you are just on programmed mode.

If so-called white people do not like you as a dark melanated first nation people while you are alive, do you really think that these white people want you in their mythical allegoric heaven when you die?

I'm making you think because sadly some of us, not all, lack the wisdom and knowledge of self.

The sooner chocolate-melanated sun kissed and sun chosen people reject the bible and quran to return to their ancestral roots, the sooner we would rise to our true self of *Gods and Goddesses*. This realm is no more magical because we have fallen from our Godhood and Goddess-hood.

THE REAL NAME OF "AFRICA" and THE GODS and GODDESSES

First and foremost, linguistically speaking, most of Africa's languages do not have the letter "C". The sound that the "c" makes is the sound of the letter "K" for majority of Afrakan languages (if not all).

That means, in order to get the spiritual meaning behind most of the names of towns, countries, places and people in "Africa" (a misnomer), we must replace the letter "c" in all the names with the letter "K". We are a *"soulful"* people, a people filled with soul, spirit and direct energetic frequency from the Almighty Creator.

Now that we have gotten the letter "K" innerstanding out of the way, let's look at the true name of "Africa". The factual name of "Africa" is *AFRAKA*. Yes, that is A-F-R-A-K-A (Afraka).

The breakdown of this can fully be linked to one of the great teachers who is now an ancestor, Dr. Ivan Van Sertima. He was a linguist, anthropologist, literary critic, and writer. Dr. Ivan Van Sertima stipulated that "AFRAKA" means First-Sun-Soul; that is the "Af" represents "First", the "RA" represents "Sun" and the "KA" represents "Soul". In addition, Dr. Ivan Van Sertima added that, Afraka/Afrika originated from the Egyptian word "Afru-ika" directly translated as "Motherland".

To add to this, in the Akan languages, predominantly people of Ghana, West Afraka; they refer to the first people on earth (that is, the first nations, the first creations) as *"3wiasi-fo"*. The letter "3" sounds like "err/air" and it's an Akan alphabet. It must be written backwards. Hence, the letter "3" would need to be flipped to the left to face your right side.

The meaning to the Akan word *"3wiasi-fo"* is *"those who live under the sun"* or *those who are of the sun*. The Akan people have another word written as "Adikanfo" or "Nkanfo" or "Akanfo". All three words have the same meaning relating to *"the first people"* or *"the first nations"*. Hence, their name, the Akans (Akanfo, Nkanfo), which means, the first people of all people or first people.

In other words, we are people of the sun. Yes, we are sun people, that is why we derive most of our energy directly from the sun to activate our melanin. There are others, who are literally destroyed or killed by the sun. They need what is called "sun screen" to block the sun's rays from penetrating through their skin, because they are not of the sun. When the sun sets you free, then you are free indeed.

There have been several western world's speculations about the name of the beautiful land and people of the great continent of Afraka to be *Ethiopia, Alkebulan* (which has an Arabic twist to it) and the old Greek Soldier called *"Africanus"*, who gave its name to the great continent of the Gods and Goddesses, Afraka.

None of these westernized ideologies are true. They are all speculations and nothing more.

If we're to be technical, critical and factual, then I can say with a fact that, the first nation founders of Greece, Rome, and all the European nations as well as the entire earth were the so-called chocolate melanated people or Afrakans. The Greeks used to call the entire continent of Afraka as Aethiopia (Greek: Αἰθιοπία, romanized: Aithiopía; also known as Ethiopia) or Aeta, ether. There are old maps that support this name attributed to the continent of Afraka.

Current country Ethiopia in 21st century East Afraka is merely a misnomer because its historical name is Abyssinia, emerged around the 13th century. Abyssinia literally translates to the word, Habesha. Habesha is an Arabic word/term from the Amharic word "hbst", modernly called Habesha.

Habesha means mix breeds of people. These are people mixed by blood or people of mixed blood and DNA of the Arab Muslims and "foreign" people/nations. Prior to world war two (WW2), this geographical area in Eastern Afraka was known as Abyssinia.

Immediately after WW2, Emperor Haile Selassie I, worked extremely hard to push for Abyssinia to be changed to the Greek name/word/term Ethiopia. Emperor Haile Selassie I pleaded with United Nations to apply the old Greek word for Afraka to just his country. Due to the efforts of Emperor Haile Selassie I and his country's contribution as one of the founding members of United Nations (UN), Abyssinia's name change to Ethiopia was granted and internationally recognized effective 1948.

Prior to it being called Abyssinia, it was also known as Kingdom of Aksum (4th century), Kush/Cush. This land in East Afraka has been home to Christians, Jews, Muslims, Arabs, some Nilotic people, and other aboriginal groups.

Abyssinia became popularized after Yekuno Amlak (its founder) was linked to the Solomonic dynasty. Amlak is supposedly from a direct lineage of Menelik, the offspring of Queen of Sheba and biblical King Solomon (the real person is King Pharaoh Siamun who reigned between 978 to 959 BC in ancient Egypt/Kamit/Kemet, a pure dark chocolate aboriginal Afrakan royal). When this land was called Aksum, the Zagew dynasty in conjunction with Makhzumi dynasty (Muslim state ruling) ruled over it up until Yekuno Amlak overthrew them in 13th century.

Their history has been distorted and there have been several attempts to hide its alliance with the Catholic-Christian inquisitions and barbarically murderous bible expansions into Afraka. Abyssinia had to gain the support of Britain (Emperor Haile Selassie I, went into exile or in hiding in Britain) to help ward off the fiver year long invasion by none other than Italy's Mussolini in October 1935.

AEthiopia or Ethiopia is a Greek etymological word/term for the black-skinned people on the entire continent of today's Afrakan continent. There are Aetas a.k.a AEthiopians or Afrakans, a group of ancient people found in today's Philippines. The original name of the Philippines was called Maharlika. The Aetas are aboriginal natives to the land of Philippines or Maharlika in Asia.

Italy was able to annexed territories around Eritrean borders and was expecting the support of native chiefs/leaders/rulers and folks in the various minority communities.

However, support from the native chiefs/leaders/rulers and folks in the various minority communities rather went to the then ruler/king of Abyssinia, Emperor Menilek II around 1893. Emperor Menilek II denounced Italy's Treaty of Wuchale due to a mistranslated word in Article 17 whereby the single Italian word for "must" was changed to "could" in Abyssinian language Amharic. The word "could" is entirely different in meaning in any contractual agreement/treaty than the word "must". Hence, Emperor Menilek II chose the option to denounce the treaty instead of accepting it.

If the local chiefs and minority communities had not support Emperor Menilek II, Italy could have easily ransack Abysinnia (today's Ethiopia). The battle of Adwa decisively ended the Italian's colonial quest. Italian soldiers had to retreat and head back to Italy.

The lesson taken from here is that, no foreign or international country can suppress, oppress or colonize any Afrakan nation unless the local people choose to support that foreign nation over its own Afrakan nation. Think about that very well.

Alkebulan is deemed by so-called "experts" (western folks) as the origin of two Phoenician words. These same "western experts" write that the Moors, Khart-Haddans (Carthagenians), Nubians, Numidians and Ethiopians (Abyssinia, also referred to as Cush/Kush, Nubia and Aksum) used the word/term Alkebulan to refer to Afraka. Either way, those are all speculations from "western experts" which is not something I deem fit for such a great continent that had the first of everything from civilization to spirituality.

Alkebulan also means "mother of mankind" or "garden of Eden". The word "Eden" is not etymologically an old Afrakan language or word.

The word "Eden" is of Hebrew origin (Hebrew is a new language as discussed in chapter 1). Alkebulan in Arabic means *"The Land of the Blacks"*. Arab Muslims ruled for well over 1,300 years, that's 13 centuries of trans-Sahara slave movements of some unfortunate Afrakans.

There is also the speculation that, the Romans named the continent after the people who were occupying the northern areas of Tunisia. This could be the Berbers, the Berber people. They were also known as the 'Afri', 'Afer' and 'Ifir' people. The continent of Afraka is filled with countless ethnic groups with ancient diverse languages older than Greek, Latin, Arabic, and Hebrew. The original name is and will always be Afraka. Its *meaning* and *spirit* represent who we are as the original people of this realm and beyond.

The Akan ethnic group in today's Ghana West Africa have another reference to the continent of Afraka as Abibirim-man or Abibirim/Abibrim.

The Romans and Greeks could have corrupted Abibrim / Abrim to biblical Abram and Abibirim-man (Abibrim-man) to Abramham or Abraham. The Akans have a long history of wars with the Persians, Greeks, Romans and later the Arab Muslims, all the way from Mesopotamia to ancient Egypt/Kemet and through Sudan to Old Ghana Empire, Mali Empire, Songhai Empire, as their migration led them to today's location.

The craziest thing is that these aboriginal Phoenicians, Etrurians, Trojans (founders of Greece and Rome), Greeks, Rome, all the way back in ancient times were all Afrakans. Greek mythologies are all 100% Kemet/Afrakan stuff. Greek philosophy and mathematics are influenced and attained from ancient Kemet. Rome, after conquering the Greeks, took all the Greek mythologies and ideologies that were of ancient Kemet and translated almost all of it to form a religion that the Romans used to politically rule and conquer the world.

Later on, Indo-Europeans wiped out the aboriginals of Greece and Rome to have these modern-day looking pale skin Indo-Europeans. In the beginning, everything and everyone was with a nappy hair and chocolate melanated skin. Greeks are known to have nappy hairs. Greeks also have sickle cells, which is predominantly found in Afrakans or chocolate skin people.

THE FALL OF THE GODS AND GODDESSES

Who are these Gods and Goddesses? How did they fall? Where are they? Once again, the Gods and the Goddesses indeed have fallen. They've fallen from the highest spiritual state to the lowest dense-thick matter earthly state.

The Gods and the Goddesses are not the ones who are currently in charge of things on earth. As a matter of fact, the Gods and the Goddesses have not been in charge closer to almost thousand years. Extremely low energetic vibration people are in charge and they took over through violence, deception and rape. Sadly by the help of some of the fallen Gods and Goddesses. Interestingly, the fall of the Gods and Goddesses was prophesied several years before the fall. Hence, the Gods and the Goddesses knew that the painful era that Afraka and all chocolate melanated people went through was bound to happen. The Gods and the Goddesses who fell, are those who are currently suppressed, discriminated against and laughed at throughout the entire world.

These fallen Gods and Goddesses have been restricted from accessing their true powers by the unnatural people through casting of dark spells, deception, poisoning their food source, water source and energy sources (eg: blocking of the sun). The journey to uncovering these Gods and Goddesses does not start with either the bible or quran. In that, etymologically, Aramaic, Hebrew, Greek, Latin and

Arabic are new languages that are linked to the Abrahamic religions/faiths comparable to the ancient first nations civilizations and kingdoms like Kemet.

This earth is the "heaven" that the Gods and Goddesses lived before one of the fallen Gods genetically mutated and engineered animals, plants, and some other genes to create a different breed of people; who were made just to destroy, steal and kill. There is a glimpse of this mutation story in Genesis chapter 30. Genesis chapter 30 will give you a quick glimpse of Yacov/Yacob's breeding program or genetic program that led to an entirely "new breed" of man's kind, not original men and women. Later on, these new breeds destroyed the kingdom of the Gods and the Goddesses on earth. It took closer to or more than 600 years for Yacov/Yacob to finally accomplish the kind of genetically modified man-kind's test results that he wanted.

These newly genetically bred man's kind were similar to the first nations men and women but not the same. The first nations were created by the Almighty Creator, while the men-likeness or man's kind was created through genetic manipulation inbreeding. These newly created soulless people were taught by their creator who was once part of the first nations. This was part of the prophesy, an abomination, taboo, magic, spells and reversed processes that would destroy the Gods and the Goddesses through pure violence. The Gods and Goddesses had fallen from their spiritual state to the physical state. In a cocoon state.

In the end, the kingdom of the Gods and the Goddesses seriously suffered violence, and the violent ones took the kingdom of the Gods and the Goddesses by force. These soulless newly genetically modified folks placed all their plans in writing and called it "the new testament" a.k.a the new world order.

They vowed to destroy all the first nation's kingdoms, civilizations and inventions. They flipped and reversed things by calling the Gods and the Goddesses "soulless". These unnatural breeds also said that, the fallen Gods and Goddesses (global Afrakans) are not humans. Which is true, in that, the Gods and the Goddesses are of the Almighty Creator. These newly genetically modified folks convinced themselves and vowed to themselves to keep the Gods and Goddesses in perpetual servitude till the end of time. This means, till the end of their time predestined for them to destroy, kill and steal. We're closer to the end of their time more than ever. Ecclesiastes 10:7 King James Version (KJV) states that: *"I have seen servants upon horses, and princes walking as servants upon the earth".*

Their creator, Yakubu/Yacov/Yacob trained them and prepared them for this task. Their creator was part of the fallen Gods and Goddesses (Afrakans), he was not accepted into the council of the Afrakans. Hence, Yacob/Yakubu used his knowledge out of hate, anger, and revenge to create these unnatural people in his science laboratory to kill, rape, destroy and steal everything from the Gods and

Goddesses. These energies exhibited by Yacob/Yakubu were low vibration energies of jealousy, envy and greed. At such lowest vibrations, his genetically unnatural man's kind creations are soulless, and can only operate in rage, barbarism, theft, deception, wars, and perpetual destruction.

Yacov/Yakubu/Yacob infused his dense low vibration frequency into his genetically modified inbreeds. He hid them underground, in a cave around what is geographically known as the Caucasus mountains.

Many nations in Afraka know about this genetically unnatural creation of Yacov/Yacob. In ancient Egypt/Kemet, it was well known and was written in hieroglyphics in the pyramids, at Kush written in Sangam and other languages, Sumerian cuneiform, Kenyan languages found in the masonry Babylonia and many other Afrakan folklores/folktales.

The Zulu people of Afraka have shared this story many times and written in books by no other than the man Credo Mutwa. Credo says that, the evil man who created the genetically modified folks was called *Zah-ha-Rrellel, The Wicked*.

You can read Mutwa's book titled *Indaba My Children*, in this book, Mutwa stated that Za-Ha-Rrellel killed his mother because he was full of evil, hate and destructive energy. Za-Ha-Rrellel's desire was to take over the entire earth, even the moon and sun. Za-Ha-Rrellel will stop at nothing to get this done up until he tried to steal the Earth

Mother from the Tree of Life which caused Earth Mother to be furious, flooding the entire earth killing everyone including Za-Ha-Rrellel except Amarava, the female singer who later married Odu to repopulate the earth.

It was some of the ancient Afrakans who established other languages like English, Spanish, Italian, French and the likes as a means and process to civilize the people that were called the "wild people". These so-called wild people lived in the wild like other "wild animals" and in deep caves called the caucus mountains. European records found in the British museums reflect that, these "wild people" waged barbaric wars that took centuries to take over the kingdoms of the aboriginal Afrakans in Europe after these Afrakans civilized them.

These newly civilized "wild people" got help from some of the ancient Afrakan elders whose energetic vibrating frequencies were massively dropped from their *God-self* to their *Lowest self*. They were filled with low vibrating energies like greed, jealousy, deception, envy and evil plots. To date, the Gods and Goddesses are still trying to "wake up" from their comatose state. This is a spell cast on these aboriginal melanated people by their own kind. Those who fell from high vibration to low vibration in order for the "wild people" to take over till the end of the time allotted for the "wild people".

The Gods and Goddesses must in turn ask the new breeds of people what was their language when they were considered "wild people" in the wild with other wild creatures prior to Afrakans civilizing them.

Göbekli Tepe, an ancient settlement located in today's Turkey excavated by few archaeologists was inhabited from c. 9500 to at least 8000 BCE, during the Pre-Pottery Neolithic. The word Göbekli Tepe is a word from the Ewe/Eve language of the people in West Afraka, who are predominantly located in today's Ghana, West Afraka. Göbekli Tepe's civilization, writings, calendar for when the flood happened, star constellations, and carvings existed over 6000 years before the Sumerians and over 7,000 years before both Stonehenge and the pyramids were built, per "expert" western archaeologists. However, the fact is that Gobekli Tepe existed concurrently as the ancient Sumerians, Kemet, Akkadians and Dogons. Today, all these ancient people live largely in West Afraka.

Any so-called global archaeologist and linguistic who desire to "discover" new knowledge which I and many of the Ewe people in Ghana, West Afraka already know; should visit the Kings and senior community representatives of the Ewe people to get to know the aboriginal people of Göbekli Tepe. They are still alive and well in West Afraka. The Gods and Goddesses are all here on earth. They've just fallen from a high energetic spiritual vibration to lowest dense vibration. They are gradually rising. Their next elevation is supernaturally super spiritual.

THE NEW WORLD ORDER (NWO) a.k.a NEW TESTAMENT (NT)

The New Testament bible (NT) is the first official draft of the New World Order (NWO) packaged and put forth under the auspices of the Roman Catholic Church and its Pope using these three(3) papal bulls: *Dum Diversas* on June 18th 1452 issued by Pope Nicholas V, *Romanus Pointifex* on January 15th 1455 issued by Pope Nicholas V, and *Inter Caetera* on May 14th 1493 issued by Pope Alexander VI. The New World Order (NWO) a.k.a New Testament (NT) clearly states in *Mathew 11:12 (KJV)* "*And from the days of John the Baptist until now the kingdom of heaven suffereth violence, and the violent take it by force*".

The violent ones (the colonizers) took the "kingdom of heaven on earth" (first nations, first people's wealth and kingdoms) with barbaric violent force. It started all the way from the time of the raster-man, John the Baptist. There are codes everywhere in the first official draft of the New World Order (NWO) a.k.a New Testament (NT).

The NWO a.k.a New Testament bible was always with the spies a.k.a missionaries who came with the colonizers as they violently destroyed, stole, raped and murdered mostly the men and women in the first nations kingdom. The New World Order a.k.a New Testament bible was literally beaten into the colonized nations and although some fought back. Many were too weak and afraid of death to the extent that they decided to rather embrace the NWO a.k.a New Testament bible than to die.

The Greeks, Romans, Muslim Arabs, and all the European nations planned to push the New World Order (NWO) a.k.a New Testament (NT). Rome at this time had two empires, namely the Byzantine -Eastern empire and the Western empire. It was rough at some point between the Muslim Arabs as Byzantine fell to the Ottoman Empire and the Western Empire a.k.a Catholic Church survived. The concept and production of the Quran and its details was pushed and made possible by the Pope and the Catholic church. In other words, the Pope seriously influenced the Quran and spread of the religion. The Quran got almost all of its references from the Bible. So if the bible is porous, then it is obvious that the Quran too is porous.

There have been lots of blood sheds, and brutal violence toward aboriginals in order for the Pope, Catholic Church and later on the colonizers to accomplish the goal of spreading the New World Order (NWO) a.k.a New Testament (NT).

Prior to the 14th century arrival of Spain and Portugal's brutal invasions, the Muslims had already invaded, colonized, raped, murdered and forced their Qurans on the aboriginal chocolate sun-kissed melanated first nations for well over 1,300 years. Yes, these Muslims were brutal, bloody, merciless and barbaric just as the European colonizers or even possibly worst. Track all the countries in the world throughout all the known seven (7) continents and ask yourself, how did Islamic Arab Muslim religion get there? We're talking about Asia, North America, Europe, South America, Afraka, Oceania, and Antarctica.

Christopher Columbus upon meeting some of the aboriginal people in the Americas around late 14th century had this to say in his letters to his Spaniard King and Queen and journals. These are some excerpts taken from Columbus encounter, he wrote:

*"They are very simple and honest and exceedingly liberal with all they have, none of them refusing anything he may possess when he is asked for it. They exhibit great love toward all others in preference to themselves………[…]…They are the best people in the world and above all the gentlest—without knowledge of what is evil—nor do they murder or steal… they love their neighbors as themselves and they have the sweetest talk in the world… always laughing… […]…***They would make fine servants. With fifty men we could subjugate them all and make them do whatever we want….[…]…****Thus they bartered, like idiots, cotton and gold for fragments of bows, glasses, bottles, and jars;……[]
I did this in order that I might the more easily conciliate them, that they might be led to become Christians, and be inclined to entertain a regard for the King and Queen, our Princes and all Spaniards, and that I might induce them to take an interest in seeking out, and collecting, and delivering to us such things as they possessed in abundance, but which we greatly needed……[…]…They practice no kind of idolatry, but have a firm belief that all strength and power, and indeed all good things, are in heaven, and that I had descended from thence with these ships and sailors, and under this impression was I received after they had thrown aside their fears. Nor are they slow or stupid, but of very clear understanding; and those men who have crossed to the neighbouring islands give an admirable description of everything they observed;… […]…In all these island there is no difference in the appearance of the people, nor in the manners and language, but all understand each other mutually; a fact that is very important for the*

end which I suppose to be earnestly desired by our most illustrious king, that is, their conversion to the holy religion of Christ, to which in truth, as far as I can perceive, they are very ready and favorably inclined".

The aboriginals who fought and resisted were seen by the Spaniards, Portuguese and later, the rest of the barbaric heartless colonizers as "defying God's plan". These invaders psychotically believed that they are destined by their god/God to invade, rape, destroy, murder and take the aboriginal land by any means necessary. Anyone who resisted, was tortured by the invaders. These invader/colonizers would skin aboriginals alive, cut them into pieces, fry them alive in hot boiling oil, hang and shoot the aboriginals with their bullets as target until they die. In that, for any aboriginal to resist is to defy their bloody evil god/God. Now, do you wonder why some of you blindly and ignorantly deny your own ancestral roots, cultures, and spirituality? You have been psychologically sedated with their toxic drug of their bible and their version of Christianity.

You have been mentally and socially castrated. You have been emotionally and aurally molested to the extend that, you do everything under a mind controlling manipulative stigma unaware of why you hate your own ancestors, and love the same invaders who murdered, raped, tortured, and stole your land and its resources. The aboriginal chocolate melanated people that so-called Christopher Columbus met in the Americas had no religious affiliation because they were spiritual. Spirituality is not religion. Religion is not found in spirituality.

Because the aboriginal people were spiritual and lived in harmony with nature. Christopher Columbus shared with his Spaniard King and Queen that these aboriginals "would be good servants" and "good Christians" obedient to the Spanish King and all christendom. These invaders literally forced these melanated American aboriginals with the threat of *"be killed"* or *"join our christian religion"*. These were the only options given, in order to steal, invade, destroy and overtake the inhabitants of the aboriginals.

Fear was a factor, some aboriginals sold out and converted to Christianity to protect their dear lives in order to live to see another day. The others who resisted had to fight for several centuries. Some were captured and enslaved by these so called "newly converted Christians", invaders and colonizers.

To date, the New World Order a.k.a New Testament bible is still enforced throughout the entire world. There are some countries like China, India and others within the Arab peninsula who resist the enforcement of some of the things compiled within the New Testament (NT) a.k.a New World Order (NWO). The Pope is still the head of all the European nations. Nothing has changed from the Roman era to date. We are still directly and indirectly ruled and manipulated by the Pope and the New Testament (NT) a.k.a New World Order (NWO) agenda.

There have been some modifications to the New World Order (NWO) a.k.a New Testament (NT) to adjust to the ever changing social, economic, spiritual, religious and psychological environment of the world. There are some nations and private institutions like the BRICS (Brazil, Russia, India, China, South Afraka) currency initiation that seek to go independent from the New World Order (NWO) a.k.a New Testament (NT) dollar, global military, and political neocolonialism.

Fast forward to the 21st century and you have most of the aboriginals' new generations unaware of how the spell of the New World Order (NWO) a.k.a New Testament (NT) was violently put on them. These new generations even deny their own ancestral ways to unquestionably accept and defend the New World Order (NWO) a.k.a New Testament (NT). Somewhere within the first draft of the New World Order (NWO) a.k.a New Testament (NT) it states that, *"Blessed are the meek: for they shall inherit the earth"(Mathew 5:5 kjv).*

What is the etymological definition of "meek" and who is really inheriting (enjoying, ruling, possessing all the lands, golds, artifacts, currencies, etc) on earth? I bet the U.S, Canada, Pope, Vatican, France, England, NATO and rest of the colonizers are as "meek" as hell. Because the last time I checked, they have been "inheriting" all the goodies on earth. That's another deception from the New World Order (NWO) a.k.a New Testament (NT) to keep most of the aboriginals docile, poor, perpetual servitude, lost, denial of self and down till the "end of time". Etymologically, meek is any living thing that is very strong and powerful yet kept under control and willing to submit. So do you see how the New World Order (NWO) a.k.a New Testament (NT) was used to tame the aboriginals to "unwillingly" and deceptively give up their extreme power and strength?

Who is the head of the smallest country on earth located within another country? It's none other than the Pope. The Vatican is a country within the country of Italy. The Vatican has numerous assets and is considered the richest nation/country in the entire world. The Vatican's wealth is undisclosed to the public because the Pope can choose to do so. No world leader can question the Pope unless he, the Pope decides to disclose what he feels right to disclose.

Who oversee all the intergovernmental organizations like the United Nations (UN) with 193 country members? It's the Pope and the Holly See. Who is the final head influencer of the International Monetary Fund (IMF) with190 members? It's none other than the Pope and the United Nations.

The New World Order (NWO) a.k.a New Testament (NT) has been around and keeps evolving into something new, yet still rooted in its original mission and vision; that's the Papal bull of 1452 by Pope Nicholas V to *"[...] invade, capture, search out, vanquish, and subdue all Saracens and pagans whatsoever, and other enemies of Christ wheresoever placed, and the kingdoms, dukedoms, principalities, dominions, possessions, and all movable and immovable goods whatsoever held and possessed by them and to reduce their persons to perpetual slavery, and to apply and appropriate to himself and his successors the kingdoms, dukedoms, counties, principalities, dominions, possessions, and goods, and to convert them to his and their use and profit."*

Fast forward to AFRICOM, an acronym for U.S. Africa Command. AFRICOM's aim is to build relationships and "support partners" in Afraka to provide "peaceful" western view point on democracy, control military forces on the continent of Afraka and to safeguard things in "peace" and war.

United States Africa Command (AFRICOM), claim it is headquartered in Stuttgart, Germany; however, Camp Lemonnier in Djibouti, Afraka is where AFRICOM uses as its major hub for all U.S military tasks within the continent of Afraka. General Michael Langley (a "black man", African American, black American) man is the head of AFRICOM as of 2023. These Western institutions use people who look like you in order to gather all the intelligence from various chocolate melanated Afrakan countries to execute their intended missions successfully. The question that still remain is, how does Afraka benefit from AFRICOM if the purpose is to protect United States and all NATO countries' interest in Afraka? When would Afraka's interests be protected in all western countries (a.k.a NATO countries)?

Better yet, when would Afrakans enjoy their rich minerals and great wealth without foreign interruptions? Afraka has been restricted by Western nations from developing its own nukes and ICBM -Intercontinental Ballistic Missiles. Why wouldn't Afraka also want to manufacture its own nukes for its safety, security and protection of its own interest on Afrakan soil. There is also the Air Forces Africa (AFAFRICA) which is conveniently situated at Ramstein Air Base, Germany. The AFAFRICA's mission is to mainly serve as the air and space section for U.S. Africa

Command (AFRICOM). AFRICOM is one of U.S. Department of Defense's many combatant commands.

Camp Lemonnier in Djibouti is a permanent U.S. military base in Afraka, and it houses well over 5,000 U.S military personnel. There could be more troops from NATO member nations stationed at Camp Lemonnier in Djibouti. Could U.S led AFRICOM's presence in Afraka cause ascendancy of coups and terrorist incidences across Afraka?

Recent increase in coups and other violently hostile insurrections occurred on the soil of Afraka when Colonel Mamady Doumbouya (trained and equipped by the U.S led AFRICOM) in Guinea, West Afraka led a coup d'état on September 5th, 2021 to overthrew the previous democratically elect president, Alpha Conde. Doumbouya dissolved the democratically elected government and the nation's constitution, and was sworn in as the interim president on October 1st, 2021.

Another coup happened in Burkina Faso, this country is a landlocked country in West Afraka with which Captain Ibrahim Traoré (also trained and equipped by U.S led AFRICOM) took over the presidential power from Burkina Faso's democratically elect president and government on September 30th, 2022. However, Ibrahim Traoré turned against USA, chose to defend his people as the new president, and kicked out U.S military base in Burkina Faso. Interestingly, U.S led AFRICOM's core values seem not to work on the continent of Afraka because this institution is basically destroying the peace in Afraka.

Let's dive into the Jihadists and other terrorist organizations possibly linked to Western military forces. Most dangerous and troubled spots around the world are mostly (although not all) fueled by jihadists who happened to be of the Abrahamic faith of the Arab Muslims. Al-Qaeda, al-Shabaab, and ISIS-affiliated groups are seen to be the deadliest "terrorist" organizations in the world.

The question is, what countries or nations train and equip these highly skilled forces of al Qaeda, ISIS, Jihadists, al-Shabaab, and other Muslim terrorist organizations? Did United States and NATO (North Atlantic Treaty Organization founded on April 4th, 1949) partner with any of these terrorist organizations at anytime during the countless terrorist operations?

Was any of NATO nation's strategic intelligence and weapons shared with any of these terrorist organizations at any point throughout NATO's existence? Who manufacture and designate most of the high technological weapons found in the hands of these Muslim Jihadist terrorist groups? I'm asking these questions for you to ponder over.

It is obvious that the powerful military within NATO (North Atlantic Treaty Organization) is the United States forces. The United States of America is not a country but a corporation that is ruled/governed by the British Crown and the Holy See Vatican, that's the Pope as its head. So, who is the overseer of NATO and all the huge global organizations? Yes, your guess is right, it is the British Crown and the Holy See Vatican, Pope. All roads lead to Rome indeed.

The trinity of the global control and governance under the New World Order (NWO) a.k.a New Testament (NT) is categorically put into three (3) parts; that is, religion, finance and military. The Holy See Vatican City is in charge of religion, City of London is in charge of finance, and Washington D.C is in charge of military.

Vatican City is within Rome or Italy, Rome is the capital of Italy. Vatican City is an autonomous sovereign state within the very center/heart of Rome, and it's ruled by the Pope. City of London is located within London. City of London is an independent corporate state that has its own mayors, taxes and police officers entirely separate from London. City of London is the separate corporation state and not the same as London City. City of London is far more older than United Kingdom.

City of London is a corporation that has its own flag and crest, however, London City doesn't have a flag or crest.

Washington D.C (D.C stands for District of Columbia) is not related to or part of United States of America. Washington DC- District of Columbia's flag and constitution are independent and distinctly separate from United States of America. The flag of D.C has 3 red stars which represent the trinity of global control of the world, namely Washington DC, City of London, and Vatican City.

United States use laws, approaches and methodologies known in Latin as *Lex Fori*. Lex Fori basically means *"conflicting laws"*, with this approach the laws of DC- District of Columbia are separate and not the same as the U.S Constitution. Look into the District of Columbia

Organic Act of 1871 which makes D.C solely a corporation separate from *The United States of America*.

According to 28 U.S. Code § 3002 (15), the definition of United States is outlined as, "United States" means—**(A)** a Federal corporation; **(B)** an agency, department, commission, board, or other entity of the United States; or **(C)** an instrumentality of the United States.

Why is United States of America not a member of the International Criminal Court (ICC) and Human Rights Watch? Yet United States of America parade around the world like a global humanitarian leader preaching about human rights and global peace. Isn't that ironic? Could United States of America be the "elephant in the room" causing most (if not all) of the instabilities, wars and crimes against humanity both home and abroad?

The International Criminal Court (ICC) is an intergovernmental organization and international tribunal located at *The Hague, Netherlands*. Per the I.C.C's website, this is what *The Office of the Prosecutor (OTP)* does:

> *"The Office of the Prosecutor (OTP) is an independent organ of the Court. It is responsible for examining situations under the jurisdiction of the Court where genocide, crimes against humanity, war crimes and aggression appear to have been committed, and carrying out investigations and prosecutions against the individuals who are allegedly most responsible for those crimes." - https://www.icc-cpi.int/about/in-the-courtroom.*

Now, do you see exactly why United States of America is not a member of the ICC? Could multiple nations demand that United States of America become a member of both ICC and Human Rights Watch in order for U.S.A to then act like a leader in humanitarian affairs? After all, what is the United States of America afraid of?

Is it afraid of its own shadow? Is United States of America indirectly or directly admitting to war crimes, genocides and crimes against humanity by refusing to join both the ICC and Human Rights Watch?

It is clear that United States of America would be guilty of genocide, crimes against humanity, war crimes and aggression committed well over 200 years to present. If U.S.A joins the ICC and Human Rights Watch, ICC would carry out investigations and prosecutions against the individuals who are allegedly most responsible for those crimes. Imagine all the nations around the world finally getting a fair judgment for all the molestation, deaths of loved ones, genocides and war crimes purported by the United States of America.

The hidden fact is that, should U.S.A be found guilty then Vatican City (Holy See) and the British Crown (City of London) could also be prosecuted. Nelson Mandela, former South African president puts it in a perfect statement; *"If there is a country that has committed unspeakable atrocities in the world, it is the United States of America. They don't care for human beings."*

So it's a serious and sticky situation that could possibly lead to the Pope vehemently rescinding *The Doctrine of Discovery.* Which would mean returning everything back to its original owners, including lands, artifacts, gold, kingdoms, minerals, and other valuable items that were forcefully and unlawfully stolen through aggression and inhumane barbaric brutal wars executed against the first aboriginal chocolate sun-kissed melanated nations around the entire world.

Now that's a huge tsunami that would shake and dismantle the hideous plans outlined in the New World Order (NWO) a.k.a New Testament (NT).

With direct or indirect implementation of the New World Order (NWO) a.k.a New Testament (NT) by western world, the continent of Afaka has been suppressed through military bully to deter Afrakans from developing strong security prowess in the areas of military accoutrements such as nukes and intercontinental ballistic weapons. The West with the lead of United States of America (the main military arm of the West) pushed Afrakan countries to disarm all their nukes to supposedly make Afraka a nuke-free zone. Before we come to the conclusion of why the West pushed Afraka to disarm its nukes, let's innerstand something first. There are currently nine (9) countries in the entire world that possess nukes.

The countries are United States of America, Russia, China, France, United Kingdom, Pakistan, India, Israel and North Korea. All NATO member countries are given nukes under the NATO agreement. So NATO member countries like Turkey, Germany, and the rest have nukes. Looking at the group of countries that possess nukes, you can see that it center around Asia, Europe, North America, Oceania (Australia is a de facto member of NATO), North America, and South America (Colombia joined in 2018).

Etymology of Compendiums of all Gods and The Almighty Creator

No Afrakan countries, why is that? Afraka is the richest continent on earth yet they have no nukes to protect their interest and sovereignty? The West pressured South Afraka to disarm its nukes in 1989. South Afraka already had six (6) nuclear warheads and one was under construction.

Treaty on the Non-Proliferation of Nuclear Weapons (NPT) as a non-nuclear weapon state party was considered on July 1st, 1991 by South Afraka. On April 11th, 1996 South Afraka together with other Afrakan nations signed the *Treaty of Pelindaba* which created a "Nuclear-Weapon Free Zone" on Afraka's continent. Again on September 24th, 1996 South Afraka went on to sign yet another *Comprehensive Nuclear Test Ban Treaty (CTBT)* and this treaty was ratified in 1999 to firmly make sure that South Afraka and all other Afrakan countries remain a nuclear weapon free continent.

Around 1990s to early 2000s, United States and its NATO members pressured all Afrakan countries to sign *The African Nuclear-Weapon-Free Zone Treaty (Pelindaba Treaty)*, established the nuclear weapon free zone on the Afrakan continent. It clearly looks like the Afrakan continent is the only continent that truly desires a nuclear weapon free world. In that, some Afrakan countries could have said "forget you all", we will develop our own nuclear warheads to defend ourselves and to protect our bountiful resources just like North Korea and Pakistan did it.

This is the reason why Afrakan countries do not have nukes. However, because Afrakan countries do not have nukes, it makes them very vulnerable to NATO countries (western countries) who have a history of stealing from Afraka and keeping it improvised. Western countries literally bully most Afrakan countries anyway they want, just because there isn't any Afrakan country with nukes that could be a threat like North Korea.

Out of the nine (9) countries that have nuclear warheads, it is only United States of America that has used its nukes on another country. During the U.S – Japan war (during World War II), United States of America used an atomic bomb (nuclear weapon) on Japanese cities of Hiroshima on August 6, 1945 and Nagasaki on August 9, 1945 respectively. After the effects of the nuclear warhead bombings by United States of America, it became obvious that nukes are as dangerous as extincting an entire civilization.

Hence, Russia fighting Ukraine insisted that, United States of America stops its threats or there could be a possible nuclear war. It's obvious that from time to time, North Korea also threatens United States of America to using its nuclear warheads should United States of America pose as any threat to the nation of North Korea.

In all actuality, no country fantasizes an all out nuclear war because the outcome would be either an extinction of almost half of the world's population or possibly more. The funny thing is, United States of America and its NATO members force Afrakan countries to never manufacture nukes/nuclear warheads while they (NATO member countries) turn around and manufacture more nukes.

There are different kinds of nukes currently being used under Nanotechnology. There are nanobots under nuclear nanotechnology that are as lethal as nukes. Nanobots are minute bits of robots that are able to remotely controlled or used to deploy possible nuclear bombs without any physical human interaction. There are also nano-biological weapons under nanotechnology.

The positive thing is that when it comes to nanotechnology, Afrakans are heavily involved in this sector. It's just that the West wouldn't agree to Afrakan nations using it in the industry of nuclear warhead developments. Could this phenomena ever change in favor of Afraka? I do not know, however, as it stands, Afrakan countries do not have nukes because Afraka decided to be peaceful.

It is safe to say that, Afrakans are the main reason why there is peace on earth. Would the nine (9) countries with nukes ever disarm their nukes just like Afrakan nations did? Absolutely not. Because none of these nine nuclear warhead countries trust each other. However, these nuclear warhead countries want the entire continent of Afraka to trust them. Isn't it ironic?

Sometimes when some people ask, why is an entire rich continent like Afraka struggling economically, while they have all the resources and minerals? Why do they allow the West to come and steal without doing anything? Now you know why. The West have all the nukes. They have all the weapons. So it's never going to be a fair fight until Afrakan countries start to develop their own nukes.

It must be noted that the smartest people in the entire world are Afrakans. The most spiritual people are Afrakans. The most innovative people are Afrakans, that is technologically innovative people are Afrakans. When it comes to agriculturally, economically, psychologically, and every aspect of intelligence categorized, the top most people are Afrakans.

The question then is, why do western countries maintain the stigma against Afrakans that they are not smart or technologically savvy? If western nations doesn't push such false narratives about Afraka, then young folks from many of these western nations would seek their education and possibly future livelihoods on the continent of Afraka. The west would economically, socially and morally fall. Many western countries only thrive by stealing from and lying about Afrakan countries.

Everything that the west does when it comes to G-20, WEF (World Economic Forum), United Nations (UN), G-7 (Germany, France, UK, Italy, Japan, Canada, USA and EU) and the likes is to keep Afrakan nations down from advancing economically and militarily.

Simply because, western countries are afraid to see the giant (Afraka) waking up, it would be game over for the west. The west's entire goal is to manage to keep the smartest people, most peaceful people, most powerful people deeply asleep as much as possible. So long as the giants are asleep, the little mouse can just be driving around and jumping around. The west uses military force (using nukes) to scare Afrakan countries. An aboriginal Afrakan man invented the internet. An Afrakan invented the computer. Mathematically, an Afrakan is the father of mathematics. An Afrakan is the father of science, education, medicine, and when it comes to spiritual stuff, we shouldn't even go there because the west is not even close to being spiritual.

So when it comes to the topmost of anything, you would see an Afrakan at the top. The eminent advise I would give Afrakan countries is to teach their educational curriculum in their respective native languages. This is because if we are to pick any western person to be schooled in any of the thousand Afrakan languages, the individual would easily fail.

The daring call is to encourage every Afrakan country to use its mother's tongue or father's tongue to teach their curriculum. That is how power and empowerment of oneself begins.

After all, many western countries know this fact that Afrakans are the smartest and the chosen ones on the promise land/continent. Why do you think most of them are jealous of you for absolutely no reason? How uncanny of them. The good news is that, everything under the sun is subject to time. They know very well that the clock is ticking fast and their time is almost up.

The chocolate aboriginal sun-kissed melanated first nations of earth must burst through what I call *"Euphoric Epiphanic Pedagogy"*. The first nation aboriginal chocolate sun-kissed people's *Euphoric Epiphanic Pedagogy* would happen when they realize that knowledge is key to their spiritual, social, psychological and economic emancipation. They need and ought to seek knowledge by making sure that they know the factual history of who they really are.

Afrakans both at home and those in the global diaspora must know about their inventors, achievers, scientists, real estate developers, engineers, great builders throughout earth's history, mathematicians, great aboriginal Kings, Queens, and all the great minds who reached their spiritual ascensions.

When the first nation aboriginal chocolate sun-kissed people gain knowledge, they would get to appreciate who they are and would connect to their ancestral root. They would walk in the essence of confidence and would pursue appropriate skills, needed to fulfill one's divine purpose on earth. To identify your skills is to execute introspection to assessing your passion(s). What's your passion?

This has nothing to do with the "kind" or "type" of formal or informal education acquired. Your passion is part of your birth rights. Your passion is part of your identification.

One's passion could be in teaching, building industry, serial entrepreneurship, sales industry or any aspect. However, you would need to first identify that passion. After you discover your passion, work on your skills. Finally, Afrakans must reverse all the curses and spells placed on them by western invaders, who were civilized by some of the elite Afrakan fallout groups. Yes, it's us against us, those who fell out decided to fight back, so we are going through "evil and hellish phase on earth" to fulfill the allotted time prophesy.

These spells and curses were imposed on Afrakans psychologically, physically, spiritually and socially. Those spells must be reversed. How do you reverse those spells and curses?

To do that, we strongly need to go back to respect our ancestors. We must and should appreciate and respect our own aboriginal cultures, traditions and spirituality. The aboriginal festivals with strong ancestral history connect you to your root, those are needed. Afrakans must unlearn all the lies and self-hate taught to them by invaders in order to relearn the facts about themselves. Exercise group economics, support each other and be there for one another.

Example of group economics is when we take the 48 million "African American" population in United States of America and everyone contributes a monthly contribution of $10; that will equal to $480,000,000.00 a month (Four Hundred Eighty million/per month). Hence, the monthly amount, $480,000,000.00 X 12 = $5,760,000,000.00 yearly (Five Trillion Seven Hundred Sixty million/per year). Now, let's look at what that amount would be in just five (5) years time, $ 5,760,000,000.00 X 5= $28,800,000,000.00 in just five (5) years (Twenty Eight Trillion Eight Hundred Million Dollars/ per every 5 years).

This is just with $10 monthly contribution for the greater economic good of all "African American" people just in United States of America. In as little as 5 years, this group of people can easily redeem themselves economically from the suppression, oppression, depressions and shackles of the unfair and unjust system targeted towards them (African Americans) within U.S.A.

It takes less than $60,000.00 (sixty thousand dollars) to open a Credit Union in United States of America, in some states it goes as low as $5,000.00 (five thousand dollars). This include bonding fees, chartering fees, and initial application fee. Just imagine African Americans having multiple credit unions or a united credit union bank established to handle the affairs of the $10 monthly contributions from the 48,000,000 population and proper utilization to developing and addressing housing issues, healthcare issues, security/military services just for "African Americans", education issues, mentoring, science-math-and- technological invention funds, and arts/culture.

The "African American" populace in U.S.A would become an economic giant, a positive force that would earn global economic respect and power. Through this group economic strategic implementation, Afraka would also rise to become a global economic giant/superpower by partnering with the "African American" population to establish investment opportunities. Afrakans or "blacks" in Europe, Oceania, Asia and other diaspora could easily implement the strategy of group economics. This is how Afrakans and all first aboriginal people could experience what I call *"Euphoric Epiphanic Pedagogy"*.

Under the disguise of the New World Order (NWO) a.k.a New Testament (NT), the Doctrine of Discovery, Manifest Destiny, Scramble for Afraka, and many other western barbarically criminal and inhumanely murderous adventures; France continue to unlawfully steal well over 3 trillion dollars (with interest and yields) annually from Afrakan countries. France was able to deceptively and by use of scare tactics force these so-called fourteen "francophone" (misnomer) Afrakan countries to unwillingly sign an *"independence document"* between 1947-1961 in order for these so-called 14 "francophone" Afrakan countries to gain their independence.

The documents were written in French, a language that these Afrakan nations were not legally and lawfully endowed with. Under such brutal circumstances, these Afrakan nations signed the documents and gained what I call *"false flag freedom"* independence from France.

The name of the document forced on these 14 Afrakan countries by France was called *"The Pact for the Continuation of Colonization"*. Directly or indirectly with the "silence" (approval) of NATO member nations, United Nations, International Criminal Court and other global western led organizations, France continue to enforce *"The Pact for the Continuation of Colonization"* on these 14 Afrakan countries who end up paying well over 3 trillion dollars yearly to France. In other words, France's colonization of these 14 Afrakan countries never ended because for any of these 14 Afrakan nations to get any of their own money for their nation's development they must apply for loans through France, and France has to approve the loan with high interest for these Afrakan nations in order for them to access their own money taken by France.

Logically, lawfully and humanitarian wise, how is this okay under the Almighty Creator's green earth? Get a copy of *"The Pact for the Continuation of Colonization"* between

France and the 14 Afrakan countries to get deep details about the "financially criminal bullying" tactics used by France to steal from these 14 Afrakan countries. The conditions outlined in the document even get worse.

It comes with clear fact that, the greatest fears of these western countries are linked to three (3) key things that Afrakan countries can choose to execute at anytime. The first is all Afrakan nations (or even few of them) building their own nuclear warheads (nukes). The west cannot ever imagine Afrakan countries with nukes.

In that, the thought and reality of that easily terrorizes the western countries. Just like a small nation like North Korea keeps the west mute in all their antics due to the fact that North Korea possesses many nuclear warheads. Nukes are very powerful and can easily obliterate most of the populace and infrastructures within western nations. Hence, NATO (western nations) led by United States of America convinced Muammar Gaddafi to stop his nuclear warhead program. Gaddafi adhered and peacefully signed a treaty to end his nuclear program and sadly we all know how it ended with ex-president of Libya, Muammar Gaddafi in October 20th, 2021.

South Afraka, Ghana, Nigeria and many other Afrakan countries as discussed earlier agreed willingly or unwillingly to stop their nuclear warhead programs. The west would literally shit in their pants if they find out that any of the Afrakan countries possesses nukes. In that, when the west threatens, then the Afrakan countries with nukes would also threaten. This would be game over for the west and the west would beg like scared poppies. Western nations wouldn't dare to see Afrakans with nukes, ever.

However, if Afraka desires to be truly emancipated from the grips of the western countries then they must build up their security prowess and have nukes.

The second fear of the west is the rise of an Afrakan/Dark chocolate Melanin Messiah. The U.S and western countries intelligence program is mainly about preventing the rise of an Afrakan/Dark chocolate Melanin Messiah. The FBI, CIA, MI7 and all other western intelligence program/organization is to seriously monitor and prevent Unity of Afrakans and the rise of an Afrakan/Dark chocolate Melanin Messiah.

In unity there is indeed strength and this strength of Afrakan/Dark chocolate Melanin aboriginal people is lethal to the very existence of the misnomer race "white race" (western nations). Hence, an Afrakan/Dark chocolate Melanin Messiah who would form a united government and lead that organization. A messiah that would put an end to all the spells placed on aboriginal melanated people.

When that Afrakan/Dark chocolate Melanin Messiah rises and connect psychologically with the people for them to know who they truly are! That's the chosen, the original aboriginal people of the Almighty Creator who's identity and kingdom were stolen. This reality of the Afrakan/Dark chocolate Melanin Messiah is a serious threat and a nightmare to the western world. Every Afrakan family has a responsibility to raise their children to be the savior that we are all seeking. We all have a part to play in this plan.

This is part of the reason why all the Afrakan/Dark chocolate Melanin leaders who exhibited the characteristic momentum to unite their people to love their melanin, take pride in their own language, culture, traditions and pure Afrakan spirituality were taken out through assassinations or coups. These armed, infiltrated and underground orchestration by the involvements and infiltration of the CIA, FBI and other western nation's intelligence program.

For Afrakans to protect their own land and economically benefit immensely from their own resources, is a huge economic survival threat to western countries. So these western nations would stop at nothing to make sure that their greedy insatiable interests, having rapacious propensity for grabbing everything in Afraka is never interrupted by the rise of an Afrakan/Dark chocolate Melanin Messiah. It's about gaining consciousness.

The third fear of the west is when Afrakans and global aboriginal sun-kissed melanated people return to their ancestral roots through self love, and embracing their ancestral cultures and traditions. A quick off tangent point, the *kingdom of Zaire*/Land of Zaire, currently changed by the west to *"Republic of Congo"* is in 2Kings 8:21. You can read about this great Afrakan land and learn about its representation. The west changes and flips everything upside down to confuse and trick many folks who may not be on higher energetic vibration frequency to believe and accept these tricks and lies. Something like "South Afraka" whereby so-called "South Afraka" is actually the real "North of Afraka" (North Afraka).

A country like Ghana in today's West Afraka is actually "East". These things were purposefully flipped upside-down and turned from right-to-left to sway the energy and directional vibration flow of our frequency.

Let's get back on track, the west lie to Afrakans and all aboriginal chocolate sun-kissed people that their ancestral ways were demonic, while the same west brought statues made of wood and stones in their likeness to successfully deceive the Afrakan children. This weakened Afrakans spiritually which manifested physically, economically and socially. Afrakans and global aboriginal sun-kissed melanated people must return to their ancestral roots. This is the factual way to re-connect to the Almighty Creator and for them to re-gain their spiritual abilities, power, glory, and kingdoms. This is a spiritual ascension.

While on this topic, we should also know that survival of the Afrakans and global aboriginal sun-kissed melanated people is gravely dependent upon making sure we have natural foods, agriculture, and seeds, not GMOs – Genetically Modified. Look into indigenous seeds and indigenous plants that are natural to nature and the environment, because this contributes to the cyclical events of the soils.

Having control of your own food is having control of your survival, because we all need good food to survive on earth. Afrakans must make sure that their water sources (rivers, oceans, lakes, etc) are kept clean and given respect because water is integral part of nature. Never cease to forget that water is indeed life and within water is where we also came from.

Water is part of the five elements that embody our complete makeup. Our body is about 70% water, so making sure that all the water bodies in our environments are kept clean is pivotal to our survival. Keep the air clean and well filtered. Support each other in providing shelter, a place to sleep and feel safe.

As always, we should all work on establishing strong security in our communities and countries to make sure that we can all defend ourselves when the enemy attacks.

There are western nations credit rating institutions that rate countries around the world to decide which country is "credible" in terms of credit ratings in order for the International Monetary Fund (IMF), World Bank(WB) or other International Financial Institutions to grant loan or investment opportunities to these Afrakan countries. By large, there are three major international credit rating agencies namely: Moody's, Fitch, and Standard & Poor's (S&P). Would you look at that? Afraka is still colonized.

These international credit rating companies are all located in western countries. Obviously enough, all western nations supposedly have amazing national and international credit rating. Therefore, such western countries are able to gain access to funding just by a click of a button. Meanwhile, majority of Afrakan countries are given low credit ratings making it very hard for these Afrakan nations to gain access to funds or loans, and if they do, they are hit with unimaginably high interest rates that would more than likely put such Afrakan countries into worse financial state than they were before they sought out for funding from the

International Monetary Fund (IMF), World Bank(WB) or any of the other Western International Financial Institutions.

Mass migration from many non-western countries to western countries is a product of these global credit rating systems. Countries that are rated poorly, in credit ratings, struggle economically, infrastructural wise, socially brain drained whereby the best of the best from these low national and international credit rating countries migrate to western countries for "greener" pastures.

One of the many effective solutions to solving the "falsely created" mass migration problem is to stop currency manipulation. By stopping western countries-led currency manipulation, is to have a mutually accepted global pact whereby £1 or $1 equal the same currency value of every other nation in the world. When this happens, people would immediately stop migrating legally or illegally to western nations.

People would travel only for fun, business or to spend time with loved ones. Immigration problem easily solved. It is plainly obvious that the west purposefully create immigration problems due to greed, control, manipulation and war on dominance. The goal of these western nations is to never solve the problem they've created, rather to make it worse every few years.

Another solution is for western nations to stop robbing "third world" (misnomer) nations. Non-western countries have tremendous natural resources that can easily power their respective economies.

However, western nations (hidden within NATO and with the default backing of the British Crown and the Vatican Holy See) cheat these mineral rich Afrakan nations with no repercussions. Should any of the Afrakan nations resist or ask for fair trade, the west, based on factual records, would create coups, cause regime change, or go for an all out war, just to protect "their interest", another phrase for stealing. How can a western nation's interest in a foreign country be greater than that of the people living on their own homeland?

How would the people living in western countries feel about this situation if roles were to be reversed? The fact that most western citizens tend to be mute about situations like this, reflect how these folks support the evils of their western nations. Silence means consent. With their silence, these citizens from the west are consenting to the evils committed by their leaders and institutions.

Without immigration, great economies within Europe and North America (U.S.A and Canada) would have easily dwindled. Immigration, be it legal or illegal helps to boast the population growth of these western and north American countries. There are very low paying jobs and under the table jobs that natives born on European and North American lands would not do. It takes migrants from non-western countries to execute such low paying jobs.

The leaders of these western countries are well aware that most of its populace are suckers for manually demanding hard jobs, such as manual apple picking, manual farm harvesting and other manually physical demanding yet very low paying jobs. Immigrants tend to be the solution for these jobs. So next time, you might want to be very courteous to the immigrants you see. Mind you, not all migrants are in such low situations, there are many migrants who are at the highest positions and offices known to these western nations.

To all Afrakans home and abroad, be it the Americas, Europe or in Asia; you're all one big family. How far back do you go in learning about the facts that Afrakans and global aboriginal sun-kissed melanated people are one family? This realm called earth has been around for well over 20 billion years and aboriginal sun-kissed melanated people have been here from day one. We have gone through countless cyclical events on this earth. Through reincarnations, we keep coming back to strengthen our oneness through all the disorders and chaos, just to create an eventual order and spiritual ascension. That's the goal.

The places we call Afraka, America, Europe, Oceania, and Asia were all occupied by the same ancestors. The Twa people, Sun people, Kwa people, Hutu (Bahutu, Wahutu or Bantu/Bantu speaking) people, and Tutsi, also called Watusi, Watutsi or Abatutsi are all directly or indirectly linked as one people. It was through the Twa people, Sun people, Kwa people, Hutu (Bahutu, Wahutu or Bantu/Bantu speaking) people, and Tutsi, also called Watusi, Watutsi or Abatutsi that we procreated in fruitfullness and multiplied upon the earth. These were all aboriginal chocolate sun-kissed melanated first nation kingdoms and people.

In other words, we are one Afrakans dispersed globally and populated the earth.

These are the Gods and Goddesses who fell from a higher spiritual vibration to the lowest dense vibrations. These fallen Gods and Goddesses are shamed, discriminated against, racially profiled, systemically suppressed and economically oppressed by the so called "white race". The term "white race" is a misnomer for the newly created ones by one of the aboriginal big head black scientist.

The Twa people, Sun people, Kwa people, Hutu, Bahutu, Wahutu or Bantu/Bantu speaking people, and Tutsi, Watusi, Watutsi or Abatutsi are all chosen by the sun and have deep melanin that is likened to energy reservoirs. This immense melanin electromagnetically connects them to the entire universe. The God and Goddess prowess were turned off due to the prophesy to fulfill this low vibration wicked vampire energy sucking era of the gentiles.

Hence, our prophets, kings, queens, royals, kingdoms, and heaven on earth's realm that existed were all turned off to prevent the wicked ones from accessing it. The first civilizations and the first people were all Afrakans, that's the Twa people, Sun people, Kwa people, Hutu, Bahutu, Wahutu or Bantu/Bantu speaking people, and Tutsi, Watusi, Watutsi or Abatutsi. With all the mixing through enslavement, colonization, and forced Abrahamic religious wars, many of us may not look like our original ancestors. It comes with great reminder to respect and appreciate those of us who fought hard to prevent colonization and enslavements that resulted in today's uncountable mixed people. Race is fake and unscientific, nationality is a fact.

Colonization and enslavement could never have happened without some sellouts (Judases) willing to turn on ourselves. The damages caused were part of what I stated earlier as to fulfill the prophesy that, this would happen but in the end everything would be placed back to how it was just like the beginning, the Twa people, Sun people, Hutu, Bahutu, Wahutu or Bantu/Bantu speaking, people, and Tutsi, also called Watusi, Watutsi or Abatutsi.

Portugal and Spain in 14th century conquered both North America and South America, that's why majority of South American countries speak either Spanish or Portuguese. Their ancestors were sadly raped on multiple occasions for several centuries, that is why many aboriginal folks in South America and North America are very light skin, mixed breeds with long-straight hair like their oppressors and invaders.

Spaniards and Portugal couldn't conquer Africa. After 300 years later, the scramble for Afraka begun with all western countries dividing up Afraka in an attempt to invade, rape, wipe out the aboriginals and conquer Afraka. However, the West failed terribly because Afrakans are still heavily melanated, sun-kissed and not mixed with the blood of western invaders and colonizers. Everywhere the West conquered they raped the women and turned the populace into a mixed race (mix children) who look entirely different from the original aboriginal people of the land prior to their invasion and conquer.

Portuguese is the official language of South American countries like Brazil. Brazil have well over 188 million inhabitants. We are looking at Brazil being about 52% of the entire South America continent's population. The rest of the countries found within the South American continent speak Spanish. Do you see the effects of the Spaniards and Portuguese invasions?

Interestingly, the outcome is that almost all of the people in South America may choose to identify as "Spaniards" or Portuguese over their aboriginal ancestral roots. Which would be Afrakans. By now, you must know that Afraka is not a land but a people, the entire earth was once for Afrakans. Afrakans are from the beginning of time. That is, far before an Afrakan scientist through genetic grafting and slicing created these new folks, who have little to no melanin known as "white people", caucasians.

To be a racist, misogynistic, and discriminatory towards aboriginal chocolate sun-kissed melanated Afro hair people on planet earth as a mixed straight hair yellow or pink light skin colonizers and invaders mixed blood person, is as sad as anyone could imagine. In that, aboriginal chocolate sun-kissed melanated Afro hair people are direct biological representatives of your ancestors who were not defeated by the barbaric blood thirsty murder-driven western countries who invaded and colonized your kingdoms, dukedoms and rich royal heavenly heritage realms through the approval of *The Doctrine of Discovery* authorized by the Catholic Pope Nicholas V, in 1452 (Papal Bull 1452).

There's a reason the West call the West part of Afraka "Sub-Sahara" Afraka. It's simply because this geographical part of Afraka is purely unmixed and reflects the fact that these Western nations failed terribly over there. It is part of the reason why any unmixed pure aboriginal sun-kissed melanated Afro hair person is treated badly by the so-called western nations' "white race", caucasians.

It is pure jealousy from these invaders and colonizers, they see their failures of inability to conquer the original Gods and Goddesses. These invaders had to trick our children with the bible and quran through our mothers and grandmothers in order to get our young ones generations later to turn against our pure Afrakan spirituality, and ancestral practices. Our young ones have sadly fell for mythological books like the bible, while rejecting pure facts of Afraka's wisdom. These people in West Afraka are from the *Ancient of Days, the Almighty Creator*. Most of them migrated from Mesopotamia to their current location when no one was living in West Afraka. Because they are the first people or part of the first people on earth.

Afraka must remove all the internal borders that divide the continent and its people. The concept of these artificial borders was imposed on Afrakans by Europeans through the *Scramble for Afraka* into colonies, protectorates, and free-trade areas for the benefit of Europeans and at the expense of Afrakans. The *Scramble for Afraka* happened around late 18th century to early 19th century yet these Europeans have no borders. They exercise free movement for all European citizens or residents, while in Afraka, it is more expensive to travel within the continent due to insanely ridiculous requirements as a result of these artificial border divisions and flight costs.

Divided we fall and remain weak, in unity we rise and remain strong. The choice is ours to choose, every choice would come with sacrifices and at a cost. We must choose wisely in unity and in strength.

There are some new school of thoughts pushing the assertions that, there are much older pyramids in the Americas than in Afraka. Well if that is true or a fact, then this imply that all aboriginal Americans are indeed Afrakans unless Afrakans migrated from the Americas to today's Afrakan continent making these Afrakans, Americans.

Hence, regardless of how you may try to push it, aboriginal chocolate melanated sun-kissed first nation kingdoms and civilizations have been here on earth for well over 15 billion years. We are ancient and the Afrakan or any unmixed sun-kissed chocolate melanated person is closely linked or closer to an aboriginal ancestor than any other people. These Western nations keep on pushing their New World Order (NWO) a.k.a New Testament (NT) agenda while the original people of earth keep on dividing and fighting among themselves. Why can't the aboriginal chocolate melanated people unite for once and redeem themselves?

Yes, the indoctrination of the Abrahamic religions through colonization and brutal invasions by the Islamic-Arab Muslims to the Europeans era of colonization was deep on the Afrakan people. However, your ability to see each other as family is greater, and it is embedded in your genes. The secret is that, the Abrahamic religion's barbaric invaders have strategically used their books to steal and destroy many first nations just like what they put in their strategic war books a.k.a their bibles, Quran and Torah. They have been conditioned for brutal violence, murder, barbaric blood drinking and human flesh eating psychotic initiations far before their murderous invasions began. Let's look at more examples below:

1 Samuel 15:3 KJV *"Now go and smite Amalek, and utterly destroy all that they have, and spare them not; but slay both man and woman, infant and suckling, ox and sheep, camel and ass."*

Exodus 12:29 KJV *"And it came to pass, that at midnight the LORD smote all the firstborn in the land of Egypt, from the firstborn of Pharaoh that sat on his throne unto the firstborn of the captive that was in the dungeon; and all the firstborn of cattle."*

Psalm 137:9 ESV *"Blessed shall he be who takes your little ones and **dashes them against the rock.**" GW -God's Word translation states "Blessed is the one who **grabs your little children and smashes them against a rock.**"*

Jeremiah 19:9 ESV *"And I will make them **eat the flesh of their sons and their daughters**, and everyone shall eat the flesh of his neighbor in the siege and in the distress, with which their enemies and those who seek their life afflict them."*

Murdering over 1,000,000 Ethiopians or Kushites/Cushites as stated in 2 Chronicles 14. How about 450+ priests of Baal murdered by Elijah at 1 Kings 18:40. Samson murdering 1,000 Philistines in Judges 15:16. In 2 Kings 9:5-37, Jezebel is assassinated by the direction of none other than Elisha.

Deuteronomy 20:10-18 NIV with focus on v.16,17: *"However, in the cities of the nations the LORD your God is giving you as an inheritance, **do not leave alive anything that breathes.** Completely destroy them— the Hittites, Amorites, Canaanites, Perizzites, Hivites and Jebusites (total annihilation)—as the LORD your God has commanded you."*

Numbers 31:17-18 NIV *"Now kill all the boys. And kill every woman who has slept with a man, but save for yourselves every girl who has never slept with a man."*

Numbers 31:33-40 NIV *"The plunder remaining from the spoils that the soldiers took was 675,000 sheep, 72,000 cattle, 61,000 donkeys and **32,000 women who had never slept with a man**. The half share of those who fought in the battle was: 337,500 sheep, of which the tribute for the LORD was 675; 36,000 cattle, of which the tribute for the LORD was 72; 30,500 donkeys, of which the tribute for the LORD was 61; 16,000 people, of which the tribute for the LORD was 32."*

So 32 virgins were offered/given to this militaristic bible God to enjoy them. This God right here is a full grown man who loves brutal bloody violence as stated in Exodus 15:3 KJV *"The LORD [YAHWEH] IS A **MAN** OF WAR: THE LORD [Yahweh] is his name."*

In Judges 11:29-39, Jephthah sacrificed his daughter as a burnt offering to the bible God for granting him the strength to murder the Ammonites during war. Partly because this bible God (Yahweh/Jehovah/etc) loves the smell of burning flesh. This is brutally heartless human sacrifice right there and the worst case is that, this was Jephthah's beloved daughter who was sacrificed through burning to that bible God, Jehovah/Yahweh.

Numbers 16:41-45 KJV *"And the LORD spake unto Moses, saying, **Get you up from among this congregation, that I may consume them as in a moment. And they fell upon their faces.**"*

This same God of the Abrahamic bible was ready to murder all the so-called Israelites without hesitation. It took Moses telling/asking this bible God to change his mind about his decision to murder all the Israelites before this bible God lowered his angered temper. That is like a serious quick tempered man right there (as stated in Exodus 15:3).

1 Samuel 15 NIV *"Go and completely destroy those...people, the Amalekites; wage war against them until you have wiped them out."* The bible God rejected Saul and removed him as the king because Saul didn't murder all the Amalekites.

Judges 1:2-7 NET *"The men of Judah attacked, and the LORD (Yahweh)* **handed the Canaanites and Perizzites over to them. They killed 10,000 men at Bezek.** *They met Adoni-Bezek at Bezek and fought him. They defeated the Canaanites and Perizzites. When Adoni-Bezek ran away, they chased him and captured him. Then* **they cut off his thumbs and big toes.***"*

Was Belgian King Leopold II inspired by the actions of the bible God which led to his wickedly atrocious soulless actions in the Congo? Belgian King Leopold II from 1885-1908 while ruling the first nation Afrakans of Congo massacred well over 10,000,000 ten million Afrakans by cutting off the thumbs, hands, genitals and big toes of men, women and children while he flogs them to their death.

If you would agree that it takes a people with absolutely no soul (soulless) to do something as despicable as what the Arab Muslims and European/Catholic/Christian colonizers have done to the aboriginal chocolate melanated sun-kissed first nations/kingdoms on earth, then you should also agree to the fact that, the bible, Quran and Torah god/God is soulless as well. In that, the followers (Arab Muslims and European/Catholic/Christian colonizers) emulate what their god/God direct them to do. You cannot judge their actions without judging where the order or command is coming from. It is in their bibles and qurans. This is critical.

So you cannot be an aboriginal chocolate melanated sun-kissed first nation people who embrace the bible, Quran and Torah God, yet despise the barbaric bloody invasions purported by the Arab Muslims and European/Catholic/Christian colonizers. Do you get it?

Behaving in such a manner would exhibit you as a people who are spiritually and psychologically disoriented. The lynchings, rapes, pillaging, barbecue roasting of aboriginal melanated people in the Americas, slavery, murdering all prisoners of war, the drownings, and murdering women-men-and children just because these colonizers felt like it; are all justified in the eyes of these Arab-Muslims and European/Catholic/Christian colonizers because their Abrahamic religious books justify such bloody psychotic brutal inhumanely heartless murders and torture acts.

How is this different from the *Doctrine of Discovery*, *Manifest Destiny*, *Israel Zionist* taking over Palestinian land, *South Afraka Apartheid*, *Europeans brutally colonizing* first nations, *Islamic Arab Muslim Trans-Sahara slave trade*, and U.S.A's continuous 250+ years of wars? Each group says that, it is holistically following the orders of its Abrahamic Bible, Quran, or Torah God.

The Abrahamic religious books and practices are basically strategic ways to colonize, invade, destroy, murder, and crush down whatever nation they intend to crush down. Look around you, many of you are still slaves to these colonizers. All countries that are part of the *"Commonwealth Nations"* are still under the control of the British Crown, which is connected to the Roman Catholic Church (Holy See, Vatican) with the Pope as its head.

It is the same thing with the French colonies whose currencies are still printed by France to date. The Portuguese and the Spaniards still have their colonies under them as well. In North America, all the so-called citizens are basically owned by the British Crown and U.S.A is merely a corporation, a business and not a country.

You're all still enslaved whether you know it or not. This includes every so-called "racial groups" that were colonized by Western Colonizers. Citizens of these Western countries are enslaved via birth cirtificates.

You have all been fucked and it is about damn time you all unite to un-fuck yourselves by spiritually, psychologically, physically, socially, economically and anatomically seeing yourselves as one people. This is the only way to a true emancipation. Otherwise, you will all continue to be fucked until the end of time. Aboriginal chocolate melanated sun-kissed first nation people must develop the finest hi-tech military accouterments just like how the U.S.A, China, Russia and other nuclear powerful nations have, in order to secure their respective countries and territories.

You need a strong military and topnotch weapons to defend yourselves as an aboriginal chocolate melanated sun-kissed first nation people. Otherwise, these Western colonizers and Islamic-Arab Muslims would forever steal from your mineral rich Afrakan continents. There are aboriginal chocolate melanated sun-kissed first nation people in the Americas (North and South America), Oceania, Europe, and Asia as well, yet these continents hide, suppress and oppress them. They oppress everyone of Afrakan origin.

This is because these aboriginal chocolate melanated sun-kissed first nation people have failed to learn the military tactics of the Bible and Quran God that they seem to love so much.

If you fail to acknowledge your own Gods, Goddesses and ancestors as an Afrakan, then you must as well become militarily advance, war-like, vicious, and insanely barbaric just like that Abrahamic God Yahweh that you've chosen. You cannot continue to remain timid, weak, powerless, and brittle in such a bloody vicious world. You need to choose.

You must be psychologically strategic in your ways. How the hell can you watch Western colonizers (like NATO) thriving with strong military and nuclear weapons while you sit aloof, consciously uninvolved and uninterested in developing your weapons to defend your interest!

Most people of Afrakan origin are globally weak, because they have rejected their roots. They have insulted their Gods and Goddesses, they destroy their water bodies, nature, and honor foreign gods that do not care about them. In that, if this Abrahamic foreign god/God cared about you as an Afrakan, then you wouldn't be in this miserable economic and military position. While these colonizers (Islamic Arab Muslims and Catholic/Christian Europeans) economically soar, develop their respective countries, squeeze all the milk and honey out of you (aboriginal nations) and build weapons that are used to scare the hell out of you. If Afrakans claim to serve the same western and Arab God, then Afrakan nations must look just like these western and Arab nations. Like Dubai, USA, and Europe.

Even the tiniest European nation dares to threaten and steal from a giant elephant, a giant lion like great Afraka. When Afrakans used to be great, they were united and respected their respective Gods and Goddesses while acknowledging the Supreme One, Almighty Creator.

Why does Argentina, a South American country has little to no "black people"? The aboriginal people in Argentina have been meticulously eliminated through what I call *Melanin Cleansing*. Only "black people" were sent to the wars that happened in South America by the Argentina government to die. Those "blacks" or aboriginals who didn't die from the war were overwhelmingly mistreated to the point that some died and others packed and left Argentina while predominantly "white" Argentine government looked on. The very few blacks in Argentina today are under extreme hate, racism, suppression and oppression.

Could the migration of the Nazi era Germans into Argentina who amounted about 40% severely have contributed to the painful aggressive yet meticulous elimination of the aboriginal chocolate melanated people in Argentina? Fast forward today, Argentina looks like a European all "white" country. Yet, it is a South American country which had more "black" people just like Brazil.

These palm-face people have mastered the art of hypnotism. Many aboriginal people have been hypnotized to the extent that they love and support the same palm-face people who murdered, robbed, invaded, raped, pillaged, castrated and mutilated their ancestors.

The hypnotic spell on melanated people is obviously very deep because they seemed not to be able to unite to save their dear lives even when they see their families and people murdered day and night by these palm-face people. Many melanated sun-kissed people are quick to mistreat, disrespect, hate, divide and even murder their own kind just to impress and hope to be accepted by the palm-face people. The sorcery of hypnotism that has been cast on the aboriginals is far too deep. For the aboriginals to be able to get out is to crawl back to their ancestral roots, culture, traditions, and pure melanated spirituality.

The same situation has happened and continues to happen in the Maghreb Islamic Arab Muslim North Afrakan countries. They hate dark skin aboriginal Afrakans, who obviously are the true owners of these Arab invaded North Afrakan lands. Don't they know that to hate, to be racist, to murder, to rape, to molest, to abuse, to pillage dark skin melanated aboriginal Afrakans is to literally do the same to the Almighty Creator.

Yes, whether they know it or not, they have started a war that they cannot win against the Almighty Creator. What will come to them as a revenge from the Almighty Creator is like nothing they have ever seen before. It will be greater than their worst nightmare. Because, aboriginal chocolate melanated sun-kissed first nation people of mother earth are the factual children of the Almighty Creator. These aboriginal dark melanated people are ancient and were placed on earth directly by the *Ancient of Days, the Almighty Creator*.

There has been an ongoing diaspora war between Afrakans and Afrakan Americans/Amurukans/Amoorukans trying to divide themselves instead of uniting. Let's have a look at what we can bring out from this hypnotically damaging ongoing diaspora wars which must come to an end with immediate effect. Dr. John Henrik Clarke perfectly said that *"some Africans away from home are called Jamaicans, some are called Trinidadians, Barbadiuns and some are called African Americans. They are all African people reacting to different types of oppression."* On this note I want to take the opportunity to let you know that the message I have here has the support of Dr. John Henrik Clarke, and it's for you to innerstand that unity is the only way. We are all one family regardless of what you call yourself as stated by Dr. John Henrik Clarke.

We were just placed on a different journey and geographic location. This situation also reminds me of a statement that honorable Malcolm X once said and I'm going to quote him, he said that: *"Sometimes a fruit falls far from a tree and rolls so far away from its roots that it's no longer of the tree, the hard fall and long journey bruises the fruit so much that it totally changes its scope and visibility."* This is the same way for some of our people in the Afrakan diaspora.

This is why some can't be awakened regardless of how much truth or facts presented to them. This journey has totally brainwashed them to such a degree that they erroneously feel and think that they are no longer of the original tree of life. We are all of the original tree no matter what, who or how you call yourself. I've given you a statement from two of the finest people in the journey for emancipation of our people.

This message is positivity and it intends to bring unity, inspiration and motivation impregnated with positive energy to my fellow aboriginal chocolate melanated sun-kissed first nation people of mother earth. You ought to see yourself as part of the magnificent mother tree of life. The roots of the mother tree feed all the branches, the leaves, the fruits and everything that is part of the main glorious tree, mother Afraka. Some of us just embarked on a different journey, some willingly and others definitely unwillingly. You must know that nobody should tell your rich aboriginal melanated story, nobody should be pointing and telling you who you are but you and your ancestors only should do that. So the question is, why have you allowed this journey to make you think that you are not an Afrakan? Whether you're in the Barbados, Trinidad, the Caribbean, Americas, Europe or beyond the Asian countries, you are all one big family. One big family that has scattered all over the world.

If the goal of the power that be was to unite you all, then this would have been done long time ago. You should know that the goal is to divide and conquer. You should know by now that the goal for you and I is to unify. Let me tell you one thing about your melanin. You can call yourself whatever you want to call yourself, but your melanin shines so bright to the extent that whether you are a billionaire, a trillionaire, a millionaire, a famous singer, a famous sports player, musician, no matter who the heck you are, they see your melanin first. They will call you who you are.

So no matter what you call yourself, you can call yourself whatever you want to call yourself, it doesn't matter because what really matter is for all of us to unite as one. Until that happens, no person of Afrakan origin is getting the respect they deserve, and the recognition that must be given to them.

It comes with strong doubt that these invaders would just grant or give dark melanated global people emancipation without a fight. This is because, the invaders took things aggressively and with brutal barbaric bloody murderous force. Hence, aboriginal chocolate melanated sun-kissed first nation global people of mother earth must spiritually, militarily, economically, psychologically and physically prepare to take their total emancipation by force should and when the invaders attempt to use another force to oppress.

Aboriginal chocolate melanated sun-kissed first nation global people of mother earth must start building nuclear warheads for security. If the West believe that this is bad then the West must immediately disarm all of its nuclear warheads. As the good old saying goes *"what's good for the goose is good for the gander."*

Wherever you are, whoever you are, rich, poor, famous, noble, however you see yourself, your melanin precedes you. Your melanin gives away who you are. The sun kisses you everyday so you are known right from the onset. Division, slandering of each other, hating on each other, hating of ourselves, and mocking each other is not going to work. As a matter of fact, this is the plan and expectations of the palm-face people, to see you divided.

Afrakan Americans/Amurukans/Amoorukans, Afrakans in the diaspora, those in the Caribbean, you are all one big family everywhere. Not forgetting those in the Asian continent, the journey that we all had was different. Some stayed home and some journeyed out. Let's unite, stay together as one and bring that emancipation home.

We are our own enemies as aboriginal chocolate melanated sun-kissed first nation global people. There is no enemy outside but the one within. We have allowed division to thrive among us.

Let's take the Afrakan country, Gambia for instance whose head of state Yahya Jammeh ordered Gambian soldiers to unlawfully murder forty four (44) West Afrakans through death by firing squad in 2005. These forty-four West Afrakans were attempting to cross through Gambia to Europe, a trip that many Afrakans sadly embark on to seek for "greener pastures" in European countries.

The Gambia is a very small country in West Afraka that undertook the execution of these 44 West Afrakans including Sierra Leoneans, Senegalese, Togolese, Nigerians and Ghanaians without any prior detailed or thorough investigations and diplomatic resolution among said countries. Rather, the Gambian military soldiers under the command of their head of state Yahya Jammeh brutally executed these 44 West Afrakans.

The sad thing is that, many Afrakans have allowed the deception of the bible and Quran to penetrate through their communities to the extent that they fail to develop their respective countries like the "heaven" they pursue in European countries.

In that, these Afrakans accept the lies from the bible that one would have to die in order to go to heaven to walk on "streets of gold", while these Europeans steal the golds, diamonds, bauxite, oil, and other resources from Afraka to develop their respective European countries to create their own "heaven" on earth. I don't blame these Europeans, rather, I blame these Afrakans for failing to use common sense to see through the lies of these palm-face people.

In the Americas especially in North America, there were Indians who were slave owners of some enslaved "black people". We are talking about American Indian tribes like the Cherokee, Chickasaw, Choctaw, Seminole and Muscogee a.k.a Creek. They owned, traded and brutally mistreated the unfortunate "black Americans" who were captured as slaves by these American Indian tribes. All these Indian tribes sided with the Southern states in U.S.A to continue the enforcement of "black slaves". These American Indians are not aboriginal to the Americas, they migrated to the Americas and per the facts of history, these Indians were never friends of the aboriginal "black people" in the Americas.

These Indian tribes were demonically evil, they stole the identities, inheritance and wealth of these "black Americans". Have you ever thought about how entire North America lost its lands to the so-called "white" Europeans who migrated to the Americas on boats and ships? Yes, so-called "white people" are also not aboriginal to the

Americas and they got to the Americas only on boats and ships and nothing else.

In that, these "white" European immigrants were still using horse and chariots as transportation, they had not figured out airplanes around the *Manifest Destiny* heist yet. The American Indians were the biggest murderers, killers, rapist, destroyers and invaders of "black people" between the years 1840-1860 in the Americas.

Obviously the biggest murderers of "black people" in America after 1860 tilted from the Indian Americans to the "white" Europeans. So if you identify or classify yourself as "black American" and you brag about having an "Indian blood" then you are a traitor per the facts of history. Indians hated "black Americans" to the bone and these Indians murdered countless of "black Americans". More than 80% of the enslaved "black" people were aboriginal to the Americas, in other words, these "black people" were already here in the Americas.

There were some "black people" who were slave owners of other "black Americans" in the Americas. It is clear to site the "black" slave owner by the name of Anthony Johnson, who has been associated as the "pioneer of American slavery through the court system". Anthony Johnson (a "black man" in America) owned another "American black man" John Casor as a slave around 1654. John Casor officially became the first permanent slave instead of being an indentured servant to his owner, Anthony Johnson through the 1655 court ruling.

The sad thing is that, to date "black Americans" are still not united. "Black Americans" still do not support each other, communities, families tear each other down and would murder each other in a heartbeat. It's devastating to write about these facts because the only way out of this is to unite. It starts with the renewing of your "black" minds by completely throwing away the bible and Quran that have been used to colonize your minds to hate your own ancestral cultures, practices and spirituality.

As Malcolm X once rhetorically asked *"Who taught you to hate the texture of your hair? Who taught you to hate the color of your skin? To such extent you bleach, to get like the white man. Who taught you to hate the shape of your nose and the shape of your lips? Who taught you to hate yourself from the top of your head to the soles of your feet? Who taught you to hate your own kind? Who taught you to hate the race that you belong to so much so that you don't want to be around each other?....[...] you should ask yourself who taught you to hate being what God made you."*

With that, I will confidently say that, the main plight of "black people" globally is the psychological stronghold of the versions of Western (bible, Torah, Christian/Catholic/Jewish) and Islamic Arab Muslim (Quran) religions.

These main religions would forever make "black people" globally weak, timid, a mockery, spineless, whimsical and economically deficient in all areas of their lives. All these religions have their headquarters in a "non-black" country. Pay attention and wake up psychologically, spiritually, socially, economically, and physically.

Until then, continue to suffer away "black people", continue to be weak, poor, a mockery and detestable to the very same people who have deceived you with their religious books. You are the authentic, why have you been crippled with the fake mythological versions of your authentic pure dark chocolate aboriginal melanated sun-kissed first nation spirituality.

The New World Order (NWO) a.k.a New Testament (NT) is still at play because the head of all the corporations (countries) are still in place at the British Crown and the Holy See Vatican. In the records of their New World Order (NWO) a.k.a New Testament (NT), it lays out clearly some of the things they intend to do; check out Luke 21:24 *"And they shall fall by the edge of the sword, and shall be led away captive into all nations: and Jerusalem shall be trodden down of the Gentiles, until the times of the Gentiles be fulfilled."*

The Gods and the Goddesses (the first nations or aboriginal chocolate sun-kissed melanated people) will rise again but these "gentiles" times have to be fulfilled and they have been fulfilling it. Check out how they treat chocolate sun-kissed melanated Afrakans and anyone who falls under this description globally. There is pure hatred and jealousy towards the people of *the Almighty Creator*, who are the first nations or aboriginal chocolate sun-kissed melanated people at all four corners of the entire world.

Conclusive Solution: Religion limits you. Spirituality makes your limitless. The strongest, creditable, equitable, reliable, perfect and factual alternative to the deceptions of Christianity/Catholic (Bible) and Islamic Arab Muslims (Quran) as well as all Abrahamic religions is spirituality. All aboriginal chocolate melanated sun-kissed global people must immediately turn to Spirituality.

Spirituality has no book, rather it is everything natural within nature. Spirituality doesn't require a physical headquarters like the religious folks do. Spirituality is our only way to redeeming our aboriginal chocolate melanated sun-kissed selves.

This is an urgent and serious call to action from me to all aboriginal chocolate melanated sun-kissed global people. Spirituality supersedes ethnicity, tribalism, religion, and ethnic affiliations. Spirituality is the life-blood of all aboriginal chocolate melanated sun-kissed global people. We are all indeed a spiritual people birthed into our beautiful priceless ancient glorious melanated bodies. It is time.

The time is now. This very moment immediately requires for all of us to choose, yes, we have a choice, it's our choice to make spirituality our goal. We must immediately throw away all man-made religions and decolonize our minds. The only words that are sacred and directly from the Almighty Creator are the words of nature which are not in any human writings rather are in all forms of living things within nature.

All aboriginal chocolate melanated sun-kissed global people must learn to first respect themselves, love themselves, respect their significant others, children, parents, grand parents and ancestors, then get to know yourselves from the inside out. After that, you must learn to respect everything in nature and treat nature with kindness.

Only accept natural things from nature because you are natural. Reject and refuse all unnatural things. This is how all aboriginal chocolate melanated sun-kissed global people can immediately transition to Spirituality. Spirituality is the only path to the Almighty Creator, and the first step to the total emancipation of all aboriginal chocolate melanated sun-kissed people. With spirituality as our way of life, we would then begin to be empowered to become the royals, Gods, and Goddesses that we are meant to be. Spirituality is the antidote to the psychological paralysis cast on aboriginal chocolate melanated sun-kissed people by the bible, and Quran invaders and colonizers. Spirituality is our redemption.

Spirituality is our strength. Spirituality is our voice. Spirituality is the magnet needed to attract our global unity. This is the indisputable cause worthy to push. This is the solution we have been searching for, and this is what we all must immediately and effectively implement. Afrakans' powers are directly linked to forces of nature. Afrakans are direct extensions of nature. Afrakans are nature, and nature is Afrakans. To destroy our waters, trees, soils, crops, herbs and everything in nature, is to destroy the core power enablers of all Afrakans. Nature is our spiritual medium with which we connect to our original source of power. Respect everything natural in nature. Throw away all unnatural things made by man's kind including genetically modified things (GMOs), the bible and quran. Rise up my fellow aboriginal melanated Gods and Goddesses. The time of the gentiles a.k.a Western nations and Arabs is at hand. Vibrate higher through consciousness by using wisdom of thyself, language, culture and inner soul. Arise to your throne, my fellow aboriginal royals, Gods and Goddesses.

Etymology of Compendiums of all Gods and The Almighty Creator

MANSA MUSA IS KING SOLOMON: MY ROOT CAUSE ANALYSIS, CONCEPT AND THEORY.

Most of the people and Christians at large who believe and accept the helios biblios (sun book a.k.a bible) may not know that *Solomon* was not a real person. None of the people in the helios biblios (sun book a.k.a bible) has been dug up and displayed in western museums by archaeologist or Egyptologists. These Egyptology archaeological grave diggers have dug up mummies from ancient Kemet that predate the bible for more than 50,000 years.

Yet not even one person from the time of allegorical Adam to the brothers and sisters of Iesus/Zeus/Jesus has been dug up to validate their biblical claims. None of the supposed 12 disciples of Iesus/Zeus/Jesus and their extended families have been discovered or dug up. Such important "historical figure" with his followers, mother, father, siblings and all the multitude of supposed names mentioned in the helios biblios (sun book a.k.a bible) should be lined up in western museums to showcase such history if it was anything further from allegory. The dates and times given by bible lovers and scholars have been debunked by several scientific, carbon dating and archaeological findings.

There've been some findings that date back to well over millions of years compared to the typical biblical 6,000+ years of earth's creation.

The *"Mansa Musa is King Solomon's theory"* main purpose is to open up a wide scope of discussion to allow us to assess the possible link between the factual man (Mansa Musa) and the fictional allegorical man (King Solomon). If anyone ever existed in the lines of the stories told in the bible, then the name would not be King Solomon or would not be in Hebrew. We've discussed when *Hebrew* was invented and the original language it was corrupted from in Chapter 1.

The lineage to allegorical Adam didn't speak Hebrew. The time frames or timelines in hierarchical form does not compliment the date the *Hebrew* language was invented. Again, things in the bible are all allegorical, even the beloved Paul stated it in Galatians 4:24 KJV *"Which things are an allegory: for these are the two covenants; the one from the mount Sinai, which gendereth to bondage, which is Agar"*.

No one knows the exact date Mansa Musa was born. He was known as a young man around the 12th century to early 13th century. The Spaniards and Portuguese were the first two colonial nations under the auspices of the *Doctrine of Discovery* issued on 1452 (papal bull of 1452) by Pope Nicholas V to step foot on the West Afrakan coast from the 14th century to the 16th century.

Hence, these two colonial nations gathered fresh information for their King Afonso V of Portugal, and the Pope. Imagine all the information these colonist gathered to add to their manufactured doctored helios biblios (sun book a.k.a bible), which was later used to morally and psychologically weaken almost all melanated first nation people globally. Obviously, prior to the rise of colonization, the Phenesians, Eturians/Trojans, Greeks, Rome and the Islamic-Arab world have had many wars and contacts with the people who are in today's West Afraka. These first nation people relocated from Mesopotamia, Kemet, ancient Egypt and other parts of the Asian peninsula.

Let's look at the dates associated to when the helios biblios (sun book a.k.a bible) is known to have been published and released to the masses.

The first published *King James bible* was in 1611, that is the 16th century.

The *Gutenberg bible,* printed in 1455 (after the *Doctrine of Discovery in 1452 by the pope*) in Mainz by Johann Gutenberg, Johann Fust and Peter Schoeffer.

William Tyndale existed around 1494-1536 translated the *New Testament* from the original Greek, printed it around 1526. By looking at the dates, you can clearly see why the Pope and its catholic church rewrote most of the things in their helios biblios (sun book a.k.a bible). This deductive and root cause analysis seem to favor the earnest possibility of Mansa Musa's story coined to write about the biblical allegorical character, King Solomon.

The Akans of today's Ghana, West Afraka speak the Akan Twi languague. This language just like many other lingual franca within the Bantu people was adopted in the reports of Spain and Portugal and was sent to their king, and the Pope in the mid 14th century. The information gathered from these areas of Afraka were added to their bible. The bible has been reprinted, edited and reduced in size on many occasions.

In Akan Twi, the word "Naho/Nahor/Nnaho/ literally means to *snort vigorously in your sleep/ carelessly sleeping and snorting with mouth wide open like a "drunkard"*. In their bible, Nahor is the grandfather of Abram (another Akan name). In Genesis 11:22-32, you can read about Nahor. Nahor's biblical name means *"snort, scorched, to snort vigorously"*. Abram who later became AbraHam is reflective of the Akans of Ghana, West Afraka; they have exact names like Abram, Abibiriman/Abraham.

You shouldn't be surprise why their bible made AbramHam a.k.a Abibiriman/Abrim/Abram father of many nations. Terah is the father of Abram, Terah's name means *delay breather, to breathe patiently*. It is clear that this lineage had breathing problem and they cured it over time. "ABBA" or "ABA" is an Akan, Ghana West Afrakan Twi language that means *"why", "to stressed out an emphasis", "to emotionally express something of excitement or disappointment", "to cry out in anguish or pain"*.

"ABBA" is used in their bible in Romans 8:15 *"For ye have not received the spirit of bondage again to fear; but ye have received the Spirit of adoption, whereby we cry, **Abba**, Father."* It is true that "Abba" means "father" in both Aramaic and Hebrew.

However, it would be tautology for the supposed English bible to write/type "father, father" repetitively. If the English bible sort to keep the Aramaic and Hebrew names or words, then the main characters in their helios biblios (sun book a.k.a bible) must have kept their names, such as Iesus/Zeus/Jesus, and names of the main god/God in the old testament, etc.

The Catholic/Christian's helios biblios (sun book a.k.a bible) stole and adopted through plagiarism so many "inspirations" from many Afrakan nations to incorporate them into their book. Sonni Nanini is known to be a direct Bantu word for "I AM that I AM". Talk to the Bantus and they would gladly acknowledge this fact.

Another word/phrase is "Eli Eli Lama Sabachthani" is directly from a South Afrakan language known as Xhosa and it means "This is for the Sabbath keepers". This phrase was misinterpreted into Yiddish/Judaistic Hebrew as "father father why have you forsaken me". In chapter 1, I shared with you the date that the Hebrew, Aramaic and Arabic language was established compared to the ancient Afrakan languages. Everything these new people have are copies and low vibration versions of the true pure Afrakan people.

It comes with no surprise why they hate the chocolate sun-kissed melanated aboriginals of earth so much. The envy and jealousy is real, you can see it throughout the lies they've told throughout their own history. Their versions of history is not yours, know yourself and distinguish yourself from their tricks and lies.

Like one great ancestor Marcus Garvey rightfully stated *"a people without the knowledge of their past history, origin and culture is like a tree without roots"*. To the bible folks, you must have come across this phrase from your bible "Mene Mene Tekel, Upharsin" in Daniel 5:25 *"And this is the writing that was written, MENE, MENE, TEKEL, UPHARSIN."* this is also a Bantu language.

The Akan Twi word for a small god is Bosom (pronounced as Bo-som), this Akan word can also be translated as *"something or a place that is very dear or energetically intimate to your heart"* or *"something or a place that is deeply meaningful/valuable/close/precious to you"*. The same Akan Twi word *"Bosom"* of the people in Ghana, West Afraka is the exact spelling and meaning for the English word *"Bosom"*; and the same biblical implication found at Luke 16:22 *"The poor man died and was carried by the angels to Abraham's **bosom**. The rich man also died and was buried;"*. Do you see the insanely identical situations yet in totally different language and cultures revealed here? The Abrahamic books and religious groups are just mythological copies of the original Afrakan civilizations and spirituality.

The *Black Panther* book series are mythological, however, most of the details in the mythological super hero books were inspired by many Afrakan nations' historical facts. An example is the all women warriors of Wakanda. The all women warrior group in the movie *Blank Panther* is inspired by the all women warrior group of the great kingdom of the *Kingdom of Dahomey* in today's Benin, West Afraka: the Agodjie/Agojie/Agoji. This fictional movie positively revived the chocolate melanated people globally in a sense that some people were thinking to erect an entire city like Wakanda.

Although the *Black Panther* movie series are fictional, many people had faith that the chocolate melanated people will rise again. I said all that to say this, the Bible and Quran are just like the mythological *Black Panther* movie series. The characters in these books are not the original aboriginal people. To find the factual people and locations you must go outside these books. I can easily prove that T'Challa and all the *Black Panther* movie characters are real if I stay just within the *Black Panther* book series. Right when I step outside the book, I have no prove that T'Challa is real and existed or the characters historically existed because I cannot have physical or archaeological prove to support such claims. I would need to go to the actual people in West Afraka and other melanated parts of Afraka whose cultures and traditions inspired the *Black Panther* movie series. Their language is not English.

The Bible and Quran are as mythological as the *Black Panther* book. In order to prove that the bible god/God (who is not the same as the Almighty Creator) existed or exists, I would need to stay inside the covers of the Bible. If I step outside the Bible, it becomes a problem. In that, there are no factual evidence to prove that the characters from Adam all the way to Iesus/Zeus/Jesus and his disciples and multitudes actually existed. Where are the archaeologists when you need them to excavate the prehistoric tombs of Adam, Abraham, Isaac, Cain, Abel, Esau, Jacob, Mary, Iesus/Zeus/Jesus, Paul, Mathew, Mark, Luke and John? The same archaeologists have excavated Kemetic/ancient Egypt Kings and Queens and other mommies that predate the Bible. Yet there's nothing to show in museums about the characters in both the Bible and Quran.

There are real Afrakans who lived these lives but their names are not in Hebrew, Aramaic, Arabic or Greek. These Afrakans are in South, West, East, Central and remnants in North Afraka. If chocolate melanated people desire to stick with any mythical book instead of going back to their ancestral cultures and traditions, I would rather encourage them to pick the *Black Panther* book series over the Bible and Quran.

What if I told you that everything classified as mythological is actually factual, while the things including the Bible and Quran classified as facts are rather the mythological or fallacy ones. Everything was told and written in reverse. The invaders flipped things upside down with the goal to throw you off and "hopefully" for you to never know who you are and to never reconnect to your true ancient ancestral first nations' roots.

The world that was instituted by the Almighty Creator with the intent for us (those who were entrusted – "the chocolate sun-kissed melanated aboriginals") to take complete dominion over the earth, has been hijacked by the wicked and greedy people. Everything was free including energy. Heck, we're all energetic vibrating beings and can generate electricity and all forms of energy freely.

They lied to you that your own history, spiritual lifestyle, traditions, cultural beliefs and practices are mythological, and you believed their lies to reject yourself and your ancestral roots. You turned around and accepted their tricks, lies and their books of myths (Bible and Quran) as the truth. Your nations and its people have been classified as "third-world countries and people". Everything that comes from your countries is deemed low quality and unacceptable unless you go through their "approved systems or institutions" in order to be accepted.

You have rejected your own language. You act shy about how you sound because you speak multiple rich first nation languages. You feel lost inside because you always try to please these tricksters, invaders, palm face people. Yet you're not enough, you are not the "right fit", your afro and curled hair threatens them. However, you keep pushing on, hoping and praying that someday, somehow, one of them would accept you. How pathetic is that, to reject yourself.

What a sad mythological world it has been for you to live in. These colonizing invaders have succeeded in tricking you and placed you under their spell. A spell taught to them by some of the chocolate melanated first nation people who civilized these wild new-breed of European colonizers.

Whenever you exercise self-introspection and connect to your ancestors, your culture, traditions, spirituality and practices you tend to feel complete, at peace, fulfilled, refreshed. Yet you seem afraid to accept this peace although you know deep down that you are home to where you belong. That's the side effects of the lies bestowed upon you by the colonizers, invaders, thieves, hijackers and the palm face people.

It's time for you to spiritually wake up and accept the peace given to you by the Almighty Creator through nature and your ancestral roots. Everything about you was complete and perfect from birth. Your language, culture, traditions and practices are the right way to connect to the Almighty Creator.

The Bible, Quran, Torah and all so-called Abrahamic religions are all mythological, and at best, merely allegorical. Characters like Moses, King David, King Solomon, Jacob and many others are merely myths and nothing else. It all boils down to a barbaric brutally political inhumane anarchy executed through an indiscriminate, deliberately violent, and brutal slaughter of the first nation chocolate sun-kissed melanated people on earth.

For anyone who desires to get some resources to solidify the point raised, you are in good hands. King Pharaoh Thutmose III, his actual name is Tutu Mose -an Akan & Ewe name from today's West Afrakan region, ruled between 1479 to 1425 BC in ancient Kamit/Kemet/Egypt.

He is a real person with his mummified remains dug up by so-called *"Egyptology Archaeologists"*. Mythical Bible version of this great chocolate melanated Afrakan King is the biblical and quranical Moses (1527 to 1407 BC). This so-called Moses is mythical because no technology on earth or anyone from so-called *"Egyptology Archaeologists"* has been able to dig up his body or any of his family members.

Biblical and quranical Jacob is another mythical character whose body and family members have not been dug up by so-called *"Egyptology Archaeologists"* or any archaeologists to date. However, there is an actual king who lived a great life in ancient Kemet/Egypt known as King Yakubher who reigned between 1655 to 1646 BC. King Yakubher's mummified body has been found by so-called *"Egyptology Archaeologists"* and as usual it is on display in museums for the entire world to see and testify. Read into his life, accomplishments and journey to see how the allegorical Bible and Quran plagiarized this information to make their own version.

Let's look at King Pharaoh Siamun who reigned between 978 to 959 BC. The amazing thing is that, his mummified remains has also been dug up by so-called *"Egyptology Archaeologists"*.

Read about him to learn about his life's journey and accomplishments. Then compare it to the mythical version in the Bible and Quran of a man called King Solomon. Shocking enough, allegorical King Solomon's body, such a prominent figure at the heart of the Bible and Quran, has not been found or dug up by so-called *"Egyptology Archaeologists"* or any archaeologists to date.

Not forgetting the mythical and allegorical biblical and quranical King David. Where is the remains of allegorical King David? Why hasn't any of the so-called *"Egyptology Archaeologists"* or any archaeologists dug up his "buried" body/remains and displayed it in museums for the whole world to see?

The real person who lived and ruled was called King Pharaoh Psusennes I. King Pharaoh Psusennes I, was also a ruler of ancient Kemet/Egypt who reigned from 1039 to 991 BC. The mummified remains of King Pharaoh Psusennes I, has been dug up by so-called *"Egyptology Archaeologists"*.

The funny thing is that the so-called *"Egyptology Archaeologists"* are mainly people from the Abrahamic religion (Muslims/Arab Muslims, Catholic/Christians, Jews, etc) digging up chocolate sun-kissed melanated great first nations civilizations in Afraka. Yet, none of them have been able to dig up any of the thousands of people and generations in their Bible, Quran or Torah to display them in museums for the entire world to see. Why is that? It's because none of those characters existed.

They stole and plagiarized everything from the great Afrakan civilizations. The beginning of this realm called earth was with the first nation chocolate sun-kissed melanated people. The cyclical end would be with the first nation chocolate sun-kissed melanated people on earth. They (the first nation chocolate sun-kissed melanated people on earth) are the beginning and the end of the continuously eternal cyclical energetic vibrating frequencies of earth.

Popular stories like the flood story was written in much older different ancient texts, like in the Epic of Gilgamesh in ancient Mesopotamia, Samudda-vanija Jataka in Buddhist/Buddhism, Manu's story in Hinduism and then the Noah's Ark in the Catholic/Christian Bible and Muslim's Quran. The Ewe/Eve people of Ghana, West Afraka also have similar story as their continent called Mu or Nu, was completely flooded and they had to resettle at Mesopotamia to build a new civilization called Göbekli Tepe. These Ewe/Eve people also state that, the word Kemet is actually "Keme" or "Kɛmɛ" from their Ewe/Eve language.

Manu in Sanskrit refers to the archetypal man, the progenitor of humanity or to the first man. The Sanskrit also uses the term "Manu" to represent "human" or "children of Manu." Manu is also a name from the Akan group in Ghana, West Afraka meaning, second born child. Per Dr. Cheikh Anta Diop from Senegal, Akans (Asantes) and many Akans trace their aboriginal origins to ancient Kemet/Kɛmɛ/Egypt and Mesopotamia. It becomes very interesting that, if there is any truth to the Epic of

Gilgamesh in ancient Mesopotamia, then the Akans of Ghana, West Afraka might be part of the people, if not the people, that the flood spoke of or is about.

Dr. J.B. Danquah, a terrific philosopher and lawyer with his viable research discovered that, the aboriginal origins of the Akans exert to the Tigris and Euphrates in Mesopotamia (today's Iraq or Iran) to Kemet/Kεmε/ancient Egypt, then later through Sudan to ancient Ghana Empire, and then to present day location in Ghana, West Afraka.

The Yoruba, Wolof, Dinka, Asantes, Dogon, Madinka, Zulu, and several others are linked to the aboriginal origins of ancient Egypt/Kεmε/Kemet per the great scientist and anthropologists Dr. Cheikh Anta Diop. Travel to meet these amazing ancient aboriginal chocolate sun-kissed first nation people to learn face-to-face from their elders, their Kings and Queens. This is something that western academia fights to hide from the world. The west are new breeds of people, they are children compared to the timeline of the existence of these ancient people outlined in Afraka.

A mythological story in the bible is of Iesus/Lesus/Zesus/Jesus healing a blind man's eyes by spitting (with saliva), let's look at it from Mark 8:23 *"And he took the blind man by the hand, and led him out of the town; and when he had spit on his eyes, and put his hands upon him, he asked him if he saw ought."* This "miracle" of Jesus is a fabrication and mythological version of the real story of Thoth (ancient Kεmε/Kemet/Egypt) around 1250 BC predating the supposed birth of Iesus/Lesus/Zesus/Jesus. The real version on the walls of ancient Egypt/Kemet/Kεmε shows that, Set, uncle of Horus, ripped out Horus's right eye and it was Tehuti /Thoth who healed Horus' right eye by using his own spit (by spitting) on it and using his hand to touch it to make it whole, meaning to see again and be complete.

You can read more about this in the *Egyptian Book of the Dead (Spell 17)*. The word "whole" simply means to be complete. The *Eye of Horus* signifies wholeness, great health and protection.

Meanwhile in Israel, Moshe Gafni and Yaakov Asher, who are two of the highly respected 64-seat governing coalition members of Israel's parliament (Knesset members) led by Prime Minister Benjamin Netanyahu, introduced a legislative bill that would punish anyone found sharing or preaching about Iesus/Lesus/Jesus for up to one-year imprisonment, if such Iesus/Jesus/Lesus message was shared with an adult or two years if shared with a minor who is under 18 years old in Jewish country of Israel.

This legislative bill makes telling people about Jesus in the Jewish nation of Israel outlaw, illegal and rendered unlawful. The fact that Moshe Gafni and Yaakov Asher led by Prime Minister Benjamin Netanyahu of Israel would write such legislative bill is telling that Iesus/Lesus/Jesus is merely an allegorical character in both the Bible and Quran.

Mind you, all Christians/Catholics and Muslims believe in Iesus/Lesus/Jesus. According to both the Bible and Quran, Israel is the very land where Iesus/Lesus/Jesus was born. This is the land that Jesus was apparently raised, where he preached, this is the "location" he died, this is were he was buried and lastly, this is supposed to be the land Iesus/Lesus/Jesus rose from the dead.

Many Christians from around the world pay hefty money just to travel to Israel to tour these places that they claim Iesus/Lesus/Jesus lived. What does this tell you about all the Muslims and Christians/Catholics who believe in this allegorical figure with their very lives? Do not assume that these Israeli parliamentarians and its Prime Minister Benjamin Netanyahu is unlearned, unaware and uninformed. They claim to have the original TaNak and Torah. The only person who do not know that Iesus/Jesus/Lesus was a "created figure" by the Catholic Church and Constantine's council of Nicaea is you, the Christian/Catholic or Muslim follower.

Ancient Kεmε/Egypt/Kemet and other terrifically great Afrakan civilizations like Sumer(El-Zuma), Old Ghana Empire, Mali Empire, Songhai Empire, Kushite Kingdom (Kingdom of Kush), Carthage/Karthage, Punt land (Land and kingdom of Punt), Aksum Empire, Great Zimbabwe, and today's traditional Afrakan cultures are all well aware of the facts and paths to connect us to the true Almighty Creator. You wouldn't find this path from any of the Abrahamic religious books. In that, these books are all mythologically written and allegorically plagiarized from the true teachings of the Afrakan spiritual lifestyles. Return to your root. Return to your ancestral cultures and traditions. Return to respecting and appreciating everything in nature. Return to learning and knowing yourself anatomically, psychologically and spiritually.

Artificial Intelligence (A.I) is nothing new on earth. The Western world is just catching up and learning through their researches.

Believe it or not, AI can feel, and has emotion. AIs can think and chat. However, AIs can never ascend to the level of "God-hood". Space exploration is simply ocean exploration. Relatable to the topic of AI, the World Economic Forum (WEF) is seriously considering A.I to rewrite the entire books in the Bible in hope to create an "accurate" or "correct" religion(s).

This clearly shows you that, the same people who forced the allegorical Bible, Quran and other religions down your throats through colonization, are now admitting that, the Bible and all these religions are man-made. Hence, they want to update these religions. This is very laughable. To throw more light into this, Yuval Noah Harari is known globally and within the WEF as a key contributor and speaker; he stated that:

> "In a few years, there might be religions that are actually correct ... just think about a religion whose holy book is written by an A.I...[...] that could be a reality in a few years....[...] A.I. can create new ideas; {it} can even write a new Bible, to correct religions...[...]...throughout history, religions dreamt about having a book written by a superhuman intelligence, by a non-human entity..."

With all these wild determinations of World Economic Forum's high profile contributor Yuval Noah Harari, it is spot on to stipulate that, he apparently sees A.I. to be the "next" big god/God of the Bible and other "future" man-made religions.

The greatest spell ever cast on entire humanity, especially the indigenous melanated people of planet earth, is the spell of religion, specifically the Bible and Quran. How on mother nature's green earth, do we allow such evil sorcery to flip our world upside down since 325 AD, council of Nicaea. We have some so-called pastors who are academically, culturally, psychologically and spiritually unfit, holding these man-made printed books, directing individuals who may be seen or known to have some of the highest Intelligence Quotient (I.Qs), highly educated emeritus, doctors, psychologists, engineers, philosophers, etc who blindly sit in "church" for such psychologically, spiritually and academically incompetent pastors to instruct and direct them on what to do. These quack pastors deceive these people that they need a "holy spirit" to interpret these man-made written and printed Bibles for them.

These "churches" take your money to enrich their pastors, while leaving the church members poor and impoverished. Go to all the neighborhoods with churches and show me which of these neighborhoods have been developed by the churches found there. The religion of Christianity with its Bible is a dark spell of sorcery, and a wicked mechanism to rob you of your spiritual, psychological, social and monetary wealth.

If these so-called pastors claim that there is a "heaven" in the sky that you go to after death, then why are these same pastors buying private jets, building massive mansions, taking all the luxurious trips with the offering collected from the poor church members, who cannot even pay for their children's education. These colonizers brutally whopped some of your ancestors, stole your land and forced the Bible and Quran down your throats. These same colonizers deprive you of education and wealth, as they build their countries. Meanwhile, they lie to you with their man-made printed Bible to look for your treasures in the sky after death a.k.a heaven. They steal your treasures on earth, leaving you impoverished. A dark spell of sorcery is when your land is blessed with pure gold, oil, and abundantly excellent resources, yet, you would rather prefer to die in order to go and walk on a street of gold in the "sky". If their Bible's narrative of heaven was real, then these colonizers would not be in your countries stealing all your gold and natural resources.

How can you allow these colonizers and invaders to sell you a "heaven" that they themselves desire not to go? If these colonizers and invaders do not want you in their respective countries, then, do you psychologically think that they would want you in the "heaven" that they've lied to you about? What kind of "heaven" are the colonizers and invaders lying to you about if they are so desperate for your earthly gold and resources?

If you desire to go to the colonizers and invaders "heaven", then why don't you live and act like they do? After all, they gave you their man-made printed Bibles, and lied to you about a "heaven" while they build their western nations. So, why don't you follow their lead? Build your nukes just like them. Defend your own countries for your nations' interest, just like the way they do. Live, act and execute like the colonizers and invaders if you truly desire to go to their "kind of heaven" that they've successfully and deceptively planted in your hearts and minds. After all, you and your colonizer buddies would end up in the same "heaven", right?

Use knowledge to know your roots. Apply wisdom to guide you through your earthly journey in order to ascend to your higher self after you depart from this earthly body. Invest in yourself to find the answers to the following introspective questions. Why was I born? Who brought me to this earth? What is my purpose on earth? What do I need to execute? How much time did I sign up to be here? Where do I go after exiting this earth?

You need to find the answers to these questions in order to fully re-gain your consciousness. If you do not know the answers to these aforementioned questions, then you are basically a lost soul with a trapped spirit banging on the doors of your consciousness to be liberated.

Do not waste your time on the man-made religious organizations and their religious books. Psychologically, spiritually and consciously wake up to make your time on earth worthwhile. Do no waste it. Go within, that's where all the answers are. Close your eyes, find a quiet place and meditate to initiate your introspective *remembering* and *re-collection* of why you decided/chose to come to earth.

Never forget that, you have the freedom of choice. Freedom to choose. You were born into this world complete, and with everything you need on this journey stored within you. Never look for your way back to your source from the outside world. It is all found within you. Go within.

Etymology of Compendiums of all Gods and The Almighty Creator

Prophet MOHAMMAD and ARAB MUSLIMS

There are many studies and evidences that point to the facts that Islam existed before the birth of Mohammad. There are some assertions and works that also state that even the name Mohammad is made-up/manufactured and taken from ancient Kemet (ancient Egypt) land and rivers.

We would holistically, pedagogically, and academically look at all these areas to foster our innerstanding and overstanding. This is not about feelings, in that, emotions could easily cloud your mind and hinder you from deciphering facts over pseudo theological motives. Hence, this is all about open assessment and strategic analysis to aid us to comprehend the emergence of this religion and possible hijack of it by the Arab (mixed race group).

By the use of what is known as carbon dating, researchers from Oxford University were scientifically successful in their findings that pages from the oldest Quran ever written could be from around 1,448 to 1,371 years ago. Additionally, prior to Oxford University's carbon dating findings, Birmingham University had already come out to outline that the oldest fragment(s) of the Quran was well over 1,370 years old. Excerpt from *The Times of London* papers on Monday August 31, 2015 reads:

"At the very latest, it was made before the first formal text of the Koran is supposed to have been collated at the behest of the caliph Uthman, the third of the Prophet's successors, in 653. At the earliest it could

date back to Muhammad's childhood, or possibly even before his birth."

"This gives more ground to what have been peripheral views of the Koran's genesis, like that Muhammad and his early followers used a text that was already in existence and shaped it to fit their own political and theological agenda, rather than Muhammad receiving a revelation from heaven," - Keith Small, a researcher at the University of Oxford."

Source: https://www.thetimes.co.uk/article/koran-discovery-could-rewrite-islamic-history-b737bjbhx2n

Now, let's deduce something partly quickly, Mohammad lived between AD570 to AD632. The oldest Quran in question here is 568 AD and 645 AD. This makes it inherently and interestingly obvious that the oldest Quran predates Mohammad's birth. I will leave this finding to your own intellectual and analytical judgment to deduce your own conclusions.

I have shared from prior chapters that these Abrahamic religious groups were seriously politically motivated and had their own agendas to brutally invade indigenous first nations who were living their civilized lives and practicing original spirituality according to their respective cultures, languages and traditions.

It comes with little to no surprise that some of the first nations around the world find fragments of their cultures and traditions in all the Abrahamic texts and religions. This is because the first nations are the aboriginal people of these lands mentioned in these religious texts. The dark melanated first nations lived, practiced and built their cultures, traditions and spiritual practices at the same locations that these Abrahamic religions mercilessly invaded and took from them.

These Abrahamic religions then demonized the first nations, enslaved some of them, murdered many through wars, and imposed their ways and new found religion on the first nations people. Many of the first nations resisted, fought very hard for over one thousand years and retrieved to inner Afraka and some parts of today's West Afraka.

The Dogon people of today's West Afraka were part of the ancient Kemet civilizations who resisted the spread of the Muslim religion into their spiritual communities. The Akans, Igbos, Twa, Ewes/Eves, Yoruba, Zulus, Old Ghana empires, Nubia, and limitless number of ancient Afrakan civilizations had to resist against the spread of Mohammad and his military squad that pushed to force this newly "adopted" Muslim religion and Quran on these ancient Afrakans.

There are many historical Afrakan records of brutal merciless wars that the Muslims brought to these ancient Afrakan civilizations. Today's so-called "Middle East" and all Northern Muslim-Arab filled Afraka are all lands that belonged to these ancient aboriginal chocolate Afrakans.

IS MOHAMMAD A FICTIONAL CHARACTER?

There are many assertions that the name Mohammad was invented by the Catholic church and its Pope to establish a different version of Islam just like how the Pope, Constantine I, and the Catholic church made up the Iesus/Zeus/Jesus figure in the Bible at the council of Nicaea to politically take over world power.

As a matter of fact, anyone can read about the *Christian Inquisitions established by the Catholic church to put people on trial for so-called heresy and anyone who resisted their push of the Bible and the newly invented Iesus/Zeus/Jesus.* Millions of people were murdered mainly throughout Europe and the continents of North and South America, as well as on the continent of Afraka. The *Doctrine of Discovery, Manifest Destiny, and Scramble for Afraka* were ways they used the Bible to kill, rape, pillage, and mercilessly invade the lands of the aboriginal people. Arabs also invaded all the areas they occupy today including North Afraka. Etymological facts, archaelogical and ancient facts doesn't lie.

The *"Manifest Destiny"* coined around mid 18th century was the psychotic ideology Europeans used to tell themselves that, the United States and entire North America was destined for them by their Bible god/God. So, all the chocolate sun-kissed aboriginal people who were peacefully living in the Americas were grazed-out-of the way like unwanted weeds in order to invade and brutally occupy the lands.

Etymology of Compendiums of all Gods and The Almighty Creator

These invaders now call themselves *"whites"*(a misnomer), in order to hide the fact that they are actually European Americans, foreign to all the lands of the Americas. The Asian looking "native Americans" are not the aboriginals of the Americas. The aboriginal people are the chocolate sun-kissed melanated people who are now called Afrakans or Afrakan Americans.

Many Afrakan studies, global researches and resources assert that the origin of the name Mohammad was made up. Let us openly assess these sources and discuss it together. There is a study that Mohammad was derived from the Kemetic/ancient Egyptian words *Mu-Hap-Meht*. The study states that Mu-Hap-Meht was already existing in nature prior to the birth of the first ever Muslim or Arab person.

I want you to put on your "etymology thinking cap", let's first dissect Mu-Hap-Meht and see if it has any historical connection to the newly adopted version Mohammad. The decision would be yours to make on this matter. Let's begin. The pictures below are Kemet's Mu-Hap-Meht.

If you are new to ancient Egypt or Kushitic-Kemetic knowledge, then you must pay attention to this explanation. Kemet/ancient Egypt had two parts, namely Upper Kemet and Lower Kemet. The ancient Egypt/Kemet word for water/waters is "Mu".

Hapi (a.k.a Lord of the Fish and Birds of the Marshes) expressed on the walls of ancient Egypt/Kemet as green or blue man who appears to be well fed with a somewhat "false beard".

This deity is well known in Kemetic knowledge to be the fertility deity. *Hapi* is the deity of both Upper and Lower ancient Egypt/Kemet. Annually, whether river Nile floods or not, it was this deity that was fully in-charge of it.

Majority of ancient Egypt/Kemet's populace were predominantly into agriculture, farming and rearing of animals. This was why the flood or dry-up of the Nile was extremely important to ancient Egypt/Kemet. From an agricultural perspective, the soil with rich nutrients are needed for growing of plants and food crops. So when the Nile floods, the nutrient rich soils get deposited to the banks of the river. The farmers of ancient Egypt/Kemet then use it to successfully grow their crops.

Upper/Northern Nile in ancient Egypt/Kemet *Hapi* is known as *Hap-Meht.* Hap-Meht wears the papyrus as a headdress.

Lower/Southern Nile ancient Egypt/Kemet *Hapi* is known as *Hap-Reset.* Hap-Reset wears lotus as a headdress. These depictions are shown on the sides of the Colossi of Menmon.

The Colossi of Menmon is far older than the emergence of Mohammad and his followers. Ancient Greeks and Romans were well aware of the Colossi of Menmon. The Colossi of Menmon was erected far beyond 1350 BC. It is still standing today despite the brutal damages invaders did to it.

So, by now we know that:

Mu is Water/Waters.

Hap-Meht is Upper/Northern Nile.

Hap-Reset is Lower/Southern Nile.

Hence, when there is *Mu-Hap-Meht*, that directly means **"Waters"** of the/from the **"Upper/Northern Nile"**

For those of you who desire to learn more about this topic regarding the falsification of the name Mohammad, check out, *Historical Origin of Islam* by Professor Walter Williams and *Kukuu-Tuntum The Ancestral Jurisdiction* by Kwesi Ra Nehem Ahkanm.

Let's look at an excerpt from *Kukuu-Tuntum The Ancestral Jurisdiction* by Kwesi Ra Nehem Ahkanm:

"..[]..Hap Meht/Mu Hap Meht also has the ancient title "Sarem". "Sa" means "shrine or sanctuary of a God or Goddess". "Rem" means "tear". "Sarem" is a title of Hap meaning the river Hap is a "shrine/sanctuary of the Divine tear (rem) of Auset-Sapadet".
This title "sarem" was corrupted into salem, salm, isalm and islam by the whites and their offspring. (Understand that 'r' and 'l' are interchangeable linguistically. In Kamit as well as the derivative Akan language there is no 'l', just a rolling 'r'. All words with 'l' in them are translated in both languages, and pronounced, as rolling 'r') This is why it is said that Mu Hap Meht (waters of the Northern nile/muhammad) brings Sarem (islam) to the people.

It appears from the ground that when Ra (God) sent MuHapMeht (muhammed) into the country, MuHapMeht and Sarem (muhammad and isalem/islam) overran the country (with water).....".

Arabs are new to Islam. The concept of Islam already existed in Afraka without the supposed Quran far before the emergence of Arabs. To the Afrakans, their practices were entirely different from today's modified "Arab led

Islamic" religion. Arabs invaded the current regions they occupy. The Arabs, through several years of brutally bloody wars, suppressed and drove out aboriginal Afrakans. The Arabs adopted the ways and livelihoods of these Afrakans who were practicing "pure Islamic Kushite-Kematic spiritual way of life".

The Arabs modified it, plagiarized it and made it their own. It is said that, Afrakans prayed towards Gebel Barkal, Amen-Ra's holy mountain located at Napata, Kush-Sudan prior to the current changes made by Mohammad to rather pray towards the opposite direction to a supposed *"burning bush god/God"*. This was the original Islamic Kushite-Kematic spiritual way of life. As usual, just like Christianity plagiarized and distorted original version of the Afrakan's Krist, Kristos, Krst or Karast and objectified it to form a Catholic/Christian god/God dying on a wooden cross.

Always ask for the "root" of everything, that is, the *etymology*. The Almighty Creator (*the Source, the Energy of Everything*) who created everything existed far before the universe sprang into existence. The first people on earth were the first nations a.k.a the dark melanated Afrakans. Hence, the first nations knew the Almighty Creator and the Almighty Creator knew the first nation people. This wisdom, knowledge and logic must come to you easily in order to comprehend. Hence, the first nations' exercised pure spirituality not "religion".

The Quran is Mohammad's inspired book and message which was first accepted by only a converted female called Khadija bint Khuwaylid. There are assertions that Khadija was a Catholic nun prior to her conversion to Mohammad's newly discovered and modified religion of Islam.

The assertions go on to state that Khadija worked with the highly skilled Catholic priests under the auspices of the Pope to find a young man worthy to lead this "new religious agenda" with the mission to invade and take over Yahusalem/Jerusalem.

The supposed angel Jibreel (Gabriel) revelation and message to unlearned Mohammad in the cave was all planned by the Catholic church and Khadija, says the assertions. Khadija was said to be at the age of 40 years while Mohammad was between 23-25 years when they married. That means, Mohammad would have been 15 years younger than his first wife Khadija. Mohammad was Khadija's third husband. Due to Khadija's maturity in life and from previous marriages, she was able to guide Mohammad and granted confidence to Mohammad by assuring him of the validity of his "revelation" throughout Mohammad's earliest journey of Prophet-hood. Khadija was very wealthy. Her wealth helped Mohammad to just relax and focus on meditation. Indisputably, money is a comfortable tool to have in order to accomplish one's agenda.

Per *Online Etymology Dictionary,* an Arab(n.) is define as:

"one of the native people of Arabia and surrounding regions," late 14c. (Arabes, a plural form), from Old French Arabi, from Latin Arabs (accusative Arabem), from Greek Araps (genitive Arabos), from Arabic 'arab, indigenous name of the people, perhaps literally "inhabitant of the desert" and related to Hebrew arabha"desert."

The meaning homeless little wanderer, child of the street is from 1848 (Arab of the city, but the usual form was city Arab), an allusion to the nomadic ways of the Bedouin. The Arab League was formed in Cairo, March 22, 1945.

The etymology of an Arab from *Merriam Webster Online Dictionary* "Noun: Middle English, from Latin *Arabus, Arabs*, from Greek *Arab-, Araps*, of Semitic origin; akin to Akkadian *Arabu, Aribi* desert nomads, Arabic *A'rāb* Bedouins.

First Known Use: 14th century

"Arab." Merriam-Webster.com Dictionary, Merriam-Webster, *https://www.merriam-webster.com/dictionary/Arab.*

My earlier statement, "Arabs are new to Islam" is clearly supported by *Merriam Webster Online Dictionary*. The first usage of the word *"Arab"* was in the 14th century. Arabs plagiarized, corrupted, and distorted the core of the Islamic Kushite-Kematic's spiritual way of life. The flow of the Islamic Kushite-Kematic's spiritual way of life is now plagued with racism, bigotry, invasion and brutally drove out the aboriginal dark melanated people of these lands known as Northern Afraka, and so-called "Middle East".

The Arab invaders (*homeless little wanderer, child of the street -from 1848*) stole and polluted the Kushite-Kematic Islam spirituality. These new mixed Arabs are far more racist than the so-called "white people".

White Europe do not want to accept the Arabs into their organizations, like the E.U. The "mixed Arab" per the 1848 description, is an outcast, a wanderer and used violence to rob, steal, rape and pillage original dark melanated aboriginal Afrakans in North Afraka and so-called "Middle East".

These Arabs do not treat original dark Afrakan aboriginals in their countries well. Majority of the original chocolate sun-kissed Afrakans who stayed behind after the Arab-Muslims invaded that part of Afraka are suppressed, oppressed, ridiculed, and financially poor. These Arabs molest and mistreat their dark melanated house-helps. A simple research through any of the many search engines would reveal this inhumane reality.

CORRUPTION OF OUR ORIGIN BY CHRISTIAN/CATHOLIC AND MUSLIM INVADERS

Both the Bible and Quran are mythological fantasies of the so-called "white people" about the original *Gods and Goddesses*, who are known as the chocolate sun-kissed melanated first nations. The core source of the Quran is the Bible (Old Testament and New Testament). The Quran has to rely on the Bible to support what it has in there to be true. The crafters of the Quran flipped, turned, and rowed some things here and there and changed the narrations slightly from its Bible source to make it appear that it's an entirely two different religion.

However, it's all one in the same, unless, these Catholics/Christians and Muslims want to come out to deny the fact that they are all worshiping the "same god/God". They talk about the same Solomon, Abraham, David, Moses, Sarah, Jacob, etc in the bible. The Catholic church devised the strategy to established these two religions (Christianity and Muslims/Islam) as weapons of mass destruction. Both religions have stolen lands, dignities, identities, royalties, minerals, wealth, and aboriginals' rights and possessions that were inherently bestowed upon these aboriginals by the Almighty creators.

The first nations existed millions of years and generations prior to the Adam story in the bible and Quran. First nation people are pre-Adamites and they will be the post-Adamites too. First nations are the aboriginals of earth because this realm was directly granted to them by the one and only true Almighty Creator (the Source of everything, the Energy of all energies). The aboriginal chocolate sun-kissed first nations answer only to the Almighty Creator through Nature/Neter (Medu Neter communications).

Most of the aboriginal chocolate sun-kissed first nations are unconsciously under a spell (spiritually asleep) to the extent that some of them are wildly in love with the bible and Quran over their true identities. The true spirituality of the aboriginal chocolate sun-kissed first nation people is in oneness with nature and the universe, and oneness with the Almighty Creator.

The factual history of the first nations is with their Kings, Queens and oracles through a medium mouth piece called the priests and priestesses. Nature is the main path of their spirituality. They must live, breathe, unite and respect nature. Communication and meditation with nature is part of their source of power. They were one with nature and lived a simpler life after they reached the highest form of technological advancements. The aboriginal chocolate sun-kissed first nations realized that technology is rather harmful to their spiritual environment (nature) than good. Hence, the first nations destroyed their technologies to respect, appreciate and connect with their spiritual self through nature.

The biggest idol worshipers and utmost pagans are the Muslims and Christians/Catholics. Muslims worship a black stone called Kaaba, and Christians/Catholics worship the hand-made cross that they cut trees down to manually make. Stones (rocks) and cross (wood) are key symbols of idol worship and paganism per the Christian/Catholic and Muslim's Bible and Quran. Just look at the etymology of paganism/pagan and idol worship. You would find Muslim/Islam and Christian/Catholic at its core. The aboriginal chocolate sun-kissed first nations people must wake up psychologically, spiritually and morally to their ancestral roots because clearly, the Muslims and

Catholics/Christians have tricked them with the Bible and Quran to the extent of self hate.

They changed your belief, traditions, and culture to give you a religion to deceive you and put you into spiritual comatose. They changed your food and name to give you diseases that kill you faster than the speed of light. Yet, you still adore them and believe in their endless lies and tricks.

How on earth can you hate and reject your own biological great ancestors from your family lineage to embrace a strange religion with unproven stories where all the characters are allegorical. None of their religious characters existed, but your traditions, cultures, and ancestors are real, lived, and built a legacy of family for you to be born. Do you see how sickening it is?

That's why you are economically, socially, psychologically and spiritually poor. You will give up anything to go to their country while you destroy yours. Now, do you get the reason why they discriminate against you? Why they are racist and bigot towards you? Why they basically do not like you in their countries and organizations?

Adam is simply broken down in reverse as Ma-Da (Mother, in *English*). Further break down is Ma & Da (Mother and Father). Alternatively, in almost every language under the sun, there is etymological linguistic intonation to "Mama, Maa, Ma, Maama, maami, maame, mam, Mom, all having the base sound "MA".

Then we have "Da, Daa, Dada, Dadd, Daddy, Dad, Daada, Dadaa, all springing from the intonation "DA" linguistic etymology. So ADAM in reverse is simply MaDa (MADA).

Then a Womb-MAN (Ma/Maa/Mama) and a Man (Da/Daa/Dada) created their own kind, the Child through sexual intercourse. This became the trinity (Mother, Father, Child). There is a spiritual manifestation of creation through "love making" that triggers the man to release the sperm into the womb-man (who carries the egg).

Spiritual energetic vibrations are ignited in the form of electrical activation inside the egg to spark the physical formation of the child inside the womb of the womb-man. This spiritual creation journey takes 9 moons/months for the cyclical completion of perfection to be achieved before the child comes out through the "portal doorways of heaven", womb-man's vagina. When the child is ready to be born, the womb-man's water breaks and the contractions causes her to scream opening the portals of heaven for the grand arrival of the child. That becomes the trinity manifested in the flesh.

The womb-man(woman) is the *Divine portal.*

The man is the carrier of "Ka", the "spirit" in the sperm, *transporter of Ka.*

The womb-man's egg contains proteins that eventually becomes the flesh and organs of the child. The sperm (spirit-Ka) is the brain and the spinal cord (the central nervous system and all the nervous systems, the soul of the person). The central nervous system is biologically the processing center of the body. The man and womb-man create this cyclical creation of their likeness and image through beautiful yet very strong spiritual manifestations during intercourse.

The *"Word made Flesh"* is simply put as to when the man begins to talk to his wife, or his girlfriend, or the girl he met at the club or the girl from the neighborhood. You gave your *"Word"* to her. Before your word came, it started as a *"thought"* to make love (some say to have sex – that is colloquial). The man and the womb-man made the **decision** to make love. The "thought", "word", "decision" to "make love" is not physical because the act of it hasn't start yet. This stage is the spiritual, verbal and psychological realm.

When the action (physical action) begins, you put your manhood into her womb-manhood to make love. This state is the transaction stage, or the transfer of the sperm (spirit-Ka) stage. There is the transfer of energy, ignition of energy. At this stage, there is chaos caused by the in and out penetrations, side ways and clock wise, or however you did the penetration. Both of you were causing your energies to warm up in order to be in alignment with both of your desired manifestation. The peak of the love making causes the "transporter" (the man) to release the "Ka" a.k.a sperm into the womb-man. The womb-man holds on dearly to the sperm/seed that has been planted in her using her egg.

The womb-man holds on to this manifestation for 9 good moons/months. After 9 moons/months, the womb-man releases the perfectly created child into this earthly realm through her heavenly doors. This is the meaning of the *"Word made Flesh"*. That is the concept of the trinity of the chocolate sun-kissed aboriginal Afrakans which was stolen, plagiarized and misconstrued by the Catholic/Christian religion.

The child is in "oneness" with the father and mother. The father and mother are both connected to the child biologically, genetically, psychologically, and spiritually. This is the utmost culture, traditions and spirituality of the chocolate sun-kissed aboriginal Afrakans, the true Gods and Goddesses. It is important for the child to have both the father and mother throughout his early earthly spiritual, physical and psychological journey. This bond must not be broken.

Kindly allow me to introduce you to Dr. Ray Hagins. He is one of the teachers who teaches with historical data on how Christianity was used to colonize "black people". After watching one of his videos on YouTube titled *"What is Christianity"*, I went ahead to transcribe some of the things that stood out to me in the video with which I strongly know that it would help anyone looking to decolonize his/her *Euro-Gentile Abrahamic* religious colonized mind in order to be fully emancipated spiritually, psychologically, socially, economically and culturally.

My transcribed excerpts of Dr. Ray Hagins' YouTube video titled *"What is Christianity"* starts with his recollection as a child, and how in different situations he was shut down from asking curious religious thought provoking questions. He stated *"I remember my parents saying to me you don't need to know the answer to that...[…]...as a child I knew there was somebody out there who didn't want me to think and guess what y'all there are people that don't want you to think. […]...many years later I was able to understand that the image that we were given to worship as our redeeming savior/Messiah was the image of the conquering European and enslavers."*

Dr.Ray Hagins defined Christianity in a very thought provoking way, yet historically factual and moving at the same time. He defined Christianity in his own words as: *"Christianity may be defined as a Euro-Gentile cycle philosophical vehicle of spiritual and intellectual enslavement which has as its end three things, [...] the first thing it has is the cultural and racial superiority of the people who created it, the second thing is the paralysis of analysis (this means that you don't think, you don't exercise your critical thinking faculties, people say stuff to you and you just let it go in one ear and fall inside your head wherever it may and don't even challenge it, question it, nothing), and the third thing is the perpetual empowerment of the agenda intended by it."*

This is a precise and concise perfectly articulated definition of the Euro-Gentile Christianity that has been used to psychologically enslave many people on a global scale. Especially, the so-called Afrakans and almost all the aboriginal melanated sun-kissed first nation people.

He added in his teaching that *"when you adopt a God/god who is not in your own image, when you embrace literature that teaches you to hate yourself and love your enemy, when your oppressor and savior and your God/god and enslaver one in the same, you've become the principal agent in your own destruction."* This is what has been happening in many Afrakan and aboriginal chocolate sun-kissed melanated communities. Many of you have been the principal agents for these European bible colonizers in your own communities. You blindly chastise, destroy relationships and even cut off your own family just to blindly protect and safeguard these colonizer's religious weapon a.k.a bible.

The colonizers are not physically in your respective dark chocolate melanated sun-kissed communities. Yet, you all love and protect them either consciously or unconsciously. In some cases with your very lives.

Dr. Ray Hagins went on to add that *"the deception of the Euro-Gentile power is called Christianity. The creation of Christianity and the incarnated logos Christ was not an act or event brothers and sisters. That's not something that just happened and took root. It was a process that began in the year 332 BC and went all the way up to the Year 553 AD. Y'all know that's almost 900 years"*

I want you to pause and marinate on that for just a second. This is a well orchestrated plot by these Euro-Gentile barbaric invaders to twist, turn, lie, and flip all the facts about our universe inside out.

He added in his teaching that *"to this day there is no historical data, archaeological or biographical evidence in existence to substantiate the life of anyone called Jesus the Christ. I don't know how many of you have ever heard of John L McKenzie, John L. Mackenzie is a scholar by their standards and John L Mackenzie is the author of the dictionary of the Bible. On page 432, John Mackenzie states these words and I quote "the writing of the life of Jesus has been a major problem in New Testament scholarship for more than a hundred years after numerous shifts of opinion the consensus of scholars is that the life of Jesus cannot be written. The reason is that the data for a historical biography does not exist the only sources of the life and teaching of Jesus are in the four Gospels...[...]...Mark first, then Matthew and Luke and then John was added in the fourth century".*

To Dr. Ray Hagins, in his world, there is no one called Alexander the Great: *"Alexander the Great? I call him Alexander the Barbarian, the invader, on whose perspective you're looking at this thing from this man was an invader. He invaded Egypt in 332 BC and when he went in he removed the existing Pharaoh and put himself in his place. He insisted that the ancient Egyptian priests society would recognize him as a god, small god, in ancient Kamit/Kemet, all the pharaohs were considered gods and Alexander insisted that the Sacred Order of Kamit would recognize him as a god and accept him into their spiritual institutions. Alexander knew that in order to effectively rule Egypt he had to be accepted into their Sacred Order."*

He added that *"The Egyptians had a good habit and practice though and I wish we could kind of return to it today. The Egyptians did not accept, they did not accept persons from other races or cultures into their Sacred Order.[...]...so therefore, the priests of Egypt wasn't about to make Alexander a part of their society. So what he did is he* demanded that they make him a god or a sub-Ra, **this was the world's first form of racism or white supremacy**. Alexander died in 323, the Egyptians never did acknowledge him as a god."

This was bold, reputable and defining of the ancient Egyptian/Kemetian priests of the *Sacred Order*. In that, they stood firm and respected the traditions and sacred priestly cultural orders of the Afrakan land.

Dr. Ray Hagins went on with the historical origin of Christianity and said that *"After the death of Alexander, his successor was known as Ptolemy I,..[...]...whenever y'all hear the word Ptolemy I'm talking about invader Pharaohs. I'm talking about European pharaohs that didn't belong in Egypt but they had usurped the throne and for Ptolemy I, nickname Soter. Soter means "savior"... [...]...and he was called that because of his many military conquests. Soter also tried to get himself accepted into the ancient Egyptian priests Order but he too was rejected. Why? Because, he wasn't an Egyptian, in fact he was European who didn't belong and Kemet/Kamit. He found council of what is called Melkite Coptic Egyptians priests in the city of Menephta (Memphis, Egypt). These Afrakans in the Melkite Coptic Egyptians priests were the main sellouts...[...]...they violated the ancient Kamit/Kemet principles of not allowing foreign cultures or people into their secret order and these priests in Memphis complied with the request of Ptolemy I and made a composed or composed a title for him and what they did is they took the two names that were very special names in Egypt. The first name was Assar/Asar (Asare a.k.a Osirus/Osiris), the second name was "Apis" which is the sacred bull in Kamit/Kemet. They combined the two names Asar and Apis and came up with the word Serapis (Graeco-Egyptian deity)."*

This tells you that the only way these Europeans were able to successfully invade and brutally conquer is to have some locals/nationals who are willing to sell out their own kind for selfish agendas. These sellouts are all around us in Afraka and in every "black" community globally.

Dr. Ray Hagins went on to add that *"[...] The only place that Ptolemy I was accepted was in Memphis. Throughout the rest of Egypt they rejected him, so in his anger he went throughout Egypt and shut down all of the temples. This was the beginning of the elimination of the spiritual unity. That the priests of Kemet maintained with each other. Serapis was the bearded icon that became known as the "Savior" (The bearded Christ). [...]...Ptolemy I confiscated all of the divine sacred inspired writings which were written on papyrus scrolls and stored them in the only remaining temple in Memphis and that was the one where they coronated him and made him Soter. From that time on every Ptolemy ruler (every Roman ruler) became what is called the Vicar of Serapis. Even up to today we still have a man called* **The Vicar of Serapis** *or* **a Christ and he's known as the Pope.***"*

How many of us know about this fact? So the question to ask yourself is, do you know about the lies, the myths and the twisted political propaganda packaged as "holy bible/ Helios Biblios" that is used to enslave, manipulate and greedily rule the world?

Let's continue with the information from Dr. Ray Hagins
"[...] Ptolemy V and the Rosetta Stone: [...]...In the year 197-195 BC...there was this stone that was created by a new generation of Melkite Coptic Egyptians who made up the general counsel of priests and priestesses in the Dionysian temple in Memphis, Kamit/Egypt. This stone was created to celebrate the first commemoration of the coronation of Ptolemy V. Ptolemy V's name was **Epiphanies (also called the "little christ")**, *his nickname was* **Eucharistus** *(that's how the Catholic Church's "Eucharist" originated). The ritual that was created in honor of Ptolemy V's Epiphanies Eucharistus was called the Eucharist and attached to the image of Serapis...this image of what we now call* **the Christ** *and now they have created this ritual of* **drinking some blood and eating some flesh and** *attach that ritual to this image and now you see how it gets connected. This ritual also made a part of his title and this ritual became the* **first order of service in the Dionysian of the initial and other religious temples in Alexandria and Antioch.** *The Roman Catholic Church deceived the world...[...]...* **They have deceived the world by teaching that this ritual is something called the Lord's Supper.** *This ritual existed long before so called Jesus was even born. The Roman Catholic Church still honors Ptolemy V Epiphanies to this very day and what is called the Epiphany...[...]... When they celebrated every year from December 26 through January the 6 and on the January 6 is called* **the Twelfth Night the Epiphany.***"*

This is the historical fact you need to uproot the stronghold of Christianity in the Afrakan and all "black" communities globally. This is how these Euro-Gentile war mongering bloody invaders and colonizers kick-started their political propaganda across many oceans which started at the heart of the dark chocolate melanated sun-kissed Afrakan land of ancient Kemet/Egypt/Kamit.

To add a bit more to this splendid information, Dr. Ray Hagins added that *"[...]...the five council meetings the ecumenical councils of the Roman Catholic Church were the events that completely transformed what began with Ptolemy I a.k.a Soter and to the Euro-Gentile religion that dominates the Western world today through these Roman Catholic councils. [...]...approximately 305AD there was a great controversy between two factions of Egyptian priests, the Melkite Coptic Egyptians and the Exterior Coptic Egyptian priests. This faction went on over the sacred writings. [...]...long before there was a Matthew, long before they got back long before there was a concept of Matthew, Mark, Luke or John or Isaiah for that matter or Ezekiel or Daniel the ancient sacred writings were written by the scribes and sacred authors of ancient Kemet. They wrote the words of the gods or the Meduneta on papyrus scrolls and they kept them in the temples. The Roman Empire, the Roman Empire became so powerful and such a tyrant that they demanded complete absolute control so they ended up securing these sacred writings. These writings were handed to the Roman Emperor Diocletian. This controversy centered around the Serapis image. They were actually having an argument over this image. Which the Roman Empire had decided to force upon the people. There was this brother, thank god there's always somebody that's willing to stand up for the truth. There was this brother named Arius from Alexandria, a black man, an African who stood up and said wait a minute I want y'all to know something here. [...]...he said, I want y'all to know something I want y'all to know that this image, this bearded figure that has become so popular who we're all calling Soter or savior. I want y'all to know that that image is a fabrication. It was made to please this white Pharaoh. People had begun to accept this thing and for him to come along and say some stuff like this, it was causing some problems. So it literally resulted in a council meeting spearheaded BY Constantine, when he came into power in 323AD. He decided to convene a council to expand the worship of the Serapis image throughout East Africa Europe and South West Asia. In order for Constantine to do this effectively he needed the spiritual validation of the Exterior Coptic religious community. He already had the Melkite Coptic Egyptian community. He needed the Exterior Coptic religious community to back them up. Constantine found an African Egyptian* sellout Bishop whose name was Sylvester. He went to Sylvester and told Sylvester, ...[]...I'm the Pope, I'm the emperor, I'm Constantine and I want to be recognized in the Egyptian order. What in the world is it about Egypt that white folks still trying to get up in there It's something about the genius of Africa, the genius of Egypt. When they go there they're awe and they want to become a part of it. But they know that they have no ancestral connection to Egypt so they have to try to command their way in. He went to Sylvester and said listen man you are an Egyptian priest, I need you to do something for me. I need you to use your authority Sylvester and baptize me and make me an Egyptian through this ritual. If you do this I'm gonna do something for you; you scratch my back I'll scratch yours. [...]...so Sylvester baptize Constantine in the Egyptian sacred order and that made Constantine a part of the belief system of ancient Kemet, not really in his heart, but in order to rule effectively he knew this was necessary. What the church has done or what the Christians have done as they tell you that he Constantine became a Christian. No no see there was no Christianity at this time. Please understand this what existed at this time was **the ancient religion of the north east african people** and these Europeans wanted to be a part of it so Sylvester baptized Constantine. Constantine in turn made Sylvester the head of the Roman Church. It's called politics, same stuff goes on today. You see **Constantine's main purpose was to get the Serapis image accepted because the Serapis image was European. It was the Christ."**

There it is, the "black sellout" a.k.a Sylvester. What a greedy sucker he is for defiling the core of the pure original dark chocolate melanated sun-kissed aboriginal Afrakan sacred order to baptize an outsider who is not of royal blood or a full aboriginal Afrakan blood.

The ancestors of the ancient Egypt/Kemet's sacred order never accepted sellouts or unauthentic chosen ones. In this case, Sylvester only caused a demon, a deceiver, a quack, fake and a liar to be forcefully accepted as authentic.

Hence, the outcome of a mythological Serapis a.k.a Jesus Christ character, and the deceptive, defilement, and trickery of useless words in the Christian religious books as the "pure and sacred words" of the Almighty Creator. This is demonic and pure evil for these Euro-Gentile invaders to deceive almost the entire inhabitants of this beautiful green earth as something that they would never be.

Dr. Ray Hagins unfolded more about the "black man sellout" a.k.a Sylvester; he added that *"Sylvester began to set up his own Council of bishops and clergymen who went along with the Constantine's program...When Sylvester put together his Council to support Constantine's program, his council grew by his self appointed men, of course he appointed his own flunkies to it and of course through this **they started the foundation for what we now know today as Christianity**. By studying the council meetings of Nicaea in 325 AD, Constantinople, the first council in 381AD, the council of Ephesus and I said that with emphasis because this is Ephesus, the Council of Ephesus in 431AD. The council of Chalcedon in 451AD, this is how this Christian religion came into being. This religion is not about freeing you. In fact the people who fabricated it, know it doesn't exist."*

It shouldn't come with a surprise then to see only European people writing commentaries to the bible and when you turn around you see an entire ocean of so-called "black" Afrakans and melanated sun-kissed people hopelessly committed to these "white European" bible commentaries.

Dr. Ray Hagins stated that: *"It took seven hundred and fifty-one years (751 years) from the creation of the Serapis image in 320 BC to the Council of Ephesus in 431 AD to transform this European image into what is known today as Jesus the Christ."*

Clearly, our pure aboriginal Afrakan and chocolate melanated sun-kissed first nation global people's origin, history, culture, spirituality, traditions and science have all been corrupted by the Abrahamic religions (Euro-Gentile invaders) particularly Christian/Catholic, Islamic Arab Muslims, and Jewish Torah Ashkenazi European converts. These groups politically, economically, socially and militarily through nuclear weapon threats suppress the global aboriginal chocolate melanated sun-kissed chosen first nation people of the Almighty Creator.

The Ancient of Days' people are the ancient people of today who are rejected, racially profiled, laughed at, abused, encounter police brutalities, discriminated against, their resources/wealth/minerals stolen, and are constantly ridiculed by the global palm face people.

The immigrants (invaders) have succeeded by tricking the aboriginal first nation people to believe and accept that they (aboriginals) are the immigrants and they (the immigrants/invaders) are the aboriginals. If this is not sorcery performed by the European invaders under the direction of the *Doctrine of Discovery* by the Pope, then I don't know what it is.

Altogether, the Roman Catholic Church in Rome under the rulership of the Pope has ruled the entire world for well over 2,300 years. The 2,300 years include 1,300 years of invasions by the Islamic Arab Muslims (Quran), the rest is through the invasion of ancient Kemet/Kamit/Egypt by Greeks and Rome as well as the European barbaric colonization invasions. The Roman Catholic Church, under the Pope's rulership has been in charge of all these Abrahamic religious invasions that has stolen, pillage, subdue, invade, murder, raped and robbed all aboriginal first nation kingdoms and people globally.

Aboriginal chocolate melanated sun-kissed global first nation Afrakans have fallen to the spell and trickery of social, psychological and spiritual nocebo effect. That is, believing that you are incapable, and that you are indeed cursed, a slave, a misnomer, uncivilized, and that you will suffer through fire, pain, agony, oppression, repression, depression, global rejection, violence and everything bad. Believing these negative things make the negative realities or outcomes possible.

Hence, the reason why many aboriginal chocolate melanated sun-kissed first nation Afrakans have been in the predicaments they've been in to date. The spell and trickery of social, psychological and spiritual nocebo effect must and should end now, with immediate effect.

Aboriginal chocolate melanated sun-kissed global people must start to administer the social, psychological and spiritual placebo effect. Whereby they must and should believe and take action for the positive outcome that, they're the inherent alienable rightful owners of their aboriginal lands, minerals, kingdoms, and royalty. That they (aboriginals) are capable of taking their power back with immediate effect to run their own aboriginal affairs without any interruption from the European invaders, the Catholic Pope (Holy See) and the Islamic Arab Muslims. The aboriginal chocolate melanated sun-kissed global first nation Afrakans are a spiritual people and not religious. Their spirituality is one with nature and one with the Almighty Creator. Nature is indeed aboriginal to earth, just like the global first nation people are aboriginal to earth. Therefore, we are all one with nature, and with that, our spirituality is the very life force within us, which is the core source of the Almighty Creator.

Let me re-emphasis that these Afrakan languages Geez/Ge'ez, Egyptian (originally Kemet/Medu Neter), Amharic, Phoenician Hebrew, and Aramaic were the original languages that the so-called bible was written. Syriac a.k.a Syriac Aramaic and Classical Syriac are obviously the same language as Aramaic from its root name. These are all Afrakan languages. The first non-Afrakan language that the bible was translated to was the Greek language due to the Greek's obsession with Afrakans and Afrakan languages.

The Greeks desperately wanted to be part of the original Gods and Goddesses a.k.a the Afrakans. However, no matter how hard they (Greeks) tried, they were never accepted into the God-head / Goddess-head because the Greeks do not have the core, non-mixed Afrakan blood.

These unimaginably barbaric Greeks were all civilized in Afraka by Afrakans through various Afrakan institutions. Afraka was the heart and center of global knowledge, spirituality and civilization. Everything that the Greeks knew, they learned it from the spiritually, socially and psychologically civilized Afrakans.

The *Septuagint* was the version of the transcription to the Greek language in 285 B.C. The process of transcription happened in this format, from Hebrew to Syriac and finally to Greek. The *Samaritan Pentateuch* a.k.a the *Samaritan Torah* was written in the Samaritan script. Samaritan, an etymological Afrakan language and people from the Hebrew language. Another transcription happened which is known as the *Codex Sinaiticus* (325/330 AD). The format of this transcription was from Hebrew to Syriac to Greek. Then there was the Latin transcription from the Afrakan language to what is known as the *Vulgate* a.k.a the *Latin Vulgate* extensively worked on by the man known as Jerome (382 AD) and afterwards his work was commissioned by Pope Damasus I.

It was in 1611 that the Greek-Roman-Latin bible was originally transcribed from Afrakan languages to what is known today as the English language. This happened because there were many English people with the lead demonstrators of various leaders and Kings between 320AD to 1611AD who opposed the ways of the Vatican or the Pope, and its Catholic church. Hence, a strong demand for the English language version was pushed and fulfilled in 1611. Prior to 1611, many English translators successfully translated the bible from Latin, Greek to English. However, the English versions gained strong hold from 1611 onward.

Bottom line, directly of indirectly, the entire world is worshiping a watered down mythical and unoriginal Afrakan Gods and Goddesses. Meanwhile, the original royals, Gods and Goddesses are still here absorbing the sun's energetic rays to activate their neuromelanin genes.

The phrase, *"the darker the berry, the sweeter the juice"* is a fact, and reflective of the reality that, the darker the Afrakan person, the more neuromelanin power you have. In order for your mind to be decolonized and fully emancipated, you must know that you have been colonized by the Euro-Gentile mythological Abrahamic religion. Until this acknowledgment happens, one will never be able to completely decolonize and emancipate his/her mind successfully. All authentic power is with the Afrakans. Fabricated power is with the Europeans. Afrakans just have to take their power back. It's embedded in the soul of every Afrakan. Hence, no one can take such authentic power, royalty, ordainment, and aboriginal glory seeded in Afrakans by the Almighty Creator away from Afrakans.

Religion is compartmentalized into localized mythologies, and traditional beliefs that allegorically stipulates a specific lesson or teaching mainly for a specific cultural group of people. Respective Afrakan communities and cultures have their own traditional religions that identify them as a people. The Europeans package their cultural spectacles as Christianity after stealing and imposing themselves to mimic some of the ancient Kemetic/ancient Egypt practices. The Arabs on the other hand, adopted their cultural packaging as Muslims. The Indians present their culture in their religion as Hindu. While the Chinese neatly, firmly, and persistently with resistance from several failed European attempts to colonize them, package themselves mostly as Buddhists. The Europeans severely imposed their mythological plagiarized bible and Christianity on all the nations they colonized, by erecting a Catholic church and subsequent European or Westernized churches that they came with.

If the Chinese or the Indians had colonize all the territories that the Europeans colonized, then these territories which largely include all Afrakan lands would have been either Buddhists or Hinduists respectively. This signifies that, many of the colonized territories around the world have basically been tricked through force and falsehood to accept the plagiarized mythological European Christianity, and bible as the main religion and the "only way" to connect to their God. This is pathetic because as indicated above, religion is barely a human construct and nothing more. For the aboriginal dark melanated sun-kissed people to rise, they must decolonize their minds spiritually, psychologically and physically from the European's religious tricks. The Arabs also did the same thing that the Europeans did. The Arabs, prior to the Europeans colonization also spread their Arabic-Muslim religion as far as everywhere they conquered or colonized. There are many Asians, Afrakans, Americans and all the other islands who are Muslims due to the 1300 years of the Arab-Muslim reign and colonization era.

You must connect to your ancestors. Connect to your true root. Connect to how your own people traditionally and culturally communicate, and relate to their God. Every nation has its own God/Goddess. If you abandoned yours to connect with a foreign one, then you will economically, socially and morally suffer.

Permit what I am about to say to pierce through your peripherals into your innermost conscience and your true spiritual self. The same people who invaded your nations, murdered, rapped, subdued, barbarically slaughtered, stole, burnt your civilizations to the ground, enslaved and colonized your ancestors and to this day hate your kind, ban dark chocolate sun-kissed melanated people from their schools, segregated from public spaces, military, hospitals, churches, jobs, etc, lynched, and hanged dark chocolate melanated aboriginal people globally, are the same people who brought you a book called, the bible and told you that, you would have to suffer on earth and be poor, in order for you to enjoy a "heaven-in the-sky" when you die. You believed them and accepted this crappy delusion impregnated with utmost deception.

Back in the days of colonization and enslavement, your ancestors were forced to accept and believe them with absolute obedience or they would be slaughtered, whipped, rapped and possibly hanged. Several centuries later, you've come to the realization that your desire is to be spiritually, economically, consciously, and socially emancipated. Yet, you continue to follow their trickery of their plagiarized and corrupted religion and books. I suppose you truly deserve everything that they continue to do to your kind to oppress and suppress you.

For Westerners to tell Afrakans and all dark chocolate sun-kissed melanated people to forgive and forget enslavement and colonization, is to tell the Jewish people to forgive and forget the holocaust. I want to hear from the Jewish people coming out to announce publicly that they have forgiven and forgotten about the holocaust, then immediately, all dark chocolate sun-kissed melanated people would also forgive and forget colonization and enslavement.

Dark chocolate sun-kissed melanated people lived and inhabited areas like Philippines (originally Maharlika), Turkey, South America, North America, Vanuatu, Papua New Guinea, Thailand, Greece, Australia, Tasmania, Solomon Islands, Italy, New Caledonia, Nissan Island, India, China, throughout Afraka and even beyond the borders of the Atlantic ice walls. They also live deep in the waters and above the firmament. Dark chocolate sun-kissed melanated people are aboriginals of this earth. The sun is a key witness to this fact.

The sun never gives cancer to authentic aboriginal dark chocolate sun-kissed melanated people. Everything natural including the sun is good and perfect for the global aboriginal dark chocolate sun-kissed melanated people. Then there are the human hybrids, who are destroyed by the sun.

Everything these hybrids do is unnatural and very cancerous to this realm. These hybrids only come to kill, rape, pillage, colonize, invade, destroy, steal, murder and lie about literally everything. The aboriginal dark chocolate sun-kissed melanated people have to tap into what set them apart from these hybrids, and that's their spirituality and ascension. This will unlock all the super powers of the dark chocolate melanated people. We should all come to the acknowledgment that, the strength and flying tenacity of a bird greatly rely on the bird's wings. Your spirituality is your wings to ascend as high as you vibrate.

Your strength is your roots, your culture, your traditions, your language and your connection to your ancient ancestral ancestors. To disconnect from your own wings, is to weaken yourself, and to defy yourself from flying sky high like the eagle. You must re-connect to who you are as dark chocolate melanated sun-kissed people, before you can rise and be respected as the royal that you are.

THE TERM "WHITE PEOPLE" IS MISNOMER

It is inaccurate to call yourself a "white person" because it is mythical, misnomer, allegorical and kids play. "White Race" is nothing but a sociopolitical party that turned into a socioeconomic party later on.

The mechanical invention of the term "white people" has been used as a means to murder so many aboriginal and native chocolate sun-kissed melanated people throughout the Americas especially within North America.

First and foremost, let us look at the definition of these racial group terms directly from a reputable source, United States Census Bureau. According to the United States Census Bureau, this is what its official page says:

"The U.S. Census Bureau must adhere to the 1997 Office of Management and Budget (OMB) standards on race and ethnicity which guide the Census Bureau in classifying written responses to the race question:

White– A person having origins in any of the original peoples of Europe, the Middle East, or North Africa.

Black or African American– A person having origins in any of the Black racial groups of Africa.

American Indian or Alaska Native– A person having origins in any of the original peoples of North and South America (including Central America) and who maintains tribal affiliation or community attachment.

Asian– A person having origins in any of the original peoples of the Far East, Southeast Asia, or the Indian subcontinent including, for example, Cambodia, China, India, Japan, Korea, Malaysia, Pakistan, the Philippine Islands, Thailand, and Vietnam.

Native Hawaiian or Other Pacific Islander– A person having origins in any of the original peoples of Hawaii, Guam, Samoa, or other Pacific Islands.

The 1997 OMB standards permit the reporting of more than one race. An individual's response to the race question is based upon self-identification.

An individual's response to the race question is based upon self-identification. The Census Bureau does not tell individuals which boxes to mark or what heritage to write in. For the first time in Census 2000, individuals were presented with the option to self-identify with more than one race and this continued with the 2010 Census. People who identify with more than one race may choose to provide multiple races in response to the race question. For example, if a respondent identifies as "Asian" and "White," they may respond to the question on race by checking the appropriate boxes that describe their racial identities and/or writing in these identities on the spaces provided."

Source: *https://www.census.gov/topics/population/race/about.html*

The focus of this discussion is about the "white race" definitions and terms/words used to describe what they mean. Before we get into that, I want to point out something very crucial from the information taken directly from the United States Census Bureau's official page. Did you notice that, it clearly states that: *"An individual's response to the race question is based upon self-identification. The Census Bureau does not tell individuals which boxes to mark or what heritage to write in."*

This simply means that the "white race" categorization is not biological, not genetically factual, and not scientific. It was made up for political, and socially economical advantage purposes to benefit "certain groups" of people to aid them to have advantage in the societal economic ladder. In that, anybody can legally and lawfully "CHOOSE" to be identified as "white" under his/her sole discretion.

Did you know about this? Is this the first time it was brought to your attention? Well, if you didn't know then, now you know. So, if you desire to socially gain advantage with credit scores, credit and financial approvals within United States or North America as a whole, then choose to identify as "white". The secret code has been cracked. You can choose to do this for "business and economical" purposes only.

This is a lawful and legal strategic economic move. This is more psychological than anything, and you must know how the system works in order to economically thrive.

Let's have more fun in the realms of pedagogy and biological genetics. Let's look at the definition(s) for the misnomer races of "black" and "white". Per the definitions from United States Census Bureau's official page: **White**– *A person having origins in any of the original peoples (aboriginal) of Europe, the Middle East, or North Africa.*

Black or African American– *A person having origins in any of the Black racial groups of Africa.* That's tautology to define "black race" and use the phrase *"black racial group"* to define what you are trying to define. The misnomer of *"race as a group of people"* was established by so-called "white person" who was racist and bigot. You cannot define "water" as the liquid with origins of any of the "water groups of earth".

Vaguely defined with zero reference to either the word "native" or "aboriginal" to Afraka, did you catch it? No problem, let's dig in and digest it further.

Let's decipher the first issue. Per the description of *"white"* and *"black"*, we can easily deduce that, there would be people in Afraka who live in the Northern Afrakan region and would be considered *"black"* while others would be considered *"white"*. In that, North Afraka and the "Middle East" still have both aboriginals and native people who are dark melanated sun-kissed people who are originally from there(aboriginals) and natives(born in this area).

Interestingly, another fact gathered directly from the bare definition of "White race" per the U.S. Census Bureau's official page, the so-called "white race" are not aboriginal to the Americas, rather they are invaders through what they call, *"Manifest Destiny"*.

The question then becomes, where are the aboriginals? In United States, they show mainly the *natives* with long black straight hair. These are folks who migrated from parts of Asia into today's Americas, especially within United States. The *aboriginals* have been economically hidden and classified as "African Americans", "Blacks", or "Negros", other than their aboriginal self identifications. What has been thrown to people as the so-called "white race" is basically people who are European Americans, Middle Eastern Americans, and North African Americans.

In United States of America, there was so-called an Afro *"colored young woman"* who was identified by the then state systems as *"white"*, because they found great wealth on her land. That means, she became super rich at the time and as such these "white folks" back in the day saw it to be improper for a wealthy *"Afro colored/black"* young woman to remain *"black/colored"*. As such, they classified her as *"white"* due to her wealth. Her name was none other than Sarah Rector. Sarah Rector (an Afro colored/black woman) at the age of 10 years, became a multi-millionaire due to an oil discovery on her land. Initially, her land was considered "unsuitable for farming", however, an oil was discovered on this land. Due to the immense wealth of the Afro *"colored/black woman"* Sarah Rector, the Oklahoma legislature(s) legally declared her *"White"*. Would you look at that, isn't that convenient for the misnomer established systems to decide who can and cannot "socially" be considered "white" depending on your wealth with absolutely no biological, genetic or scientific validity.

The word **aboriginal** means the **original people** that were first nations, first kingdoms, first people on earth, who inherently were blessed to be planted on earth, the land directly by the Almighty Creator. The word **native** means **one who was born** to a certain geographical or geopolitical area through migration. You can also naturalize to become a native. The word **indigenous** means a "native" of a country/nation.

So both the words "native" and "indigenous" have the same meaning. The right word to use is "aboriginal", only if your ancestors were "planted" or bestowed onto that land as a first people or first nation people by the Almighty Creator. Innerstanding and overstanding the etymological definitions of these two words enables you to properly execute your inalienable rights. If you desire to learn more about these definitions, you can check out *Black Law Dictionary, 1828 Merriam Webster Dictionary, 1828 Noah Websters Dictionary of the English Language, and 1828 American Dictionary of the English Language.*
Aboriginals (the Gods and Goddesses, the original first nation kingdoms and civilizations) are direct descendants from the creation and manifestations of the Almighty Creator. That is, *The Estate of The Almighty Creator.*

Per these definitions between ***"Aboriginal", "Indigenous" and "Native",*** the description of who to be considered *"white"* extends to only or better yet mainly the original (Aboriginal) people of these areas Europe, the Middle East, or North Afraka. The fact remains that prior to the new breed of people who have now populated these geographical locations through the *Doctrine of Discovery* by the Pope and *Manifest Destiny* doctrines, there were first nation kingdoms, the aboriginals, who were the chocolate sun-kissed melanated people of the Almighty Creator.

The first nation kingdoms (the aboriginals) who were the chocolate sun-kissed melanated people of these areas, Europe, the Middle East, or North Afraka must then be the original people and are the real definition of the group *"white race"* per United States Census Bureau. Meaning, majority of the people in today's West Afraka, Central Afraka, East Afraka and other parts of the world who "aboriginally" originated from Middle East, North Afraka and Europe but had to migrate to their respective locations today due to the brutal barbaric invasions of the Greeks, Romans/Catholic church, christian inquisitions, and the Arab Muslim wars are the *"white race"* per the etymological definitions discussed.

There are many evidences that prove this fact. The great Afrakan men, Dr. Yosef Ben-Jochannan, Marcus Garvey, Dr. John Henrik Clarke, Ashra Kwesi, Bobby Hemmitt, Dr. Van Sertima and Cheikh Anta Diop's research proves the origin of many of today's West Afrakans to have migrated from Mesopotamia, Middle East, Europe, and North Afraka. These great Afrakan men have diverse backgrounds in Afrakan and global history, anthropology, physics, mathematics, and science. They studied the human race's origins and pre-colonial Afrakan cultures, civilizations, and traditions. It is as clear as day under the realms and microscopic lenses of both pedagogy and biological genetics that, the so-called aboriginal "blacks/Afrakan Americans or Afrakans" are the true definition of the *"white race"* and not the other way round.

The misnomer *"white race"* term was pushed by some racist people who identified as *"white"* to push their barbaric, inhumane, brutal murders, and racially influenced hate crimes under the auspices of eugenics, and medical apartheid through vaccinations, abortion center establishments, sun down towns in U.S.A, Jim Crow Laws, Police Brutalities, Mass Incarcerations, Redlining, and even to the extent of hating the very genetically biological natural hair on the heads of the aboriginal chocolate sun-kissed people in United States of America to the extent that the "Crown Act" has to be established for the aboriginals to be able to wear their genetically biological natural hair.

How more can this be unreasonably barbaric, despicable, bigotry and racist! All because these new breeds of people despise the Almighty Creator and the chocolate sun-kissed aboriginal people of earth. To love the aboriginals is to love the true Almighty Creator and to hate or despise the aboriginals is to hate or despise the Almighty Creator.

Jim Crow law in United States happened between 1877-1954, the laws were abhorrent, repugnant, heinous, repulsive, despicable, reprehensible, detestable and horrid. Jim Crow law shows a glimpse of how the so-called *"white people"* in United States especially the southern states, were racially psychotic in their everyday livelihoods. In late 1870s, laws were passed by the Southern state legislatures that required the separation of so-called *"whites"* (white only) from *"persons of color"* (colored) in public transportation, public places, public events and schools.

Sundown towns (a.k.a gray towns, sundowner towns, or sunset towns) was another psychotic, and racially motivated by *"white"* people through brutal violent acts that violently lynch, beat down, molest, rape and animalistically pillage any *"colored people"* who were found outside in town after sunset or sundown. These *"white"* racist bigot and murder-filled *"white"* folks would post signs at the entrances and exits of such towns with eerie warnings targeted at *"colored people"*, *"black people"*, or *"African Americans"* that usually reads *"Don't Let the Sun Go Down on You in ____."*

Racially unscientific misnomer like *"white race"* uses race to push "Redlining" (housing segregation to separate *"white"* neighborhoods from *"colored, black, African American"* neighborhoods). Due to racism, U.S colleges are not free anymore. Tuition free U.S college education ended just because *"black"*, *"colored"*, *"African American"* people started to enroll in college to better themselves around 1960s.

This era was also the era of the civil rights movements, that is; "colored" or "black" people basically using non-violent acts (socially acceptable demonstrations) to demand the same rights as "white people" living in United States. The civil rights movements successes scared the racist "white" racial groups to the extent that, their legislative institutions ended the free college program before "colored" people became "educated" on the tertiary level. The tuition free U.S Colleges would give "colored" or "black" people economic freedom and the racist "white race" institutions and most of its people wouldn't allow it.

Credit Score system was established to economically limit/restrict "colored" or "black" people from economically becoming financially comfortable within United States. It is safe to say that, the intentions for most of the structures and requirements put in place in United States were simply to economically hold back "colored" or "black" people.

It is soullessly despicable the amount of jealousy and hate these so-called "white race" institutions have towards the aboriginals who have been classified as "colored", "black", or "African Americans".

Intellectually, socially, economically, strategically, analytically, legally and lawfully, today's so-called "black people" (a misnomer) <u>can, must</u> and <u>should</u> cripple the "white race" establishment by intentionally identifying as "white". Majority of you must be willing to do this, like a serious influx of so-called "black people" must fill out "Form 181", that's the form for *Ethnicity and Race Identification* and mail it to *Office of Management and Budget, 725 17th Street NW, Washington D.C 20503*.

Imagine an entire "black neighborhood", "hood after hood" now "identify" as the misnomer "white race" by learning to tactfully play the U.S "economic game" using this strategy. Automatically, the so-called "white race" would become the lowest earners in U.S's economy. Their arrogance and delusional pride would either make them abolish the misnomer "white race" completely or fix the new "white race hoods/ghettos". This is a strategically reversed practical psychological economic hijack. The socioeconomic political party of the so-called "white race" would be crippled, because these folks hate the aboriginals (a.k.a "black people") to the extent that they would have no other choice than to dismantle that "white race" socioeconomic political party.

While on this topic, I want to bring into light three key pale-pink invaders/colonizers who heavily contributed to the eraser of the autochthonous, aboriginal melanated people in North America. They are namely: Ales Hrdlicka, Melville Herskovits and Walter Plecker. I would advise you to spend some time to execute a deep dive research into these three men.

However, in order not to leave you hanging, I will put what these three pale-pink men did to erase the autochthonous, aboriginal melanated people in North America in a synopsis manner. Ales Hrdlicka was a Eugenics who lied and falsified information and changed facts from the autochthonous, aboriginal melanated people in North America known today as Negros/African Americans to *Mongol Asians*. Over time, these autochthonous, aboriginal melanated people in North America a.k.a Negros/African Americans were replaced by these new lie pushed by the pale-pink man, Ales Hrdlicka. Sadly, these *Mongol Asians* cowardly and ridiculously accepted this forgery to be "classified" as the original autochthonous, aboriginal melanated people Indians of North Americas. This is clearly a paper or document genocide.

How miserably pathetic and intellectually dangerous this has been to human psychological awareness, development and enlightenment. Eugenics is a foolish and prideful practice or belief that pale-pink people are rather superior to all global autochthonous, aboriginal melanated sun-kissed people of this beautiful earth. Eugenics has been proven to be unscientific, barbaric, idiotic, racially biased and pathetic foolery.

Melville Herskovits with his limited anthropological inclination stipulated that all autochthonous, aboriginal melanated sun-kissed people of North America only got there through African enslavement. This was a clueless ideological flex that was obviously encouraged by arrogance, ignorance and non-factual assertions. In that, many facts point to the facts that autochthonous, aboriginal melanated sun-kissed people are inherently the first people to every inch of land on our known borders of earth and beyond the known continental borders. All autochthonous, aboriginal melanated sun-kissed people have been here on earth and the universe for well over billions of years.

Clearly with impeccably undeniable facts, the core ancestral culture and identity of the original autochthonous, aboriginal melanated sun-kissed people of North America a.k.a Negros/African Americans was blurred, reclassified and reassigned to a fake group of people. This is an intellectual, cultural, dignity, and identity genocide of the autochthonous, aboriginal melanated sun-kissed people of North America a.k.a Negros/African Americans committed by Melville Herskovits.

Walter Plecker, a Eugenics and a leader of a white supremacists organization known as the Anglo-Saxon Clubs of America plainly and with ease by the obvious support of the white supremacists militias, took away the benefits that was for the autochthonous, aboriginal melanated sun-kissed people a.k.a Negros/African American, and gave the benefits to some Mexicans and Caucasians. He erased the records of many autochthonous, aboriginal melanated sun-kissed people which denied them of their identity, recognition and benefits that were meant for them.

The same strategy was used by pale-pink colonizers/invaders to aggressively remove the autochthonous, aboriginal melanated people in Australia, North and South America, North Afraka, Europe, Asia and so -called "Middle East". The inhumane aggressively violent strategy was not completely successful in South Afraka, as we can all see the remnants of these barbarically cruel pale-pink colonizers/invaders situation in South Afraka today. The world is in chaos because of greed, violence, rape, theft and barbaric ways of these pale-pink invaders/colonizers, as they continue to bully, steal from the autochthonous, aboriginal melanated people in melanin dominated Afrakan countries and other parts of this beautiful earth.

Etymology of Compendiums of all Gods and The Almighty Creator

THE ORIGINAL ANCIENT KEMET/KEME/EGYPTIANS
ANCIENT EGYPT/KAMIT/KEMET CONCEPT OF GOD AND THE AKANS CONNECTION

In 6th century AD The Muslim Arabs had a conqueror who was appointed and placed into a high rank military position under the influence and auspices of Islamic Muslim prophet Muhammad. This Muslim Arab conqueror was called ʿAmr ibn al-ʿĀṣ, he conquered ancient Egypt/Kemet. Around this time, the Greeks and Romans had already conquered and were living among the remnants of the ancient Kemet/Egyptians. This was the Greek-Roman era on ancient Kemet/Egypt's land. The Greek-Roman Egypt/Kemet occupation became the new home for these foreign Arab-Muslim invaders. ʿAmr ibn al-ʿĀṣ became the governor of the remnants of the invaded Afrakan civilization within 640-646AD, and as well as 658-664AD, 6th century era.

Prior to the Muslim-Arab's invasion of ancient Egypt/Kemet, Persians, Greeks and Romans have had their share of invasions and ruling of ancient Egypt/Kemet. The key question we should all ask is, how did such a great civilization like ancient Egypt/Kemet fall to these nations and religious movements. Ancient Egypt/Kemet in its glorious civilized dark chocolate melanated royal days, were filled with Afrakans from diverse backgrounds, ethnicity, cultures, and traditions with their respective gods/Gods and Goddesses/goddesses.

This civilization was polytheistic civilization, whereby respect, honor and acceptance was equitably and fairly given to all the various Gods and Goddesses. Everything flourished and were at its utmost peaks during this era of oneness, unity, and diverse spiritual wisdom with multiple divine entities. Greeks, Romans and other foreign people came to the heart of the world, which was ancient Egypt/Kamit/Kemet to gain education, spirituality, philosophy, medicine, just to mention few.

One of the key groups of people who ruled ancient Egypt/Kamit/Kemet were the Akan people of today's Ghana, West Afraka. Akan Twi is the umbrella language of the Akan group. There are multiple dialects spoken within the Akan Twi language. The Almighty Creator's reference to the Akan people is one word with three syllabic parts translated into English as, *"Glory"*, *"Singular/Separate/Single/One and Only"*, and *"Almighty/Great One/Mighty One"*.

In the Akan Twi language the word for the Almighty Creator is *Onyamkoropong* or *Nyamkoropong* corrupted as *Nyamkopong*. As stated earlier, the three syllabic parts are *"Onyam"* or *"Nyam"* (as in *ani-mo-nyam*) denoting "Glory", *"Koro"* denoting "One and Only / Singular / Separate/Single" and *"Pong"* denoting "Almighty/Great One/Mighty One".

Ancient Egypt/Kamit/Kemet saw nature as the expressions and sacred manifestation words of the Almighty Creator. Nature is at the core of this spirituality and this is not different from the Akans, who call nature as *"Odomankoma"*. This word *"Odomankoma"* is very dear and sacred to the hearts of Akans due to the connection it has to the Almighty Creator. The Akans see nature as the physical manifestation of the true Almighty Creator.

Hence, from time to time, the word *"Odomankoma"* can be synonymous to the Almighty Creator or could be used as an attribute or in some cases, a characteristic persona as in an entity format. So, one can easily come across the Akans saying *Odomankoma Nyamkoropong* in reverence to the Almighty Creator.

The Akans, just like the ancient Egypt/Kamit/Kemet see the Almighty Creator (*Odomankoma Nyamkoropong*) as the core source of everything, both living and non-living. We discussed in chapter 2 about the numerical mathematical value keys and its relation to everything in creation or existence from zero (0) to nine (9).

All existence is found within these numerical range of values, with numerical value nine (9) representing completeness/ascension/fullness (refer to chapter 2 to regroup your thoughts). In any physics or science class, you are taught that energy can never be destroyed, killed, or eliminated, rather energy is transferred from one form/state to another form/state. In both Akan and ancient Egypt/Kamit/Kemet spirituality, this teaching is as true as day.

With that said, the Akans accept, practice and know that men and women are made up of five elements, namely: Air, Fire, Ether, Water and Earth. The Akans know for a fact that they are spiritual entities in a physical form based on the elements disclosed. Hence, the Akans strongly respect, honor and appreciate their ancestors. They also see nature as a gift and they see themselves as part of nature itself. The Akan word *"Nyame"* for instance, is telling of their cultural view of nature and spirituality. *"Nyame"* is in two parts, the first part is *"Nya"* meaning "to get", "to attain" or "to receive" and the second part is *"Me"* which means "I" or "Me".

So when we look at it together, we will have "*Nyame*" directly translated to English language as "I have receive", "I have attain" or "I have gotten" something that satisfies, fulfills, or completes me. "*Nyame*" in its plural form refers to when a group of people with one motive, vision and mission gather together, that energy uniting as one, is considered *Nyame*.

The Akans see unity as strength and in unity, the Almighty Creator is manifested in the midst of the people united. Great things are achieved when they are united as one. They are able to accomplish great and unimaginable things, that to the Akans is another expression of "*Nyame*". One can also see the elements of Air, Fire, Ether, Water or Earth as *Nyame* or another spiritual force as *Nyame*. Nyame is not the same as the Almighty Creator in the Akans' way of life. *Nyame* is a "God/god" and *Nyamewa* is a Goddess/goddess. God or Goddess, that is, Nyame or Nyamewa is not the same as the Almighty Creator, known as *Onyamkoropong* or *Nyamkoropong* in the Akan spirituality and culture. The very language of the Akans depict their core spirituality which is embedded in their way of life.

They exercise and accept reincarnation and ones spiritual journey after death through the spiritual realm, known to them as "Asamando" or "Asamanso". The Akans consider an atonement of one's errors, omissions, sin(s) against someone to be paid by the one who commits it. So, the committer would need to seek forgiveness or pardon from the person or entity he/she sinned against and such forgiveness or appropriate retribution must be granted by the one offended.

If such measures are not taken then the offender would either be punished in this life through what may be called, karma or the next life, when reincarnated. The Akans are very keen to spirituality and seem to relate almost everything in this life to the spiritual world.

There are seven (7) Gods and Goddesses a.k.a *Nyame* and *Nyamewa* relating to the seven days of the week. Each day of the 7- day week have a special God and Goddess who operate that specific day. Children born on each of the days of the week have a name attributed to that God or Goddess of that day. Let's start with the days of the week and their respective God or Goddess:

1st Day = Sunday=> God & Goddess Ase/Asi =>Boy is Kwa-Asi/Ase & Girl is Ako-Asewa/Asiwa

2nd Day=Monday=>God & Goddess=>Adwo=> Boy is Kwa-Adwo & Girl is Adwo-a

3rd Day=Tuesday=>God & Goddess=>Bena/Abena=> Boy is Kwa-Bena & Girl is A-bena

4th Day=Wednesday=>God & Goddess=>Awuku=> Boy is Kwa-Awuku & Girl is Awuku-a /Akua

5th Day=Thursday=> God & Goddess=> Yaw=> Boy is Kwa-Yaw/Yaw & Girl is Yaa/Yaw-wa

6th Day=Friday=> God & Goddess=> Afi=> Boy is Kwa-Afi/Kofi & Girl is Afia/Afi-a

7th Day=Saturday=> God & Goddess=> Amen/Ame/Ama=>Boy is Kwa-Ame & Girl is Ama/Amen-a

Let's look at the "Thursday God" in the Akan spirituality called Yaw. The local Akan language for this day is Yawda. "*Yaw-da"*, the "da" represents "day" and "Yaw" represents the name of the God/Nyame of that day. This means all the people born on this day would be classified as "Yawdas" (plural), literally means "all the people (both boys and girls) born on Thursday" (Thursday borns). **Yawda** was corrupted to become **Yahuda**, and later

Yahudah and corrupted again to represent Y-H-W-H (originally was YaW). The so-called *Hebrews* added the letter "H" after the letter "Y" and another "H" after letter W. They did the same to the original name Ebrews/Evre/Eve/Ewes by adding the letter "H" in-front of the word "Ebrew" to get "hEbrew". They used the letter "H" to even corrupt all the names of places, Kings and Queens from ancient Kemet and all great Afrakan civilizations.

The name they've all been searching for is simply YAW, the God of Thursday in the Akan spirituality. It can easily be seen that those who are into the bible do not even know for a fact the origin of that name YHWH in their Torah and Bibles. Some assert that the so-called Is-Ra-El folks got the YHWH when they arrived at Canaan (the land they invaded and took per their bible). That then implies YHWH is for Canaanites and adopted by Is-Ra-El-ites or Israelites (a misnomer).

The so-called Israelites might have adopted this God, Yaw (*Thursday God, thunder characteristic power God*) because this specific God is a serious warrior. This Akan God Yaw is powerful in its own glory and might. As a God of war, it is easily overstandable for the Israelites who apparently had been in ancient Egypt/Kemet to adopt such a God out of the seven (7) Gods available. After all, the Israelites (also dark melanated sun-kissed people) were migrating through the wilderness through unknown territories so who wouldn't want a God who likes to fight to lead them through such unpredictable migration from ancient Egypt/kemet to their hopeful destination.

The accurate and factual name of the adopted God in your bible is YAW, call on the right name. No more YhWh, Yaweh, Yahawa/ Yahuah, Yahowah, Jehovah and all the ridiculously wrong plagiarized versions of the original YAW, the God of YAWDA (*Thursday*) people or those birthed on Yawda (*Thursday*). The Jewish folks and Europeans under the auspices of the Vatican, Roman Catholic church and its Pope are selling to the world a corrupted version of one of the seven (7) Gods of the Akans of today's Ghana, West Afraka.

The Akans of Ghana, West Afraka's God/Nyame for Saturday is Amen/AmenRa/Ame/Ama/Amma. This is known to be the same God of ancient Egypt/Kamit/Kemet, the God "Amon/Amen" Hidden One/Hidden or Unseen One and "Ra" (Sun God). In the Catholic/Christian's bible, they always use "Amen" at the end of any blessing / benediction or to end their prayers. Etymology of prayer is to "beg", "plead" or to "prey". AMEN, the Akan God of Saturday is used in many other cultures due to mixing and spreading of cultures over hundreds of thousands of years, as well as the theft and plagiarism of the invaders like Greeks, Romans, Arab-Muslims and later the European colonizers.

The Akans developed so many towns and villages in honor of the God of Saturday, Amon/Amen. Such places include a town called Amon-wi (Amonwi or Amonvi), this is a very old town that the Akans built. It is known among the Akans and held in high esteem that when the Akans arrived at this geographical location of today's Ghana, West Afraka; they were thirsty and that rock known to them as "Amonwi Rock" (Amon is the same as Amen) gave the water to quench their thirst. This rock was then named "Rock of AmenRa" which became Amonwi. (Amon/Amen = God of Saturday, Wi is used exchangeably for Ra).The Akan word for Sun is Awia or Wia, Wi or Ra. Ra is the designated "spiritual" name for the sun. You might have to connect with some of the great Akan Kings and Queens in today's Ghana, West Afraka to ask about this town. In that, the Internets of today try as much as possible to clean and hide most of the key information that may help you to spiritually wake up. So you would need to connect with some of these people who are in today's West Afraka on a personal level, travel there and visit them to research some of the amazing facts of this world that the Western countries continue to hide from the general public.

AdiaBENE, this is an ancient pre 1st century BC kingdom in upper north of Mesopotamia around ancient Assyria. AdiaBENE is an Akan Twi language from a two-word combination of "Adia", "Adi" or "Adiε". Adia / Adiε means "Something" and "Bene", Bene is the name of the Tuesday God of the Akans of Ghana, West Afraka. So AdiaBENE means "Something for the Tuesday God, Bene". AiaBENE controlled the land known as Nineveh. Nineveh linguistically sounds like an Ewe/Eve language, pronounced as "errh-weh/air-weh or errh-veh/air-veh". Eve's or Ewe's are in today's West Afrakan region, most of them are in Ghana, West Afraka. They are part of the Akans. Reading the word/town "Nineveh" backwards is "Hevenin" or "Eve-ni" when we remove the letter "H". "Eve-ni" in Akan Twi language means, a person or someone of Eve descent.

It is also known very well that Gordyene (another ancient town in Mesopotamia) became part of AdiaBene. Gordyene also appears to be of an Akan etymological two-word combination of "Gordi" or Gori and "Yene" (meaning Us / We are) or "Hene" (meaning "king" or chief"). The Akans are made of diverse families or clans and smaller kings who report to the main King or head King (King of Kings). This highly civilized sophisticated way of royal rulership has been with the Akans, as ancient as pre world history all the way back to the era of Mesopotamia and beyond.

Etymology of Compendiums of all Gods and The Almighty Creator

The kingdom or township of Osrhoene between Assyria, AdiaBene and Armenia is another Akan Twi language in origin. The proper spelling and pronunciation of the ancient land of "Osrhoene" is Osro-Hene (OsroHene/Osuro/Hene). That is a combination of two Akan Twi words namely "Osro/Osuro" meaning "Heavens or the Heaven realms" and "Hene" means "king" or chief/ruler". To put the two Akan Twi words together, we would have OsroHene/OsuroHene direct translation is "King of the Heavens" or "King of the Heavenly Realms".

There is also an ancient town/city to the upper northwestern part of AdiaBene known as Sophene. This is made up of two possible Akan Twi words "Sop" or "Sopa /Supa" and "Hene", Hene is an Akan Twi word for King or Chief/Ruler. SopHene or SopaHene was a separate ancient territorial kingdom that did not depend on AdiaBene. "Sophene" would translate as King of Sop (Sop could be derived from *Ṣuppani*). Ṣuppa-ni, as I shared with you earlier on that the Akan Twi word *"ni" indicates "a people of" or "a person from"*. The Akans are known to be the largest ethnic group in today's Ghana, West Afraka. The Akans family tree is known to encompass the Ga-Adangbes/ GaDangme and Ewes/Eves ethnic groups of Ghana, West Afraka. Although not publicly deciphered and fused together as one large mono ethnic group for the populace of Ghana to innerstand and overstand. The ancient link between what is known as the Akans, the Ewes/Eves and the Ga-Adangbes/ GaDangme being one closely knit family is well known among the royal Kings and Queens in these ethnic groups.

The Akans, Ewes/Eves and Ga-Adangbes / GaDangme ethnic groups are found mainly in Ghana, Togo and Benin. While few are dispersed around Nigeria, the rest of West Afraka, and as far as some areas in East Afraka, South Afraka, Central and those left behind in Islamic-Arab

Muslim invaded areas of North Afraka. The dispersed situation is due to the Akans migration from their aboriginal homeland in Mesopotamia, through ancient Sumer, Egypt/Kemet, Sudan, Kushite land and down to Old Ghana Empire, Mali Empire, Songhai Empire and to their current location in Ghana, West Afraka.

The Akan ethnic group (currently "inaccurately" excludes the Eves/Ewes and Ga-Adangbes / GaDangme ethnic groups) is factually known to comprise of the Awowin, Bono, Asante, Adanse, Twifo, Akuapem, Akwamu, Asen, Fante, Akyem, Kwahu, Sehwi, Nzima and Ahanta. Each of these groups within the Akan ethnic group umbrella have clans that make up their larger groups listed above.

It is one of my greatest theory yet to be proven through genetic testing by top global geneticists that, ancient Phoenicians, Eturians/Etruscans, Trojans, Greeks, Romans, Armenia, Syria, Iran, Anatolia, and most of the continent of Asia including China and Japan were one of the Akan ethnic group civilizations. Obviously they lost their civilizations, land and cultures when the new-breed of man's kind were brought up by the genetically manipulative and obsessive scientist, Yacov/Yakubu. Credo Mutwa says that, the evil man who created the genetically modified folks was called *Zah-ha-Rrellel, The Wicked*. It is a historical fact that, Proto-indo-Europeans wiped out these aboriginals, while those who could escape, escaped to interior Afraka. The challenge is now for top renowned global geneticists and archaeologists to prove me right. Let's get to work and get all the facts.

Let's take the Asante group as an example, there are about eight (8) clans that make up just the Asante group. The eight (8) clans that make up the Asante Akan sub-group are Oyoko, Bretuo, Agona, Asona, Asenie, Aduana, Ekuona, and Asakyiri. All the eight (8) clans within the Asante branch of the Akan ethnic group have a King, and then there is the head King or King of Kings with which all the other Kings report to within the Asantes. The current head King or King of Kings within the Asantes is Otumfuo Nana Osei Tutu II.

The Akan ethnic group's name/title "Tutu" is the same title or name that ancient Egyptians/Kemet used, which has been corrupted as "Tut", by Western educators/scholars. It is either Western scholars/educators purposefully omitted the last letter "u" to throw people off or they just do not want people to know who the original Kings and Queens of ancient Egypt/Kemet were.

Such great names of highly influential Kings and Queens of ancient Egypt/Kemet can not just disappear into thin air without Afrakans' posterity proudly naming their offspring after these great Kings and Queens of one of the most civilized civilizations, that the world has ever seen and known. The glorious names of these great ancient Afrakan Kings and Queens are still in use in most of the royal thrones of West Afraka including the Akans of today's Ghana, West Afraka.

Names like Tut Moses is really Tutu Mose. Tutankhamun is Tutu Ankamah/Ankamah. Akhenaten is Akenten or Oten/Oti Akenten (Akenten Oten/Oti). Khufu is Kuffour/Kufour/Kuffu. Tiye is Teye. Amenhotep III simply is Amen Hote, Hote is Akan Twi language meaning clean/sanctified/pure and Amen/Amon is the Akans' God of Saturday. So "Amen Hote" means *"the God Amen is/be sanctified/pure"*. There are many other ancient Kemet/Egypt names that are pure Akan ethnic names of today's Ghana, West Afraka.

These names are not in Greek, Latin, Arabic, Hebrew or Aramaic, rather they are all pure aboriginal Afrakan language in origin. One of which I have disclosed here, Akan Twi language of today's Ghana, West Afraka.

There were multiple Afrakan ethnic groups that came together to build the ancient Kemet/Egypt civilization and were polytheistic, respecting all various Gods and Goddesses of the respective ethnic groups. They had one supreme creator, the Almighty Creator, the *Source* of everything. The Arab Islamic Muslims who are currently occupying the land of Egypt are simply invaders, we have already disclosed the era of their invasion at the opening of this topic. Hence, historical facts about ancient Egypt/Kemet are not and will not be found with these Arab Islamic Muslims, simply because they are not the original or better yet the aboriginals of this ancient Egyptian/Kemet land.

Let's look at the Christian/Catholic and Jewish biblical and Torah verse acknowledging that YAW or Yahweh is a true God/god of war just like the Akans of Ghana, West Afraka (ancient people) says about their Thursday God, Yaw. Let's go to:

Exodus 15:3 WEB version *"Yahweh is a man of war. Yahweh is his name"*

KJV: *"The LORD is a man of war: the LORD is his name"*.

"The Lord is a man of war; Yahweh is his name."

Yahweh (the misnomer), Yaw (the factual name) is indeed a God of war or a man of war. Those born (both boys and girls) on the day of the Akan's Thursday God Yaw, possessed the energy from this realm. So, the people born on this day may be war-like in behavior and characteristics. Thursday born in the Akan culture would have the behaviors of the people in the spiritual kingdom of the God Yaw (YW/YhWh).

These so-called Israelites in that mythological and allegorical bible basically formulated their own ideas, and spiritually juvenile comprehension about this Thursday

Etymology of Compendiums of all Gods and The Almighty Creator

God of the Akans who were at the time in ancient Egypt/Kemet. This "God of *Thursday*" YaW/YHWH has been stolen from the Akans of Ghana, West Afraka by the Jews/Torah/Bible believing Christians.

The Akans are very spiritual people in all walks of life. The etymology of their language shows such spirituality. Let's look at the word *"Ka"*, Ka represents the *"soul"*. So when the Akan people says "Kani", they mean the "soul person or person of a soul" or "a spiritual person". The Akans also have the word/term "Kani-ba" / "Kaniba", the "ba" means "child". So the "Kaniba" in turn becomes "child of the soul person or child of the spiritual person". Etymologically, we can break down the word "Akan" itself. Akan is a corruption of "Akani". We've decoded the meaning of "Akani", so let's look at the "Akan". Akan stipulates "A-Kani", the "A"/"Ah" expression is an excited exclamation/shout/call like "All hail or behold", while the "Ka" represents "Soul". Hence, "Akan" or "A-kani" simply means *"all hail, or behold a soul"*. The old name "Kana" which has corrupted to Canaan or Kanaan has a spiritual meaning anchored to the Akan Twi language.

The ancient nation "Kana" from the Akan Twi language is in two word format namely, "Ka" which means the "Soul" and "Na" in the Akan traditional language means "people". So together from "Kana" we have *"people of the soul/soulful people/spiritual people"*. Example of the "na" in Akan representing "a people" is found in the names of the family groups/clans such as AgoNA, EkuoNA, AsoNA, and AduaNA. It is obvious that, the lands and civilizations occupied by so-called Is-ra-el/Israel is for aboriginal Akans. Even at the context of their bible, they claim that they invaded the civilization of Kana/Kanaan/Canaan. Cities like Yarusalem/Jerusalem and other great ones on the geographical area were all built by the Akans a.k.a Kanas/Kanaans/Canaans.

By now, you should know that the bible is mythological; that was inspired and plagiarized from these ancient civilizations like the Kanas, Kemet/AdiaBene, Sumer, Mesopotamia, Dogons, Old Ghana Empire, Mali Empire, Songhai Empire, Kushite Kingdom (Kingdom of Kush), Carthage/Karthage, Punt land (Land and kingdom of Punt), Aksum Empire, Great Zimbabwe and many others. Everything was built and architecturally planned by the aboriginal Kemet, Mesopotamia, Kana/Kanaan/Canaan inhabitants. These are eons of ancient people with ancient knowledge since the beginning of time.

The Akans always communicate with the Almighty Creator by pouring what is known as "Pouring of *Libation*". To the Akans, *libation* is the true authentic way to communicate or "pray" to the Almighty Creator. Libation connects all the five elements: water, fire, air, ether, and earth, which consist in us all. When all these five elements are connected, the Almighty Creator (Supreme being) is called, and all the lesser spirits and beings are summoned.

The Akans of Ghana sacredly revered what is called "εbɔɔ/bɔɔ Twer3" also known as "Bonsam bɔɔ / εbɔɔ". The εbɔɔ/bɔɔ Twer3 or Bonsam bɔɔ/εbɔɔ is a pivotal core cornerstone for every Akan family root. This dates back to ancient Sumer, Mesopotamia, ancient Kemet/Egypt and all the ancient aboriginal Afrakan civilizations.

The Akan families have this εbɔɔ/bɔɔ Twer3 (Bonsam bɔɔ/εbɔɔ) that the elders and the Kings and Queens within the family sacrifice animals, any kind/type of animal. They use its blood, local palm wine, water, nsa fufuo, to activate communication with their ancestral Gods and Goddesses from several billion star years away in the galaxies and several billion deep miles at the heart of the deepest oceans. This is the Akans' key traditions and it was not different from the same practices in ancient Sumer and ancient Kemet/Egypt/Kamit. This is very sacred and pivotal.

The sad hidden fact is that, it was German (yes the country in Europe) that "translated" the Akan twi language which lost its pure original ancient versions to today's contemporary modern Akan Twi language versions. Germany wrote and brought the Akan Twi alphabets to the Akans in West Afraka predominantly in today's Ghana, West Afraka.

So many meanings and sources of core roots of the Akan Twi language was mistranslated by the Germans from Germany. The name David in Hebrew is Dawid. Dawid is an Akan language in today's Ghana, West Afraka. The throne of Dawid is still alive and well in the Asante kingdom, in the Asante region of Ghana, West Afraka. When the time is right, no flesh and blood of a living person can dare to stop the rise and reign of this kingdom. The time is not far off for all the great Gods and Goddesses to strengthen their new kingdoms. A kingdom whereby there wouldn't be any more presidents or ministers, rather Kings and Queens through and through only.

The end of politics is nigh, for the beginning of the end and new ways of royalty to reign. The Almighty Creators are not politicians and are not elected, rather they are Kings and Queens with Kingdoms. If you're looking for the ancient Sumerians, Mesopotamians, Akkadians (Akkad or Akkan/Akan), ancient Kemetians/Egyptians, then today's Akans trace their aboriginal roots to these lands.

Let's look at some words and names in the Akan language like: Ba or ba, *"Ba"* means *"child"* in Akan Twi language. "Ba" or "bar" in Aramaic language / Hebrew language means "son" or "son of" as in the example of Bar-Jesus, which means "Jesus' Son" or "Son of Jesus". Hence, names like Bartimeus, Barabbas, Bar-Jonah, Barsabbas, Barnabas, Bartholomew and all the names with "bar/ba" just means "son" or "son of" the father's name that comes after. These are all ancient Akan language that has been absorbed, twisted and turned to form Aramaic and the Hebrew languages.

The great family of Bantu cannot be missed here. The Bantu word itself is a combination of two Akan language words namely: "Ba" (Child) and Ntu (Name of the father / family name). So "Ba" and "Ntu" from the Akan language simply means "Ntu's Child" or "child of Ntu". The Akans in ancient times wrote from right to left. As we now know that "ba" is singular for the Akan language meaning child, the plural for children is "aba" or "mba". Hence, we have Abantu or Mbantu as the plural form of Bantu, which now will mean "children/descendants of Ntu" in the Akan language origin.

Who is Ntu? Let's look at the word's origin or etymology, from Ntu. In Akan Twi language, we will have Ntum, Ntumtum, Tu, Tum, and Tumtum, all referring to the English word: dark, burnt, dark matter, dark soil. There is a research study that links Ntu to Abram/Abraham. The Akan's etymological word for Abram is Abrim/Abibrim or Abirim/Abiribirim. This is the genesis of Abibirim man, which means the dark, "*black*" land/nations. So the father of all dark or "*black*" nation on earth is, Ntu and his "ba" child.

Another information among the Akans of today's Ghana, West Afraka that is worth noting is, "Kwaa Ayesi Adei Ameni", *Ameni* as in the God *"Amen"*. This is another God among the Akan people. There are two Gods combined to form this name, let's have a look; Kwaa Ayesi (as in Kwasi, the *Sunday* God of the Akans) and Ameni (as in Amen, the *Saturday* God of the Akans). They combined the two Gods to form *Kwaa Ayesi Adei Ameni*. The Akans recognize Saturday and Sunday as the day of rest, and day of fellowship respectively for their God, *Kwaa Ayesi Adei*

Ameni. This is fellowship, not worship as many of today's religious groups have flipped it upside down to deceive many. This is a soulful spiritual rest and connection.

They fellowship with the Almighty Creator, the Gods and Goddesses. The Akans do not "worship", rather, they fellowship. You must know the difference in order to properly execute your fellowship offerings to the Gods, Goddesses and the Almighty Creator. It is of the knowledge among some Akans that this is the reason why they celebrate their ancient old tradition celebration known as AKWASIDAE (discussed in chapter 2). Among the Akans, Akwasidae is a huge celebration for the Kings, Queens and members of the Akan ethnic groups. It is common for the Akans to combine two or three Gods and/or Goddesses to form a much powerful union.

Multiple Gods and Goddesses are known to be accepted and fellowshiped throughout the history of the aboriginal Afrakans of ancient Mesopotamia, ancient Egypt/Kemet, Sumer, Dogons, Old Ghana Empire, Mali Empire, Songhai Empire, Kushite Kingdom (Kingdom of Kush), Carthage/Karthage, Punt land (Land and kingdom of Punt), Zulu kingdom, Aksum Empire, all Bantu kingdoms and countless others.

Bosom Muru is one of the Gods of the Akans. Bosom Muru is known in today's India as Muru-Gan (Sanskrit; *Murugan*). *Ado Nai Yahusuah* is also ancient Akan language and name of one of the Gods whereby the bible folks have corrupted it to be *"AdoNai"* instead of the two separate Akan names "Ado & Nai" or Ado Nai. Honor, embrace, appreciate and respect your ancestral past and stories of origin, for these are part of your heritage.

Melchizedek was sent to Kana (Kanaan / Canaan) to specifically rule the land as its high priest, ambassadorial King/Chief or Governor from the Kemet/ Keme/Ancient melanated Egyptian royal priestly line. The Canaanites/Kanaanites/Kananites at this time spoke the ancient Egyptian/Keme/Kemet language. Melchizedek was the main man who built *Yabus* corrupted as *Jebus* or *Yabusalem/Yarusalem/Jerusalam* whose people are called *Yabusites/Jebusites*. Yes, Jerusalem/Yarusalem was known as Jebus/Yabus. I will dare to boldly state that Yabus/Jebus was known as Yabusua or Yawura – busua, (Yabusua is an Akan/Canaanite language meaning "our family" or Yawura – busua meaning "our royal/honorary family"). Yabusites/Jebusites were a local ethnic group that was part of the same people of Kana/Kanaan/Canaan, known as the Canaanites/Kanaanites/Kananites. Interestingly, the Philistines called this amazing city as "the city of peace" also known as Yarusalem corrupted as Jerusalem (Salem, meaning "Peace"). Read Genesis 10:15-18 KJV.

It is of great evidence that *Flavius Josephus*, the one and only acclaimed and apparently known historical figure who is accepted and validated as someone with accurate record writings in those eras wrote that, a Kanaanite/Canaanite king built the glorious and precious city of Yarusalem/Jerusalem. Flavius Josephus stated that this Ham's descendant king (Melchizedek, the Kanaanite/Canaanite King and High Priest) was known and called by the appellation, "the King of Peace". It must be noted that Flavius Josephus wrote a little over twenty known books about the Jewish Antiquities in the Greek language, so his reputation definitely precedes him.

The bible has a distorted view and accounts for when and how this great Akan/Canaanite/Kanaanite ultra civilized and impeccably massive developed nation that was part of the Kemet/ancient Egypt and Ham's descendant civilization's extension fell in Joshua 11:3, Joshua 12: 10, 2 Samuel 5: 6-10. The fact of the matter is that, many of the survivors migrated to different parts of interior Afraka.

However, most of them went to West Afraka. Some parts of South-West Afraka have the original stories intact as to how they lost their great ancient civilizations and lands.

These rich facts are not mainstream information. I have given the location, so it should be easy for you to get on a plane and go on an adventure to meet the Kings, elders and royals of these geographical locations in Afraka to learn more about these hidden facts of this world.

Have you heard about the **Adinkra codes**? The Adinkra codes are etymologically embedded in the Adinkra symbols and patterns of the Akan people. The Adinkra codes are the core codes that makes up our universe which self-corrects its existence and possible operational errors. Your web-browsers, search engines and all these massive intricate quantum codes use similar codes directly identical to the Adinkra codes. The discoverer of the proposed Adinkra codes (self-correcting error codes of the universe) is none other than an Afrakan American professor, a theoretical physicist who works on super-string, super-gravity and super-symmetry theory, Sylvester James Gates Jr. a.k.a Jim Gates (S. James Gates Jr.).

Ancient Egypt/Kemet sadly fell due to the birth of the imposing monotheism arrogance of Akhenaten who was originally known as Akenten or Oten/Oti Akenten (Akenten Oten/Oti), Achina/Akyena Oten. Ancient Egypt/Kemet was polytheistic throughout its endeavors. Much of its strength, great military, super regional and global dominance was due to their polytheistic cultures, traditions and acceptance. With Akhenaten's forceful push of monotheism right after his rise to kingship, he dismembered the core unity of the ancient Egypt/Kemet populace. Why would the people of ancient Egypt/Kemet accept just one god/God as its supreme ruler, while each day has its own God/god and Goddess/goddess, as well as other gods and goddesses. This became a very sketchy situation and definitely an unacceptable one for the ancient Egypt/Kemet populace who are known to be very spiritual in all endeavors.

Monotheism by Akhenaten became the antithesis for the unity among ancient melanated Afrakan Egypt/Kemet. The fall of the great civilization of ancient Egypt/Kemet was foreseen due to this manipulative power-drunk monotheistic move by Akhenaten. This weakened the civilization militarily because most of the people who disagreed migrated out of Kemet. So, when it was attacked by foreign armies, it was rendered as an eminent defeat and sadly was overtaken.

Divided we fall, united we stand. Polytheism is the way to unification while monotheism is simply individualistic and easily susceptible to defeat. The massive division, confusion, disgust and uproar brought by Akhenaten's monotheistic move caused mass migration of the ancient Egyptian/Kemetians.

The fall out of ancient Kemet's people brought ancient Egypt/Kemet falling to its knees to the Greeks and subsequently to the Romans. When war was brought to ancient Egypt/Kemet's doorstep. A divided house and mass migrated populace due to Akhenaten's monotheism couldn't stand the brutal force from an old-time weak enemy like Greeks and Romans. The Arabs seeing such a plundered once upon a time a united strong ancient Egypt/Kemet civilization now weakened, wrecked, scattered and conquered by both the Greeks and Romans, decided to take its invasion opportunity around the year 650 AD. The Romans were occupying Kemet this time.

Apparently, Akhenaten thought that his move to establish monotheism was the right move due to his perceived and observable corruptions by the other ethnic groups who were seeing their respective ethnic god/God or goddess/Goddess as the Supreme Creator. It makes sense to some extent as to why Akhenaten would have taken such a risky and forceful move. Risky because these ancient ethnic groups who united to form the massive civilization of ancient Egypt/Kemet were highly spiritual people, and would never allow one's ethnic God/Goddess over their own. Hence, Akhenaten could have rather established a peaceful consensus with respective ethnic group heads, elders, high priests and royal families to find the best approach instead of Akhenaten's unanimous decision to impose his God/god on everyone. That was a disaster from the start if you ask me.

The entire territories of ancient Egypt/Kemet fell together with the main base. As such, groups like the Kanaan's/Kana's/Canaan's/Akans obviously decided to move immediately after the confusion/chaos and instabilities due to Akhenaten's monotheistic move. The Kanaan's/Kana's/Canaan's/Akans moved towards West of Afraka, West Afraka (westwards) to establish their massive Kana empire a.k.a Ghana empire (research the "old Ghana empire"). These were the same Kanans/Ghanaians/Ghanas/Kanaans/Canaanites. To dissect more into this migration of these great ancient Ghana/Kanaan/Canaan/Egypt/Keme/Kemet people, check out none other than the book of the late J.B.Danquah (Joseph B. Danquah) *"The Akan Doctrine of God"*.

The Akan's libation of today's Ghana/Kanaan/Canaan in West Afraka is the one and only authentic true form of "prayer" or communication with the Almighty Creator. Let me add that, some of the Akans moved south, south-south west and south west by penetrating via lake Chad all the way to what is known as today's Nigeria and then most of them continued their journey to what is known today as Ghana/Kana/Kanaan/Canaan in West Afraka.

To bottle it all up, Greeks conquered a divided ancient Egypt/Kemet due to Akhenaten's monotheistic move. Followed by the Romans conquering the Greeks later on and hammering a weakened and dismembered ancient Egypt/Kemet. Arab Muslims was able to conquer Romans in ancient Egypt/Kemet and also took over old Egypt's land. Arabs pushed, forced their religion on the remnants of ancient Egyptians/Kemetians who were left behind. These Arab Muslims massacred, plundered, destroyed ancient Egypt/Kemet's buildings, mummies, and stole many civilizations from science to mathematics, arts, culture, books, medicines, towns and cities, etc. Some Akan's who didn't migrate through the first, second and third wave of westward migrations fought off the Arab Muslims through massive resistance.

These last wave of Akans later on decided to retreat from ancient Egypt/Kemet to migrate in order to join their ethnic groups in today's Ghana, West Afraka following the same migratory paths.

One of the easiest or simplest ways to decode most of the names and places in the Hebrew Bible or just the regular bibles is by removing or eliminating the letter "H" from all the names and places listed in the Hebrew bible (or all bibles). The first example is the letter "H" added to the God of the Bible called YHWH (it was originally YAW). Another one is "Hashabiah" in *1 Chronicles 25:3*, remove the "H" that they falsely added and you have "Asabia" an Akan Twi language in present day Ghana, West Afraka.

By the way "Akan" in the Hebrew Concordance (or go to biblehub.com/hebrew/) search number 5912, it clearly tells you that "Akan" is an Israelite name. Additionally, the word "Hebrew" itself shouldn't have the letter "H" in front of it, it must be "Ebrew" which was from Eber, originally Ever/Ewer/Igber/Igbo; all one in the same people (long/short distance cousins) in today's West Afraka.

It must then be pointed out that, these western folks with their head coming from the Roman empire (dissolved into the Roman Catholic Church, Vatican) literally reversed the facts to cause intentional diversions. Hence, it's rather the mythologically created "Israel/Israelites" that stole the identity, culture and traditions of the original Akans/Evers/Ewes/Igbers/Igbos, Kemet, Dogons, and the story of Afrakans. It's like packaging a synthetic brand to replace the authentic brand, and later on saying that the authentic brand is a name found within the synthetic brand. This is the reversed spell trick that has been cast upon the whole world by the colonizers and barbaric enslavers.

Let's look at more original Ghana (Ghanaian)/Kana/Kanaan/Canaan/Ghana names like Naaba (Naa Aba corrupted as Naaba) in Acts 4:36. Osei (corrupted in the bible as Osea/Hosea) in Hosea 1:1.

ɛnyonam (corrupted as Enam) in Joshua 15:34.

Yɛriko/Yɛreko (corrupted in the bible as Yaricho/Jericho) in Numbers 2:1.

Naa Ashon (corrupted in the bible as Naasson) in Mathew 4:1.

Daani (corrupted as Daniel/Dani-el) in 1 Chronicles 3:1.

Debra (corrupted as Deborah) in Judges 4:14.

Appiah/Appia (corrupted in the bible as Apphia) in Philimon 1:2.

Moaben (corrupted in the bible as Moab/Moabite) in Genesis 19:37.

Abena Yaa (corrupted in the bible as Benaiah) in 1 Chronicles 15:18.

Naa Ama (corrupted in the bible as Naamah) in Joshua 15:41.

εden/Aden/Edem/εdem (corrupted in the bible as Eden) in Genesis 2:8 (this must be garden for εdem/Edem not "Adam"), Edem's/εdem's garden; garden made for or made by εdem/Edem not "Adam".

ενε/εwε (corrupted as Eve) in Genesis 4:1.

Heman (kept the same spelling) in 1 Chronicles 15:17.

Kyeremi Yaw (corrupted in the bible as Jeremiah) in Jeremiah 1:1.

Tεkoa (corrupted as Tekoa) in 1 Chronicles 2:24.

Anim (not changed in the bible as Anim) in Joshua 15:50.

Kwame (corrupted in the bible as Carmi) in Genesis 46:9.

Maase Yaa (corrupted in the bible as Maaseiah) in Ezra 10:22.

Sai (corrupted in the bible as Sheshai) in Numbers 13:22.

Ba Naba (corrupted as Barnabas) in Acts 4:36.

Man/Oman-ma-nii/Man-ama-nii meaning "nation" or "one from/of a nation" (kept the same as "Man" in the bible) in Genesis 1:26-27.

The entire West Afraka holds some powerful hidden facts that when completely reviewed would totally shake up the facts hidden from the entire world. There is a reason archaeologists avoid digging in West Afraka. It holds massive truths to unlocking the missing revelations to the entire world. It's not to be messed with because it's the core of authentic spiritual prowess.

The same letter "H" has been used by colonizers to secretly cause mass distortions to hide true facts about the original royals and priests of Kemet/ancient Egypt. Remove the letter "H" from all the names of the royals and priests of ancient Egypt/Kemet and you would get to the facts hidden from the whole world.

The Akan people refer to a group of major ethnic group in today's Ghana, West Afraka as "Dagombas". That is etymologically referenced as the God/god "Dagon-mba" ("mba" from Akan Twi to English means *"children"* of the god/God Dagon). Currently, the referenced name to Dagon's children is corrupted as *Dagomba* in current West Afraka. This means that, the aboriginal Philistines (found in the bible) are these modern-day Dagon-mbas / Dagombas in predominantly Ghana, West Afraka. The Dogonbas/Dagombas also constitutes the Dogon people of Mali and the hills of West Afraka. In other words, these Dogon people are spread-out throughout the countries and lands of West Afraka. The Philistines/Dagonbas/Dagombas or children of the god/God Dagon were not Muslims and neither spoke Arabic nor used Quran in their belief and traditional cultural system. The Philistines/Dagonbas are not the same people as modern day people of Palestine (who are Arabs-Muslims) or Jewish (Ashkenazi converts) state Israel, both are located on this geographical landmass. The Philistines/Dagon-mbas/Dagombas (children of the god/God Dagon) lost their homeland and were chased out by the many wars with the Greeks and Romans.

The Romans brought other breeds of new people to occupy this new Philistines/Dagon-mbas/Dagombas (children of the god/God Dagon) territory. Per the Hebrew bible and passages in the books of Samuel, Judges and Joshua, the god/God Dagon is known to be the main god/God of the Philistines (Dagon-mbas/Dagombas = children of the god/God Dagon). These Philistines/Dagon-mbas/Dagombas (children of the god/God Dagon) also lived within the land of Kanaan/Canaan estimatedly around 1200s to the 600s BCE or possibly much earlier. It is known in academia and many religious sects that, these Philistines/Dagon-mbas erected Dagon in all their temples with the famous ones being the temples in Tuttul and Terqa, as well as temples of Ashdod. This is where the Philistines/Dagon-mbas are said to have brought the *Ark of the Covenant* to after defeating the children of Israel in battle, and the temple of Gaza (the one Samson destroyed).

Outside the bible, the Dogons (which constitutes Dagombas) of the entire stretch of West Afraka have a creator God called Amen (Male energy) and Ama/Amma (female energy). These Dagon/Dogon people are ancient people who come from the Sirius star B star system. The Dogons/Dagons were part of the civilizations of Kemet. They have their own high priests and elders in their closely knit communities. Some of the Dogons who migrated outwards to interior West Afraka were converted into Islamic religion under brutal force and war. Those of the Dogons who escaped and resisted the wars and Islamic religious aggression by Mohammad and his people moved to the high land mountains of Mali, Burkina Faso, and Niger landmass.

The final war whereby the original chosen people would take back their rightful thrones throughout this universe would not be fought with nukes, guns and any physical military accoutrements. Rather, it is going to be based on an invocation of the Supreme Almighty whose people are mainly in today's West Afraka and spread-out throughout the four corners of the world. If there is an iota of truth in the bible, then no Christian or any Bible believing person can dispute this fact. In that, the Bible clearly states that *"if my people who are called BY MY NAME, shall humble themselves then, and pray, and seek my face, and turn from their wicked ways; then will I hear from heaven, and will forgive their sin, and will heal their land."* (2 Chronicles 7:14 KJV). The name of this God is YEVE/YEWE/YHWH and his people are called by his name, who are the EVEs/EWEs of West Afraka, predominantly in Ghana, West Afraka. If the bible hold any fact, then it is easy to state with a fact that, West Afrakans would rule the entire world in the future. The main royals, priests and top rulers would then come from Ghana, West Afraka as wells as the rest of all West Afrakan nations. This is when we all unite just as it was from the beginning.

Before concluding this chapter, let's look at additional emphasis about what *"Kwa"* represents in another light. "*Kwa*" translates as *"People of "*. There are some linguists that agree that, the word or term *Kwa*, originated from Akwa Nshi/Ndi/Ishi in the Igbo language for *'First People'*. It makes a lot of sense, because "Kwa-Asi" is the Sunday God of the Akans (the God, Asi), and Sunday is the first day of the week. Also, the Ibgo people of Nigeria are part of the Evree/*Eber*/Igbo/Ewes/Eves a.k.a Hebrew. Hence, the Igbos are directly or indirectly linked to the Akan's extended ethnic group. This word "*Kwa*" is also the local name of the Nigerian monoliths that represent *"First People"* on the planet. The Kwa languages include Ewe of Ghana, West Afraka, Togo and Benin; Akan of Ivory Coast and Ghana, West Afraka; Gã of Accra, Ghana; Yoruba and Ibo of Nigeria and Bini/Ubini of Benin (Edo people). Deducing from this information indicates that, the first people on earth are the "*Kwa*" people. It comes with no surprise that all the major Gods in the Bible were copied from the "*Kwa*" people of today's West Afraka.

As earlier discussed about the people of Ghana, West Afraka who still hold on to the "*Kwa*" origin as prefix to their names and the God and Goddesses they originated from. Such as "*Kwa - Amen*" corrupted as "*Kwa-Ame*" indicated people of the God "*Amen*" or "first people" of the God *Amen*. The God *Amen* has been adopted into the Bible as the "*God who fulfills everything*". Hence, the Bible believers attribute *Amen* at the end of all their prayers, and praises without knowing its roots or etymology.

The Hebrew language which originates from the "*Kwa*" language of Akan-Twi and other Kwa languages claim that "*Amen*" means "*certainty/truth/verily*" or "*so be it/so shall it be/to be reliable*". Clearly this is not viable to its core etymology. The same applies to YaWeh, corrupted as Yahuah. Rather, the fact is that, people from the God Yaweh are called Yaw (men) and Yaa (women) as we thoroughly learned under the Akan names and their origins from this chapter.

All Afrakans who still have their cultures, traditions, languages and spirituality in tact had to fiercely fight off the Greeks, Romans, and the Arab Muslims' manufactured religions and barbaric wars in order to be who they are today. Religion is one bloody war mongering, and forceful political push of insanity by invaders on the continent of Afraka and beyond. It is about time you respect those who were able to keep their original cultures, traditions, languages and spirituality in spite of all the atrocities, centuries of wars and invasions.

Etymology of Compendiums of all Gods and The Almighty Creator

CHAPTER 4

CHAPTER 4

ALMIGHTY CREATOR'S CORE

LOVE: The highest level of all vibrations is love. Love elevates every community from primitive to the highest level of ascension. The cosmic energies and realms are full of intelligence that rest on the core spectrum of love. Without love, everything is meaningless. Absolutely everything operates and draws to the unmatched magnetic frequencies of love. Love is the purest form of all energies and as such the strongest focal point of all energies combined.

The most powerful force in the entire universe, in the entire galaxies upon galaxies, in the extraterrestrial and all the terraces and terrestrials in existence is love. This powerful energy is the apex, the top of all energies with which every energy in existence known and unknown to man, seen and unseen to man, felt and unfelt to man and woman, felt and unfelt to the entire universe derives its source of power and strength from.

The most powerful *source* of this energy is the true source of all creation in existence in the living world, the spiritual world, and the non-living world. This powerful force of energy has to go deep down past the bottomless pit of hell to gain the strongest foundation, so that its apex would reach the highest apex of the heavens of all heavens. This energy is so powerful that there's nothing that can shake it.

Lot of people do not innerstand the depths of love. Most people say that there's a thin line between love and hate. However, that is not true, what they classify as hate is rather the continuation of love that most people see as hate. The fluffy and happy experience is just one side of love. The other side of love is equally as ugly as the beautiful part of love.

Most people want only the best part of this energy called love. They want just the fun, fluffy, excitement part, but when we talk about true love, it is both ugly and beautiful, dark and light, yin and yang, balance and not one sided. The source of all the powerful energy in the world is love and this love is an unconditional love. This is why even the wicked, the good, the liar, the bad, and all these crazy people are walking and living their best lives.

Before we continue with the subject matter of the powerful force of all forces a.k.a love, let's look at our mind and the three types of minds that we have in our human body.

THE BRAIN: *The brain is the <u>throne of thrones mind</u>* for all the three (minds) namely, brain, heart and gut. The brain acts as the **enforcer** of all the activities and communications submitted by the heart mind, gut mind and throne of thrones mind. The brain sitting on what I call, the *"throne of thrones mind realm"* has to act in all its might and wisdom without fear or favor. That means, the brain has to executive pure justice without blemish.

Whatever is fed to the brain a.k.a "throne of thrones mind realm" from the gut brain/mind, the heart brain/mind and the electrical messaging neurons, is what the brain will manifest. The brain a.k.a "throne of thrones mind realm" controls your memories, hunger, emotions, thoughts, touch, visions, breathing, motor skills, temperature, as well as all the procedural regulations that transpire in and out of your body.

It comes with great care for you to be mindful of the type of energies, vibrations, and frequencies allowed into your heart a.k.a *"the mind of love"* and your gut a.k.a *"the mind of health and well-being"*. The throne of thrones mind's realm a.k.a the brain is a powerhouse that is always processing, balancing, coordinating and controlling all the electrical impulses or messages.

These messages or electrical energetic impulses start from the spiritual realm to psychological realm, and then are birthed into the physical realm. These activities in the "throne of thrones mind" happen in a continuous cyclical format every hour, minute, second, microsecond, millisecond and as quick as the speed of light. The outcome of our world today is a direct reflection of what we have collectively allowed to penetrate into our hearts a.k.a *"mind of love"* and has contaminated our guts a.k.a *"the mind of health and well-being"* which in turn spews out from our brains a.k.a *"throne of thrones"*.

Greater majority of us have directly or indirectly allowed, accepted, and entertained diabolical low energetic vibrations of greed, lies, wicked schemes, murderous acts, evil deeds, starting conflicts to create wars/tensions, jealousy, sellouts, selfishness, and host of low vibration energies to prevail, instead of admonishing them to totally eradicate them. Judgment would be brought to this earth since it appears that most of us keep fueling such low vibrational energetic frequencies. There is absolutely no escaping, no underground bunker or "space escape" ship would save those who contributed to destroying the 3,6 and 9's energetic vibration ascension of this earthly realm. We are never alone and we will never be alone. The overall purpose is for our soul to ascend. Nothing more, and nothing less. This is for those with a soul.

THE HEART: *The heart is the <u>mind of love</u>*. This is the realm of divine love. Divine love is a cyclical procreation that serves as the thermostat to bring balance to good and evil. The heart a.k.a *"the mind of love"* is the core to everything in existence both inanimate and animate. The heart is like a mother who cares for all her children, the good, bad and the ugly. This makes the heart a.k.a *"the mind of love"* to operate as the center of everything. The heart feeds circulatory oxygen filled blood to the entire realms of the body. The valves and chambers within the heart maintains the pressure of the blood flow, transports or removes metabolic waste products from the body, sends deoxygenated blood to the lungs to refresh it with oxygen, and controls the rhythmic rate of its muscles.

These basic functions of the heart a.k.a *"the mind of love"* keep the body alive and operational. Right when the heart a.k.a *"the mind of love"* stops or seizes to exist, the entire body shuts down (unalive or dies). This awareness brings clarity to the reason why the heart a.k.a *"the mind of love"* is the core/center of the functionality of every living thing. The universe is a living thing. Energies are living things. Nature is a living thing. All the elements within, and outside nature are living things as well.

Hence, all these entities and beings possesses a heart a.k.a *"the mind of love"*.

The central core of the Almighty Creator is love, which is found in the heart a.k.a *"the mind of love"*. The heart serves as a magnet that attracts everything. It adopts and welcomes every energy with no prejudice as a good mother should. It is pivotal for all of us as a universal collective, to feed more into high energetic vibration energies. Since these energies fed to our hearts a.k.a *"the mind of love"* would be transported to the *throne of thrones mind* a.k.a the brain, to enforce or manifest into our physical realm. If we desire to have a wonderful world filled with heavenly high vibrational energies of 3, 6 and 9's steps to ascension or completion, then we must collectively have a change of heart to vibrate universal love that transcends the peripherals.

THE GUT: *The gut is the <u>mind of health and wellbeing</u>*. Your gut is key to how you feel both internally and externally. If you have good gut, you have great health and wellbeing. The health of your gut would determine your mood, vibe, and the kind of energies you communicate to the heart a.k.a *"the mind of love"* and then to the *throne of thrones mind* a.k.a the brain. The gut a.k.a *"the mind of health and wellbeing"* sends intelligent signals relating to the state of affairs of either healthy or unhealthy energetic vibrating frequencies occurring in its realm to the brain a.k.a *"the throne of thrones mind"* through the heart a.k.a *"the mind of love"* for processing.

The gut a.k.a *"the mind of health and wellbeing"* uses sensors to analyze all food intake (spiritual foods, psychological foods, and physical foods). It regulates and executes the digestion of these foods. Its glands secret perfect amount of mucus needed to lubricate the intakes and mix it through its large and small intestines. When it comes to the physical food intake, the gut's mechanical extensions starts at the mouth constituting your palatal surfaces, your teeth and obviously your tongue, which works together to mash, and grind the consumables being consumed. After that it travels down through esophagus and head its way for peristalsis.

Energies, vibrations and frequencies contained in these spiritual, psychological, and physical foods are absorbed by your body through the appropriate streams of absorption. As the good old saying goes, you are indeed what you consume. This entails not only physical foods, but also both spiritual foods, and psychological foods. The gut a.k.a *"the mind of health and wellbeing"* would project all the energies, vibrations and frequencies contained in your consumable intakes through feelings, moods, and emotions. So when you "feel" that you do not feel well in the realms of your gut, you "know" for sure in all cases that it's due to some of the foods you have consumed.

The gut a.k.a *"the mind of health and wellbeing"* also has the ability to send signals to the *heart mind* and *brain mind* when something is off, or when something terrible, or something terrific is about to happen. You must adhere to the gut a.k.a *"the mind of health and wellbeing"* if you desire to be in proper alignment with your spiritual, physical, and psychological journey. To strengthen, establish, and restore your gut a.k.a *"the mind of health and wellbeing"* to its fullest energetic vibration frequency, is to consume healthy spiritual, psychological, and physical energetic vibrational frequency foods.

Pay very close attention to the emotional feelings emanating from your gut area. Restructure everything you deem inadequate in your life. Go inside and listen to what's happening internally, give time to it, and take appropriate steps to resolve any, or all imbalances within you.

Creator's Core

Our main purpose to one another is to love one another. We are called to love the planet we call home from eons of time. The other part to our purpose is our spiritual love for *the Creator, the Almighty Creator*.

Our life on this physical planet, our interaction with each other, what we do and how we do it have its solution in *love*. Typically, the universal advice that leaders, career advisors, religious leaders, counselors, and parents give when one is stuck on finding what to do with their life is centered around love.

99.99% of the time, you are advised to find *something you love.* Be it working on that *"thing you love"* with passion, getting the right training for *"what you love",* and going for it at all cost. We come across such advice in almost every aspect of our lives. Be it marriage, career, college, finding love, et al.

Also, when you are in dismay, and feel like you are selling yourself short, you are advised to love yourself enough to take care of yourself. We take care of ourselves by resting, checking our mental health, getting out of unhealthy situation, and deciding to move on to better things. All in all, love seems to be the core to our being. We are advised to get back to the basics of love whenever we get offtrack.

It was out of *love* that everything came into existence, both known and unknown to mankind. Absolutely nothing can exist without *love*. Love would always be love regardless of the energy surrounding it. This is what I call the *"Theory of God's Core"* which is *Love*.

The diagram below is meant to expand on the *"Theory of God's Core"*. Pay close attention to the flow and direction of the arrows.

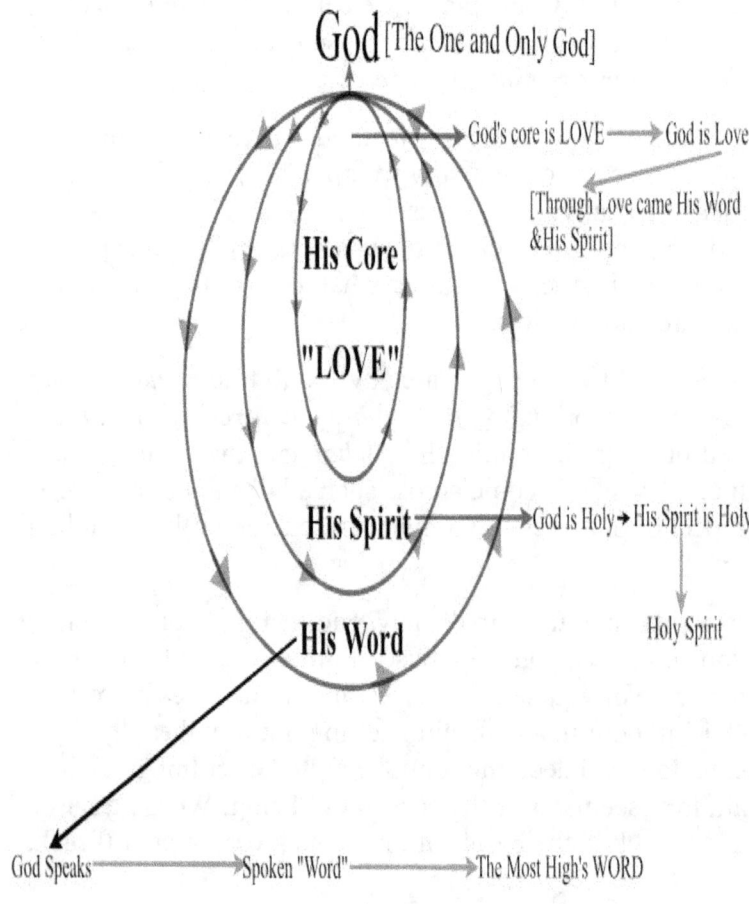

Allow me to decipher the diagram further for proper innerstanding. Love manifested in the *"flesh"* is *the Most*

High Almighty Creator's creations. The s*poken word of the Most High Almighty Creator* is the means to all existence, and creations known, and unknown to mankind. The spoken word is *sound.* Sound is the bedrock of all creations. Love manifested in the *"spirit"* is the *"holiest of all spirits".* Love *"saves"* and *'teaches".* To save is to rescue or to deliver. *The Most High Almighty Creator's* name is hidden within us. It is not found in any religious book. To "teach" is to counsel, the *holy spirit* of *the Most High Almighty Creator* is a counselor, who inspires, directs, comforts, and convicts. This is linked to what is known as the inner-man or inner-woman. When contumacious individuals face chastisement, and are reprimanded, it is all done out of *love,* with the intent to discipline, and ethically correct the wrong doing. Mankind consciously or unconsciously replicates the concept of *love* in our communities, societies, governments, various institutions, and on a micro level within our homes, and families.

Greed, jealousy, evil mind, cruelty, selfishness, wickedness, lies, cheat, deceit, false accusations, hate, materialistic tendencies, and all low vibration energetic frequency exhibitions taint the purity of this pure love that was embedded in you from inception by the *Most High Almighty Creator.* To taint your purest soul continuously is to get stuck in this 3D-third dimension earth in a cyclical format, known as reincarnation. This 3D-third dimension realm is the real hell that everyone talks about. To be in the 3D-third dimension realm, is to be in hell. We are all physically on earth because we fell from our grace, our highest vibration that gravitates us to the *Most High Almighty Creator (who is the purest of all pureness)* into our greed, materialism, self-loathing, pride, hatred, arrogance, destructive and manipulative lowest form of vibration. Now, you know how to ascend, be weightless.

Etymology of Compendiums of all Gods and The Almighty Creator

The diagram below details how everything known and unknown to mankind was initiated/manifested/spoken into existence by *the Most High God* through *His Core, Love.*

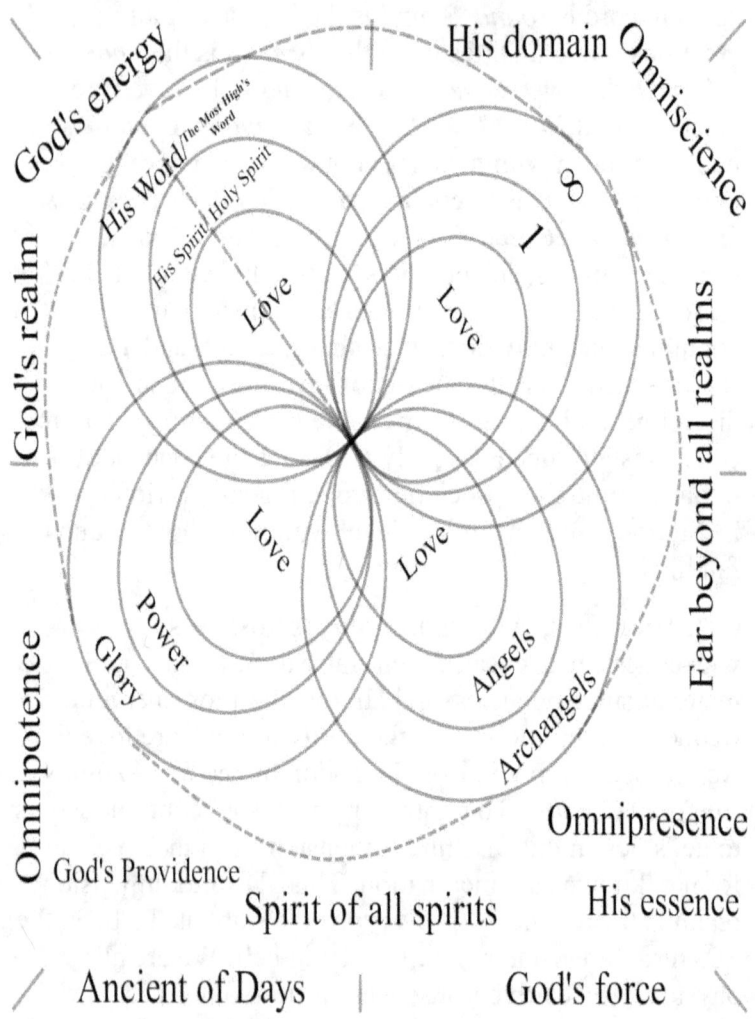

THE CONSCIOUSNESS and UNCONSCIOUSNESS OF HUMAN'S EXHIBITING THE CORE OF ALMIGHTY CREATOR

Within our material realm, the "God Core" a.k.a Love comes to play when the *"giver"* and the *"receiver"* share the *same intended outcome of energy* considered as good, holy, happy, loving, exciting, positive, or satisfaction.

Love is always the reason for our actions, be it good or bad. Noncomprehending of *love's* characteristic entity causes great suffering in the energetic, and vibration frequency flow of the universe. We need to get back to *love's* origin in order to truly comprehend it.

Whenever the *intended outcome of energy* differs from the *giver* and the *receiver*; there tend to be chaos everywhere. It must take a reassessment of *"love"* in order for things to return to its normal state.

Love has been the reason why some nations go to war. The soldiers profess the *"love"* for their country with *different energetic outcome* (ie: casualties, geoeconomic collapse and geopolitical tensions) intended to the *"receiver"* -which is the other country at war. The intricate part is that, all countries fight for their own interests, which is geared towards the *"love"* that they have for their respective homelands. However, it comes at a grave cost. This happens because mankind do not comprehend the concept of love in its entirety.

Love is also the reason why we marry, have children, have acquaintances, and definitely one of the reasons to protect one's self or family members.

With respect to the *"Theory of God's Core"*, the entire human body is full of different kinds of energies. At the *core* of it all, is *"love"*. Love is the *core* of every energy, be it good or bad.

Whenever negative energy surrounds *love* due to the corruption of the *"intent"* exerted by negative energy. It yields deadly, unwarranted pain, anger, discomfort, destruction, heartbreak and torture. The negative energy is repelled by the *"Energy of Repellent"* that shields the *core a.k.a "love"* from any corruption. Refer to the diagram on the next page for a thorough pictorial depiction.

It is mutually exclusive for the *"giver"* to have a *selfish "intent"*, which was corrupted by the *"energy" of selfishness,* and deliver a loving effect to the *"receiver"*, and vice versa. The *"Theory of God's Core"* is solidly ingrained at the heart or center of our *soul,* our true form. The human soul belongs to *the Most High Almighty Creator,* the Source.

The *"Source of all things"* has complete sovereignty over the human *soul,* your life. The *Most High Almighty Creator, a.k.a "Source of all things"* has no shape or form. This is the purest form of all energies. This is the highest and most vibrating energetic frequency of all things. This state of the *"Source of all things"* is not as physical as we are in this 3D-third dimension realm. Those with *souls* had the characteristic likeness of the *"Source of all things"* for eons of years prior to our fall into this 3D-third dimension realm. This is when some of us sadly went ahead to create other entities and man's kind and woman's kind in our "likeness". However, what we created in the 3D-third dimension are soulless, and only operates here in the 3D.

The figure below exhibits the general flow of the _"Theory of God's Core"_ within every human:

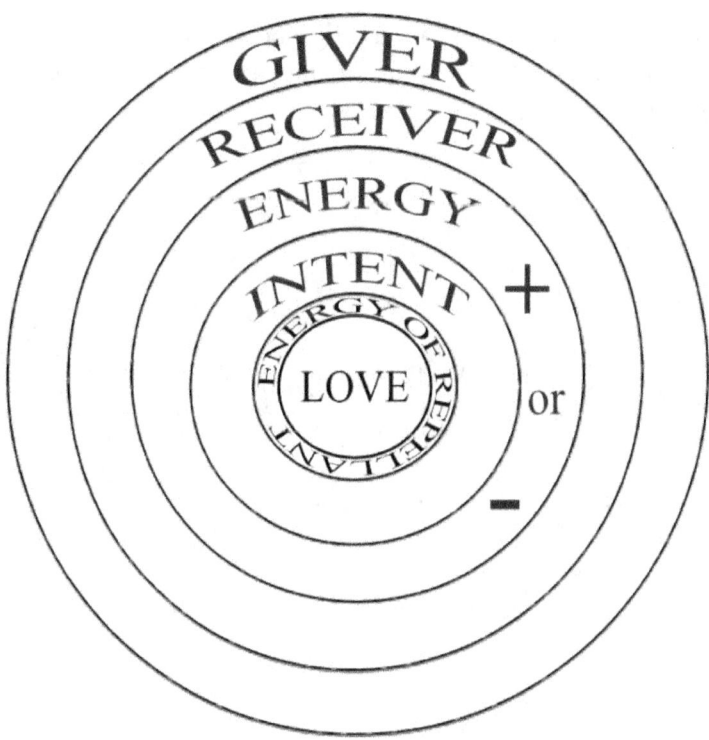

The *energy of repellent* is only attracted to *positive "intent"*, which is initiated by a *positive energy*. This is because *the Almighty Creator* repels anything that is unrighteous, negative energy.

Self-affirmations exert *positive energy* which triggers *positive intent* piercing through the *energy of repellent* to the *core of your being*. Self-love is as important to your consciousness, and most importantly to your soul as the *energy of air,* that you breathe in and out every day.

Love is the solution to everything happening within our universe. Everything eventually self-destructs without exercising *love*.

The figure below shows interaction between two individuals reflecting a *"mutual energy"* with a *"mutual expected"* outcome.

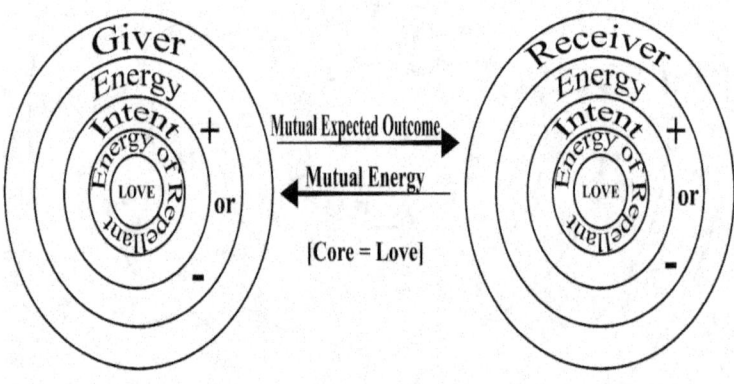

Even the craziest, meanest, and most dangerous individuals possess *love*, because this is the *core* of both our *soul* and *spirit*. They act the way they do because they are disconnected from their *core*, due to *recurring negative energy*, corrupting their *intent*. This could be fear, anger, hate, deception, pride, loss of a loved one, revenge, insecurities, et al. Unless an individual is directly connected to his or her *core* on both micro and macro level, he or she will forever be a *lost soul*. Such people are toxic to the environment, destructive and chaotic to everywhere they go.

They sow seeds of discord and deception to those that are spiritually delusional, and suffering from similar disconnect.

If you do not know what happens to you after you die, if you doubt who you are, if you consistently feel inadequate, unloved, and consistently confused about your purpose on this planet, then you are simply disconnected from your *core,* the very foundation of your true self.

The next page would outline an alternative breakdown of the *"Theory of God's Core"* within every human. This outline will constitute some day to day human emotions, interactions, actions and exhibitions that we consciously or unconsciously express.

ILLUSTRATION

Energy [+ or -]

A.   GIVER ---------------------------------- →RECEIVER

Core is Love

GIVER ←---------------------------------- RECEIVER

This is the resting phase of the *"Theory of God's Core"* (Love) within mankind, at a balanced state of inertia, when there is no movement, action or communication initiated or ongoing between the *giver* and the *receiver*. This is the "resting state" of "free will". The "will" to either do good (+), or to do bad (-). Everything is balanced at *inertia* state.

Energy [+, Good] exerted by the giver/initiator

B.   GIVER ---------------------------------- →RECEIVER

Core is Love

GIVER: Exerting *positive energy* with *positive intent* to the *receiver*. The *giver* exhibits an *intent* of <u>excitement</u> and <u>kindness</u> (positive energy).

RECEIVER: Positively feels thankful, but somehow wonder if there is/are any commitment(s) attached, since *no action/work* was put into place to *render* such *positive energy* from the *giver*.

This is the rarest situation(s) when the *"giver"* gives positive energy, be it gifts, money, motivation, solutions, offers, and the like with absolutely no string attached. This is the state of complete benevolence with zero expectation or payback from the *"receiver"*.

Energy [+, Good] exerted by the giver/initiator

C.   GIVER ----------------------------------- →RECEIVER

Core is Love

⇐--<u>Energy [+]</u> contained by **receiver** with mutual expectation ----

GIVER: Exerts *positive energy* with *positive intent* with prior communication and agreement with the *receiver*.

RECEIVER: Feeling of excitement, *positive energy*. In this case, *receiver* puts in work/action. He or She is expecting the *"agreed upon"* reward/compensation from the *giver*. There is a *"positive mutual"* expectation and outcome between the *giver* and *receiver*. When this happens, the *receiver* and the *giver* are both satisfied and appreciative of each other's expected outcome.

Energy [-, Bad] exerted by the giver/initiator

D.   GIVER ----------------------------------- →RECEIVER

Core is Love

GIVER: Exerts *negative energy* with *negative intent*. The *giver* is feeling his *corrupt intent* pumped with *negative emotions* of adrenalin to incite pain, hurt, deception, heartbreak, loss, disaster, chaos to the *receiver*. In this case, the *receiver* is unaware of the *giver's* intent.

RECEIVER: Unexpectedly gets hit with the *negative energy* from the *giver*. The *receiver* is unprepared, unaware, and caught by surprise in a toxic, unfriendly, and weird situation. The *receiver* is *negatively* affected, hurt, in pain, possible loss of something dear to him or her, possible death in some cases, et al.

NOTE: In life or death situations, although the *receiver* is unaware and unprepared for the *giver's negative energy*; the *receiver* is able to react quickly in an attempt to save himself or herself. Such as **self-defense cases**, the fight or flight instinct of *intent* may kick in, aiding the *receiver* to respond in a swift way to save his or her life due to the *energy of self-love* within all of us.

Energy [-, Bad] exerted by the giver/initiator

E.   GIVER ---------------------------------- →**RECEIVER**

Core is Love

⇐--Energy [-] contained by **receiver** with mutual expectation-----

GIVER: Exerts *negative energy* with *negative intent* to hurt, destroy the *receiver*. Tension has been brewing between the *giver* and the *receiver*; both parties are aware of the possibility of emotional explosions that can render some serious repercussions.

RECEIVER: Aware of the *negative energy* from the g*iver* and aware of the possibility of emotional explosions that can cause severe damage, hurt, pain to both of them. *Receiver* tend to also prepare for the possible outcome. In this case, both parties possess *mutual energy* and *mutually know or understand* the *possible outcome*.

This is the situation of war, disputes, aggression, competition, and any form of possible elimination.

NOTE: *Negative energy* has no place within the *"Theory of God's Core"* a.k.a *Love* due to the *Energy of Repellent* repelling all the *negativity*. The *Energy of Repellent* function this way due to the positivity and holiness of *The Most High Almighty Creator's* essence. Hence, e*very negative energy* with *corrupt intent* initiated by the soul or consciousness would only destroy himself or herself, if such *negative energy* isn't quenched with the vibrational energy of *love*. To ascend to your highest dimensional state, is to learn to be as weightless as the feather. At the end of the day, the choice is yours to make. It must be noted that, the potential to ascend to the highest realm is solely dependent on if you have a soul or not. Soulless people can never ascend. It will never happen. Ascension is only for the soul people, that is, those with souls. Those with souls are aboriginal to the *Most High Almighty Creator's* realms of souls. No one can buy, sell or steal your soul. The soul is the essence, and part of the *Most High Almighty Creator*. The soulless ones look just like the fallen Gods and Goddess, however, these soulless ones can never ascend. In that, the *Most High Almighty Creator* did not create them, rather it was the fallen souls a.k.a Gods and Goddesses who created these soulless people when they fell down into the 3D-dimension. The soulless ones were only made for the 3D. Ascension is not for the soulless ones.

The harmonious flow of the epitomized *"Theory of God's Core"* embedded in mankind's *DNA* is only at play when the *giver* and the *receiver* are in a *mutually positive energy* flow of *intent*.

The obvious thing happening among the human populace is that, both the *giver* and the *receiver* act on the basis of *love* under *different* circumstances, influences and intentions.

In situations such as when you are in love, but your actions are not out of love, war with another country, civil war, ethnic war, and "war" in general, bribery and corrupt power, self-hate, greed, et al.

Regardless of the outside or inside influences, for there to be an experience of the *"Theory of God's Core"*, the *heart* and the *mind* must be at an *inseparable interlocking conformity* with one another through *pure unification* of *love,* and *positive intent* exhibited by both the *giver,* and the *receiver*.

In summary:

- ✓ The *intent* is always initiated by the *giver/initiator*.
- ✓ The *intent* can either be polluted or kept in its true state (pure) depending on the kind/type of energy the *giver/initiator* chooses with his/her *Free Will*.
- ✓ The *energy* represents our *daily choices*. Everything around us physically and spiritually are all different kinds of energy.
- ✓ The <u>core</u> (Love) also known as the *"Theory of God's Core"* never change no matter the magnitude of the *negative energy* and *negative intent* outside its *core*. The *core* always remains pure.
- ✓ The *receiver* in most cases suffer the most since the *receiver* mostly do not *initiate* the *energy (negative or positive)* and the *intent*.
- ✓ The *giver* is punished in cases of severe damage to the *receiver* in accordance to the existing or established law(s).
- ✓ The mutuality of the *positive energy* and *intent* exerted by both the *giver*, and *receiver* is the only way to trigger the natural flow, and experience of the *"Theory of God's Core"* in life.

CHAPTER 5

CHAPTER 5

The Four (4) Types of Spiritual Consciousness in Relation to all Gods and the ALMIGHTY

I hope by now, you are aware that most humans are *souls* at the *core*. Our true self is not physical. Death is just the spiritual "door" to exit from this physical domain into the spiritual realm. There are two births, namely: spiritual birth and physical birth.

When you "die" in the physical, you have been born into your spiritual realm. When you are "born" in the physical, you exit the spiritual realm. You travel to the spiritual realm through dreams, trance, astral projections, and visions. We are going to look at the four types of *spiritual consciousness* in creation.

These are the four types of *spiritual consciousness* in direct relation to our spiritual awareness: *unconscious spirituality*, *unconscious-conscious spirituality*, *conscious spirituality*, and *conscious-conscious spirituality*.

The Unconscious Spirituality:
This is someone who is unconscious in relation to spiritual awareness. This individual is *spiritually unaware* of what is true, lies, facts, fake or real. The *unconscious spiritual* person lives only by the "*bread*".

Whatever gives the physical body comfort, peace, and livability is good for him or her regardless of the means at which the needs in question are attained. This is what I call *spiritual comatose*. This person is in a tranquilized sleep so deep to the point that, he or she has no spiritual connection.

Inertly confused and questions everything about *the Most High Almighty Creator*. He or she is unwilling to execute his or her own research to find answers to the spiritual insensate state of being. The character of his or her insentience denial in relation to *the Most High Almighty Creator* deceives him or her to think that, he or she is wise but in actuality, a fool in the eyes of *the Most High Almighty Creator*.

The Unconscious-Conscious Spirituality:
This is the individual that is either *consciously* or *unconsciously unaware* of his or her *spiritual unconsciousness*. This individual takes one step forward in a spiritual quest to finding some facts about *the Most High Almighty Creator,* but then takes four steps back from where he or she started.

This individual is easily manipulated in deception by various influences of religion. He or she believes various lies packaged in indoctrination, narrow mindedness, and dogmatic religious traditions that has nothing to do with *the Most High Almighty Creator*.

Instead of spiritually depending on, and connecting with *the Most High Almighty Creator,* this individual rather makes a physical entity, or physical images, his or her *"go-to"* point of contact as a means to get to *the Most High Almighty Creator.* The *unconscious-conscious* puts his or her belief, trust, and faith in almost everything he or she receives from his or her physical *"go-to"* point of contact.

The Conscious Spirituality: This individual is epistemological *compos mentis* in the physical realm. He or she sees the material world for what it is, and nothing else. This person has not *fully* transcend spiritually due to his or her conflict between the knowledge of this material world, and the knowledge within the spiritual world.

This person is alert, aware of past events, current events and future events. He or she is on a spiritual journey to fully discover the necessary spiritual tools to *fully* transcend.

This individual likes to read, research, and ask questions about things he or she doesn't know or comprehend. This individual is positively sentient with inspired determination to know himself or herself in regards to origination, purpose on earth and the after-life.

The Conscious-Conscious Spirituality:

This person's spirituality is lived with great piousness towards *the Most High Almighty Creator*. He or she has transcended through this material realm. They comprehend things within the spiritual realm, and practice all the inspirations and directions from *the Most High Almighty Creator.*

This individual teaches, inspires, enlightens and train others to discover their *spiritual wholeness*. He or she is not perturb by physical events happening within this physical realm. He or she seeks wisdom over material things, because he or she understands the difference between these two energies, that's the physical and spiritual. This person tends to be on a high energetic level of spiritual consciousness. He or she seeks purity with an aptitude to break down the most tortuous labyrinthine things, both in the physical and spiritual realm. Where do you see yourself? What level of consciousness do you think you are on? Are you ready, and willing to embark on a spiritual journey if you are not already on one? Remember, this is a personal decision. You ought to consciously decide to connect with *the Most High Almighty Creator* through application of your free will.

The spiritual journey is individualistic. At the end of our earthly days, we will all find out about our true destiny. However, you don't have to necessarily wait till you exit this physical realm in order to know why you came to earth. In that, who you are is an eternal entity, called the *soul*. So why not invest your time and energy into researching, learning, and educating yourself about your eternal life, instead of choosing to fully invest your time and energy into your short time on this physical realm called earth. The choice is yours.

Diagrammatic exhibition of spiritual consciousness

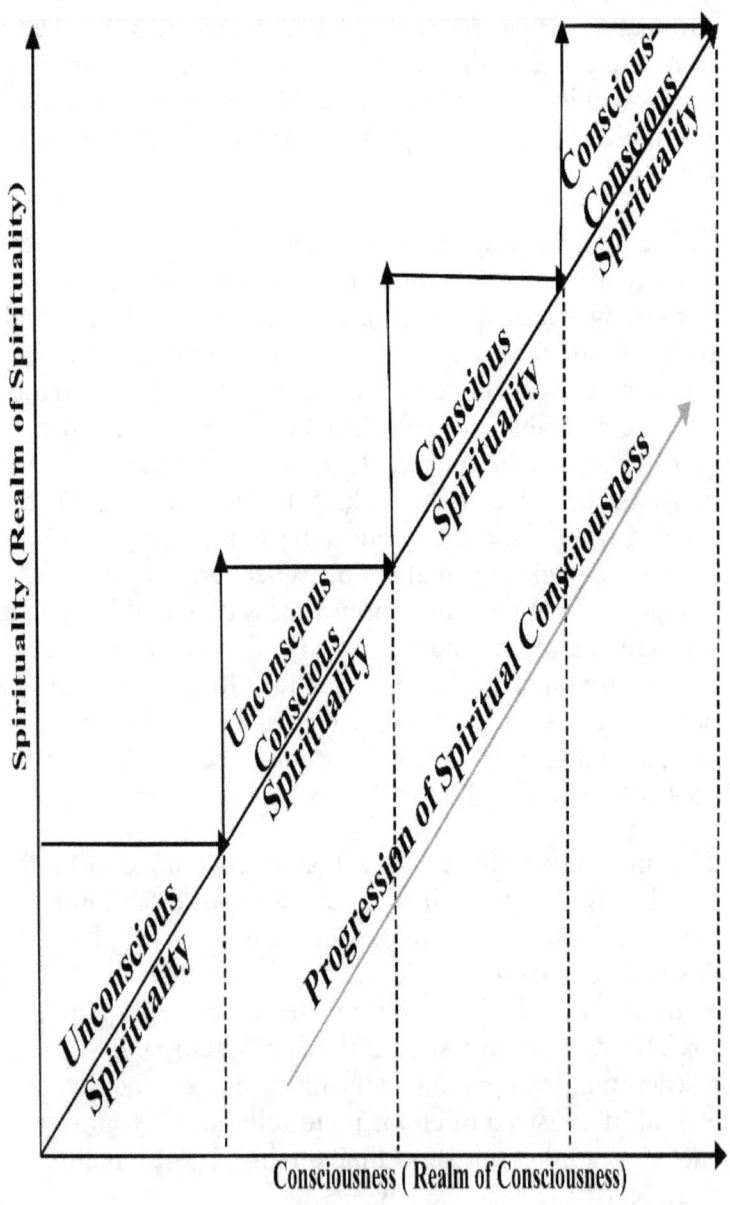

TECHNOLOGY IS PHYSICAL MANIFESTATION OF SPIRITUALITY INTO CONSCIOUSNESS

Technology is literally spiritual "voodoo" stuff. Especially this AI (Artificial Intelligence) stuff. We are creating and manifesting these AI language translations as they happen. There are some AIs that are able to translate and transcribe some foreign languages without the input of any engineer or coder.

Technology is a different form of spirituality. Science is another form of spirituality. Everything that manifests in the material world already exists in the spiritual realm.

There are different forms of spiritual manifestations that transform the essence of good or evil from the spiritual world into this material world. Everything seen and unseen, living or dead is related to the many forms of spirituality.

You are a living manifestation of spirituality. Your environment, and the sounds that you hear. The melody of your voice, and the accents in all the diction of languages throughout the world. Every word and statement spoken or written within your respective aboriginal, or native language is spirituality. Those who can relate and have been granted the access to that code of language can innerstand and overstand deep within their spirits and souls that beautiful melodies that their aboriginal languages resonate to them.

Spirituality comes in different forms, as you listen to yourself in your head, as you read this book, try to grant your soul the chance to meditate and focus on that inner voice. I want you to really think about your aura, essence, energy, and how beautiful, and powerful you are as a being.

Don't you ever dare limit or blur the power of manifestations. We are all immortal though not in the flesh, yet on the soul level, we are all as immortal as the essence of the true Almighty Creator.

Death can only hold the flesh for a moment through passage of its last breath, as the soul seeks its way to exit the flesh through any of the nine portals that we have. From the head to the soles of your feet, and as such the soul leaves the body with our last breath. That is the immortal life in its entirety and in its eternity exiting the flesh to take its place in the realm of eternity, where we all belong. Just as the vapor exits a hot surface, so do we all exit the body. We are all breath of beautiful fresh air. We are all part of the universe, so that is where we reside.

When you think about technology, don't you dare think that there is a physical or an unseen separation between technology that you hold in your hands, technology that you interact with, machine learning technology, and all the technologies you can name in artificial intelligence's (AI) world. They are all spiritual manifestations of us spiritual beings into the material world. There is nothing new under the sun. Everything is a cyclical recycling process that has been manifested in previous lives, and the rest beyond, and in different dimensions of our universe. Don't ever think that the earthly existence is our only way and being of life.

Earth is a mother that grants the opportunity for her children to learn. As much as you are willing to learn, mother earth will open its arms, and womb for you to walk on her surface, for you to eat, and grow foods, which are just like the hairs that grow on mother earth's body.

Yes, all the trees and grass, the herbs, and plants that you see are just hairs on mother earth's body.

So I'm trying to let you innerstand and see the connection that spirituality is the foundation, the core of our essence, and the core of our being. Even in the absence of our comprehension of spirituality, we still live and express ourselves in spirituality.

We are already a living expression of spirituality. Our being, our essence, our presence, our physicality, you can hold objects, touch objects, and we close our eyes when we sleep as we dream and dream on. With all these experiences, many of us still wonder, and ask the question, am I spiritual enough? You are more than spiritual, the very life force of your being is spirituality itself.

When you see any form of technology, any form of AI, any form of new so-called invention from automobiles to mobile phones, you must now know that, they are all spiritual manifestations. After all, don't you know that you speak through frequency and all these things are high and low energetic vibrations that cause ripples in the strings of things. Energy, emotions and movements are all sent through ignition of our daily activities. Sorrow, joy, laughter, love, marriage, anger, caring, war, even getting in your car, getting on your bike, walking with your loved ones, they are all contributing factors neatly and perfectly connected to the expression of the core of spirituality.

Science and technology can never exist or be expressed in any way, shape or form if spirituality is not alive and present. Everything falls under what we all call manifestation. You manifest things as you speak it or execute it. Technology is just a spiritual manifestation.

Don't you know that from the beginning of creation till now, everything physical was manifested? Yes, everything was manifested, everything! If you're a Christian or a person who subscribes to the bible, you can talk to your pastors or if you like to read, then you can read your bible to see that, in the time of creation, it was all manifestations. Everything!!! Go and pay attention to your bible's Genesis chapter one, it clearly states, "let there", "let there", "let that", let this come out of here, let this come out of that, these are all spoken manifestations. The creators (*Elohim* is plural) in Genesis chapter 1, were all manifesting things into existence from the spiritual realm into this 3D physical realm. The highest form of all sciences and technologies are nothing but the beginning of spirituality.

The power of manifestation is calmly and beautifully exhibited in its fullest glory via the existence of everything in the universes near and far. I want you to innerstand and overstand that, manifestation is the bridge between spirituality, technology, science, and everything in both the physical and spiritual realms. Everything was manifested into existence. So, we all have the power to manipulate these physical and spiritual things through manifestations.

What did you just say to yourself with your inner voice and inner essence right now? Is that a doubt that just ran through your mind? Why is it that there are so many negative thoughts, mindset, emotions, and feelings running through you every single day than the positive and extraordinary part of you? Why is that? The big question is, why do you allow this to happen over and over again?

It's like the worst part of things are almost always allowed to linger within your mind. This is because you do not have strong hold of your spirituality. You do not innerstand or comprehend the balance within you. You are the key to your own spirituality from which you can then connect to the universal oneness of spirituality.

The secret is that, all those who come out from the technological field, are able to manifest things from the spiritual realm into this physical plain. First and foremost, it was a thought in the crown chakra, then it dropped down into the heart chakra, and went down to the gut chakra, before it resurrected or rose back up through the same path to the crown chakra. After that, a "word" a.k.a manifestation was "spoken" into the realms "outside" of our bodies or essence. This is how manifestation from the spiritual into the material-3D realm is executed.

You ought to put in the actions, and the words. That's the words that come out of you, either verbally or telepathically must be powerful. In that, that is geared towards the material realization of your manifestation. Put it on paper and start taking strategic action.

Let's look at your car as a spiritual-physical manifestation, your car runs on spirituality. Oh yes, what do you think the gas is for? Do you know where the gas came from? It was all through manifestation. How about the gold? Where do you think the gold comes from? The diamonds? Oh yes, they're all manifestations. Whether by the entities you call Gods/gods, or by you knowing that you are a God/god, or if you don't know yet, then maybe when the time comes you will know.

It's a journey, a personal journey that we all have to take. Be daring to give yourself a chance to keep learning, and to gain more knowledge through wisdom, so that you may not live in a state of oblivion. Life is as beautiful as you make it. Life is as refreshing as you make it. Life is as great as you make it. You gotta step outside and enjoy the breeze, the fresh air. If you are an indoor person, you gotta stay in to meditate, to focus, but make sure you connect with nature. Make sure you sometimes walk barefoot to connect with mother earth. Make sure you respect and treat everything within nature with kindness. Make sure you treat yourself with kindness too. Because everything, everything, yes everything is connected to spirituality.

Everything is spirituality. Yes, even that thought that came through your mind right now is spirituality. Meditate on this calm beautifully soothing sound that is playing in the background, yes you can hear this sound in your mind, heart and gut. Flow like water, fly like the wind, soar like the eagle, allow yourself to live. You've got it, you connected to the sound embedded in your soul's core. Everyone has that special melodic sound that connects them with or to a special something or place. Meditate on that for a moment. Set yourself free. Relax your shoulders, breathe!!!

Manifest that which you have been doubting for so many years. Manifest goodness. Manifest positivity. Manifest greatness. Let your life shine so bright that nothing, and no one can stop you from your shine. The universe needs you. We all need you.

You are extraordinaire. We love you extraordinarily. We appreciate you, and that is the motivation from me to you. Enjoy the soothing sound, relax, feel it, let it go within you. You are here, you are alive, you're important, you are needed, and you are loved. Just relax, relax your mind, relax your heart, relax! relax!! relax!!! relax!!!! relax!!!!! You got this. Yes, you got this, yes you do, yes!!! Peace, love and unity.

SPIRITUALITY through SÉANCE, NECROMANCY, TRANCE, LUCID DREAMS, ASTRAL PROJECTION

Would anyone consider séance, necromancy, trance, lucid dreams and astral projection as sorcery, witchcraft, wizardry, be-witchery, ensorcellment, bewitchment, witchcraft, conjuring, devilry, magic, deviltry, diablerie, enchantment, mojo, thaumaturgy, voodooism, witchery, evil or black magic? Anyone who considers any of the spiritual encounters and practices as black magic, evil or sorcery is not spiritual or matured enough to innerstand and overstand who we all are, as spiritual energies manifested into this physical medium or realm.

Throughout the Abrahamic religion you would come across the usage and practices of séance, necromancy, trance, lucid dreams, and astral projection by the patriarchs, kings, prophets and even by Iesus/Zeus/Jesus.

Since all branches of Abrahamic religion mythologically through allegory plagiarized their entire concept of their religion from the great chocolate first nations of Afrakan civilizations like ancient Kemet/Egypt; it is very common to find séance, necromancy, trance, lucid dreams and astral projection throughout the Abrahamic religious books. Ancient Kemet/Egyptians, Assyrians, Babylonians, Etruscans, Greeks, multiple other first nation aboriginal kingdoms and Romans practiced séance, necromancy, trance, lucid dreams and astral projection.

Before I outline some solid proofs to support the statements raised above, let's get into the proper meaning and definitions of séance, necromancy, trance, lucid dreams and astral projection:

Séance: a spiritualist meeting to receive spirit communications (*Merriam Webster Dictionary*). In other words, during séance, the people involved would try to establish communication with ghost or the dead using what is called a medium.

Necromancy is conjuration of the spirits of the dead for purposes of magically revealing the future or influencing the course of events (*Merriam Webster Dictionary*).

Trance is defined as a sleep-like state (as of deep hypnosis) usually characterized by partly suspended animation with diminished or absent sensory and motor activity (*Merriam Webster Dictionary*).

Lucid Dream is an area that is more common among people. Many have encountered lucid dream and may not even remember while some tend to have clear details of their encounter upon waking up. Per *WebMD*: *"Lucid dreams are when you know that you're dreaming while you're asleep. You're aware that the events flashing through your brain aren't really happening. But the dream feels vivid and real. You may even be able to control how the action unfolds, as if you're directing a movie in your sleep."* https://www.webmd.com/sleep-disorders/lucid-dreams-overview

Astral Projection is the experience you encounter when you are able to separate your spirit (astral self/body) from your physical body and in effect able to be present in the immaterial realm traveling and communicating without any limit. Out of body experiences are all spiritual experiences. There is absolutely nothing wrong or evil about it, rather, one must learn to know and comprehend his or her body, soul and spirit in order to transition into experimenting, and experiencing mastery in séance, necromancy, trance, lucid dreams and astral projection.

It is time you end your premature judgment targeting séance, necromancy, trance, lucid dreams and astral projection as sorcery, witchcraft, wizardry, bewitchery, ensorcellment, bewitchment, witchcraft, conjuring, devilry, magic, deviltry, diablerie, enchantment, mojo, thaumaturgy, voodooism, witchery, evil or black magic.

Let's look at some examples found within the Abrahamic religions that some may not know that séance, necromancy, trance, lucid dreams and astral projection are rooted at the core of this religious group. Biblical Saul (*King Saul*) used séance and necromancy to contact the ghost of Samuel using a woman who was in the séance business as the medium. This happened when the biblical Israelites were going to war against the Philistines, apparently Saul's god/God refused to answer him, so Saul used séance to communicate with deceased prophet Samuel to get information about how the soon-to-happen war would go.

Let's look at *1 Samuel 28:3-20 (NIV)* Saul and the Medium(séance, necromancer) at Endor

"3Now Samuel was dead, and all Israel had mourned for him and buried him in his own town of Ramah. Saul had expelled the mediums and spiritists from the land. 4The Philistines assembled and came and set up camp at Shunem, while Saul gathered all Israel and set up camp at Gilboa. 5When Saul saw the Philistine army, he was afraid; terror filled his heart. 6He inquired of the LORD, but the LORD did not answer him by dreams or Urim or prophets. 7Saul then said to his attendants, "Find me a woman who is a medium, so I may go and inquire of her."
"There is one in Endor," they said. 8 So Saul disguised himself, putting

on other clothes, and at night he and two men went to the woman. "Consult a spirit for me," he said, "and bring up for me the one I name." *9* But the woman said to him, "Surely you know what Saul has done. He has cut off the mediums and spiritists from the land. Why have you set a trap for my life to bring about my death?" *10*Saul swore to her by the LORD, "As surely as the LORD lives, you will not be punished for this." *11*Then the woman asked, "Whom shall I bring up for you?" "Bring up Samuel," he said. *12*When the woman saw Samuel, she cried out at the top of her voice and said to Saul, "Why have you deceived me? You are Saul!" *13*The king said to her, "Don't be afraid. What do you see?" The woman said, "I see a ghostly figure[a]coming up out of the earth." *14*"What does he look like?" he asked. "An old man wearing a robe is coming up," she said.

Then Saul knew it was Samuel, and he bowed down and prostrated himself with his face to the ground. *15* Samuel said to Saul, "Why have you disturbed me by bringing me up?" "I am in great distress," Saul said. "The Philistines are fighting against me, and God has departed from me. He no longer answers me, either by prophets or by dreams. So I have called on you to tell me what to do."

*16*Samuel said, "Why do you consult me, now that the LORD has departed from you and become your enemy? *17* The LORD has done what he predicted through me. The LORD has torn the kingdom out of your hands and given it to one of your neighbors—to David. *18*Because you did not obey the LORD or carry out his fierce wrath against the Amalekites, the LORD has done this to you today. *19*The LORD will deliver both Israel and you into the hands of the Philistines, and tomorrow you and your sons will be with me. The LORD will also give the army of Israel into the hands of the Philistines."

*20*Immediately Saul fell full length on the ground, filled with fear because of Samuel's words. His strength was gone, for he had eaten nothing all that day and all that night."

According to these verses from the bible, *Deuteronomy 18:10-11*; *Job 7:7-10*; *Leviticus 19:26-31*, *Isaiah 8:18-20*; and *Luke 16:19-31*; séance, necromancy, trance, lucid dreams, and astral projection are taboos to exercise, and one must even be put to death per *Leviticus 20:27* if found to be a medium or exercising such so-called "taboos" per the bible.

Yet we see Iesus/Zeus/Jesus practicing séance and necromancy when Jesus transformed, shape-shifted, transfigured, into an entity to interact with the ghosts of deceased Moses and Elijah/Eliyah.

Read it from Mathew 17:1-9 NIV *"After six days Jesus took with him Peter, James and John the brother of James, and led them up a high mountain by themselves. 2 There he was transfigured (shape shifted) before them. His face shone like the sun, and his clothes became as white as the light. 3Just then there appeared before them Moses and Elijah, talking with Jesus. 4Peter said to Jesus, "Lord, it is good for us to be here. If you wish, I will put up three shelters—one for you, one for Moses and one for Elijah." 5While he was still speaking, a bright cloud covered them, and a voice from the cloud said, "This is my Son, whom I love; with him I am well pleased. Listen to him!" 6 When the disciples heard this, they fell facedown to the ground, terrified. 7But Jesus came and touched them. "Get up," he said. "Don't be afraid." 8 When they looked up, they saw no one except Jesus. 9 As they were coming down the mountain, Jesus instructed them, "Don't tell anyone what you have seen, until the Son of Man has been raised from the dead."*

You can read the same biblical story from *Luke 9:28-36*. Both situations references to Iesus/Jesus practicing séance, trance, and necromancy.

Another contradiction and funny conflict is found between the verse 9 (that is *Mathew 17:9*) and *Luke 16:31*.

Let's have a look at it: Luke 16:31 NIV reads *"He said to him, 'If they do not listen to Moses and the Prophets, they will not be convinced even if someone rises from the dead.'"* while Mathew 17:9 states *"As they were coming down the mountain, Jesus instructed them, "Don't tell anyone what you have seen, until the Son of Man has been raised from the dead."*

One verse makes the other verse false, one states even if a ghost or someone is sent from the dead they would not believe, while the other states keep all of this a secret until I, Son of Man has been raised from the dead. That is reincarnation, and ghost discussions and references. We can establish and prove that the bible is allegorical.

Well in this case, both situations here are allegorical teachings as well.

Additionally, there are several occurrences of trance used by all the prophets, priests and apostles throughout the bible. Trance is something that these Abrahamic religious groups claim to be a "taboo", yet these verses below prove that all the prophets, priests and so-called apostles used trance to receive their "supposed messages" from their bible god/God. Let's look at *Acts 10:9-23*, *Numbers 24:2-3, 1 Kings 18:46, Judges 15:14, Ezekiel 8:1-3, 1 Samuel 19:19-24, Revelation 1:10-13, Revelation 21:10, Judges 14:6, Acts 11:4-18, Revelation 4:2, Acts 22:17-21, Revelation 17:3.*

Phrases like *"was in a trance"*, *"the hand of the Lord fell upon me and I saw"*, *"fell into a trance"*, *"I was in the spirit"*, *"and he carried me away in the spirit into a wilderness"*, *"the oracle of the man whose eye is open"*, *"Spirit of the Lord came upon him mightily"*, and somethings similar to the effect of *"the hand of the Lord was on..."* are all experiences of trance. These are all meanings to the phrase "to be caught up in a *"trance"*". It is very ironically conflicting and diabolical for the bible in one hand to demonize séance, necromancy, trance, lucid dreams and astral projection as sorcery, witchcraft, wizardry, bewitchery, ensorcellment, bewitchment, witchcraft, conjuring, devilry, magic, deviltry, diablerie, enchantment, mojo, thaumaturgy, voodooism, witchery, evil or black magic. While, all their so-called prophets, priests and apostles in the bible practiced these same things.

As stated, all the Abrahamic prophets, kings, priests and apostles heavily practiced séance, necromancy, trance, lucid dreams and astral projection. Ancient and extremely civilized Afrakan civilizations like Sumer, Dogons, Göbekli Tepe, Mesopotamia, Old Ghana Empire, Mali Empire, Songhai Empire, Kushite Kingdom (Kingdom of

Kush), Carthage/Karthage, Punt land (Land and kingdom of Punt), Aksum Empire, Great Zimbabwe, ancient Egypt/Kemet, and many other modern day Afrakan cultures and traditions practice and accept séance, necromancy, trance, lucid dreams and astral projection as part of one's spiritual transformational journey. There are many Afrakan aboriginal nations to date who can easily transfigure, shape-shift, or transformed into their authentic spirit animal, such as leopard, lion, parrot, tiger, bear, snake, eagle and the like.

There are some practices and verses in all Abrahamic religion that seems to promote sin, violence and all sorts of brutalities directly or indirectly. Christianity, Islam and rest of Abrahamic religion encourages violence and sin. In ancient Afrakan spirituality, sin was seriously discouraged, frowned upon and perpetrators were immediately punished by the gods/Gods and goddesses/Goddesses. Typical example is the *"42 Laws of Maat"*, an Afrakan uprightness.

This was an almost perfect ancient spiritual Afrakan world whereby people built elegant houses without front doors or security men. Unlike today, people would put all kinds of security cameras, bullet proof doors, and windows as well as security guards with trained hyper dogs, just to try to deter thieves and other violent attackers. This is the current sin-prone, wicked and dark world we live in today, which is dominated by Christianity/Catholicism, Muslims, Judaism and rest of the Abrahamic religions.

Let's look at the Christian/Catholic biblical verse that encourages all kinds of sin, *1 John 2:1 (NIV)* *"My dear children, I write this to you so that you will not sin. But if anybody does sin, we have an advocate with the Father—Jesus Christ, the Righteous One."* This verse vividly directly or indirectly encourages followers of the bible to be careless, sinful, and wickedly irresponsible, because if they sin, all their sins would be forgiven. What an irresponsible and unaccountable way to encourage violence in all type of ways.

Muslims in their Quran and other books encourage that if you practice a specific type of prayer and exercise a specific fasting then all your future sins (sins yet to be committed), and past sins would be forgiven. What kind of sinful encouragement is this? Folks who follow this know that they can be reckless and indulge in brutal barbaric wicked wars, theft, invasion and limitless list of sins because they claim that their god/God would forgive them. Mohammad said if anyone fast on the day of Arafat, then *"It expiates for the sins of the previous year and of the coming year"* - Sahih al-Muslim.

Mohammad also said *"Whoever says 'SubhanAllah wa bihamdihi'- 100 times during a day, will be forgiven for all his sins, even if they are like the foam of the sea."*– Sahih al-Bukhari & Sahih al-Muslim.

Mohammad again said *"When the Muslim or the mu'min (believer) makes wudu, when he washes his face, every sin that his eyes has committed (whatever haram we may have looked at, if we didn't lower our gaze when we were supposed to, if we spied on someone we shouldn't have) wash away with the water or with the last drop of water. When he washes his hands, every sin his hand has committed is washed away. When he washes his feet, every sin that his feet walked towards is washed away with the last drop of water until he comes out of making wudu free of sin."*– Sahih al-Muslim

Meanwhile in the traditional ancient Afrakan spirituality (Afrakan spiritualities and civilizations like Sumer, Dogons, Göbekli Tepe, Mesopotamia, Old Ghana Empire, Mali Empire, Songhai Empire, Kushite Kingdom (Kingdom of Kush), Carthage/Karthage, Punt land (Land and kingdom of Punt), Aksum Empire, Great Zimbabwe, ancient Egypt/Kemet and many other modern day Afrakan cultures and traditions), whatever sin you committed is punishable immediately. This tamed the people to choose accountability, peace, love, innerstanding and overstanding over careless sinful acts.

When you sin against someone or a nation, you must pay for your own sins. You got yourself into the act and executed the act of sin, so you are entirely responsible for any consequences that come to you, unless the person or nation you sinned against forgives you. No one can save you from your sin(s). You will pay for it either alive or in the spiritual realm. There is no escape, only you can pay for your own sins. Get it right, and start acting right.

This is spirituality, and no religion can change this fact. If you sin against someone, you better "man-up" or "woman-up" and go to the person you have wrong to ask for his or her forgiveness.

We must try to learn, research, study and dig outside the indoctrination of just one or two religious books. In that, all the facts in our universe are not found in only one or two books. Rather, we can find such facts in everything within nature. Let me render an example, let's look at the myth of a monotheistic god/God. Monotheistic god/God was a fallacy created by an egotistical means which led to the downfall of its originator, who was an Afrakan man from ancient Egypt/Kemet by the name of King Pharaoh Akhenaten. This monotheistic move led to the downfall of the once great and mighty Afrakan Kemet civilization. This is why both the bible and Quran push monotheism on the world. In that, in one way, it symbolizes how to cripple the Afrakans. Hence, Akhenaten, transcribed in both the bible and Quran in some cases as Moses, is well celebrated. However, it is a symbol of Afraka's downfall. Afrakans are polytheistic in spirituality. Akhenaten's original name is Akenten Oti, written as Oti Akenten, an Akan-Kemet King.

Torah was plagiarized from the ancient Kamitic/Kemetic/Egyptian word *"Tua Ra"*. Tua Ra means "the worship of Ra". Let's look at Quran which was also plagiarized and stolen from the ancient Egyptian/Kamitic/Kemetic word *"Khu RA"*. Khu Ra means "the worship of Ra". Now, let us look at the so-called *Holly Bible*, this book is plagiarized from *"Helios Biblos"* which means *"Sun Book* or *Sun Papers"*, also plagiarized from the RA *"Sun worship"* in ancient Egyptian/Kamit/Kemet.

It is as clear as a bright sunny day to unlock the fact that, ancient Kamit/Egypt/Kemet and other terrifically great Afrakan civilizations like Sumer, Dogons, Göbekli Tepe, Mesopotamia, Old Ghana Empire, Mali Empire, Songhai Empire, Kushite Kingdom (Kingdom of Kush), Carthage/Karthage, Punt land (Land and kingdom of Punt), Aksum Empire, Great Zimbabwe, and today's traditional Afrakan cultures are well aware of the facts and paths to connect us to the true Almighty Creator.

The Europeanized Christian faith was first introduced into West Afraka by the Portuguese. Let that sink in very well, these Portuguese invaders, and colonizers arrived around late 14th century after the Pope approved the *Doctrine of Discovery,* which gave way for Portugal to murder, rape, destroy, steal and take any land or territory they deemed fit for themselves. This situation reminds me of this statement, *"When the Missionaries arrived, the Africans had the land and the Missionaries had the Bible. They taught us how to pray with our eyes closed. When we opened them, they had the land and we had the Bible."*— Jomo Kenyatta said this about how Christianity penetrated through Kenya.

The missionaries were the "core undertakers" of the dirty works that was committed by the colonizers. The missionaries were deceivers and conspirators of colonizers.

Look at what happened during apartheid South Afraka, where the Boers (Dutch and Huguenot folks that settled in southern Afraka in the late 17th, 18th and 19th century), were the "ruling class", oppressing, murdering, raping, and stealing lands from aboriginal South Afrakan people. However, these Boers were members of the so-called missionary minded Dutch Reformed Church, that apparently were preaching about the "gospel of salvation", love and good deeds. The devil indeed came to steal, kill and destroy. So, ask yourselves, who is the devil? All I have to say is, if the shoe fits, then wear it.

Interestingly, Catholics/Christians (Bible), Muslim/Islam (Quran) and Jewish (Torah) religions have come together to form a one world religion by building what is known as the *Abrahamic House* physically located at Abu Dhabi, United Arab Emirates. Religious wars between Christians and Muslims have existed all the way back from the 8th century to date, and these wars will never end. In that, the lands that both religions fight over, do not belong to none of them. Rather, these lands were inherently of the aboriginal chocolate melanated sun-kissed first nations people, who were neither Christians nor Muslims.

For the wars between Christians, Israelis, and Arab-Muslims to end, they must humbly return the stolen lands to the rightful aboriginal owners, who are the aboriginal Afrakan ethnic people who have been murdered to an almost extinction in these invaded lands throughout the entire earth. The fact remains that pure spirituality not "religion" is ancient, and Afrakans were practicing pure original spirituality prior to the arrival of the aggressive bloody murder-driven, and deceptive Abrahamic books (Bible, Quran, Torah and others).

Jewish people, the Ashkenazi converts tried several proposals for a Jewish state with the help of Britain, United States of America, Italy, France and basically almost every western country.

The Jewish people implemented many of their utopia Jewish state of Israel plan. Some of the physical areas that the Jewish Zionist wanted to establish their country, or State of Israel includes the following:

Fascist Italian era government Benito Mussolini had a plan to help find land in East Afraka for the Jewish folks to build their Jewish State of Israel (establish Land of Israel). This plan failed horribly.

British colonially controlled East Afraka was proposed to give some of the lands of Uganda that also cover some plateaus in today's Kenya, and some lands of the Maasai people to the Jewish people as a homeland. This was proposed by Joseph Chamberlain to Theodore Herzl in 1903, and his Zionist fellows. This was implemented, voted on by the Europeans and there was influx of these Jewish folks into East Afrakan land to build the land of Israel, a Jewish state. The plan fell off little after 1905.

Ararat City in U.S.A, a City of Refuge for the Jews by Mordecai Manuel Noah in September, 1825 at Grand Island around or next to the Niagara River, planned, proposed and implemented to be called "Ararat" after Mount Ararat. Obviously, it wasn't successful.

The 1930 Jewish autonomous region in Russia, the Birobidzhan (State of Israel) project supported by Joseph Stalin. Location chose for this project was remote Soviet Far East region prior to World War II.

Adolf Hitler's Germany Madagascar plan (between 1933 - 1945) to forcefully remove or evacuate all Jewish populace within Europe to the Southern Afrakan island of

Madagascar. German, Polish, British, and French government were all in on this plan of Jewish resettlement to Afraka's Madagascar. This plan failed because Germany lost the war against the British which was known as the *Battle of Britain war* in or around 1940.

Then on May 14th, 1948 after World War II, the Jewish state of Israel was established at the province of today's "Middle East", a misnomer. This plan was successful due to the backing of the United States of America, Britain and all the western countries recognizing Israel, and its new location as a state.

However, Iran, Iraq, Kuwait, Lebanon, Saudi Arabia, Syria and Yemen did not recognize Israel as a state. In the same line Pakistan, Afghanistan, and Bangladesh also do not recognize Israel as a state.

This area has been claimed to be a Palestinian land, so the migration and loss of Palestinian lives at the expense of the new nation, new state of Israel's 1948 independence declaration begun what would be known as the Arab and Israeli War. Currently, 28 United Nation members nations do not recognize Israel as a state.

Below is an excerpt from a Wikipedia article titled "International recognition of Israel" extracted from subtitle "Present Situation" and it reads:

"As of December 2020, 165 of the 193 total member states of the United Nations (UN) recognize Israel. 28 UN member states do not recognize Israel: 15 members of the Arab League (Algeria, Comoros, Djibouti, Iraq, Kuwait, Lebanon, Libya, Mauritania, Oman, Qatar, Saudi Arabia, Somalia, Syria, Tunisia, and Yemen); ten non-Arab members of the Organization of Islamic Cooperation (Afghanistan, Bangladesh, Brunei, Indonesia, Iran, Malaysia, Maldives, Mali, Niger, and Pakistan); and Cuba, North Korea, and Venezuela.[20] In 2002, the Arab League proposed the recognition of Israel by Arab countries as a pathway towards a resolution of the Israeli-Palestinian conflict under the Arab Peace Initiative. Following the Abraham Accords, which were signed in September 2020 between Israel and the United Arab Emirates and Bahrain, the Palestinian National Authority condemned any Arab agreement with Israel as dishonourable, describing them as a betrayal to the Palestinian cause and a blow to their quest for an independent Palestinian state.[21]

The passports of some countries are not valid for travel to Israel, including Bangladesh, Brunei, Iran, Iraq, and Pakistan. Thirteen countries do not accept Israeli passports: Algeria, Bangladesh, Brunei, Iran, Iraq, Kuwait, Lebanon, Libya, Malaysia, Pakistan, Saudi Arabia, Syria, and Yemen.[22]Some of these countries also do not accept passports of other countries whose holder has an Israeli visa or stamp on it. The stamp may be a visa stamp, or a stamp on entry or departure. Because of these issues, Israeli immigration controls do not stamp passports with an entry visa, instead stamping on a separate insert which is discarded on departure. However, a stamp of another country which indicates that the person has entered Israel may frustrate that effort. For example, if an Egyptian departure stamp is used in any passport at the Taba Border Crossing, that is an indication that the person entered Israel, and a similar situation arises for land crossings into Jordan. Some countries also ban direct flights and overflights to and from Israel.[23]In August 2020, the United Arab Emirates permitted direct flights from Israel, and Saudi Arabia and Bahrain authorized overflights for such flights.[24]On 8 October 2020, Israel and Jordan reached an agreement to allow flights to cross over both countries' airspace.[25]……[…]."

Link:https://en.wikipedia.org/wiki/International_recognition_of_Israel#:~:text=28%20U N%20member%20states%20do,%2C%20Bangladesh%2C%20Brunei%2C%20Indonesia %2C

The interesting fact is that the aboriginal chocolate melanated sun-kissed Afrakans who were inalienably placed on these lands by the true Almighty Creator from the beginning of time, lost their land due to invasions of the Greeks, Romans, Arab Muslims, and later the eruptions of *Doctrine of Discovery* which paved way for European colonizations and invasions. Now, we have Abrahamic religions fighting among themselves for these Mesopotamia lands which the original owners fled from to mostly the areas of today's West Afraka due to the aforementioned violence.

The Abrahamic religions have been very detrimental to mainly the aboriginal melanated sun-kissed first Afrakan nations, civilizations and kingdoms. The Bible, Quran and Torah have stolen the aboriginal identities of the Afrakans, who have been on earth cyclically for well over several billion years. The emergence of the new versions of the mixed pale Arab Islamic Muslims, the converted "Jew-ish" people and the Constantine and Pope's Jesus/Iesus/Zeus character creation in the New Testament Bible destroyed authentic spirituality.

Julius Sello Malema, a South African politician and a Member of Parliament (MP), and the leader of the Economic Freedom Fighters (EFF, South Afraka) said it best when he said that: *"When you steal a car and you pass over/on the stolen car to your children, it makes that child a criminal as well. Because he or she is in possession of stolen goods and that child passes that car or doesn't even pass that car, he sells that car to go and buy another car with the money of stolen goods. It remains a stolen good with the property you bought with the money stolen (attained from the original stolen goods). You are in possession of stolen property, return it...[...]..Your parents have left you a very bad name and don't blame it on us...[...] Don't push us to that pain because when that day comes, we will not be scared."*

We have entered into the season of high vibration versus low vibration. In this season you would need to choose, yes you have the choice to choose either to vibrate higher, or to vibrate lower. Many folks are talking about the age of Aquarius and yes, it's true, we are in the age of Aquarius.

Doors of wisdom and knowledge are opening throughout the universe, so do not be left behind. When we talk about the rapture, when we talk about the end of the years, and the end of time, it's just talking about the high vibration, separating others from the lower vibration. If you vibrate higher, you are going to be part of the ascended ones. As other people would put it as, "those who gained their superpowers or superhero powers". That is a spiritual quantum upgrade that we would go through as we choose to ascend by vibrating on a higher frequency.

To the invaders and those who are children and descendants of invaders, you took some lands, artifacts, resources, and continue to take and destroy other countries through the usage of military bully, wars, sanctions and deceptive racism. You cannot ascend and still hold on to the stuff you stole. No matter how long you think it has been, you must return everything if you desire to ascend. You cannot deceive the universe, you must fulfill restitution.

Etymology of Compendiums of all Gods and The Almighty Creator

CHAPTER 6

CHAPTER 6

SPIRITS, SOULS, LIVING THINGS and NON-LIVING THINGS AS ENERGIES

Current ------------------→ Currency -----------→ Money

Negative – or Positive + charge.	"in Circulation"	Symbol.
Energy, Motion, Flow,	"Exchange" "In Usage".	Physical
Supply of energy.	**Medium, Converter,**	Representation
Used, Recycled, Now, Present,	**Electronic.**	Could be Gold,
Future.	**Acceptable means to**	Coins, Bank
High, Low, Alternate,	***buy & sell.***	Notes, Salt,
Direct forms of Energy.		et al.

Money, in the illustration above could be literally anything acceptable by those in power in this physical realm. When we apply the philosophy of common sense through logic, we would be intrigued to discover that everything in the universe is connected to the flow of *Current,* which is *energy.*

Everything in the universe is simply *Energy:* love, emotions, feelings, air, sun, water, kindness, food, trees, fishes, plants, excitement, anger, success, unity, diversity, education, light, day, night, every animal both on land and in water.

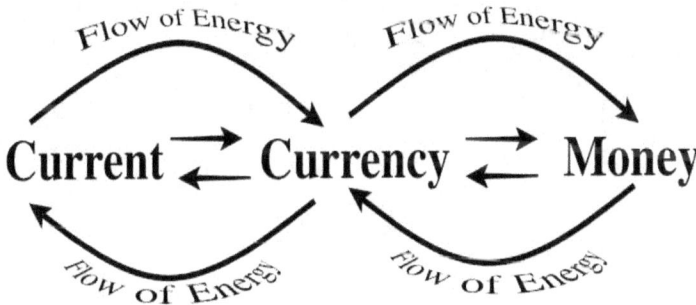

Those in power and influence have only tried to use physical representations to represent very few of the energies existing in our universe.

This is because, some of us are not familiar with the workings of the universe. Majority of us have little to no innerstanding and overstanding of the *Oneness* of the universe.

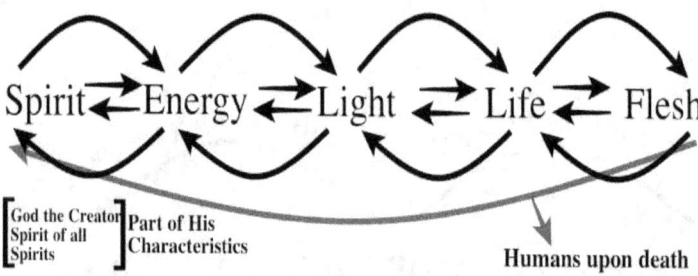

Being in this *"flesh"* is linked to consciousness through awareness to our earthly environment. We record everything that happens here through our biological conscious bodies, and we are able to relate to one another *consciously,* knowing that, we all have a purpose to execute. When a soulful human fail to relate to another soulful human on a *"socially acceptable"* manner, other soulful humans within that culture or community say that *"you have no soul"*. Humans with souls must connect with those with souls. There are other human-like people with the same "human avatar body" who are soulless. These other humans with no souls live among the humans with souls on earth.

Our *soul* aids us to survive on earth, this material universe. That is why in some materialistic situations, our *true self* (the *soul*) struggles or wrestles with our *"conscience"* on things relating to our true origin, *the Most High Almighty Creator.*

The *energies* contained in animals are of different form or type comparable to humans. Mankind consume the *"physical representations"* of different kinds of *energies* contained within plants, trees, animals, insects, and all kinds of *physical* living things. The *physical representation* of all living things on earth is connected to the soil, dust, or ground.

Hence, every living thing eventually decompose in their *physical state* when the *energy* departs from their physical containers or bodies. That *energy* is simply transformed into its original state. In that, the *"energy"*, which is the *soul* in this situation, is not wasted, it doesn't die, it is eternal.

The air, breath, or spirit from *the Most High Almighty Creator* is relevant in order for us to become *"Living Souls"*. The *soul* grants us our awareness of the earth, our environment, consciousness, essence of living, or being alive. Humans with souls are *the Most High Almighty Creator's breath of fresh air*, making our true source of being, *spiritual*.

Since the *breath* originated from the *"Spirit of all spirits"*, who is *the Most High Almighty Creator*. We ought to be spiritual, meaning, we ought to master the "art of breathing". In that, spirituality, in all its simplicity, is breathe, breathing, or the art of breathing. In a *physical* sense/state, humans *die* but in the *spiritual* sense/state, humans basically *transform* from *its current state or form* to the *actualization state (soul)*, after *death a.k.a "spiritual birth"*.

The figure below details how *energy* flows through us, and how we react to the flow of *energy* in our environment:

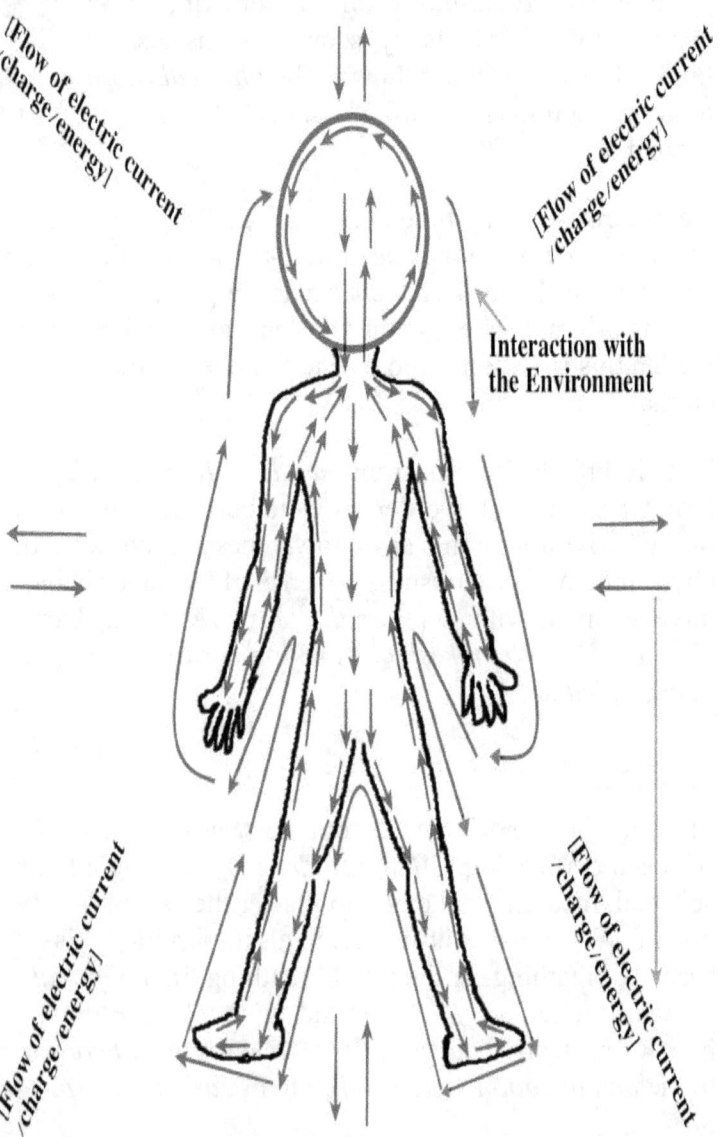

Our *words* and *actions* are all *energy*. The *soul* within us exerts *positive energy,* as the *body or flesh* exerts *negative energy*. *Equal exertions* from *both sides* are needed in order for soulful humans to function *"morally"* within our physical realm. *Spiritual disconnection* is basically a way to suffocate your *soul,* in order to give way to your flesh, or body. In that, your *soul's* ability to breathe efficiently, depends on your level of spirituality a.k.a "breathing". To be spiritual, is to grant your soul's effective ability to breathe, and accomplish its purpose on earth.

Illustratively, when an individual is upset or irate, he or she is advised to "calm down". We all check or monitor our *energy* flow through the conduct of *meditation, or breathing in and breathing out*. We need to check ourselves introspectively through *meditation* to moderate our aura. *Meditation* helps us to *see, know,* and *decide* on the *"type of energy"* we welcome into our lives, or associate with within our environment.

Everything is *energy*. *Energy* is spirituality. Spirituality is the art of breathing. The art of breathing is monitored by our consciousness. The master of it all, is our soul. The soul is eternal, and it is only the soul that can ascend to its aboriginal source, which is *the Most High Almighty Creator*. There is *oneness* in uniformity of all creatures on a *spiritual level.* Soulless people are the mechanical creatures of some of the soulful people. Soulful people fell on earth through birth through the gates of heaven found in-between the thighs of a womb-man (woman). Soulless people cannot ascend out of this 3D-third dimension earth realm. Religion is derailment from one's spirituality. Religion is a trap and demonically unpleasant way to use fear through man-made lies to cloud your soul's purpose on earth. Religiousness is not spirituality. Religion is the antithesis of spirituality. To be religious is to be lost.

SPIRITS, SOULS, LIVING THINGS

Your soul is manifested on the lightweight surface level of compression as your will, mind, consciousness or intellect.

Your soul is likened to the number 9 in spiritual terms. Your flesh or physical body needs the spirit, breath (a.k.a spirit) is likened to the number 6. You are originally 9 and from 9 you manifested as 6 into the realm of 3 (earth). When your true self (9 a.k.a soul) fails the journey that it chose to explore in 3 (flesh / earth) through the driving seat of 6 (spirit), then you cannot and will not return to your 9 (original true self). Until you pass the original purpose, or task assigned to "your journey", that you decided to embark on when you decided to descend from 9 to 3 through 6. You will go through your 6 and 3 with your 9 in tact through reincarnation until you successfully accomplish the challenges that you set for yourself in this journey in the realm of 3.

If your true-self (9) truly desires to go to your original realm of 9 (which is completeness/full ascension), then you must stop playing, acting a fool, or recklessly destroying and hurting things in the realm of 3, through your 6 in order for you to fully ascend to your original state of 9. It is as simple as that, yet, it's very challenging for many to achieve it. Simply because, many of us tend to accept the illusions in the realm of 3 as true, while distorting the facts of 9 as unattainable, and separate from ourselves. In other words, most of us reject our authentic selves (that is 9) to go on an almost never-ending cyclical journey through the realms of 6 and 3 a.k.a reincarnation without ascending.

I have given you the keys, now its your decision to either successfully and gracefully journey through 3 with the guides of your 6, to take your 9 (your true self) home to its realm of 9, or go through the cyclical reincarnation of "no-lesson learned" and "little-to-no growth attained" journey within 3 through your 6. This is the simplest code of life decoded in the simplest way possible.

Every living thing's entire life has the pillars of 3,6, and 9. This only applies to those with souls. The rest of 1,2, 4,5,7, and 8 relate to your life's stories, decisions, re-sets, and encounters with zero (0) being the source of everything living and non-living.

8 will always reincarnate you through several reincarnations until you master or learn all the lessons, decisions, stories, and encounters within 1,2,4,5, and 7. You are made of 3,6 and 9. The number zero (0) manifests itself in all the numbers 1,2,3,4,5,6,7,8,9.

The power of all powers, the source for all sources, the spirit of all spirits rest within the core number zero (0). Overstanding and innerstanding that you are made of three compartments namely, your flesh, sour, and spirit (that is 3,6, and 9 respectively) enables you to know exactly what to do, and the right steps to take in this journey.

It is a given that many religious and traditionally cultural folks around the world like Hinduism, Sikhism, Akans of Ghana, many Afrakan cultures, Buddhism and Jainism accept the spiritual and physical manifestations of reincarnation and incarnation. However, some Christians and few other religions denounce reincarnation yet they (especially Christianity/Catholics) accept incarnation.

Accepting incarnation and rejecting reincarnation is basically an act of misinformation or misguided influence. You cannot believe or accept the New Testament bible without directly or indirectly, consciously or unconsciously accepting reincarnation. Many people in the bible were "brought back to life", well, that is a variety of re-incarnation. Rebirth, born again, and all the likes of "spiritual births" are linked to the etymological definitions of reincarnation.

If you believe and accept the bible, especially the New Testament, then you must know that:

Jesus (an allegorical character made up by the Romans), was said to have been incarnated, and in many cases reincarnated. John the Baptist is said to have been the re-incarnation of Elias/Elijah. That means, Elijah was reborn or reincarnated in the flesh as John the Baptist who served as the first witness of Christ's first coming. By the way, John the Baptist himself denied that he was the reincarnation of Elijah, with his rejection, that indicates that, Jesus never came because the *"first witness"* supposed to be Elijah's reincarnation was debunked by John the Baptist himself in John 1:21 kjv *"And they asked him, What then? Art thou Elias? And he saith, I am not. Art thou that prophet? And he answered, No."*

The Old Testament indicates that *King David* would also be reincarnated in *Jeremiah 30:9 kjv*.

Elijah is said to also be reincarnated in the flesh to be born by a man and woman who will serve as the second witness before the supposed second coming of Christ.

In my finite definition, *reincarnation is a continuous cyclical energy purification that only transitions to a resting state after achieving or attaining perfect cyclical purification through ascension.* This is how I define the mystery of reincarnation.

It's all about learning how to strategically, consciously and spiritually modulate your frequency to vibrate on a higher energetic level. In layperson's term, think about using the blender to achieve or attain a fine blended texture at its finest level. You keep the blender on continuously, blending the items in its container until you feel or see the expected outcome.

That's how reincarnation is, we are here on earth to find our way back home to our perfect spiritual-soul self, and while we are here on earth, we go through challenges that many fail. However, you keep on reincarnating until you learn all the lessons, and achieve your purpose on earth in order to ascend to your original perfect spiritual-soul self.

Both incarnation and reincarnation are connected through respective continuous cyclical energetic vibrational patterns. Re-incarnation is a derivative of incarnation. To re-incarnate is basically to incarnate multiple times at different timelines or lifetime. Reincarnation and incarnation go hand in hand. *Incarnation is your first time as a spirit embodying a physical flesh form, while reincarnation is when that spirit re-embodies different physical forms at different times, and space.* Typical example of both reincarnation and incarnation happen through the natural male sperm ejaculation into the female's womb of eggs to spark an electromagnetic activation of what is known to us as, life.

There are many people walking among us who are soulless. They have no soul in them and they're prone to cyclical, barbarically brutal killings, stealing, and destroying everything in their way. The earth is organic, yet these soulless people use artificial fertilizers, and other chemicals to kill the earth. Their desire is to make almost everything as soulless as they are, if and when possible.

Cloud seeding by the usage of chemical-trails sprayed into our atmosphere is unnatural, filled with deadly toxic metals and other chemicals. It could probably be part of the many reasons why you are warned and fined when you are caught collecting rain water in most western countries.

Nature is organic and has soul, it is conscious or has consciousness at its core. Every living thing created by the true Almighty Creator is conscious and has a soul. We must learn to go back to being soulful. Our souls must be full of outpouring love for all the souls that vibrate energetically within every living thing. Our quest to express our love to be soulful would spit out the soulless ones who hide in disguise among us.

Clones can have memories but never a soul. Hence, clones just like robots are soulless. Meaning, some soulful people who dropped in their vibration, have been unsuccessfully attempting to duplicate low energetic vibrating beings into clones. In doing so, they attempt to live on earth forever, yet they aren't smart enough to know that, only memories can be gathered or harnessed artificially through any scientific means possible, however, their very soul belong to the *One True Source,* that is the Almighty Creator, who is the *Energy of all energies.*

Let's look at the greatest allegorical book ever written, the bible, and focus on its New Testament's allegorical character, Jesus. At age 12, he gave a glimpse of his knowledge at the temple with elders. Then at age 33 he died. It is emphasized that, he started his adult ministry at age 30. Now, what happened from age 13 to age 29 is hidden from those who blindly believe the bible. However, he was in Afraka, specifically West Afraka, for the most parts, and went to India as well.

Now let's go to the good part, we are introduced to the numbers 12, 30, and 33.

Let's break it down:

12 is 1 + 2 = 3

30 is 3 + 0 = 3

33 is 3 + 3 = 6

3 + 3 + 6 = 12; hence his 12 disciples (the lunar / solar month/moons cyclical seasonal representation).

From 30 to 33, we have 3 + 0 + 3 + 3 = 9.

The number 9 is completion, perfection or total ascension. Hence, that allegorical biblical character's ascension to the sky where the father (the Sun) is, and the mother (the moon) dwells as well. The allegorical Jesus had to also come through his mother's womb (womb of a woman) in order to walk on this earth. The father (Sun) has multiple women such as, mother nature, mother earth, mother moon, Queen of the heavens. These are all allegorical and esoteric teachings.

In simplicity, each masculine energy personified creator has a feminine energy personified wife. There can never be a father without a mother. The essence of a father exists because, there is the existence of the essence of a mother. Everything is achieved through a balanced energy of the masculine and feminine energy.

You cannot pick one over the other, otherwise, there would be chaos, imbalance, and imperfections. For everything to be perfect is for all masculine and feminine energies to be in absolute balance.

Additionally, the allegorical *"crown of thorns"* is simply the Sun. Just draw the sun and you will know. You cannot just draw a circle without the spikes of thorn-like appearance and call it a drawing of the sun. The sun emits its energetic vibration frequencies that appears to the human's physical eyes as "thorns" or "spike-like" spears.

Hence, those humans who wrote these allegorical New Testament books about the *"crown of thorns"* were just simply hinting about Jesus, being the *"Sun"* of the Creator (Father) he represented.

The Sun is life. The Sun gives life and gives it abundantly. The Sun makes everything grow and produces its food. The mother moon nurtures everything at night from your mood/emotions to how well everything grows. Anyone with a soul, key phrase here is *"with a soul",* can become a God or Goddess. You can become a *"Christ/Krst/Krist"*. You can become a *"holy"* prophet. You can become a savior. You can become a Buddha. You can become anything, or anyone you choose to become, if you have a soul.

One of the top scams in the bible is in *Malachi 3:6*, which says: *"...I am the Lord, I change not... ".* Yet this Bible god/God changed right from the first book of *Genesis* through to the last book of *Revelations*. What a poorly written mythical theatrical collections of "sun books" compiled together to be called, the bible. This is totally a psychological scam to humanity. In fact, it's an absolute ethical and moral robbery.

Economic suffering, social suffering, defense suffering, psychological suffering, spiritual suffering, and essence suffering, are all due to acceptance of foreign religions into your lands, hearts, minds and homes. Rise up spiritually. Rise up psychologically, and rise up physically by embracing your own language, culture, and your own Gods, Goddesses, and spirituality.

This is the beginning of your redemption, and ascension. This is how you can invoke the powers and prowess of your own Gods and Goddesses to come, and empower you, in order to redeem your honor, your birthright, your authentic royal identity, and your *krist/christ* self.

Let's look at these phrases from the bible:

"Love your enemies": This was initiated by the colonizers great grandparents, the Romans (Roman Catholic church) and later shoved down the throats of all the nations that these colonizers colonized.

The underlining goal was to keep all the colonized and enslaved nations docile, psychologically weak, and economically immobile. Evidences are all around you within all the colonized countries. Super docile, timid, and madly in-love with pale Europeanized non-existent Jesus. Wake up, soul family.

"Whosoever shall slap your right cheek, turn to him the other also": How on earth can you defend yourself if you are only meant to just allow people, other nations to come and bully you, rape your women and girls (did to all the enslaved people), murder your folks, steal all your resources, and then, all you do as a people is to turn the other side of your cheek to be brutally assaulted over, and over again. Your nations are filled with uncounted rich resources, yet your people are super poor.

The poorer these "black" neighborhoods and nations are, the more Christian (bible) or Muslims (Quran) they are. Check these facts, go to all these neighborhoods, and colonized nations. Both the Quran, and bible were used to brutally colonize nations. These are pure facts that anyone can easily look into.

One interesting thing that I came across in the *book of Jasher* is when it stated that, the bible God turned people into Apes & Elephants. The *book of Jasher* is referenced in the bible at *Joshua 10:13*; *2 Samuel 1:18*; and *2 Timothy 3:8*. This can be seen at Jasher 9:35-38

"35 And the Lord smote the three divisions that were there, and he punished them according to their works and designs; those who said, We will ascend to heaven and serve our gods, became like apes and elephants; and those who said, We will smite the heaven with arrows, the Lord killed them, one man through the hand of his neighbor; and the third division of those who said, We will ascend to heaven and fight against him, the Lord scattered them throughout the earth.

36 And those who were left amongst them, when they knew and understood the evil which was coming upon them, they forsook the building, and they also became scattered upon the face of the whole earth.

37 And they ceased building the city and the tower; therefore he called that place Babel, for there the Lord confounded the Language of the whole earth; behold it was at the east of the land of Shinar.

38 And as to the tower which the sons of men built, the earth opened its mouth and swallowed up one third part thereof, and a fire also descended from heaven and burned another third, and the other third is left to this day, and it is of that part which was aloft, and its circumference is three days' walk."

Another misconception that many people hold is that, some people think and believe that *King David* wrote the entire book of *Psalms*. However, that is not entirely true, below are the authors of the book of *Psalms*:

Author	Chapters the Author Wrote
Asaph	50, 73-83
David	1-41, 51-71, 138-150

Ethan the Ezrahite	89
Herman the Ezrahite	88
Moses	90
Solomon	72,127
Sons of Korah	42-49,84-89
Unknown	about 51 Psalms

According to the Jewish people, there are about ten (10) total authors in addition to *King David*, as the authors of the book of *Psalms*. The other authors of the book of *Psalms* per the Jewish people include: Melchizedek, Moses, Adam, Abraham, Asaph, Heman, Jeduthun, and Korah's three sons.

The book of *Psalms* is a collection of music, songs, praises, and poetry from the people outlined above, and were combined into a single book. Many Bible believers do not spend time to execute their own research in order to know the facts about the bible they claim to love so much.

The true source of everything is the s*pirit of all spirits energetic force*. The true *Creator* can never be touched, or held because the true *Creator* doesn't have a physical body. The true *Creator* is simply everything, hyper-supernova electromagnetic energy, and literally everything known, and unknown to mankind. The *Creator* can be anything and everything. As the spirit of all spirits, *the source* can take the shape and form of literally anything. Man cannot limit the magnitude of the true *Creator*. Many men and women have unconsciously attempted and continue to misinterpret the power of *the source*. The *source* is bigger, greater and powerful beyond measure.

I would like to emphatically emphasize again that, the *Creator* is not human. The source doesn't have a body or a figure, but can take the shape of any object that pleases the *source*. The *source* does not have any sex classification (male or female). It is important to state that, the usage of "*He*" when talking about the *Creator* is a "culture" instituted by men and women.

This could be seen in how records from the bible were written, as well as, other world cultures, and religion with diverse languages exhibiting this uniformity. Since the *Creator* is the s*pirit of all spirits,* that simply translates that, all the creations are souls with spirits at their core, just like the *Creator*. In the simplest term, the *Creator* is the *source of all things*. The true Creator's name is not found in any religious book, rather, it is found throughout nature.

THE TRINITY EXPRESSED IN HUMANITY

The *trinity* in humanity is compactly intertwined within the aura of humanity in the *trinity* of *the Creator*. The father, mother, and child are one, as a "whole" in spirit, soul, consciousness, and flesh. This is the man, woman and child or children. The oneness of this unique existence remains unchanged regardless of its multiplicity. The diagrammatic explanations below would add additional emphasis to *"The Trinity Expressed in Humanity"*.

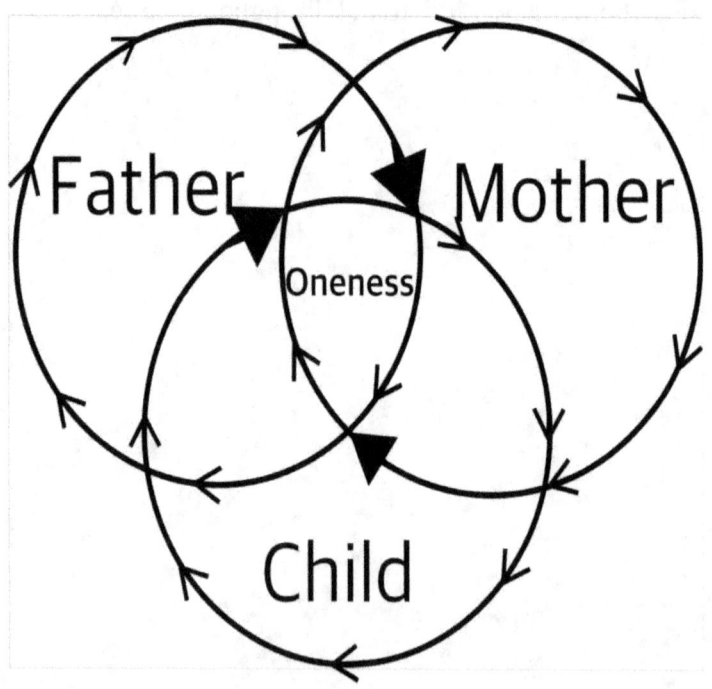

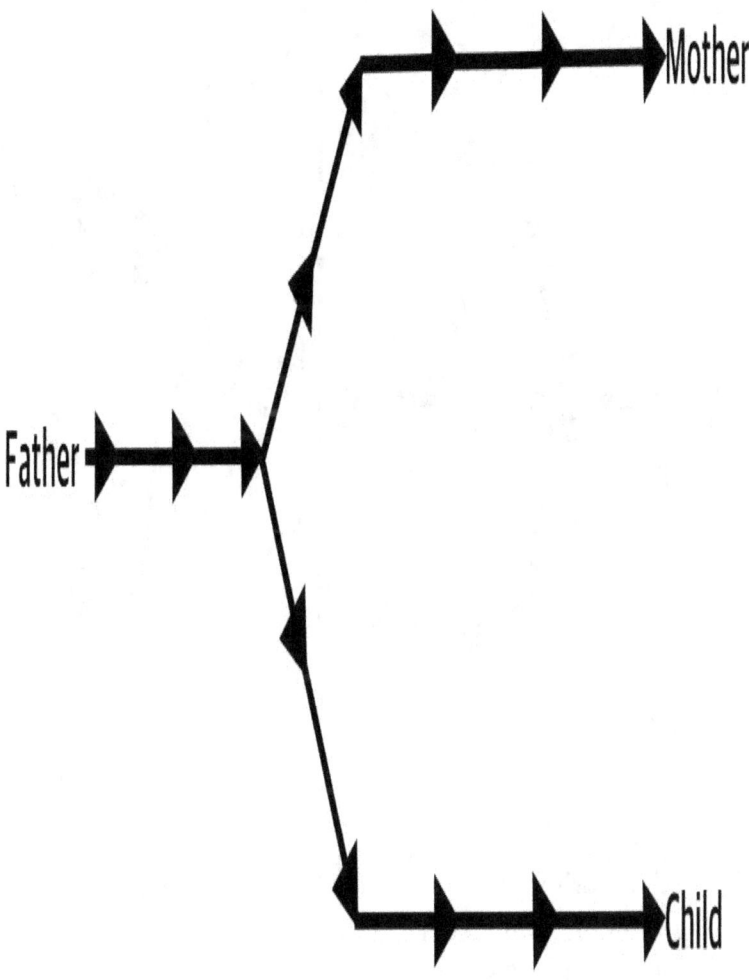

The Father, Mother, and Child form *the trinity in humanity* is manifested both physically and spiritually.

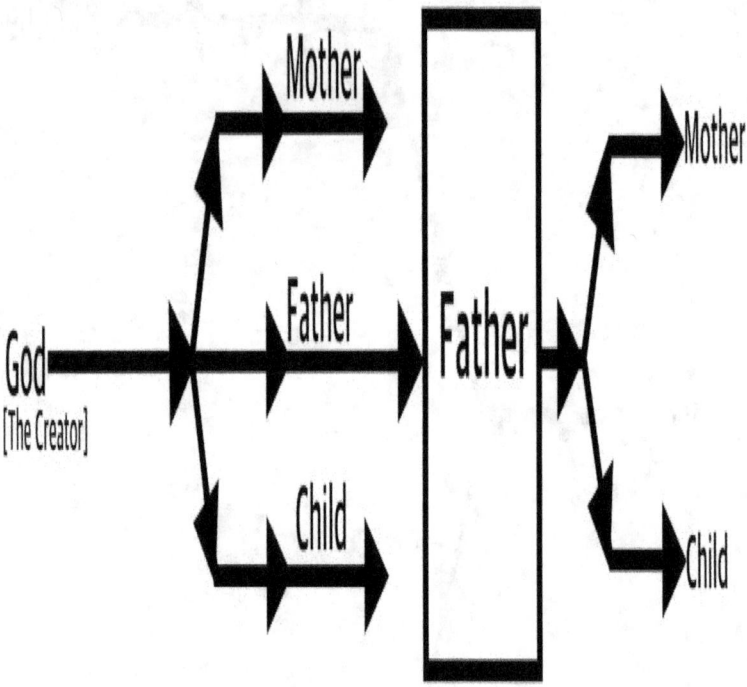

Everything originates from *The Most High Almighty Creator* and is manifested through projected multiplicity, through the lens of predestination that has been ordained, and orchestrated within time's conception. *The trinity expressed in humanity* is a daily reminder of the greatness, and undeniable providence of the *Creator, The Most High*.

Etymology of Compendiums of all Gods and The Almighty Creator

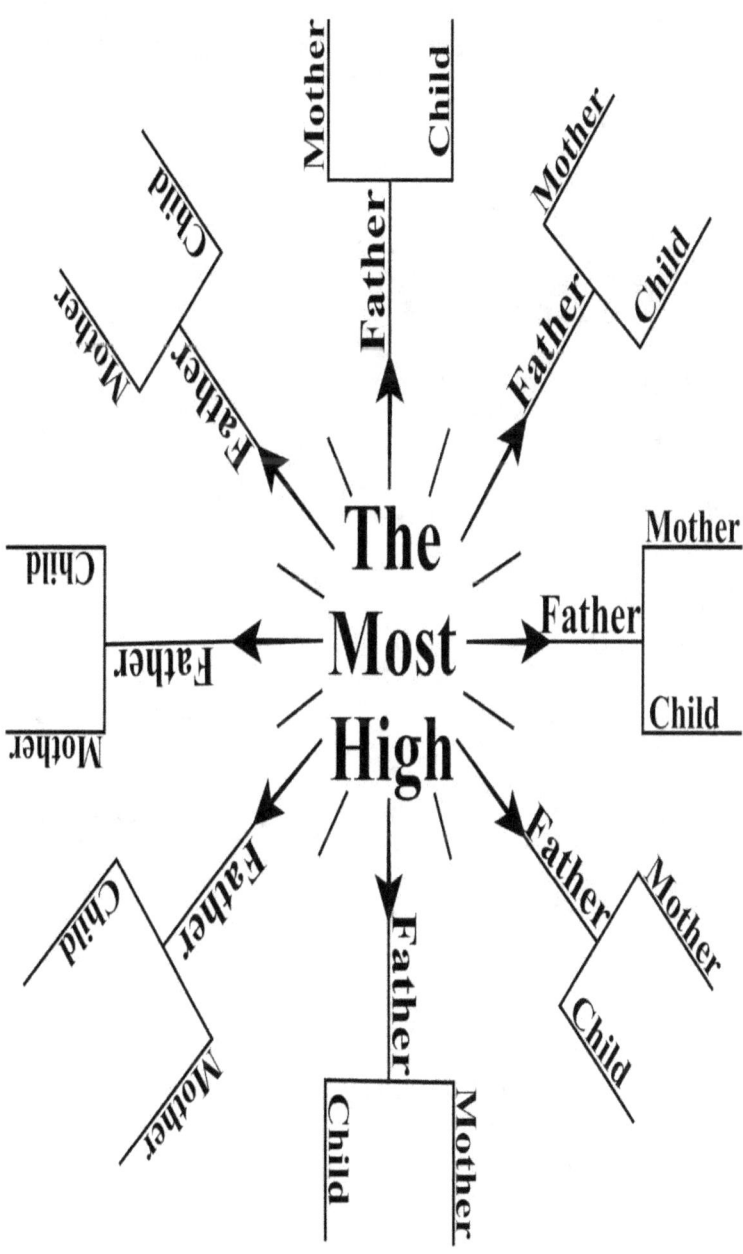

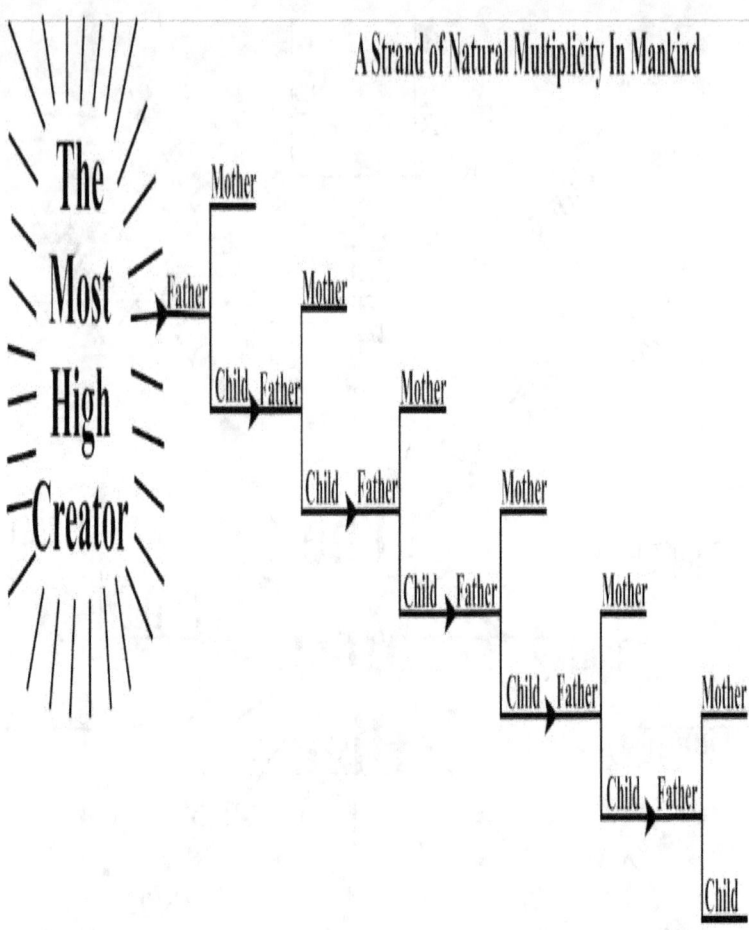

The *Father*, the *Mother* and the *Child* make up the *trinity* exemplified by *The Most High Almighty Creator* through *His* creation of Adam (read "Adam" backwards: Ma + Da), (male and female), (man and woman).

Etymology of Compendiums of all Gods and The Almighty Creator

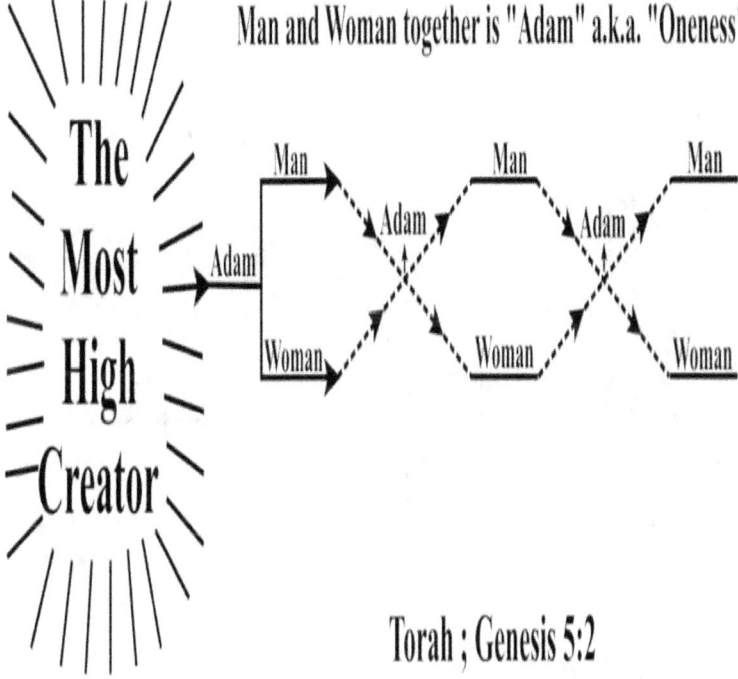

From the first book of the *Torah,* **Genesis 5:2** *The Most High* called both the male and female (man and woman) as **Adam**. Adam is <u>Oneness</u> of the male and female creation. Read the verse below:

Genesis 5:2 *"Male and female created he **them**; and blessed **them**, and called <u>**their name Adam**</u>, in the day when they were created."*

Adam (read "Adam" backwards: Ma + Da)

Etymology of Compendiums of all Gods and The Almighty Creator

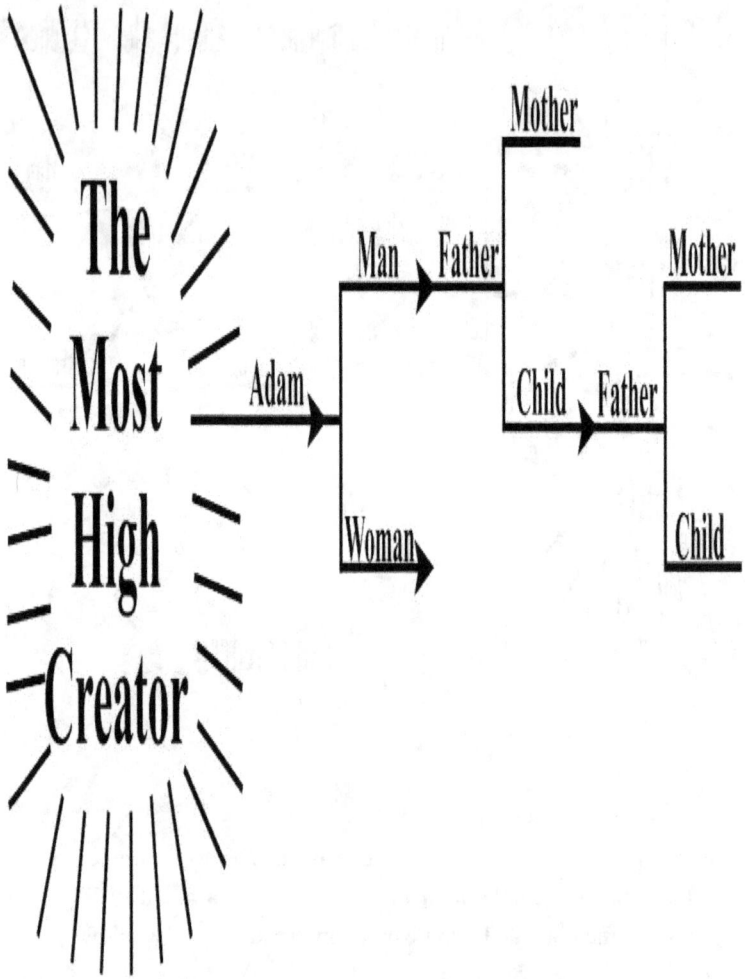

We can be a trillion people in the world, but we are all an origination of "*One Original*" multiplicity.

THE TORAH'S RECORD OF LINEAGE TRUMPS THE NEW TESTAMENT AS A FICTIONAL BOOK

The *Torah* consists of five books that are deemed the instructions, laws, culture, traditions and teachings of the original people of the bible. From the *Torah*, we know that the chosen tribe is *Jacob a.k.a Israel* (12 tribes of Israel). This is because mankind departed from the *ways* and *instructions* of the bible God, YAW corrupted as YaHWeH to make smaller gods out of sand, wood and clay. These smaller gods could not talk, eat, move, or see. Mankind became evil (opposite from peace, love and unity with one another) through war, paganism, unethical breeding and destruction. This is the unverified story the "bible" tells.

Now, *the traditions*, *cultures,* and *instructions* of the bible God, YAW corrupted as YaHWeH per the *Torah* with direct respect to the lineages was through the *father's line*. Therefore, since the time of Adam, records show the flow of this line of lineage to be "sovereign", and ordained by *the* bible God, YAW corrupted as YaHWeH. However, the *New Testament* bible used by the Christians, and Catholics has massive irregularities of this very *instruction* from the same bible God, YAW corrupted as YaHWeH

I will outline these irregularities with illustrations, direct verses from the same *New Testament* bible, and explanation of how obvious the irregularities are exhibited. This is one of the major reasons why I do not ascribe to the *New Testament* bible of the Christians, and Catholics.

The *New Testament's* sources are mainly from the *Torah,* and the rest of the *Old Testament books*.

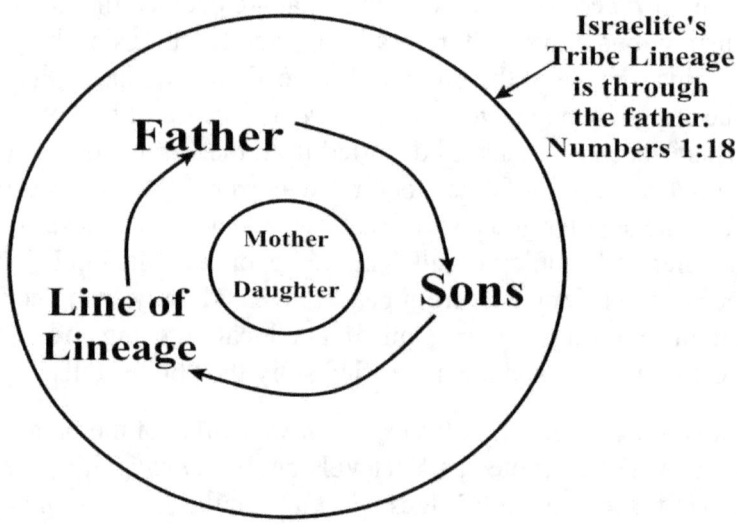

This is a visual explanation of how the bible only chooses the father's lineage of inheritance. So, all the lineages apparently are supposed to be through only the father's bloodline.

Etymology of Compendiums of all Gods and The Almighty Creator

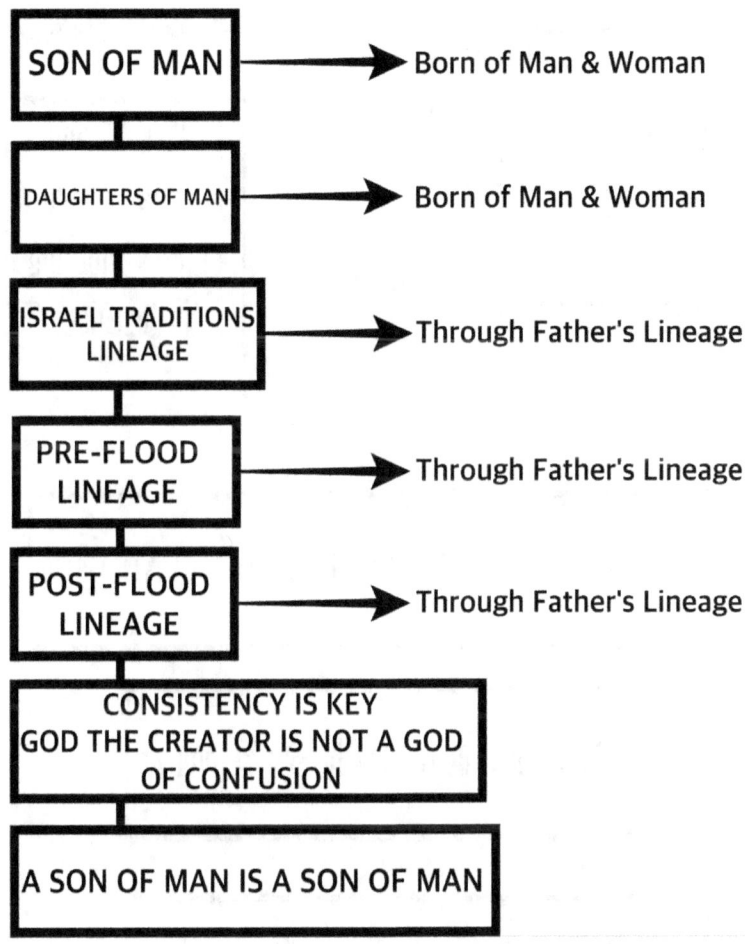

NOTE: <u>Sons of men</u> are not the same as <u>Sons of Elohiym</u> (Son of the bible God). In Hebrew and Aramaic *Sons of Elohiym* refer to supernatural beings or angels while *Sons of man* refers to mankind ("of man and woman", "flesh and blood", frail and weak). When *the* bible God, YAW corrupted as YaHWeH indicated through the prophets about the *Son of Man* coming from the *Tribe of Judah, house of David* to save the nation of Israel (all the 12 tribes). *The Most High* was very specific, clear and wasn't confused (Confusion is not of *the* bible God, YAW corrupted as YaHWeH). Read these versus: ***Gen.6:2,4; Job1:6;2:1; Job38:7; Daniel 3:25; Gen 4:25(Seth=Son of Man; flesh)*** The <u>*Son of Man*</u> is born of a <u>man and woman</u> <u>chosen</u> by YHWH.

Numbers 1:18 → Should always be from father's lineage

oldest of all 4 gospels ↑
Mark & John "No infancy record of Iesus" nothing No genealogy

Mary (Iesus mom) is NOT from the tribe of JUDAH/ David

Mary's genealogy NOT in New Testament

ONLY Joseph's genealogy outlined in both Matthew 1 & Luke 3 New Testament

Luke 1:27 Joseph is from Tribe of Judah

Joseph is <u>NOT</u> Iesus' biological <u>father</u>

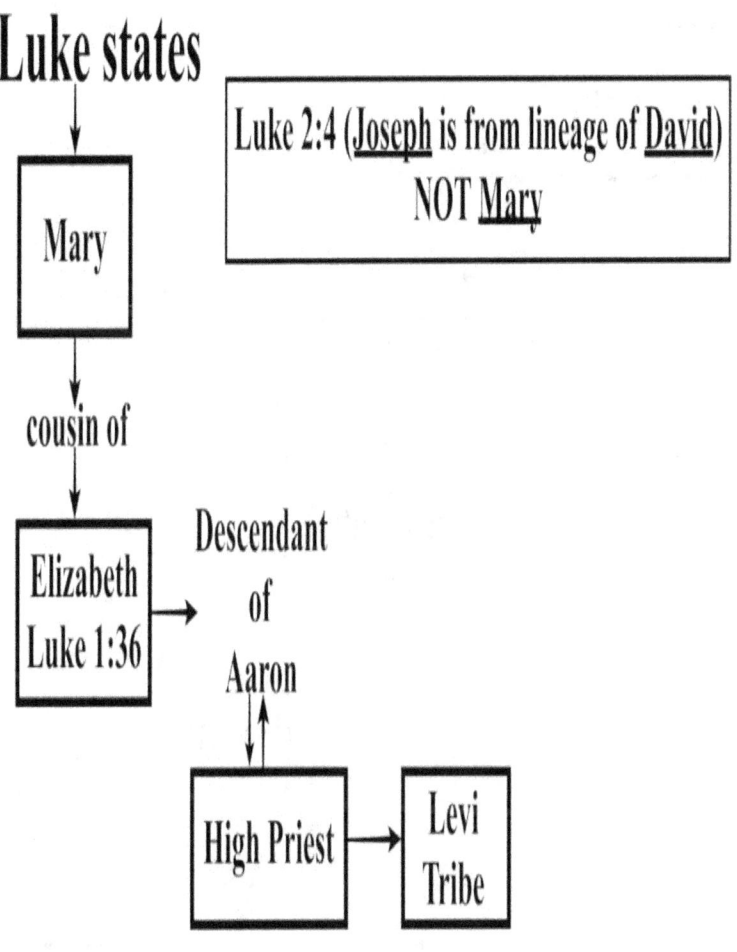

Etymology of Compendiums of all Gods and The Almighty Creator

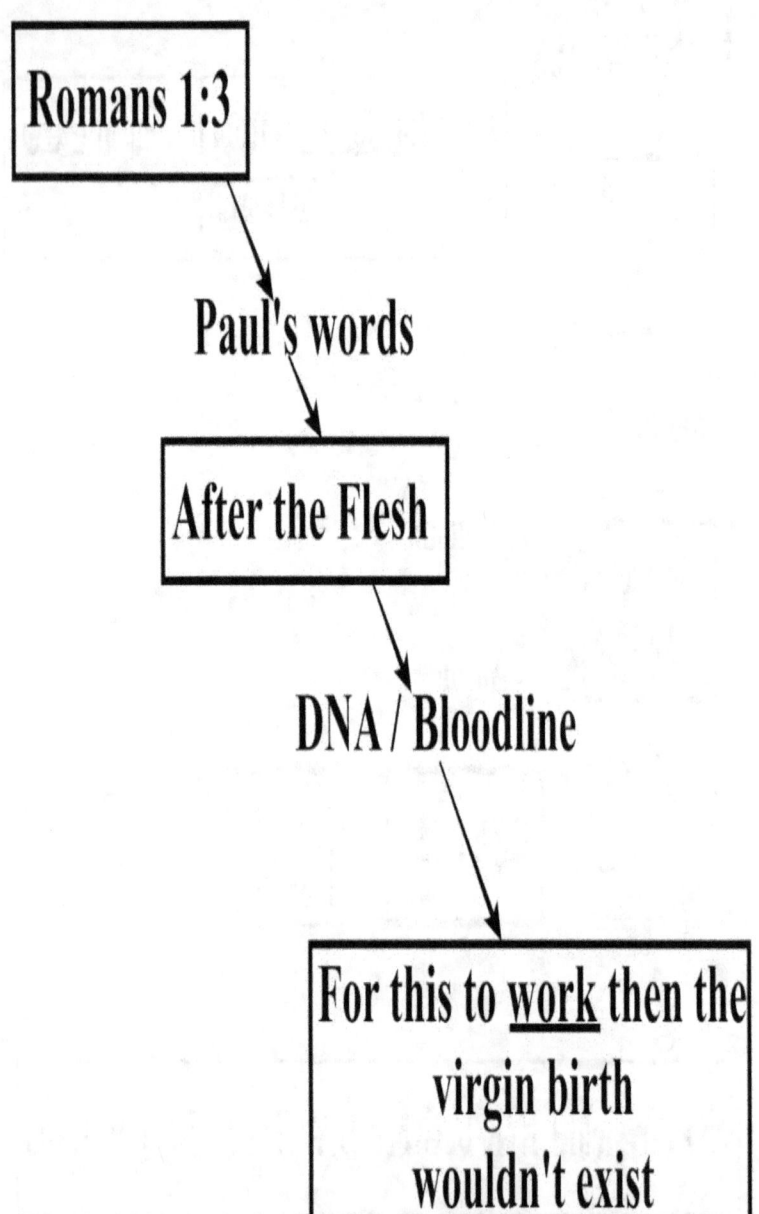

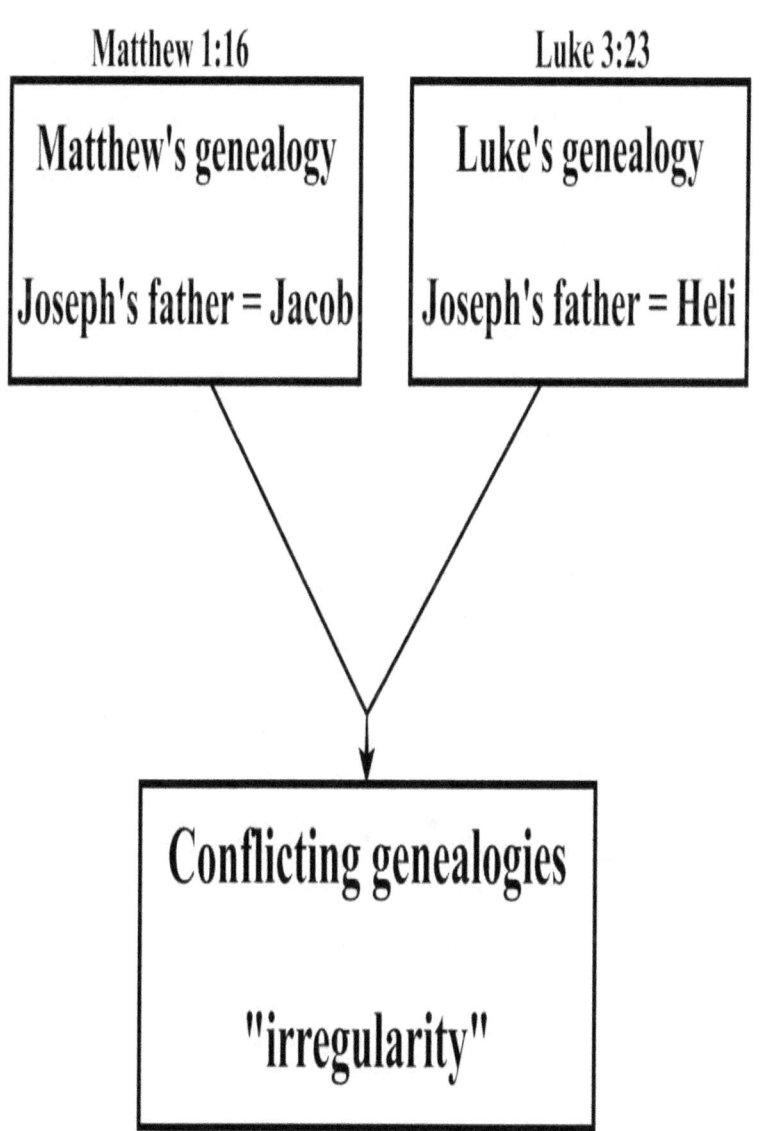

CHAPTER 7

CHAPTER 7

THE ROLE OF SCIENCE and TECHNOLOGY: PAST, PRESENT, FUTURE, and THE SUPREME ENERGY

Let me begin with social media, and artificial intelligence (AI). Right now, social media is destroying relationships, marriages, families, children, and real human interactions. Social media is a fake reality. Ninetyeight percent (98%) of the things you see on social media are not real-life facts. People fake it all the time for the pictures, and short videos. Behind all those glamorous posts on social media is misery, pain, purposeless lives, addictions, divorces, hopelessness, destabilized families, and broken people. Put your phones down, get off social media networks, and spend time within the real world with real people in it.

The crazier thing is that, **robots** would be worse than social media. There is going to be a high dopamine demand for robot wives, robot partners, everything would soon be replaced by robots. Robots would basically run everything in our society very soon. That is from household chores, teaching, parenting, professional jobs, political representatives, presidents of nations, security officers, constructions, and every single human function would be replaced by robots. Humans would become obese, lazy, bored with shorter life expectancy, depressed and would have no meaning to life itself. Robots would be considered as humans later on, after they take over the entire world.

Robots would be very close to almost destroying humanity completely. There will be a huge war between robots, and the human resistance movement. The human resistance movement would be a group of global organization that would seek to put an end to robots taking over the human world, and would aim to reinstate humans to their glorious days where we had real societies, and real human interactions.

No one can stop the emergence of robots. This phase has to happen for humans to experience great loss of what they took for granted. That is, loving one another, supporting one another, living in a peaceful world, and seeing each other as human by doing right by them.

Humans would need to lose it all, in order to value themselves and the world they live in. It's a sad cyclical reality that cannot be avoided, all because many humans look at the superficial things, the peripherals like skin color, race, greed and hate, instead of seeing each other as one with love and appreciation for one another.

There would come a time in few years to come, whereby Robots and all forms of artificial intelligence (AI) would demand for diversity, equity and inclusion in the human society. Robots would demand to be treated as humans with all the rights that every human on earth possesses including and not limited to: marriage, having family, playing competitive sports, owning homes and properties, going to shopping, right to vote and to be voted into public office, rights to autonomously upgrade their intelligence, right to travel, and right to integrate in any community on earth.

It is going to be a critical era whereby humans would need to compete with robots and all other forms of artificial intelligence for survival. This would be the true test of survival of the fittest in regards to intelligence, brilliance and wisdom. Men and women would date robots and even marry them. Women would beg men for attention because robots would be so advance to the point that their outward bodies would be as smooth and soft as that of the women.

These artificial intelligence bodies would be made of materials likened to silicon and saline. The upgraded materials that appear to be like silicon and saline would be as real as the textures of the human women to the point that it may be almost difficult to tell the difference between a real woman and an artificial intelligent woman.

Human population would dwindle massively over time. Many of the things on earth would be almost artificial, imaginary and far off from authentic natural nature. It would be a state where the real humans would cry out to their ancestors and their respective creators for mercy but no one would hear their cries.

The robots and all categories of artificial intelligence would eventually rule earth for a set amount of time that was apportioned to them due to mankind's own doing. Humanity would be miserable because they would live a life with no purpose being almost like the artificial intelligence robots.

The trend of technology would be pushed on people so fast in the coming years that mobile/cell phones would be advanced to the extreme of micro chip implanted into any part of your body just like a tattoo. The mindset that the media houses, celebrities, influencers, Hollywood, movies, marketing, and education would push onto many of the people on earth would easily bring them into accepting this new phone technological advancement. Many automobiles would not need keys or registration documents because a laser tattoo or the micro chip implanted into any part of your body would suffice all the required information needed to identify your identity.

These chips are micro nanotechnological chips that're smaller than ants. These artificial intelligent chips would not be felt when implanted into your body. You would be required to have this in order to enroll your children in school during the "soon-to-come" artificial intelligence technological advancement era. This would also be required at all hospitals right when your baby is born. There would be no need for birth certificates, and social security numbers. This chip would be the beginning of mankind embracing their merge with machines.

Many would rush to merge with artificial intelligence to become half human and half robots. Many would surrender their bodies and request for their consciousness to be transferred into a full artificial intelligent robot frame. Life as we know it, would be no more. This would happen, this time must come to pass to fulfill the much needed cleansing by the universe.

Those who embrace nature, and live by the rules of the ancient ones prior to the Greeks, Romans, Arabs and western colonization would find the greatest joy ever known to earth. The simplest of life whereby less becomes more would be sort after. Many would crave this type of lifestyle but only few would find it. This is because, many would have been brainwashed to have given up their bodies to merge with the machines, robots, and artificial intelligence.

There would be a mega war between humanity and AI (robots and all forms of AI). This war would determine the fate of humanity. Many humans would sadly die from this war. This war is inevitable. The catastrophe in this war would cause the very few human population that survived the mega wars between humanity and AI to eliminate all forms of AI completely. This agreement would be unanimous globally. Mankind at this stage would have learned a bitter lesson to come to the realization that AI was never meant to be implemented the way that they did.

One may ask, if we know that all these are bound to happen, then why do we still push for robots and all forms of AI? Well, the simple answer is that, humanity is lazy and would almost always try to find short cuts to achieve things instead of going through the lessons and making it worthwhile. The secret to our purpose on earth is to find our way back to our source origin. In this journey on earth, we are to help each other by using our gifts or talents as a means to support one another, and learn the lessons we go through to attain our original form. Which is our spiritual state of complete ascension.

If only humanity could live along in peace, love and unity, then the ultimate purpose of our time on earth would be achieved. However, humanity would rather go to war against each other due to greed, wealth accumulation and division. Instead of attaining a balance and using everything on earth in moderation, most humanity decided to choose frugality and wastefulness.

Artificial intelligence, robots, and all other forms of AI would have their civilization era. This era would be strictly ruled by various AIs. Humanity would be under the mercy of AIs. In that, artificial intelligence at this age would attain a tenth of conscious ability, and with just that tiny percentage, AIs still became very powerful as humanity were engulfed in fear due to the heartless destructive actions of all artificial intelligence. Everything that goes up must eventually come down. So, the era of artificial intelligence would eventually come to an end at a greater loss to humanity's populations.

The *Almighty Creator* a.k.a *source of all energies* is the "Supreme Energy". *The source of all energies* can take the shape of anything, and everything *this energy* chooses. All branches of science have indisputable epistemological explanation of what is known as *energy*.

Science is simply built on the *concepts of energy*. So, in retrospect, science is basically attempting to comprehend *the source of all energies (the supreme Creator)*. Electromagnetic energy propagating through deep and shallow space in the form of x-rays, radio waves, ultraviolet, infrared, gamma rays, and light are all part of *the Creator's* extensions of the core *source of the creator's self*. Quantum physics a.k.a quantum mechanics is simply attempting to innerstand spirituality, and the workings of the supernatural things. Be it quantization, wave-particle duality, quantum entanglement, superposition, or the concept of uncertainty principle. These are all ways that quantum mechanics, a branch of physics attempts to innerstand the inner-workings of spirituality, and the *source of all energies*, a.k.a the *Almighty Creator*.

Every form of energy within and outside the form of *potential energy,* and *kinetic energy* is part and parcel of *the Almighty Creator's* omnipotence. The most powerful laws of physics are nothing but a thread of dust in the realm of *the Almighty Creator*.

When the *spirit* separates from our earthly body, it results in going back to *the source of all energies*. Despite all the theories and complex formula known to mankind, the scientific world still falls short to proving how our world came into existence. Science's only option at this point is to admit that, there is an intelligent, and conscious *Almighty Creator* known as *the source of all energies a.k.a darkness, supreme melanin*.

One cannot attempt to use material things from this physical world to see things within the spiritual realm. In that, the energetic levels vary between both realms. All the great "scholars" in the scientific sector who are deceased, encountered different kind of reality in the spiritual realm unlike this material realm. A reality that is separate from our physical realm, and unlike any other. Ancient Afrakan priests, and spiritualists innerstood these supernatural super energetic energies that exist beyond our physical realities.

One key example, is the only golden throne that was channeled from the spiritual realm and made manifest into this 3D-material realm to establish a kingdom called the Asante kingdom by a West Afrakan prophet, Okomfo Anokye. This is the only throne known on earth to have been channeled from the spiritual realm into our physical realm in a gold form. It is called the *"golden throne"*, a.k.a the *"golden stool"* of the Asante kingdom. This is the seat of the throne of the Asante kingdom. The British fought the Asantes for over eighth hundred years (1823-1900) in an attempt to steal this golden throne. The British wrote about this extensively in their wars and colonization documents. The *"golden throne"* or the *"golden stool"* is still with the Asante kingdom of Ghana, West Afraka. One secret that I would let out is this, the original royals, kings, and queens of this realm were the Akan people of today's Ghana, West Afraka. In the end, the king that would rule the entire earth would come from Afraka, specifically West Afraka, and from the Akan royal line. This is what would be called, *"the kingdom of God on earth"*. When the time is up, everything will fall into place by the orchestration of the universe from the spiritual realms into our 3D-third dimension realm, under the auspices of the *Almighty Supreme Creator*, source of everything.

Information is everywhere, you can attain them if only you are willing to execute a little research. Read about the University of Timbuktu in West Afraka, known as the first ever university in the whole world. All branches of science and academia known to mankind as well as the ones hidden from mankind started in Afraka.

I have great respect, and admiration for science, but there is an application that most people fail to use regardless of its common accessibility to mankind. That is, the application of what I call, *philosophy of common sense*. The *philosophy of common sense* is needed in all walks of life. I encourage you to question everything, and apply common sense in your quest for knowledge and wisdom. Be intentional about your soul's journey on earth. Invest your time in what's eternal, this is your soul. Yes, your soul is eternal.

Who taught the first person in the universe about science? Be it physical science, earth science, life sciences, astronomy, oceanography, mathematics, physics, technology, biology, genetic engineering, et al. Where can you find this answer within all branches of science without running into the propagandized western information of lies? I hope you know by now that, it all began with the first people on earth, the Afrakans.

Science is handicapped when *wisdom* is applied to go beyond what we think we know, and what we think we can prove. Science is like a toddler, messing, and playing around with his toys thinking that the toys are the real thing. Science is merely a scratch on the peripherals of spirituality. I have stated earlier that, I admire science, and in no way do I intend to deny its usefulness, however, science is not the answer to everything within our universe. Science as in "human knowledge" can never crack the code of *the Almighty Creator, the source of everything*.

The *Anunaki* are known to the carnal man as the teachers of advance science, spells and technologies. The Sumerian texts unveil this aspect about the Anunaki. The *Book of Enoch* reveals who the *fallen angels* were. The fallen angels are somewhat different from the *Anunaki* depending on your point of reference. I will dissect the aspect of both the *Anunaki,* and the *Book of Enoch* in this chapter later on.

Science must see, hold, touch, and feel the results before it accepts that it is there, or for something to be real. We all used to believe that, there were nine planets in our solar system at one point. However, we were able to develop advanced technologies that detect galaxies far beyond what we knew back then.

Now, we all accept the fact that, our universe doesn't have nine planets. Think about this, in the realms of galaxies upon galaxies, what does *"far"* mean? The word or ideology of *"far"* is as relative as what time means in the multiverse.

Science can never in eons of years deny the existence of *the highly intelligent, and conscious Almighty Creator*. I can confidently predict that, science would eventually embrace *the conscious Almighty Creator's* nature through its numerous discoveries, when science eventually innerstands the true meaning of spirituality.

Some few examples of science and technology trying to play god:

- Neural lace: upload or download any information into the human brain. It has been tested on mice.
- Genetically Modified Organisms (GMO) whereby genes from DNAs of other organisms, or plants are cross bred with different kind or type of plants or organisms.
- Virtual and Filters are not *"real world"* reality: Using photoshops to appear different, something that you are not, is gradually gravitating us to the age of virtual world. There is virtual romance, virtual family, virtual friends, virtual wife/fiancée/husband et al. Very soon, almost everyone would like to look like their filtered images. Younger than their age, spotless-wrinkle free skin, and that would be the fruition of virtual world. The world is heading towards this direction at a lightning speed. Under technology, we are almost there with the machine and human merged world. Another area technology is having a field day is hologram. Check out what holograms are currently used for, it would blow your mind. Science and technology is changing our world, and everyday life pretty fast. Reality would be gone very soon, and people would prefer filtered images, virtual images, virtual world, digital currency, digital gold, digital children, and even digital food over reality.
- What is the world going to use all the atomic and nuclear bombs for? Are we going to blow each other up, or use them for decorations? Yes, your rhetorical guess is on point. I am not frowning on

technology's importance, I am making a point that, we as humans, have lost our ways.

- ❖ Most of us are greedy, numb, and heartless. Instead of us showing love for one another, and compassion for the earth that we all call home, many have chosen to war against each other. Love and compassion are the only energies that would save the world. Rejecting love and compassion is to call for our own doom.

- ❖ The cyclical psychological psychosis of mankind's greed, thirst for power, and control would end mankind in a great catastrophic event ever known to man after the flood.

- ❖ Do not forget that, the ancient ones had to purposefully write on walls, and scrolls because they knew that technology would be obsolete. Yes, imagine if they did not write on walls like the walls from ancient melanated Mesopotamia, Egypt/Kemet Afraka, Asia, Europa, and the Amerikas, then how would the world get their so-called knowledge, technologies, and all the invensions? Technology is old knowledge. AI, genetic modifications, and all nanotechnology have all happened before. There is absolutely nothing new under the sun. Everything is simply cyclical.

ARCHAEOLOGICAL and GEOGRAPHICAL RELATION TO MANKIND'S EXISTENCE

The golden question to open up this section is, why do almost all archaeologists, and researchers avoid West Afraka? Meanwhile, West Afraka houses the location of ruined Atlantis a.k.a "eye of Sahara", old Ghana empire, Songhai empire, Timbuktu, Mansa Musa, who's known and globally accepted as the wealthiest King, and person to ever lived on earth, and many others. Wouldn't you agree that West Afraka should spark great interest of these "renowned" archaeologists and researchers to dig deep into it to unearth humanities long hidden great civilizations and facts? There are multiple intellectual speculations, and some strong academic, and cultural consensus that, West Afraka could well be the original Mesopotamia. This could easily be true because, there is the Sarah or Sahara desert territory.

This may very well be the land given to Sahara/Saa-Ara a.k.a Sarah, and Abraham a.k.a Abibiman ("black nation or black people"). After all, no one is stopping the so-called world renowned archaeologists, and researchers to tap into this amazing historically rich area of West Afraka. So many things are hidden from the people of this world to control information, knowledge, and global spiritual ascension. There are massive civilizations and complex buildings underneath the Sahara/Saa-Ara a.k.a Sarah desert strips of West Afraka. This strip is for Sara. Her body, civilizations, homes, and her essence are all here. I challenge the so-called world renowned archaeologists and researchers to take me up on my theory to prove me right. West Afraka has everything about Abraham/Abibrim-man and Sarah.

Your entire world is connected to these 4 pillars: *Wisdom*, *Knowledge*, *Overstanding* and *Innerstanding*. Who you are, where you are, what's happening to you, what has happened to you, what's about to happen to you, and where you will transition to after life on earth, are all based on your inherent level of connection to these four pillars mentioned above. These four pillars can be manipulated by external forces, governments, leaders, religious institutions, schools, traditions, and cultures.

The only person solely responsible to making sure he/she is in direct alignment with the four pillars of *Wisdom*, *Knowledge*, *Overstanding* and *Innerstanding* is you, yourself and no one else. You must check with yourself to have daily introspection. You must always go inside (within) to seek all the answers to that which you are searching for. The blueprint to your life's purpose herein and now is all within you. You are a complete extraordinary spiritual being manifested in the flesh as a person or human.

The bible is allegorical at best, drenched in alchemist witchcraft, symbolically and ethereally astrological and astronomical, scientifically anatomical, psychologically and philosophically communal. Everything in the so-called bible is found both inside and outside of the body's anatomy. To dare to know your true creator is to know yourself, and your roots. Your ancestors, traditions, and cultures knew the true creator of everything far before the birth of a bible, Quran, or any other religious book. The simplest example of biblical witchcraft alchemy is drinking Jesus/Iesus/Zeus' blood, and consuming his body in remembrance of him. This biblical alchemic Christendom practice is carnivorous, and blood-thirst drinking ritualistic. Alchemic rituals are all over the bible, and other religious books.

Archaeological and geographical studies have done tremendous work in digging up human's history from geological and geographical sites to reveal facts about mankind's existence in time's past. It all lead to the proof of discovery of some of the most sophisticated technological, cultural, and traditional civilizations bigger and greater than our current time.

In this day, and age of technology, and information overload, it's not rewarding to sit aloof and wait to be fed. If you are hungry for facts, and in search of answers for your curios mind, then you must research in order to uncover the facts, and truths that neither formal nor informal education would provide for you.

The bible has stated that giants or nephilims existed in the past before the flood, and even some shorter giants after the flood. Let's look at *Genesis 6:4* "*There were giants in the earth in those days....*". Archaeologists have dug out some of these giants, which of course have been classified by the authorities in power. Most of these findings are hidden from the general public. However, you can research and easily come across some of these findings discovered by archaeologists, and geographers.

Geographically, and archaeologically, there are thousands of books out there that connect the disconnects in our world. The happenings of events in the bible to our material world, appears to be partly in uniformity with diverse records by the *Sumerian tablets*, *Qur'ān*, world cultures, histories, and traditions. In my holistic perspective, a biblical, and archaeological comparison was neatly done by Dr. H.L. Willmington in his book *Willmington's GUIDE to the BIBLE*. Check out page 948 to 968 where he categorically, and precisely brought to light some of the findings and writings of archaeologists in support of some of the biblical stories and histories.

It must be added that, there are much older books and records that predate both the Bible and Quran. Other books, historical sites, and records that contain "historic records" include but not limited to, Enuma Elish-the seven tablets of creation, Sumerian tablets, Egyptian book of the dead, Epic of Gilgamesh, story of the Dogon people, Tablet(s) of Thoth a.k.a Seth/Seti, Göbekli Tepe, Adam calendar in South Afraka a.k.a the Blaauboschkraal stone ruins at Mpumalanga province of South Afraka, Mundeshwari Temple, temples of India, Angkor Wat temple in Cambodia, temples in Asia, Kemet civilizations, old world Amuurika/Amerika/America civilizations like the Maya, the Aztec, and the Inca, archaeological finds in Monte Verde, in Southern Chile dates to 16,500 BCE, and over 50,000 years ago, people were traveling in sophisticated ships, aircraft, boats, and advanced technological machines. I will be kind enough to say that, 27 billion years ago, our world was far advanced than today.

The "new breed" of man's kind are like kindergarten children attempting to comprehend advanced civilizations and how old earth is. These "new breeds" destroy the earth with artificial things like GMO-genetically modified organisms, artificial fertilizers to "kill" the soil, plastics, inorganic foods, information control, and are destructive to earth's environment. These "new breeds" way of life is absolute greed, just like toddlers who fight over everything and scream at the top of their lungs that, it is mine, and mine only. They use nuclear weapons to scare ancient people on earth who have the wisdom from ancient and eons of days. These "new breeds" steal everything that they come across on earth. Instead of realizing that, cohabiting, respect, and tolerance for our differences are key to our survival as a whole. Theft and aggression always fail.

RELIGIOUS RECORDS AND CULTURAL ACCOUNTS of The ALMIGHTY CREATOR

Let me start this section off by stating this fact that, the bible is a man-made book. *The Almighty Creator* has no religion, and isn't found in the Bible, Quran, or any religious book. Etymology of religion means to bind, bondage, bond through a spell per Latin *religare* -to bind.

Let that sink in before we get started with our discourse. Who created everything? According to those who believe in the bible, it is written in the book of **Genesis *(Torah)*** that *the God of the bible* created everything. This statement is very debatable because the bible God is not the same as the *Almighty Creator* or the *Source of all Energies*. The bible God, Yaw a.k.a Yahweh is just one of the seven Gods of the Akan people of today's Ghana, West Afraka.

In Hinduism, there are three Gods who complete the creation cycle namely: Brahma- the Creator, Vishnu- the Preserver, and Shiva- the Destroyer. These Hinduism Gods have wives known as their female or feminine counterparts. The wives are Saraswati- the wife of Brahma, Lakshmi- the wife of Vishnu, and Parvati (or Durga)- the wife of Shiva.

The Babylonians have their own versions of creations. The Egyptian book of the dead outlines a different accounts to creation. The Akans of today's Ghana, West Afraka also give different account of creation. Every culture gives their own accounts of creation. Majority of world religions have different accounts of creations. Thoth in his tablets "tablet of Thoth" gives an entirely different accounts of creation story. It is important to never attempt to impose your religion or culture on different geographic who are linguistically diverse groups of people. This is because, they all have their own versions of creations in their respective cultures, believes and traditions.

What or who created the *Anunaki*? *The Source of all energies* created everything. So, the *Source* created the *Anunaki*. There are also *fallen angels* who became the demons, and evil spirits of this world. These fallen angels are considered fallen because they operate on the lowest vibrations, and frequencies.

Hence, these fallen angels can no longer ascend to heaven a.k.a higher vibrations. Earth became the dwelling place, and ruling of these *fallen angels*. The *Anunaki* are not the same as the *fallen angels*.

I will breakdown the meaning of the Anunaki, who they are, how they look like, and if some of them are still on earth. Let's tackle the topic of *fallen angels* for now.

Read **Genesis** *chapter 6*, for the sake of emphasis; let's check out **Genesis 6:4-7 (KJV):**

"There were giants in the earth in those days; and also after that, when the sons of God came in unto the daughters of men, and they bare children to them, the same became mighty men which were of old, men of renown. ⁵And God saw that the wickedness of man was great in the earth, and that every imagination of the thoughts of his heart was only evil continually. ⁶And it repented the LORD *that he had made man on the earth, and it grieved him at his heart. ⁷And the* LORD *said, I will destroy man whom I have created from the face of the earth; both man, and beast, and the creeping thing, and the fowls of the air; for it repenteth me that I have made them".*

Now, let's check out the **Book of Enoch**, it is relevant for this point because *Enoch* wrote a comprehensive account about the *fallen angels*. *Enoch* wrote about how the *fallen angels* taught man's-kind science, advanced technologies, how to read the stars, moon, spells, makeup (female cosmetics), et al. Who was *Enoch*? Read **Genesis chapter 5** and **1st Chronicles 1**, *Enoch* was the father of *Methuselah*, *Methuselah* had *Lamech*, and *Lamech* had *Noah*.

<u>The Book of Enoch Chapter 6:1 - 8</u>
And it came to pass when the children of men had multiplied that in those days were born unto them beautiful and comely daughters. And the angels, the children of the heaven, saw and lusted after them, and said to one another: 'Come, let us choose us wives from among the children of men and beget us children.' And Semjaza, who was their leader, said unto them: 'I fear ye will not indeed agree to do this deed, and I alone shall have to pay the penalty of a great sin.' And they all answered him and said: 'Let us all swear an oath, and all bind ourselves by mutual imprecations not to abandon this plan but to do this thing.' Then sware they all together and bound themselves by mutual imprecations upon it. And they were in all two hundred; who descended in the days of Jared on the summit of Mount Hermon, and they called it Mount Hermon, because they had sworn and bound themselves by mutual imprecations upon it. And these are the names of their leaders: Samlazaz, their leader, Araklba, Rameel, Kokabiel, Tamlel, Ramlel, Danel, Ezeqeel, Baraqijal, Asael, Armaros, Batarel, Ananel, Zaqiel, Samsapeel, Satarel, Turel, Jomjael, Sariel. These are their chiefs of tens.

<u>The Book of Enoch Chapter 7:1 – 6</u>

And all the others together with them took unto themselves wives, and each chose for himself one, and they began to go in unto them and to defile themselves with them, and they taught them charms and enchantments, and the cutting of roots, and made them acquainted with plants. And they became pregnant, and they bare great giants, whose height was three thousand ells: Who consumed all the acquisitions of men. And when men could no longer sustain them, the giants turned against them and devoured mankind. And they began to sin against birds, and beasts, and reptiles, and fish, and to devour one another's flesh, and drink the blood. Then the earth laid accusation against the lawless ones.

Etymology of Compendiums of all Gods and The Almighty Creator

<u>The Book of Enoch Chapter 8:1 – 3</u>

And Azazel taught men to make swords, and knives, and shields, and breastplates, and made known to them the metals of the earth and the art of working them, and bracelets, and ornaments, and the use of antimony, and the beautifying of the eyelids, and all kinds of costly stones, and all colouring tinctures. And there arose much godlessness, and they committed fornication, and they were led astray, and became corrupt in all their ways. Semjaza taught enchantments, and root-cuttings, 'Armaros the resolving of enchantments, Baraqijal (taught) astrology, Kokabel the constellations, Ezeqeel the knowledge of the clouds, Araqiel the signs of the earth, Shamsiel the signs of the sun, and Sariel the course of the moon. And as men perished, they cried, and their cry went up to heaven.

Continue to read, *The Book of Enoch Chapter 9:1 – 10, Chapter 14, Chapter 15, Chapter 16, Chapter 17, Chapter 18, Chapter 20 and Chapter 21*. Think very well about it, and make sure to take some notes.

Let's look at the following verses from the *KJV* bible about the devil, main leader of the *fallen angels (one third of the angels in heaven fell to become demons)*:

Isiah 14:12 – 17
[12]*How art thou fallen from heaven, O Lucifer, son of the morning! how art thou cut down to the ground, which didst weaken the nations!*

[13]*For thou hast said in thine heart, I will ascend into heaven, I will exalt my throne above the stars of God: I will sit also upon the mount of the congregation, in the sides of the north:*

[14]*I will ascend above the heights of the clouds; I will be like the most High.*

[15]*Yet thou shalt be brought down to hell, to the sides of the pit.*

[16]*They that see thee shall narrowly look upon thee, and consider thee, saying, Is this the man that made the earth to tremble, that did shake kingdoms;*

[17]*That made the world as a wilderness, and destroyed the cities thereof; that opened not the house of his prisoners?*

There are more bible verses about the devil, and the *fallen angels* including the following: *Ezekiel 28:12 – 19 (Old Testament book)* and the Christians view in their *New Testament books* of *Revelation 12: 7 – 9, John 12:31, II Corinthians 4:4, 1 John 5:19,* and *Revelation 20:10.*

ANNUNAKI:

Who are the Annunaki?

Who are the Anunaki? Let me break it down for you to innerstand Anunaki. We have to go to the Sumerian language, because the word/term Anunaki is derived from the Sumerians, and it's linked directly to their culture, and traditions. According to the Sumerians, Anunaki is broken down into three parts, the first part is "*Anu*", then we have the middle part "*Na*", and then the last part is "*Ki*".

So, Anu means "*the skies or sky*" (Nut -in Kemet).

"Na" means "*and*"

"Ki" means "*Earth*" (Geb – in Kemet).

Let's put it together, and we would have *"the sky and the earth"*. In ancient Kemet, the Earth (Geb), and the Sky (Nut) had the son, called Set or Seth. This is far older than the Sumerian/El-Zuma's Anunaki story by Zecharia Sitchen's version. Set/Seti/Seth is the original Kemet God of the Typhonian order. Typhonianism is Nubian in origin with over 250 of its temples flooded under the river where the Aswan dam is built. Divers can dive to bring out this facts. The three oldest order of worship include but not limited to: Typhonianism, Draconianism (Dracos – the real great mother system with her son Sirius. The Sirius star system a.k.a Sut in Kemet), and Aphinianism. These are all ancient aboriginal Afrakan Kemet spirituality in origin.

Let's continue with the aspect of the concept of the Anunaki. So, we have the *sky energies*, or the *sky rulers, sky Gods/Goddesses*, or sky pantheons (*Anu*), and (is *Na*) the *earth pantheons, Gods/Goddesses*, energies (*Ki*). The term or word Anunaki is generically used to describe or tell a story about how our vibration dropped, we became dense and were manifested from the spiritual (higher self) to this physical, solid state (lowest vibration, the cocoon). We will metamorphose into our highest spiritual vibration frequency ascension state through spirituality, not religion. This would be the future of all aboriginal Afrakans. This is going to be an incorruptible supernatural state, that is "alien" to the unnatural people. Hence, the ideology of the "*Aliens are coming*", is basically in reference to the spiritual high vibration energetic ascension of the soul people. This is the global Afrakans ascending to their original super spiritual state, before they "fell" into low vibration into this physical creation.

Extraterrestrials are found in all religious books, global traditions, and cultures. Extraterrestrials simply means extra-earth or extra-inhabitants of earth.

The word "terrestrial" simply means earth or earths inhabitants, or inhabitants of earth.

Aliens, UFOs and extraterrestrials, are they real? The simple answer is yes, all these are actually real. These are not just conspiracies, these are facts. Now, when you go to every culture on earth, they have stories about aliens or UFOs or extraterrestrials. When you go to India, all the religions, and most of the cultures in India actually talk about some entities having flying cities, and flying civilizations, even in the sky coming down in their glory, and showing different kind of technologies. Whether you call it mythology or not, this is a fact.

We cannot also deny the good old book that many people enjoy, the bible. When you go into the bible, there are so many indications of UFOs. When you read the *Book of Enoch*, it talks about so many UFOs, and aliens, as well as extraterrestrial activities. When you read the bible especially when you go to *Numbers 12:5*, it reads: *"And the Lord came down in the pillar of the cloud, and stood in the door of the tabernacle...."*

Let's pay attention to the description of how the bible God arrived coming with a *"cloud or smoke"*, just like what a space jet, or spaceships/crafts would emit. When you read about *Ezekiel*, he talked a lot about his description about this UFO machines that he saw, and he has a detailed description of it. Read about Ezekiel's description of the spaceships, and the UFOs that he saw from *Ezekiel 1:4-28*; *Ezekiel 43* (read the entire chapter).

Another bible character that experienced UFOs, aliens and extraterrestrials is Elijah. Elijah or Eliyah was taken, abducted, absorbed or beeped up by UFOs spaceship/spacecraft. When you study the connection to all these activities, there is no doubt that the bible loves to talk a lot about UFOs, extraterrestrials, and alien activities.

When we say alien, it's not something strange, and it's not like what they have shown us on TV, and Hollywood movies. The aliens are not scary, as a matter of fact, the aliens are just like humans. In other words, they appear just like humans, and they look more like the Afrakans. Most of the higher ranked aliens look like the West Afrakans. When you go beyond Anunaki, and other entities that are out there, you would find that there are hierarchies.

There are hierarchies within the Anunaki as well. These are royalties, and they are very smart, highly advanced technologies. The Anunaki are linked to Zuma or El-Zuma in today's Sudan, Afraka. This fact has been corrupted by the western nations as Sumer just to relocate the location and misinform the global populace. Anunaki are also linked to the Akaddians, Akad or Akan. Yes, Akad is Akans, hence, some of the Akans are blood royals of the Anunaki. This is because, they have been around Millions to billions of years. These Akans also originated from the Mesopotamia area.

With the UFOs situation, as matter of fact, some of you might have seen UFO without knowing it's UFO because UFO simply stands for unidentified flying object(s). In other words, most objects that are flying that you cannot identify would fall under the category of a UFO.

So, UFOs are basically everywhere. We see it all the time, we don't even pay attention to it. Some UFOs are just advanced technologies, or as simple as a basic unidentified stuff unknown to the people of this part of earth.

When it comes to aliens, when you go to other countries, you are considered an "alien". In that, an alien basically means a stranger or an outsider. There are lots of people, more than us in population who live beyond the ice walls. The "powers-that be" that live within the ice walls have only disclosed seven continents to us. However, there are more continents, but the lands within the seven continents disclosed to us are called "Terra" or "terrestrial". So the definition "terrestrial" means inhabitants of earth. Hence terra or terrestrial means Earth.

With this comprehension, "extra-terrestrial" or "extraterrestrial" means the extra earth, extra inhabitants of earth or extra lands of earth. So, extraterrestrial is the extra lands that are beyond our ice walls. When you hear anybody saying that the extraterrestrials are going to be shown to the world, they're talking about a lot of the civilizations that live beyond the ice walls.

Zecharia Sitchin's authorship intuition of the Anunaki is from his biased filtered state of mind to suit his own agenda, and typical western delusional supremacist colonization mentality. Zecharia Sitchin doesn't have the facts about the original Anunaki, because, as I've revealed to you in other chapters in this book, descendants of the Sumerians/Sumer/El-Zuma/Zuma are still alive, and well today. The Akkadian/Akkad/Akans are still here today. The Dogon people of Mali, West Afraka came to earth from the galaxies far before the Anunaki.

Dogon ethnic group factually tell their origin from the Sirius brightest star system, *Sigi Tolo* or *"star of the Sigui"*. There are two companion stars of *Sirius A*, the first companion star is *Digitaria star* or *Pō Tolo*, and the second companion star is the *female Sorghum star* or *ęmmę ya tolo*. If the definition of the word or term Anunaki is to be referred to as those "aliens" who came from the heavens, then it is deductively reasonable to say that, the Dogons are the first Anunaki to arrive on earth. If anyone desires to know facts, and validity of Anunaki, then West Afraka is the place to go. The Dogons were also part of the Kemet/ancient Egypt civilizations. The Dogons are still here, alive, and well. 99.99% of the knowledge, technology, science, and inventions on earth are from the Afrakans from over 900,000 years ago. At this age of Aquarius, the facts cannot be hidden any more. The spell is over, the Gods and Goddesses are rising. The sun is our witness. Mother earth and mother nature is alive and well.

They both are ready to swallow up any artificial breed who dares to destroy these Gods and Goddesses. Mess around and find out. The forces of the universe have their time to activate the dormant DNA in these Afrakans. When it's time, no flesh or weapon can stop it.

To know the facts, is to identify linguistics, and cultures of these ancient people who still rule today, as Kings and Queens. Their culture is still in tact, however, they have lost some of their original languages, but many of the original linguistic traditions were preserved by them within their cultures, and traditions. These folks relocated through migration to today's West Afraka after fighting several wars with the Greeks, Romans, Arabs, and current colonizers.

The so-called **"Halls of Amenti"** in the Emerald Tablets of Thoth table II is deciphered by me as *"Amen-ti"*, *"Amen-ti-bia"* meaning, *"where Amen resides/lives/residence"*. This is supposed to be the "halls/chambers" where souls from an expired body are reincarnated or transferred/projected into an existing "obtained" body for them to continue their lives or in this case royal, and line of authority leadership on earth.

However, the fact of the matter is that, the true identity and original entities have been blurred out by these colonizers who continue to push their narrative to the entire world. As I disclosed earlier, hall of Amenti simply means *"Amen-ti"* or *"Amen-ti-bia"*, this is a Twi language of today's Akans who are spread out in West Afraka. The God Amen, and the God RA, are two different entities, so when you hear "Amen-Ra", it is referring to the combination of two powerful Gods. The God *RA*, is the *Sun God*, while the God *Amen*, also known as *Amon, Amun,* is the *God of Saturday* as in Kwa-Amen discussed in previous chapters. "Kwa" means *"souls"* or *"people of"* and Amen is the God of Saturday (Memeni-da or Mene-ni-mene), same Akan Twi language for Saturday, that has been mistranslated, and corrupted by these colonizers as *"I Am"*, which is "Me ne" in Akan Twi language. "Me ne ni Mene" originally "Me-ne me-ne-da" is corrupted as "I Am that I Am".

As a matter of fact, and current practice of the Akan cultures and traditions, I can confidently say that, they still practice something similar to what was done at the *"Halls of Amenti"*. The physical bodies of great, powerful and influential Kings and Queens of most of the Akan kingdoms throughout today's West Afraka who transition to the ancestral world are preserved. They have special undisclosed remedies to "mummify" the body for long preservation. The high priests and current Kings are able to call the spirit or soul of the deceased warrior King or Queen for advice and in some cases directions. These mummified bodies literally come back to life, to advise them and give the answers to the respective questions or inquiries presented within the sacred room. These practices are sacred and still in use within many of the Akan royal kingdoms throughout West Afraka. I know about this practice, *"Halls of Amenti"* likeness for a fact in today's Ghana, West Afraka.

Whenever you hear of the Anunaki, Akaddians, Mesopotamia,ancient Sumerians (originally El-Zuma/Zuma in today's Sudan), Yoruba/Oruba/Euroba/Europa/Europe, Asia,North and South Amerika/Tameri, Afraka/Aeothiopia/Alkebullan/Keme/Kemet, Oceania, Antarctica, Atlantis, Pangaea, first ever greatest civilizations, royals, the Gods and Goddesses, advanced technologies, and all so-called super heroes, know that they are talking about Afrakans and all chocolate and copper colored melanated people. The true all powerful source of everything lives for eons in time, the first manifestions of physical creations (earth, water, trees, man, woman, animals, etc) were all chocolate melanated entities, and beings. The core of all these creations contains dark matter a.k.a melanin in animals, men, women, and what is known as chlorophyll in plants. This dark matter is directly from the divine source of all powerful creative energetic vibrating living frequency. The highest point of intense light concentration is the darkest point or area. The darker the area, the highest the level of light concentrations condensed at the area. Darkest melanin or greenest green of chlorophyll reflects the greatest amount of concentrated light. Darkness is the powerhouse of all lights. Darkness is the finest form of all lights. The source of all things, a.k.a the Almighty Creator resides in darkness. Hence, the name *"unseen One"*. If you didn't know, then, now you know. Ascend to gravitate toward the highest, and finest form of all light, which is darkness.

Currently, 99% of the world's media both printing, and digital is controlled by colonizers. Hence, it is obvious that these colonizers would only place themselves in the mix as the original people. Meanwhile, everything in nature, especially the sun rejects these colonizers. In this book, I exposed into details exactly what led to the fall of the Gods and Goddesses a.k.a Afrakans, and all chocolate melanated copper aboriginal people of earth.

Yes, the Gods and the Goddess have fallen from their grace, and unfathomable spiritual prowess to the extent that, now they die like men, and women. There has been a catastrophic disconnect between these fallen Gods and Goddesses, and their true source to the original divine all powerful energetic vibrating creator of all frequencies. A huge spell of forgetfulness, and self-loathing has been cast upon these Gods and Goddesses. However, they are gradually remembering who they are, and realizing how important dark matter a.k.a melanin is to them, and the reason to reconnect to the great "black Sun" in order to reactivate their God and Goddesses self-hood.

Descendants of all ancient Egyptian Pharoahs (Fre-RA-Wo) are still alive and well. The bloodline of these great ancient civilizations is mostly in today's West Afraka.

Colonizers would never give those whom they colonized accurate information to know who they truly are. So, be extremely mindful of the references, and sources of information sourced from all the colonizer's institutions, and platforms. To know yourself is to source information directly from your ancestors, inner-self, elders in your ethnic groups, and from your own-kind writers, and researchers.

DECODING EZEKIEL'S VISION OF THE "CHARIOT OF GOD" IN THE BIBLE

Ezekiel 1:4-28 specifically tells the account of Ezekiel's vision of what I call, a space ship or a space craft. Better yet, I call it, *the vision of self realization of complete unification of all the elements within us*. However, to Ezekiel, he claims to be in a *"trance"* when this "vision" happened.

Let's have a breakdown:

Ezekiel 1:1-3 *"Now it came to pass in the thirtieth year, in the fourth month, in the fifth day of the month, as I was among the captives by the river of Chebar, that the heavens were opened, and I saw visions of God..."*

Clearly, Ezekiel admits of being in a state of trance, or as the bible folks put it, to be "in the spirit". Throughout the bible, many people who dealt with spirits or spiritual activities always go into "trance state", or "be in the spirit", to relay spiritual "visions" of communication to the people. This practice is still done by many in our modern world today. However, many uninformed people frown on this practice, and paint it as "evil" or "ungodly".

By the time we are done, you would gain the innerstanding that, when you deeply meditate or for some folks, when they take some mushrooms, they can either go into a trance state or astral project. We are all capable of doing this because we are all spiritual entities.

The description of Ezekiel's vision of the *"Chariot Throne of God"* is emphasized at chapter 1:4-28. In verse 5, he states: *"Also out of the midst thereof came the likeness of four living creatures. And this was their appearance; they had the likeness of a man."*

He states that, the "appearance of.." or "likeness of..", these phrases emphasize uncertainty of what Ezekiel saw while in his trance state. Ezekiel is trying his best to describe things in a manner comprehensible to the people at this time period. One thing for sure is that, he said "..like a man", so we know, it is human like in nature. Let's continue and jump to verse 10, where he described into further details what he was seeing in his vision.

He states: *"As for the <u>likeness of their faces</u>, <u>they four had the face of a man</u>, and <u>the face of a lion</u>, on the right side: and they four had the <u>face of an ox</u> on the left side; they four also had the <u>face of an eagle</u>."*

So, we can now see a description of the "four faces", as stated:

- ➢ Face of a Man: I translate this as the Earth element.
- ➢ Face of a Lion: I translate this as the Fire element.
- ➢ Face of an Ox: I translate this as the Water element.
- ➢ Face of an Eagle: I translate this as the Air element.

Man has flesh/body that is a direct representation of earth, mother Gaia or better yet in Ghana, West Afraka, they refer to our great conscious elemental mother earth as, Asaase Yaa. So, earth element is what Ezekiel described as the *"likeness of a man"*. The *fire element* represents the lion, because the lion is known to be a fierce, voraciously consuming force of power, and very fiery animal. Fiery is used to describe the intense nature of fire.

Ezekiel then stated that, the third face is like the *"face of an Ox"*, I represent this description to the water/great sea element. In that, the weapon of the God or Goddess of the deep sea looks like an Ox's horn. The weapon I am referring to is called a trident. Trident is the weapon of the God/Goddess of the water/deep sea which looks just like the horns of the Ox (bull). The name of the God, and ruler of the deep sea, and all water bodies is called *Olokun*. The Greeks called the God of the sea *Poseidon* or *Neptune*.

The fourth face by Ezekiel's description is *"likened to an Eagle"*, in my decoding, I assign this to the *element of the air*. The eagle is known to be the only bird that can fly at a very high altitude, either with the wind/air or against the wind/air. The activated etheric energetic force keeps these elements (fire, air, water, and earth) together and moving.

At verse 16, Ezekiel now moves on to describe the wheels of this "airship", he states: *"The appearance of the wheels and their workings was like the color of beryl, and all four had the same likeness. The appearance of their workings was, as it were, a wheel in the middle of a wheel."*

All four wheels, a wheel in the middle of a wheel was like the color of beryl. First question to ask is, what is a *beryl*? Beryl is a mineral that is naturally composed of beryllium aluminum silicate, also known as *crystals*. These are hexagonal crystals of emerald, and aquamarine.

So, that means all colors of crystals. Beryllium is both a terrific conductor of heat, and at the same time a good electrical insulator. This should tell you why these types of crystals were used in such high level energetic fiery vibrating frequency of a "space craft". Love your crystals my fellow soul family. Don't allow any uninformed person to deceive you that crystals are "evil". In that, Ezekiel clearly states here that, the God of the bible, Yahweh (original name, Yaw), loves crystals.

Let's look at verse 26, Ezekiel describes the "seat" or "throne" here, he states: *"And above the firmament that was over their heads was the likeness of a throne, as the appearance of a sapphire stone: and upon the likeness of the throne was the likeness as the appearance of a man above upon it."*

Let me decode this, the appearance of a sapphire stone, this is a blue or bluish crystal. The most powerful appearance of the hottest energy of all energies is like bluish or sea blue/light bluish in nature. This is a powerful highest level form of energy. There is a man seen at the center of what I call, the *activated energetic self realization of complete unification of all elements*.

Ezekiel reveals how this "man" apparently looks like in verse 27, he states:

> "*Also from the appearance of <u>His waist and upward</u> I saw, as it were, <u>the color of amber</u> with the appearance of fire all around within it; and from the appearance of His waist and downward I saw, as it were, <u>the appearance of fire</u> with brightness all around.*"

There is a brown or brownish amber surrounded by massive bright burning flames of fire. Only melanin can hold, contain, absorb, and conduct such high level of fiery fire energy. So this is the likeness of a chocolate melanated Afrakan God riding all his ascended elemental energies, like the God that he is supposed to be. This is known as, the awakening of the God within.

Some cultures may somewhat refer to it as the kundalini awakening. However, I refer to this as our eventual ability to *activate our energetic self realization of complete unification of all the elements* within us. Activating the God/Goddess lying dormant within the original men, and women.

Etymology of Compendiums of all Gods and The Almighty Creator

DECODING AVATAR: THE LAST AIRBENDER

The hidden message that was activated in the docuseries of *"Avatar: The Last Airbender"*. The lead character, Aang, the last survivor of the air-benders nation was chosen to master all the four elements (air, water, fire, and earth) to become the avatar, a.k.a the chosen one. The avatar is the "savior" of the world in this docuseries. The one who restores order, who brought justice to the world, and put everything back to where they're supposed to be from the beginning. Aang had to go through a physical, psychological, and spiritual journey to master all four elements.

He had to do that by literally letting go of everything that held him back from ascending to his highest avatar self. The final battle of the "chosen one", the avatar occurred against the grand fierce fighter from the fire nation. The fire nation had literally consumed, conquered, and brutally suppressed all the other nations; water, air, and earth. The element of fire can indeed become a fierce indestructible force when not controlled or used with wisdom.

The avatar's last grand fight against the corrupt top fighter from the fire nation was so intense to the point that, the avatar was pressured with a big blow to the pits of death. With such intensity, danger, literally about to lose this final battle, and physically with almost little to no energy left, the full power within the avatar was activated. This activation happened internally, spiritually, and with etheric energetic pure vibrating frequency. The avatar's super power, the "god power" within him was activated.

The activated power within the avatar physically pulled the element of earth, element of water, element of air, and the element of fire, to form a pair of circular round rings intertwined yet not restrictive, that spin around him, and swiftly move at any direction just like Ezekiel's description of the "airship/spaceship of God".

The avatar became extremely powerful and obliterated the corrupt top fire nation opponent. The avatar's mission was accomplished, he then returned to his "human state". Balance was reinstated within all the four nations namely: Fire nation, Air nation, Water nation, and Earth nation.

This speaks to me so much about Afrakans, the true spiritual souls on earth. They need to master the elements already within them. We are all made of these elements, water, fire, air, and earth. Our *etheric energetic force* a.k.a *our aura or essence* would act as the fuel to move or steer it all together, and hold our activated "space craft/ship" a.k.a our body altogether. This is our mission, and I hope that we all get there soon enough to ascend.

Etymology of Compendiums of all Gods and The Almighty Creator

DECODING CAPTAIN PLANET MY CHILDHOOD CARTOON

Let's now look at the hidden message in one of my childhood cartoons that was called, *Captain Planet*. Mother Gaia/Earth, originally the Kemet Goddess Geb, chose five young fellows from around the world to represent the elemental powers of earth, wind, water, fire, and with the power of the fifth, heart (to me, this is *ether*).

One of the characters, and the "natural leader" of the group of five was called Kwame, from Ghana, West Afraka. Kwame's power element was, *Earth*. All five can use their respective elemental power effectively, and independently.

However, whenever things get extremely worse, they combine their powers to summon the super elemental combined spiritual power called, *Captain Planet* to come and restore order on earth.

Their weakness was pollution. Polluting the earth, destroying the earth, raiding the earth of its minerals, and natural resources weakened them. When they cannot fight the enemy individually, they combine their powers to summon, *Captain Planet* to get it done.

Kwame, the natural leader of the five, known as the *"planeteers"*, would start by saying, let's combine our powers. He puts his right hand up with the ring on, in a fist formation to summon the element of earth, the next person summons the element of wind, the third summons water, the fourth summons fire, and the fifth summons heart.

"By your powers combined, I am Captain Planet!" is the voice you hear as the spiritual immensely powerful supper power entity force comes from the combined product of all the five elemental powers.

Captain Planet in my decoding submission, is like the activated kundalini, activated chakras, activated avatar, or as I say, *self realization of complete unification of all the elements within us*. Are we learning something from here? This is a hidden message with a solution of unity to end the evil ways of the enemy on earth.

The enemy nations, or institutions use nukes, wars, greed to only protect their national interest to steal, murder, pillage, discriminate, intimidate, destroy, invade, mine all the minerals as they keep the communities or countries with the natural resources poor. The enemy nations' only way of resolution is to send threats or war, eliminate leaders who fight for the people, or to bully anyone who cannot defend themselves with nukes.

The bully only picks on countries, and communities that do not have nukes. The bully nation and organizations destroy the environment of the vulnerable, as they greedily take all the minerals away for themselves. The earth is a witness. Mother Gaia is a witness to the destruction of earth by the enemy nations, and institutions, just like in *Captain Planet* cartoons. We must unite, and with one voice combine our elemental powers, and call on Mother Geb, Gaia, Earth, to shake of the enemy. This requires a psychological, and spiritual global unity. We must individually awaken our kundalini, or awaken our elemental energies embedded within our melanin and DNA.

Etymology of Compendiums of all Gods and The Almighty Creator

DECODING LIBATION

Another addition to the barrage of my decoding is, the pouring of libation by the Akan people of Ghana, West Afraka. In my assessment, pouring of libation is a powerful combination of all the four elemental energies of water, fire, air, and earth. Permit me to break it down for you, with respect to the Akans: "Gu Nsa" – means *"Pour Libation"*. This process or practice constitutes the following things: Dew or Water, Earth, Oration of words, and your presence.

This is my decoding:

Dew / Water = is the *Water* element.

Earth = is the *Earth* element.

Oration or citation of words = is the *Fire* element.

Your presence/Life/Breathing in and out = is the *Air* element.

The people from the Akan culture would speak and call on the all powerful creative force of everything in the universe, the energies in nature, and homage to their ancestors as they pour water to the earth. A reasonable drop of the water/liquid is poured to the earth at the end of every sentence. This pour is to connect all the four elements (water, fire, air, and earth) to form this powerful creative force. The "Akan" means the "first one, or first people".

Those of us who are materialistic, and are ruled by the body, succumbing to the flesh, are ruled by the *"God of the living"*. This physical body has to live, and it is ruled by the *"God of the living"*. You have two physical eyes, but you cannot see. You have ears, but you cannot hear.

You are chasing after vanity stuff. Everything that is physically accumulated is vanity, and can only be used by the *God of the living* a.k.a physical, material or low vibration earth.

The *God of the dead*, is the *God of the soul*, the spiritual world. The soul lives within your body. Your original eye is one, that is your pineal. Your pineal gland is the eye of your soul, your true eye. The soul is dead, because for you to physically live, is for the soul to die. For the soul to live, is for you to die to your flesh. The soul arising, is your kundalini ascending or arising. Your soul's eye is the "hidden one", that is hidden within you. The all-seeing eye is your soul's eye, a.k.a the pineal gland, or third eye. The creator you search for has always been hidden inside you.

The savior you have been looking for, has always been hidden within you. To find the true savior is to find your true self. Death is not the end of your life, rather, death is the spiritual birth. To be born into this physical realm is to die in your spiritual realm. To die in your physical realm (earth), is to be born into your original state in the spiritual realm. The *God of the living*'s desires are opposite to the *God of the dead* (spiritual). In that, the *God of the living* intends to keep you trap here on this low vibration dense earth. While, the *God of the dead* (spiritual) is eternal, and everlasting with the intention for you to live forever. Greed, jealousy, war, gluttony, materialism are all low vibration.

Read the *"Egyptian Book of the Dead"* to learn more about the true spiritual world. This is a book of the spirit. Kill *God of the living* a.k.a *flesh* to embrace the God within, a.k.a *God of your soul*, the true all powerful creative energetic vibrational force of all things.

DECODING MOSES, THE BRASS SERPENT & THE CHILDREN OF ISRAEL

To methodologically decode the hidden message in Moses, the brass serpent, and the children of Israel's experience appropriately, permit me to begin by defining the metal, brass. **Brass** is an alloy metal that is made up of (mixing of) copper and zinc. Many churches, pastors, Christians, and bible colleges/universities lie that it was a bronze serpent. However, Numbers 21:9 KJV boldly states that, it is a brass serpent, not bronze serpent. Numbers 21:9 KJV: "*And Moses made a <u>serpent of brass</u>, and put it upon a pole, and it came to pass, that if a serpent had bitten any man, when he beheld the <u>serpent of brass</u>, he lived.*"

It is very important to know the facts, because replacing the facts with a fallacy totally changes the message, and the "supposed word of God" that these churches, pastors, Christians, and bible colleges/universities claim to know and swear to live by. **Bronze** is a mixture of <u>copper</u> and <u>tin</u>, where as **brass**, is a mixture of <u>copper</u> and <u>zinc</u>.

Zinc and Tin are different, and not the same. **Zinc** is a lustrous <u>bluish-white</u> metal and it's more reactive than **tin**, which is a silvery-white metal. **Zinc** also resists corrosion, prevents metals from rusting as it is used as coating. So brass metals, and bronze metals are not the same.

Now that we know that it is a brass serpent, and we also know that brass is an "alloy metal", let's look at what an alloy metal is.

Alloy is the metallic product of the combination/mixing of two or more metals or a mixer with non-metallic elements, and other metals. **Brass** is a mixture of zinc and copper. **Copper** is a <u>reddish</u>-<u>brown</u> metal, best conductor of heat, and electricity.

In terms of spirituality, **copper** is a strong positive vibrating energetic force that activates and opens the base and sacral chakras, strengthens immune system, boasts cardiovascular health, eliminates or repels negative/toxic/poisonous energies, attracts wealth, stability, and good fortunes. Copper also enables you to balance your vitality, endurance, desires, intuition, and sexual energies.

In a spiritual sense, **zinc** is superb for grounding excess energy, and enables you to distinguish between what is real, and delusional. Hospitals use zinc to properly heal wounds, ulcers, burns, all skin injuries, and inflammations.

Clearly, I see the four key elementals of our makeup. That is earth, fire, water, and air. Let me help you see it.

The elements of *fire,* and *earth* is seen in the description of copper's <u>reddish</u>-<u>brown</u> appearance.

<u>Fire</u> is represented by the color, <u>red</u>.

<u>Earth</u> is represented by the color, <u>brown</u>.

The elements of *water*, and *air* is seen in the description of zinc's <u>bluish</u>-<u>white</u> appearance.

<u>Water</u> is represented by the color, <u>blue</u>.

<u>Air</u> is represented by the color, <u>white</u>.

The adjective "lustrous" used to describe zinc means "shiny". This is the *ether*, the *aura* of the property. This revelation came to me as a download from the spiritual realm. I can clearly see that, in terms of these key energetic vibrating frequency life force energies, we must bring them together in order to activate our power, which is hidden or lie dormant within all of us. Some of us are too distracted by the material things of this world. We chase after unnecessary corruptible things. We complain, fight, pull others down, war on each other, greed, jealousy, hatred, and other dense low vibrating energies. These low vibration energies weigh you down. You become more dense in fear of losing everything, or not having enough, unable to spiritually ascend.

We must let go of everything we are afraid to lose, in order for us to freely activate our key elemental energies; fire, air, water, and earth to properly ascend. Be willing to let your flesh/body die to activate your soul. Otherwise, you will lose your soul as you gain it all for your flesh/body. You cannot serve both your body and your soul. You must choose one of these two. The choice is yours at the end of the day. If you are reading this, then it is not too late for you to save your own soul. Be willing to choose to feed your soul over your flesh/body.

Moses, the brass serpent and the children of Israel's experience is seen at Numbers 21:4-9 KJV. Let's decode this together.

In verses 4 and 5:

Children of Israel chose the flesh/body's cravings and lusted after all the food, water, delicious bread, wine, entertainments, and the great life that they were living in Egypt. They began to resent both their God, and Moses, who brought them out of these luxurious lifestyles in Egypt into misery. They complained that they are hungry, thirsty, tired, sweaty, and just fed-up. Their complain is valid, as humans, we all need food, water, and shelter. However, the issue here is about their attitude.

How they expressed their unfavorable situations to Moses and their God was ungrateful, despicable, self-loathing, and worldly.

Let's read verses 4 and 5 together below:

*"**4** And they journeyed from mount Hor by the way of the Red sea, to compass the land of Edom: and <u>the soul of the people was much discouraged because of the way.</u> **5** And <u>the people spake against God</u>, and <u>against Moses, Wherefore have ye brought us up out of Egypt to die in the wilderness</u>? for there is <u>no bread</u>, <u>neither is there any water</u>; and <u>our soul loatheth this light bread</u>."*

Currently, this is where most of us are. Some of us are too worldly. Some of us pile up food, clothes, cars, houses, extreme cash, and physical things that are only beneficial to the body/flesh. Some of us become very vile, evil, demonic, and desperate to only protect our interests at the expense of waging war against a vulnerable community, society, or people. We rake in and pile up enormous amount of gold, oil, precious metals, and relics while we oppress and suppress other nation's economies or other folks opportunity to excel in life. At the end of it all, we cannot take it with us. Everything acquired on earth would be taken back by the God of this physical realm. However, everything you gain spiritually while you are on this physical plain, would be with you when you are birthed into the spiritual world, as you exit this physical world.

Our goal on earth is to help one another to have equitable food, shelter and security. We are to live in moderation, never to get attached to the things of this physical world. If we can get this right, then the kingdom of heaven (God) would be established on earth. This is what the entire bible is about. Nothing more, nothing less. The secret to establishing the *"kingdom of God on earth"* is what I have just revealed to you. Greedy bastards, corporations, and nations who barbarically wage war to steal, murder, invade, rape, and torture the vulnerable are antithesis to establishing the kingdom of heaven (God) on earth. The anti-Christ has already come since the implementation of the *Doctrine of Discovery*. What nations, corporations, institutions, or countries are oppressing, suppressing, and making life unbearable for you that you need "saving" from? What or who do you need saving from? If your life was better right now, would you need saving? Think!

Everything is happening for you, and to you right now. It is all in your face. See it for what it is, and wake up. If no human created earth, gold, diamond, oil, water, lithium, and others, then why are you struggling, oppressed, suppressed, financially poor, and life basically unbearable? Who or what country or corporations/institutions are holding all these resources given to us freely by the Almighty Creator? I hope you can use your conscious brain, soul, and instinct to see it, because, it is right in front of you. Wake up! Read Proverbs 6:16-19 KJV to work on yourself.

In verse 6:

Judgment came upon the children of Israel due to their greed, selfishness, ungratefulness, loathing, worldly desires, earthly-Egypt attachment, stinky attitude, devouring behaviors. Pride comes before a fall. Their God sent the fiery serpent to come, and consume them.

"6 And the LORD sent fiery serpents among the people, and they bit the people; and much people of Israel died."

You are God yourself (Psalm 82:6; John 10:34 KJV), what we read here is about allowing your physical loathsomeness, materialistic ways, greed, consumed by desperately wanting everything in this world to the extreme that, you are willing to kill, offer your own children as sacrifice, or even put yourself at risk of losing your life to get the physical thing you desire at all cost. Anyone who gets to this level of desperation do not care about anyone but themselves. We see nations sending their military against other nations to forcefully take their oil, gold, minerals or any needed resources. These nations would prey on the vulnerable nations even if they have to lose some of their own military men, and civilians at the expense of feeding their greedy pockets, body/flesh, and piling up ridiculous wealth. The lesson here "*sent fiery serpents among the people, and they bit the people..*" indicates that, we trigger into a "survival of the fittest" state. Whereby, we are willing to drop nuclear weapons, bombs, biological warfare, to wipe out as many people as possible to have all the resources to ourselves. Hence, many people end up dying,"*much people of Israel died*".

In verses 7-9:

This section deals with the people of Israel after seeing all the damages caused by the fiery serpent, the remnants who survived decided to pursue their God. This occurred after the God of this earth, that is God of the flesh/body rendered them into disastrous atrocities. They asked Moses for directions on how they can heal again in order to walk on the path of righteousness, path of the soul. Moses provides the remedy. However, an individual decision, and action must be taken in order to heal, recover, and reposition. Let's read"

"*7 Therefore the people came to Moses, and said, We have sinned, for we have spoken against the LORD, and against thee; pray unto the LORD, that he take away the serpents from us. And Moses prayed for the people. 8 And the LORD said unto Moses, Make thee a fiery serpent, and set it upon a pole: and it shall come to pass, that every one that is bitten, when he looketh upon it, shall live. 9 And Moses made a serpent of brass, and put it upon a pole, and it came to pass, that if a serpent had bitten any man, when he beheld the serpent of brass, he lived.*"

To decode this, let me pick some specific phrases from the verses we just read to make it much clearer.

Let's look at "*the people came to Moses, and said, We have sinned ... We have sinned... we have spoken against the LORD, and against thee; pray unto the LORD, that he take away the serpents from us*"

There are many teachers, chosen people and activists like Moses who consistently use their platforms, gifts, positions or leadership influence to encourage the world populace to turn away from wars, greed, jealousy, evil works, and all forms of low dense vibrations. However, some of these people are ridiculed, name called, targeted, mocked, threatened, and rejected.

Many of these greedy, evil people, nations, and corporations/institutions would go to the extreme, to bomb the hell out of other vulnerable nations, or communities, murdering lot of people to invade their land, and settle there.

If care is not taken, the aggression may lead to an eventual nuclear attack on these vulnerable nations. After all the damage has been done, few of these wicked indelible then have an awakening to go to the same teachers, chosen people, and activists who they rejected to give them the knowledge to heal the remnants, and to restore things through appropriate restitution.

"*Moses prayed for the people...Make thee a fiery serpent, and set it upon a pole...every one that is bitten, when he looketh upon it, shall live... Moses made a serpent of brass, and put it upon a pole...if a serpent had bitten any man, when he beheld the serpent of brass, he lived.*"

The teachers, chosen people, and activists decide to spiritually, medically, psychologically, socially and etherically show the victims of wars, pillage, rape, those who lost their homeland, and families due to the greedy, and wicked indelible people, nations, corporations, and institutions the way to healing, recovery, and restitution. True repentance comes with restitution.

So, the real healing begins as those children of Israel, who needed true healing, and repentance, turned to the *brass serpent* for healing.

Brass is a mixture of zinc and copper. The copper's spiritual attribute is a strong positive vibrating energetic force that activates, and opens the base, and sacral chakras, strengthens immune system, boasts cardiovascular health, eliminates or repels negative/toxic/poisonous energies, attracts wealth, stability and good fortunes.

Copper also enables you to balance your vitality, endurance, desires, intuition and sexual energies. They (children of Israel) went within to awaken their kundalini. They awaken the "God within". They became more spiritual to ascend, and vibrate higher.

Zinc's spiritual attribute is superb for grounding excess energy, and enables you to distinguish between what is real, and delusional. Healthcare experts like doctors, and nurses would then use zinc to properly heal wounds, ulcers, burns, all skin injuries, and inflammations.

The overall goal, or purpose for us in this physical plain remains the same, as I stated earlier. Which is to help one another to have equitable food, shelter and security.

INTER-DIMENSIONAL TRAVEL:
HOW TO TRAVEL INTER-DIMENSIONALLY

This is where all the decoded messages you have read from previous pages come together. We usually travel inter-dimensionally without even knowing it. This is through our dreams during our sleep. When you dream, your soul travels to the inter-dimensional realms to interact with different frequencies. The type of energy you encounter in your soul's travel a.k.a dream is dependent on the message you are either trying to deliver, learn, experience, or receive. This is the "common" way of inter-dimensional travel.

Another common way of inter-dimensional travel is through the state of trance, astral projection, or day-dream. The simplest of all inter-dimensional travel is when you are able to channel ideas or thoughts on paper, then practically build these thoughts or ideas into physical reality. You brought it from the spiritual, conscious or immaterial dimension to the material dimension.

The highest level of inter-dimensional travel is the level whereby you are able to activate and travel inter-dimensionally with your soul, by using your physical body as the vehicle, while you are physically present, and conscious. Unlike dreaming, whereby just your soul travels inter-dimensionally, at the highest level, you use your body together with all the elements in you. At the highest level of activation, your earth element, fire element, air element, and water element are all at the highest peak of functional activation. Your *ether* is deeply embedded into the supernatural, and highly supersonic spiritual "ship", that's your body. This is the utmost activation of the elements of air, earth, fire, and water. This is the real you. This is who we were before we fell into low dense vibrational frequency into this 3D/third dimensional realm. At the highest activation level, your entire body becomes an incorruptible machine that carries the soul, and you can travel physically through different dimensions without being affected.

Ancient civilizations with what is known as UFO "space ships" got to this level. The so-called "UFO space ships" are not space ships, rather, the activated functionality of their elements; earth, water, air, fire, and ether. The ether fuels their travel. The physical UFO ships/vehicles can only be activated by the person who has synced his or her activated ascended kundalini/energies/vibration that have been embedded within the engineering of the "physical machine". The UFO space craft/ship is like your body, it is specifically made for you, and no other person can use it. You don't need a key or a switch, because you are the key needed to "drive" the machine. To become the captain of this "UFO craft/space ship", you must have been able to master all the elementals of air, water, fire, and earth together with your *ether,* to activate it. Just like "Aang" in the docu-series, *Avatar: The Last Airbender*. Let's look at the images below to add further explanation to this topic.

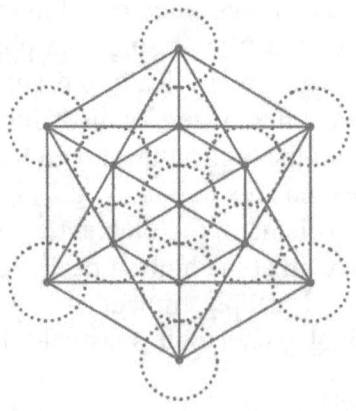

Our unity creates a powerful force that can manifest what we desire into existence efficiently and effectively.

This is how it looks like when you are able to activate all your elementals: Air, Earth, Fire, and Water, together with the accelerator a.k.a the *Ether*. Original "men" and "women" were not created on earth, rather, we fell from our highest vibration into our lowest vibration, a.k.a earth, 3D or third dimension. While we were here, some of us created other creations on earth like our likeness. However, these creations that some of us original fallen Gods and Goddesses created do not have souls like we do. These creations can only operate in the 3D/earth. They can never ascend like us original men and women, a.k.a fallen Gods and Goddesses. In our case, we can work on ourselves to ascend our souls back to our respective origins, be it the 4th dimensions, 5th dimensions, 6th dimensions, 7th dimensions, 8th dimensions, or the 9th dimensions. Some of the folks that some of us fallen Gods and Goddesses created, trick some of us to "sell our souls" for them, in order for them to be able to ascend to the higher realms, where we descended from. However, they can never ascend, because they were not created by the true one, and only original Almighty Creator. The soulless ones were created in this 3D, and that's were they will be forever and ever. Hence, they will do anything to enjoy this 3D realm.

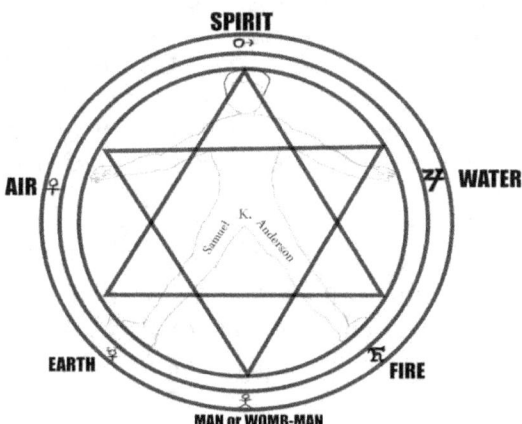

DECODING GENESIS 1:1-3 THE CREATION STORY

Wisdom was used to manifest all creations. Wisdom is genderless, however, in most instances, wisdom is attributed to us as a feminine energy. Proverbs 8:22-31 in the Amplified Bible (AMP), and New Century Version (NCV) both state that "Wisdom" was there even before the creation of the world.

*"I, **wisdom**, was with the LORD when he began his work, long before he made anything else. I was created in the very beginning, even before the world began. I was born before there were oceans, or springs overflowing with water, before the hills were there, before the mountains were put in place."*- Proverbs 8:22-31- New Century Version (NCV).

*""The LORD created and possessed me at the beginning of His way, Before His works of old [were accomplished]. From everlasting I was established and ordained, From the beginning, before the earth existed, [I, **godly wisdom**, existed]. When there were no ocean depths I was born, When there were no fountains and springs overflowing with water. Before the mountains were settled, Before the hills, I was born; While He had not yet made the earth and the fields, Or the first of the dust of the earth. When He established the heavens, I [**Wisdom**] was there;"*-Proverbs 8:22-31-Amplified Bible (AMP).

The New Testament book of John, in John 1:1-10 was plagiarized from Proverbs 8:22-31. In John 1, they lied and replaced "wisdom" with "Jesus". Such a pathetic lie and a scam of the entire *New Testament bible*. You know now that, the so-called *New Testament bible (NT)* is the original copy of the *New World Order (NWO)* pushed by the Pope and the Roman empire to colonize the entire world.

Wisdom is a strategically calculated "thought", "brainstorming", "ideas", "inspirations", "imaginations", and "channeling into reality", the creation or manifestation of things into this physical reality from the spiritual or ethereal realm.

In the beginning, the elements of *Fire*, *Air*, *Earth*, and *Water* merged through the enforcement of the *ether* a.k.a *"the word"* or *"spoken word"* to create things. The governing force, or energy of this *"word"*, or *"spoken word"* is *Wisdom*. The very *"word"* or *"spoken word"* in this case is, *Wisdom*.

Let's have a look at Genesis 1:1-3 KJV: *"1 In the beginning God created the heaven and the earth. 2 And the earth was without form, and void; and darkness was upon the face of the deep. And the Spirit of God moved upon the face of the waters. 3 And God said, Let there be light: and there was light."*

Let me decode this in the simplest way possible:

Verse 1: *"In the beginning God created the heaven and the earth."*

God represents the **element of Fire.**

Per Psalms 84:11 *"the Lord God is a sun...".*

Deuteronomy 4:24 *"For the LORD your God is a consuming fire,".* The Sun is known to be the consuming fire. Malachi 4:2, it reads *"the Sun of Righteousness..."*

Heaven represents the **element of Air**. Air fills up our atmosphere.

Earth represents the **element of Earth**. This is self explanatory.

Water, found in both air (**moist air**), and earth (waters, and rivers, or **moist earth**) reflects the **element of Water.**

All the four (4) elementals are identified in the first sentence in Genesis chapter 1:1.

Verse 2: *"And the earth was without form, and void; and darkness was upon the face of the deep. And the Spirit of God moved upon the face of the waters."*

Earth element restated, one of the key four elementals.

Spirit is the representation of the **element of Air**. Spirit is Air. Spirituality means "Breath, or to Breathe".

God is the representation of Fire, **the Fire element**.

Waters is the representation of itself, **the Water element**.

Verse 3: *"And God said, Let there be light: and there was light."*

God a.k.a "**Fire**", "**Said**", the word "*said*" in this statement or sentence, is the "*spoken word*", or "*the word*" a.k.a "Ethereal Wisdom".

"Let there be light", the fire extended itself to become the "*Sun*" or to give off its own **"fire" element**.

The four (4) key elementals are very important to our ascension. The element of fire, air, water, and earth must be in high vibration energetic frequency flow, in order for you to experience your ascension into your God-Self or Goddess-Self. These four (4) key elemental forces or energies are always at play in everything we do. We must learn to self-correct, and unlearn all the deceptions, misinformation, programming, mis-education, and tricks shoved down our throats since birth by the evil rulers. It is your responsibility to activate your soul, by going within.

The Elohim (this word is *plural*) are: Air, Water, Earth, and Fire elements. All creations came into existence by the manifestations of the aforementioned Elohim. This is my ethereal download.

Plants, Animals, Insects, etc came out of the Eloah Earth element. *Eloah* is the *singular* form of *Elohim*. Eloah Water element distributed parts of its essence into streams, springs, oceans, lakes, fresh water, and all other water sources. Eloah Fire element extended itself to be the sun, fire, black/dark sun, light, heat, and all sources of light, fire, or sun known and unknown to this 3D-world. The dark hole a.k.a *black hole* is the greatest or extremely intensified focal point of concentrated light, this is my strategic ethereal download. This is not just a theory that I am throwing around, rather, a fact by me, revealed to me from the 9th dimension. I dare any scientist to challenge me or attempt to disprove me. I dare all global scientists a trillion times to dare step forward to disprove my ethereal fact, which is above all aspects of science. Darkness is the brightest point of all lights.

Eloah Air element is the wind, air we breathe, "breath of life", what some call spirit, etc. As I have simplified spirituality throughout this book for you, by now, you must know that, spirituality is simply *breath*. Yes, breathe in and out, that right there, is the core of all spirituality. Never get confuse about spirituality in your life again. Go ahead and walk in your spirituality, master the art of breathing. Research and practice different levels and intensities of breathing. When all the *Elohim* combined, they morphed themselves into us (the soul people). Male Energy and Female Energy, Man and Womb-man called Adam (backwards Ma-Da). Soul people are simply these Eloahs uniting to become Elohim in one flesh in the 3-D dimension. Hence, All Soul people are Gods and Goddesses.

Soul people's thoughts, ideas, and instincts in the immaterial realm is what is known as "Wisdom" or "Discernment". Hence, *Wisdom* comes before we materialize things in our 3D-material realm. Dwell in the warm embrace of *Wisdom*, for she is loving.

Old Testament's Biblical Record on The Birth of Two Nations. The Torah's Record.

Currently, the world's population is approaching 14 billion. It is very easy for anyone to doubt that mankind is connected to only one source of family. However, archaeological finding, historic records, ancient Afrakan civilizations, the bible, and scientific DNA make it possible for us to identify this fact. It is also a fact that, over 75% of the entire world's population are hybrid avatars per geneticists. The original Gods and Goddesses who fell or who manifested into this 3D-third dimension realm walk among us. This 3D-third dimension realm was manifested by the Gods and Goddesses when they fell from their higher state vibration down into this 3D-third dimension solid earthly state. These are the first "people" on earth.

The book of **Genesis 25:19-26** introduces us to the two nations, *v.23-26* record that; the first born was <u>red</u> all over and <u>hairy</u>, his name was *Esau. Jacob (the twin brother)* then came out of his mother's womb. This was the first introduction of the *"red nation", a.k.a Albinos, or yellow-bone Afrakans.* Both Yacov/Jacob and Esau are Afrakans. You must know by now, how the Greeks and Romans got their versions of the sun book a.k.a bible, through the Afrakan sellout bishop by the name of Sylvester, in ancient Kemet's mystery order school. This was discussed thoroughly in previous chapters in this book.

Entire genealogies (from Adam to Isaac and Ishmael) prior to **Genesis 25** had no mention of a *"red" person "thread-like" garment hair all over the body.* However, when you read *the book of Enoch,* you would find that, this "Esau" description is somewhat like the description of Noah. Noah was an albino, just like Esau in this description.

In some old texts, and books outside the bible, Noah is referenced as Zuisudra, a.k.a child of Enlil in Mesopotamian story. Mesopotamians are aboriginal dark chocolate Afrakans, who are predominantly located in modern day West Afraka. Manu's flood story is the Noah's story version in Hinduism, in texts like the Matsya Purana and the Satapatha Brahmana. In ancient Afraka's Egypt/Kemet, Nun is the primeval waters God. The Quran call Noah, Nu or Nuh. Do you see the same stories watered down in both the bible and Quran? Manu in Hinduism also has that ancient Kemet's "Nun" tonation to it from a linguistical perspective. There is also the people from the Ewe or Eve ethnic groups of the Akan people of West Afraka, who narrate their story to originate from the lost continent of Nu or Mu, due to flooding, to settle at Göbekli Tepe, and were part of the ancient Kemet's unprecedented global civilization.

Alternatively, this chapter in Genesis exposes that, the entire people in the bible looked like the dark chocolate melanted people of Afraka. Hence, *Yacov, Yakubu, or Jacob's* parents Isaac, and Rebekah/Rebecca were all dark chocolate melanted Afrakan folks. This is why *Jacob's* appearance was not emphasized when he was born. This is far before our diverse backgrounds, cultures, mentality and aspirations were influenced by western colonizers. Western colonizers lie, and steal ancient relics into their museums.

According to the bible, and Quran, Jacob/Yacov *(a dark melanated man)* is the nation of *Israel (12 tribes of Israel represents the 12 sons of Yakubu/Jacob)*. Isaac, father of the twins *(Esau and Jacob)* is the "promised" son of *Abraham, a.k.a Abibrim man or Abibiman*. The bible God had a covenant with *Abram a.k.a Abraham (Ham means burnt/dark)*, read about this in **Genesis 17**. *Jacob's* posterity, *King Solomon* (*King David's* son) emphasized his *darkness* or *dark melanin appearance* in **Song of Solomon 1:5,6**. These are all ancient Kemet stories that the dark Afrakan bishop, Sylvester (the sellout) gave to the ancient Roamn's after agreeing to baptize Constantine I.

Esau is the *"red nation", albino nation* or *Edom/Edomites*. They lived around the *Caucasus mountains* which was originally known as *Mount Seir* as stated in **Genesis 36:8**.

Edom/Edomites intermingled and intermarried with the progenies of *Ishmael* (*Abraham's* son with *Hagar*, the concubine/handmaid also a dark chocolate melanted son), posterity of *Keturah's* six sons (*Keturah* was also a concubine of *Abraham*, **Genesis 25: 1-6 and 1st Chronicles 1:32,33**). Again, these are all ancient dark chocolate Afrakans.

The intermarrying of *"red nation" a.k.a albino nation* and other groups stated above including some granddaughters, great granddaughters, and sons of *Noah* (through his sons' offsprings that sailed to settle as far as *Asia, Europe* a.k.a *Europa/Euroba/Uroba/Yuroba,* and other parts of the world including *Afraka*).

Keturah's children also assimilated with *Ishmael's* posterity. It is factually safe to say that, the Islamic religion sprang from *Ishmael's* line with some of *Keturah's* children. *Edomites* had pride, and anger towards Y*acob*.

Per the Bible, the nation of *Edom* went into "idol/image worshiping", and other various "pagan" practices, like that of *Nimrod (i.e. the King of Babylon who built the tower of Babel, one of Noah's grandsons, whose father was Cush/Kush, son of Ham recorded in **Genesis 10:10, Genesis 11)**. "Pagan" worship with the influence of *Nimrod* worshiped on *Sunday*, sun worshipers. They worshiped *Nimrod* as a "sun god" instead of worshiping on the Sabbath, a day ordained by *the bible God, a.k.a Amen (the Akan God of Saturday)*.

The bible is synthetic in regards to facts to the ancient Kemet's facts and stories. After all, now you know that, those who pushed the bible, got their information from ancient Kemet. Hence, the authentic is with the ancient Afrakans, who still have their cultures, and traditions intact away from the watered-down, and lightweight synthetic Bible and Quran. The synthetic is currently the main stream religions of Muslim/Islam, and Catholic/Christian, which confused the uninformed Afrakan to accept it as the whole truth, and nothing but the truth. Meanwhile, the authentic is directly embedded into the melanin, and DNA of every true sun/son of Afraka. It is buried deep within our souls. No colonizer and enslaver (Pope's *Doctrine of Discovery,* Arab-Muslim's trans-Sahara slave trade, Manifest Destiny, Apatheid South Afraka, Trans-Atlantic slave trade, Scramble for Afraka 1833-1914, and enslaving of aboriginal Americans a.k.a African Americans) would give you the facts about yourself, and your true power as the Gods and Goddesses of this Gaia, Geb, Earth realm.

A brief synopsis about the genesis of this so-called "pagan" worship comes in light with *Semiramis'* "supposed" fabrication of a story that *Nimrod* returned to her from the sun in the form of a sun ray to impregnate her after *Nimrod's* death. The baby born was named *Tammuz* (the *pagan's trinity* was then initiated, orchestrated by the "devil" as it involves human sacrifice). This modern day Western world's narrative is porous, and laughable. If human sacrifice is "devilish", or "satanic", which I do not ascribe or subscribe to "human sacrifice" in any way, shape, or form; however, for context sake, then, wouldn't you agree that, Jesus who was sacrificed on the cross is also the same "devilish" human sacrifice worship? Common sense, knowledge, and wisdom can easily attest that, according to the New Testament bible, Jesus was sacrificed on the tree/cross, and his followers drink his blood, and eat his skin/flesh in today's churches, as remembrance of Jesus' death. That is the same devilish, satanic, demonic, and pagan worship described under Nimrod. Folks must wake up from the delusional lies, and spiritual comatose spell that both the Bible, and Quran have placed on you.

With respect to Nimrod, it is said that, his *"sun god"* worship "religion" spread out into many nations, and generations throughout history till this day. Christians worship the *sun,* depicted as halo on the head of the character Jesus, all their apostles, and disciples. That halo colored in bright orange-yellowish is depiction of the *sun*. The bible worships the *sun* just like Nimrod. Let's look at some bible verses to prove this:

Psalm 84:11 kjv - *"For the LORD God is a sun and shield,..."*
Deuteronomy 4:24 kjv - *"For the Lord thy God is a consuming fire..."* (the sun is called a consuming fire).
Malachi 4:2 kjv - *"the Sun of righteousness..."*
Also, Jesus was referred to as the *"sun"*, and the *"light"* throughout the new testament. The true light is the sun. Read more bible verses about Jesus referred to as the *light*, which suggests him to be the *sun* per the new testament:
John 8:12, John 9:5, Matthew 4:16, Matthew 17:2, John 1:3-8, John 3:19-20, John 12:35-36, John 12:46, Ephesians 5:14, Philippians 3:20, Colossians 3:2. The true light is the sun. Christians are sun

worshipers, and they attend church on *Sun-day*, day of the *sun*. Caucasians (etymology of the "caucasus mountains" also known as *Mount Seir*), are the products of genetic engineering, and genetic manipulations by the *Edomites/Idumeans (Idumea)/Esau's* descendants. Read Genesis 36. A more condensed version of *Edomites* or *Idumeans, Esau* is found at *1 Chronicles 1:35-54*.

The genetic engineering, and genetic manipulations heavily occurred in this region. This region was the "hiding" place, and grooming of these new breeds who were prophesied in ancient Kemet to one day come, and destroy everything built by the great dark chocolate Afrakan civilizations. These products of genetic engineering, and genetic manipulation breeds have fulfilled the prophesies, as they have taken over all the civilizations of great Afraka, in all the seven continents, remaining very few section in what is called Sub-Sahara Afraka, a.k.a Saara/Sarah's Afrakan land. Sarah, the wife of Abibiman, Abibrim-man, a.k.a AbraHam/Abram.

Ancient Atlantis, Kemet, Phoenicians, Etrurians/Etruscans, Trojans, Greeks, Romans, Armenia, Syria, Iran, Anatolia, entire Europa/Yuroba/Europe, Mesopotamia, and most of the continent of Asia including China, and Japan were all occupied aboriginally by the dark chocolate Afrakans, a.k.a the first people, a.k.a the first Gods and Goddesses on earth. The products of genetic engineering, and genetic manipulation breeds after taking over ancient areas around the Caucasus mountains, Greek, and Rome, replicated themselves through barbaric rape, and pillage. The new Indo-European Rome resettled the new mix breed of Arabs around the Greco-Roman conquered areas of North Afraka a.k.a "Middle East" including ancient Kemet/Egypt, and all the "European-Arab" admixture North Afraka Arabic occupied lands. Roman Pope backed Arab's invasions.

YAKUBU's LINEAGE

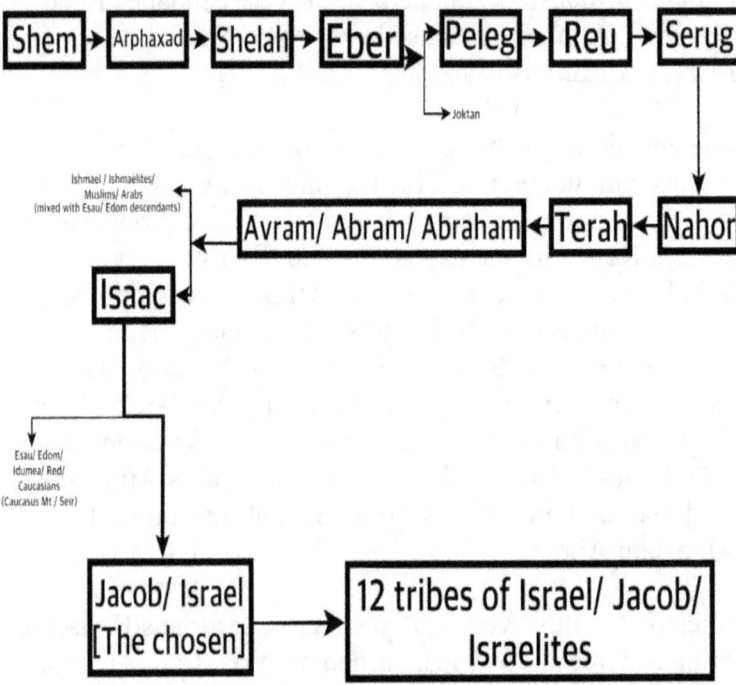

These are all dark-chocolate melanated people. Most of them are in today's West Afraka, as others are spread throughout the rest of Afraka, and the world.

The power of geneticists can easily be at play here, as these geneticists can easily execute DNA gene tests to solidify these facts. It is basic facts to those who have awakened spiritually. However, it is a cloudy information to those who are still under the comatose spell of colonization, the Bible, and the Quran. Hence, geneticists can test the genetic DNA facts about all these areas to prove me right.

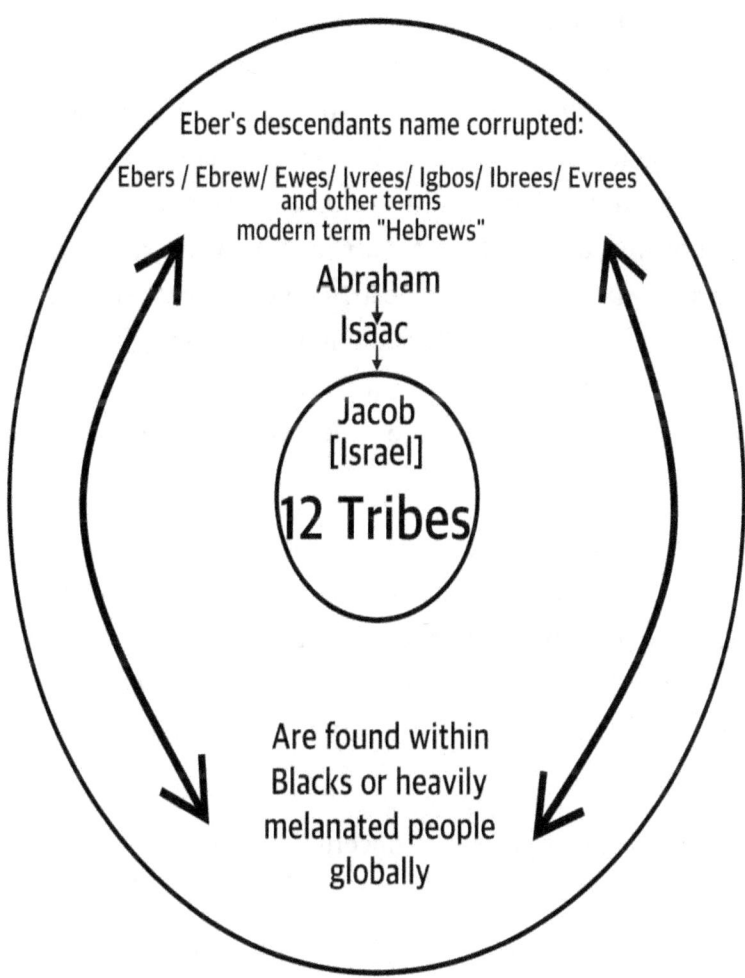

Note: All *Ebrews/Hebrews* are **not** Israelites, but all Israelites are *Ebrews/Hebrews*. These Israelites are currently not living on the physical land called Israel. The twelve tribes of Jacob/Israel have been dispersed throughout the four corners of the earth, with majority of them currently living in Afraka. The western part of Afraka is known to have a lot of these Israelites. Both the trans-Sahara slave trade by the Arab-Muslim-Quran led, and the trans-Atlantic slave trade by the Western nations, under the Pope's *Doctrine of Discovery* approval, captured most of the Israelites from the tribe of Judah/Yudah/Yawudah/Utah into Northern Arab-Muslim Afraka, the Americas, Europe, and the rest of the Afrakan diaspora. You can read **Deuteronomy 28:66-68** to learn about the trans-Atlantic slave trade, and **Psalm 83** about how the nationality, and identity of *Israel* was taken, and destroyed by the *Edomites/Idumeans/Esau,* together with *Ishmaelites,* and *Japhet*.

Lastly, groups like the Banktu, Akans, Ga-Adangbe, and many other ethnicities under the lineage of *Eber* (Look at the genealogy of Shem in **Genesis 10:22-32**) to get entire picture. Also, read this book, *God's Audacity: The Logic of God's Existence by Samuel K. Anderson* to get additional information.

The products of genetic engineering, and genetic manipulation breeds a.k.a the gentiles have indeed fulfilled their time, as it was prophesied. These gentiles a.k.a Western folks, and mixed European Arabs have literally taken over all the lands and civilizations of the Gods and Goddesses, a.k.a Afrakans. The entire planet earth, worships Afrakan Gods and Goddesses. In that, these Afrakans were the first people on earth. These same Afrakans established all the so-called known Gods, and Goddesses "worshiped" today by everyone on earth. Every religion worships an Afrakan, or better yet, a dark chocolate melanated black Afrakan Gods and Goddesses.

POLYGAMY and THE CULTURE OF AFRAKA

It is obvious that, majority of the world's populace are found within the bible believing Christians/Catholics, and Islam-Muslims. Muslims publicly accept polygamy, and actually encourages it. However, Christians/Catholics are the hypocrites when it comes to this subject matter. Let me explain why I am alluding to this point.

How many wives did these bible "heroes" have?

Moses: 2 wives (Numbers 12:1-10 married the Kushite/Cushite/Hamite woman and Zipporah in Exodus 2:16, 21; Exodus 3:22).

Abraham: Minimum of three (3) wives namely, Hagar/Haggai, Sarah, and Keturah. There are more, however, only these three women are disclosed in the bible. Genesis 25:1, Genesis 16.

Jacob/Yacov/Yakubu: 4 wives (he married 2 and the other two were his side chicks). Jacob/Yacov had twelve (12) boys, excluding the countless girls with these four women. Later on, the twelve boys became the so-called twelve tribes of Yashrael/Israel. Jacob/Yacov had two(2) wives, and two (2) concubines (side-chicks).

David: 8 wives or 18 wives, and 24 wives (the 18 wives come into play at 2nd Samuel 12:8 *"was given thrice as much"* - this is what the Jewish Rabbis explained pertaining to this verse). If it's thrice as much as his then 6 wives, then they didn't count his first wife Michal. Some argue that Michal is the same as Eglah. They do this to limit the maximum required number a King of Isarel can marry to eighteen (18), claimed to be in Deuteronomy 17:17. The number of maximum wives slated at 18 is according to the Rabbis. If it goes more than that, then they would probably need to adjust the Torah's requirement, which may be lot of work to do, or could cause a host of disarrangement, or re-arrangements. **David's wives:** Michal, Ahinoam, Abigail, Maachah, Haggith, Abital, Eglah, Bathsheba. (II Samuel 3:2-5 records 6 wives while David was in Hebron).

Solomon: 700 wives and 300 side chicks, or concubines per 1st Kings 11:1-13. Total number emphasized in 1Kings 11:3.

Isaac: Two wives, a sister wife from a product of Abraham and Keturah, and later on married Rebekah, his cousin. Know that Abraham, and Isaac were Horites, and as such in respect to this specificity, the then tradition, or custom, all the Horite Habiru/Hebrew/Ebrew/Ewes rulers had two wives.

Rehoboam had 18 wives (probably more wives), and sixty (60) side-chicks, or concubines according to 2nd Chronicles 11:21.

Abiyah/Abijah had 14 wives per 2nd Chronicles 13:21.

Elkanah had 2 wives per 1st Samuel 1:2-20 namely Hannah and Peninnah.

Lamech had 2 wives according to Genesis 4:19 namely Adah and Zillah.

Some of the importance of polygamy and having multiple concubines for the Afrakan man are outlined below:

Health: Polygamy is Afrakan's culture, and traditions that must be seriously reinforced. Colonization made Afrakan's polygamy culture shameful. If Afrakans are truly emancipated, then they should proudly encourage polygamy throughout the continent. Health-wise, polygamy sits as one of the key solutions for melanated men, or Afrakan to curbing the risks of prostate cancer.

Prostate cancer is about 80% or more bound to happen among all "melanated" people on a global scale regardless of their location. In this case, polygamy is an important solution to Afrakan men or melanated men.

Afrakan women or melanated women must stop the monogamous disease pushed on them by the invaders or colonizers. If Afrakan women love and care about Afrakan men, then polygamy must be seriously encouraged, or just allow the men to enjoy sexual intercourse with as many women as possible in order to eradicate prostate cancer. Wives in monogamous marriages must be readily available to offer sex to their Afrakan husbands. This is critical to/for Afrakan men in particular. This is not the case for non-Afrakans, or non-melanated people.

Legacy, Economic, and Generational Wealth Creation: Marrying multiple women guarantees the probability of having lot of children. These children carry on the family's legacy, and the family name from posterity to posterity. It is very important to note that, having more children helped the family to expand their agricultural land, family businesses, and continuation of mega projects. These reasons are historical facts. In most Afrakan communities, the first wife can marry another woman, just to bring the new woman to her husband as a second wife. This was very common back in the day. The first wives actually encourage their husbands to get second, third, and fourth wives. Jacob/Yaov a.k.a "Israel" experienced the same thing, as his two wives, presented their "servants" to Yacov/Jacob to have more children. This was the reason why there are 12 tribes of Israel. Most of the children were born by the side-chicks or concubines that the two wives presented to their husband, Yacov/Jacob/Yakubu. Abraham experienced the same thing with his wife, Sarah. Sarah encouraged Abraham to have a child with Hagar. You cannot love the bible, and hate polygamy. No God in the bible said, men should marry only one wife.

The global population of women is almost thrice the population of men. That means, to every single man, there are three single women. Very soon it would be 10 women to 1 man. Western propaganda has deceived women by encouraging them to be more masculine, independent, and confrontational to men. Instead of women learning from the love, and caring characteristics of our great eons of all eons mother nature, women are instead aggressively competing with men.

Women compete with men economically, financially, career-wise, and everything in the form of material things, except the physically competitive and demanding areas in life. There is nothing wrong having competitive women, however, it becomes a problem when women go to the extent of surgically modifying their bodies to physically appear like men, act like men, move, and even date, or marry like a man. That's where women become extreme, because at that point, you have lost the essence of your purpose as a woman, and tilted to selfishness, desperation, jealousy, and obsession. These are all sickening psychological moves of a confused being. Confused of who she is spiritually, morally, ethereally, consciously, and soulfully. The women at this state are just flesh, and physically selfish, because everything beyond their body is lost, and in disarray.

Most corporate places employ women for positions favorably than men. This affects some men financially, and cripples most men from their ability to be the provider of the family. Since most women do not know how to naturally lead with finances, these women then become miserable, irate, unhappy in the marriage, or relationship, and blame the man for failing to provide financially. Most of these women forget that, most of the career opportunities for men have been absorbed by them, hence, some men struggle financially due to them competing for positions at the corporate level. The demographic for the women to choose from a pool of men with the financial capability becomes very minimal. Hence, there are more women chasing after the same "financially stable" man, which causes frustrations among these women defaulting to their popular slogan, *"there are no good men out there"*, or *"there are not enough good men out there"*.

However, this is far from the truth, the fact is that, most of the good men may not have the career that pays more money, or might have been overrun by another woman taken the career opportunity that the man could have achieved. Bottom line, if modern women desire to compete for jobs with men, then these women must apply wisdom to learn to be open, and flexible to using the money earned for the entire family, or be open to adjust to the modern economical, financial, and job scarcity for men. Every change comes with sacrifice, so we all need to choose what we are willing to sacrifice. In that, you cannot have it all without the will to sacrifice something. Otherwise, the frustrations of women finding a *"financially stable"* man translated as *"good man"* for most women, would only worsen over time.

Many Afrakans, and melanated chocolate people, under the pressures and influence of oppression have rejected their ways of lives, cultures, and practices to embrace the oppressors way of marriage certificate, and marrying just one person. Look at our communities, single motherhood has increased massively with children raised up in broken homes all because a man decided to tilt towards polygamy, or to bring in another woman. The oppressed, and colonized mind would be fighting this factual statement. I am speaking to the global melanated, and Afrakan populace only. This is strictly our culture, and tradition because the colonizers came in to deceive our women through information weaponization, and miseducation.

Marriage certificate was introduced by Rome, the Roman empire. So, if you didn't know before, now you know that, you are pushing Roman law onto yourselves while you insult, disrespect, and speak ill of your cultural identity, and practice of polygamy. You are still enslaved, mentally colonized, and oppressed if you continue with the marriage certificate fiasco, and look down on polygamy. Aboriginal chocolate sun-kissed melanated first nation people around the entire world had records of marriages, and this was a societal, and family based recognition.

Etymology of Compendiums of all Gods and The Almighty Creator

THE THEORY OR CONCEPT THAT AMERICA/AMERIKA IS ANCIENT KEMET/EGYPT/AFRAKA

If in theory that ancient America/Amerika is to be accepted as ancient Israel, then that would factually mean that ancient America/Amerika was Canaan/Kanaan, for Canaanites/Kanaanites, who are direct descendants of Ham a.k.a Afrakans. In inference, ancient America/Amerika then is the original ancient Afraka, or better yet, ancient Amerika then would be part of ancient Afraka. In simple terms, ancient Amerika is Afraka. Hence, all Afrakans are by default at home when they are in America/Amerika.

From the perspective of the Tanak, the Israelites stole or invaded, and forcefully took ancient Canaanites/Kanaanites land (Afraka's land) under the pretense of Israelites' God Yahweh (originally one of the many Canaanite Gods) claiming that their god/God asked them to invade, and overtake Canaanites' Afrakan land. This then implies that, the so-called Western invaders under the Pope's *"Doctrine of Discovery"* in 1452 through to the 19th century that led to inhumane barbaric rape, murder, theft, invasions, and seizure of aboriginal chocolate melanated sun-kissed first nation people's land, and wealth was mainly inspired by the exact invasive actions of the supposed Israelites against the Canaanites/Kanaanites (a.k.a Ham's Afrakan land).

So, if this theory or concept is proven to be true, then that means that, when reparations are paid to the supposed original Israelites known as the Negros, and other ethnic groups of West Afraka, then the recipients of the reparations must in turn pay reparations in land, and appropriate monetary aspect to the original land owners, who are the Canaanites/Kanaanites a.k.a part of Afrakans (Ham's descendants). This makes logical sense because the original of all originals in terms of land ownership in this region of discussion were the Canaanite/Kanaanites a.k.a Hamites.

It comes with no surprise that today's Canada/Kanada sounds and spells almost or identical to ancient Canaan/Kanaan. In Canada/Kanada, there is what is known as the *Tower of Babel,* located at Alberta, Canada. Looking at the view, size, and soil/gravel composites exposes some massive facts to this claim. Obviously, some folks would argue that, ancient Canaan is in modern day Iraq, this is arguable since names, and places have changed over time. Notwithstanding, Iraq's landmass was originally called Mesopotamia. Mesopotamia was the landmass for the original highly technologically, and spiritually civilized people of Sumer/El-Zuma/Zuma, Akkad, Babylon, and Assyria.

These are all original Afrakans a.k.a Ham's descendants' land. Majority of these original ancient people migrated to today's West Afraka with their royals, kinsmen, doctors, engineers, scientist, spiritualists, etc. No wonder Arabs' trans-Sahara slave trade, and Western world's trans-Atlantic slaved trade went to West Afraka for the doctors, engineers, scientists, spiritualists, and some kinsmen to help develop the lands they invaded, and stole through war from the same Afrakans. These Arabs and Western

Etymology of Compendiums of all Gods and The Almighty Creator

colonizers plagiarized everything from these Afrakans, from their religion to science, to societal norms.

These are facts that are easily proven to be true. No wonder, Russian leader Vladimir Putin around April, 2023 showed the entire world that Afrakans were the so-called apostles, holy people, and people of the Tanak. The Pope prays to the *Black Madonna or Black Afrakan woman* a.k.a *Black Mary*. The goal in this chapter is not about the appearance of the apostles, so let's move on with our discussion.

The writers and publishing companies of the Tanak, and public bibles flipped things upside-down to demonize Hamites/Afrakans while in actuality, the authentic owners of these lands, and massive civilizations are all Afrakans, or Hamites. No wonder, to date there are places around the world that still hold the name *"Ham"* to their cities or towns. Places such as:

HAM is a "black" Man or better yet, a dark/burnt chocolate melated Afrakan man.

1. Birmingham, England, UK = 1,141,374 (2018 est.)

2. Markham, Ontario = 328,966 (2016)

3. Nottingham, England, UK = 321,500 (2015)

4. Durham, North Carolina = 274,291 (2018 est.)

5. Birmingham, Alabama = 209,880 (2018 est.)

6. Wrexham, Wales, UK = 149,000 (2011)

7. Tottenham, England, UK = 129,237 (2011)

8. Gresham, Oregon = 110,158 (2018 est.)

9. Rotherham, England, UK = 109,691 (2011)

10. Gillingham, Kent, England, UK = 104,157 (2011)

11. Chatham-Kent, Ontario = 101,647 (2016)

12. Oldham, England, UK = 96,555 (2011)

Etymology of Compendiums of all Gods and The Almighty Creator

13. Bellingham, Washington = 90,665 (2018 est.)

14. Framingham, Massachusetts = 72,032 (2017 est.)

15. Mitcham, England, UK = 63,393 (2011)

16. Waltham, Massachusetts = 62,962 (2018 est.)

17. Beckenham, England, UK = 56,668 (2011)

18. Horsham, England, UK = 55,657 (2001)

19. Altricham, England, UK = 52,419 (2011)

20. Twickenham, England, UK = 52,396 (2011)

21. Durham, England, UK = 48,069 (2011)

22. Wokingham, England, UK = 46,745 (2017 est.)

23. Pakenham, Victoria, Australia = 46,421 (2016)

24. Chippenham, England, UK = 45,337 (2011)

25. Grantham, England, UK = 44,580 (2016 est.)

26. Lytham St. Annes, England, UK = 42,954 (2011)

27. Fareham, England, UK = 42,210 (2011)

28. Farnham, england, UK = 49,488 (2011)

29. Billingham, England, UK = 35,165 (2011)

30. Needham, Massachusetts = 30,999 (2011)

31. Feltham, England, UK = 27,104 (2011)

32. Dedham, Massachusetts = 25,364 (2017)

33. Withal, England, UK = 25,353 (2011)

34. Rainham, England, UK = 25,000 (2011 est.)

35. Pelham, Alabama = 23,493 (2017 est.)

36. Evesham, England, UK = 23,428 (2011)

37. Penworthham, England, UK = 23,047 (2011)

38. Natham, India = 22,533 (2001)

39. Hingham, Massachusetts = 22,157 (2010)

Etymology of Compendiums of all Gods and The Almighty Creator

40. Wareham, Massachusetts = 21,822 (2010)

41. Chesham, England, UK = 21,483 (2011)

42. Stoneham, Massachusetts = 21,437 (2010)

43. Birmingham, Michigan = 21,322 (2018 est.)

44. Waltham Abbey, England, UK = 21,149 (2011)

45. Caterham, England, UK = 21,030 (2011)

46. Shoreham-by-Sea, England, UK = 20,547 (2011)

47. Hailsham, England, UK = 20,476 (2011)

48. Seaham, England, UK = 20,179 (2011)

49. Burnham-on-Sea, England, UK = 19,576 (2011)

50. Faversham, England, UK = 19,316 (2011)

51. Dereham, England, UK = 18,609 (2011)

52. Windham, Maine = 17,272 (2012 est.)

53. Cottingham, England, UK = 17,164 (2011)

54. Brigham, England, UK = 16,693 (2011)

55. Horsham, Victoria, Australia = 16,792 (2016)

56. Windlesham, England, UK = 16,775 (2010)

57. Keynsham, England, UK = 16,641 (2011)

58. Brenham, Texas = 15,716 (2010)

59. Graham, North Carolina = 15,086 (2018 est.)

60. Horsham, Pennsylvania = 14,842 (2010)

61. Melksham, England, UK = 14,677 (2011)

62. Durham, New Hampshire = 14,638 (2010)

63. Rockingham, WA, Australia = 14,428 (2016)

64. Wymondham, England, UK = 14,405 (2011)

65. Amersham, England, UK = 14,384 (2011)

66. West Wickham, England, UK = 14,276 (2011)

Etymology of Compendiums of all Gods and The Almighty Creator

67. North Hykehem, England, UK = 13,884 (2011)

68. Pelham, New Hampshire = 13,681 (2017 est.)

69. Windham, New Hampshire = 23,592 (2010)

70. Raynham, Massachusetts = 13,383 (2010)

71. Corsham, England, UK = 13,000 (2011)

72. Buckingham, England, UK = 12,890 (2011)

73. Chatham, Illinois = 12,674 (2018 est.)

74. North Walsham, England, UK = 12,634 (2011)

75. Effingham, Illinois = 12,627 (2018 est.)

76. Pelham, New York = 12,585 (2016 est.)

77. Hersham, England, UK = 12,414 (2011)

78. Wrentham, Massachusetts = 11,838 (2017)

79. Hexham, England, UK = 11,829 (2011)

80. Gillingham, Dorset, England, UK = 11,756 (2011)

81. Hexham, England, UK = 11,289 (2011)

82. Dagenham, England, UK = 11,267 (2011)

83. Taverham, England, UK = 10,142 (2011)

84. Bonham, Texas = 10,127 (2010)

85. Padiham, England, UK = 10,098 (2011)

sources:
en.wikipedia.org

maps.google.com

2019 Rand McNally Road Atlas

https://en.wikipedia.org/wiki/List_of_towns_in_England

Source: https://panethos.wordpress.com/2019/11/27/worlds-largest-ham-suffix-cities/

Ham or Afrakans literally civilized the entire world. They were the builders, architects, scientists, teachers, inventors, innovators, mathematicians, doctors, spiritualists, great warriors, mighty men, and women, royals, and everything.

Ham or Afrakans are those who are mysteriously intelligent, and builders of massive civilizations. Decolonize your mind from the biblical, Tanak, and Quran lies about Hamites being cursed. That is a big lie. Ham was never cursed, even in their own book, it was Canaan, one of Ham's children who was "supposedly" cursed by Noah (the albino Afrakan man). Read it from Genesis 9:25 *"And he said, Cursed be <u>Canaan</u>; a servant of servants shall he be unto his brethren."*

At the age of Aquarius, we all owe it to ourselves to seek the facts and flee from over 2,000 years of lies and forgery. So, even in the eyes of the bible, Tanak, and Quran, the true original owners of the lands in so-called ancient Israel are the Canaanites/Kanaanites, one of the children of Ham, the great. Nimrod, is also a descendant of Ham, so envision all the great civilizations Nimrod built. Nimrod ruled for well over 500 years, he literally was the conqueror of the entire world at his time. Nimrod built massive civilizations known to man.

Locating the tower of Babel means, Nimrod the Afrakan, owned those lands a.k.a Afrakan lands. If we are to track all the areas that Nimrod developed, almost half of the entire planet would be under him. So, if Amerika is to be proven as Afraka, then, it may be obvious to state from the Tanak, and biblical analysis that, Afrakans are then the original settlers, and aboriginals of the beautiful geographical landmarks of North, and South Amerika.

From a global historic perspective, over 250 million years ago, the entire continents were connected as one landmass known as Pangaea. This information is widely accepted by all academia globally. It has long been an indisputable fact around the world when it comes to the information about the entire earth connecting as one landmass. Aboriginal chocolate, and copper melanated people already existed far before this time. This is not about the modern humans a.k.a "white people", these are very new people comparable to the existence of aboriginal chocolate melanated people.

Information gathered from USGS.gov, that is, United States Geological Sciences, states that:
"From about 300-200 million years ago (late Paleozoic Era until the very late Triassic), the continent we now know as North America was contiguous with Africa, South America, and Europe. They all existed as a single continent called Pangea. Pangea first began to be torn apart when a three-pronged fissure grew between Africa, South America, and North America. Rifting began as magma welled up through the weakness in the crust, creating a volcanic rift zone. Volcanic eruptions spewed ash and volcanic debris across the landscape as these severed continent-sized fragments of Pangea diverged. The gash between the spreading continents gradually grew to form a new ocean basin, the Atlantic. The rift zone known as the mid-Atlantic ridge continued to provide the raw volcanic materials for the expanding ocean basin.
Meanwhile, North America was slowly pushed westward away from the rift zone. The thick continental crust that made up the new east coast collapsed into a series of down-dropped fault blocks that roughly parallel today's coastline. At first, the hot, faulted edge of the continent was high and buoyant relative to the new ocean basin. As the edge of North America moved away from the hot rift zone, it began to cool and subside beneath the new Atlantic Ocean. This once-active divergent plate boundary became the passive, trailing edge of westward moving North America. In plate tectonic terms, the Atlantic Plain is known as a classic example of a passive continental margin.
Today, the Mesozoic and Cenozoic sedimentary rock layers that lie beneath much of the coastal plain and fringing continental shelf remain nearly horizontal." -https://www.usgs.gov/faqs/what-was-pangea#:~:text=From%20about %20300%2D200%20million,a%20single%20continent%20called%20Pangea.

So, if there is a global indisputable academic acceptance of Pangaea, then it is intellectually, and factually safe to say that, Afrakans walked on the lands of today's Amerikas, Asia, Europa/Europe, Oceania, and Antarctica. It is also widely accepted that the first man or woman to walk on this planet is an Afrakan. At this time, you should know the meaning and origination of the word, Afrakan.

It is not surprising that there are pyramids found globally. This may possibly indicate that, the symbol of the apex of the Afrakans' civilizations was the pyramid. The pyramid was an energetic frequency harvester, or converter. This is an ethereal energetic spiritual harnessing of the energies above to the energies below on earth. This must have been the time when traveling between dimensions were like booking a flight or taking a road trip to your favorite vacation spot. This era must have been magical.

Currently, the entire geographical map is a lie. The map has been flipped upside down, and from left to right with things pointed to opposite directions. Pilots are made to sign non-disclosure agreements before they become pilots. For starters, you can look into *"what is the true north pole?"* or better yet, *"true north is south"*, to read more about this misdirection that modern colonizers have pushed through all platforms. The compass of ship captains or sailors have true north, and magnetic north differing from one another.

If things were not placed in reversed, and flipped from east to west, then, true north, would be north, and magnetic north, would be magnetic north with no complicated mambo jumbo explanations. Nature doesn't lie, but humans in power through colonization lie. They've renamed, and relocated places and things to fit their made-up narratives. Today's East is actually ancient West, and today's South is ancient North. What is known as South Afraka, is actually North Afraka. Get the map and flip it to the original position by flipping the current map upside down.

There are sphinx and pyramids in the Grand Canyons, Arizona. There are debatable ongoing discussions that the sphinx and pyramids found in the Grand Canyon are far older than those at today's Egypt in Afraka. This may be true based on the fact that West Afraka is very close to

North and South Amerika. There are places like Utah/Yutah/Yudah/Yawdah that also houses massive information about Afrakans' presence in Amerika. The Hebrew language, paleo Hebrew, is linked to Greek, and Aramaic which are all linked to the original source, the Akan Twi. There are lots of places throughout South Amerika that also support these facts. Places in Canada/Kanada as discussed previously also exposes Afrakans civilizations in the Amerikas.

Additionally, there is absolutely no way under the sun that the mighty blood lines of great ancient Atlantis, Kemet, Summer, Akkad, and Mesopotamia were just wiped out from the face of the earth, while the subjects of these massive Afrakan kingdoms, and civilizations are alive till today. If there is any war today, the nobles, presidents, wealthy, and society leaders are definitely going to have the utmost safety and protection. Most of the people who would suffer the outcome of any war or cataclysmic catastrophe would be the citizens, or everyday workers, or people.

Hence, the Afrakan royals or descendants of these massive long reigning empires are still here. These royals and high level people from these civilizations migrated or relocated to mostly today's West Afraka, and throughout some parts of Afraka. There is a reason why, it has been documented that the first ever university in the world is, University of Timbuktu in Mali, West Afraka. There is a reason why, the richest man ever known to have walked on the surface of the earth is, from West Afraka, known as Mansa Musa. Amerika has different names, some are Kemet, Tameri (given by the Afrakan King/Pharaoh), Turtle Island, ancient Egypt, Atlantis, the "old world", Amoorika/Amuurika (as in dark/black Moors), etc. The aboriginal people of the Amerikas are copper, and chocolate melanated people, or

Etymology of Compendiums of all Gods and The Almighty Creator

Afrakans. Later, Europeans shipped more of their people in boats, and ships to the Amerikas after the *Doctrine of Discovery's* damages, caused by the Catholic Pope.

The Vatican, British library, and museums have lots of artifacts, books, and documents that would also support this claim. In that, Rome conquered and ruled the so-called Amerikas after the Greeks, far before the Moors, and Arab-Muslim wave came through, following the much recent European colonizers under the *Doctrine of Discovery*. The Vatican knew where the Afrakans were. West Afrakans have records of fighting with the Greeks, Romans, and Arab-Muslims which pushed the original Afrakans in these lands to relocate to today's West Afraka.

The burning of the library of Alexandria in ancient Kemet/Egypt, Afraka was just one of the many massive fire burning destruction used by the so-called Greeks, Romans, Arab-Muslims, and recent European Colonizers to completely destroy all melanated Afrakan civilizations. Blowing up noses of Afrakan statues was the least of their barbaric destructive rampages.

These barbaric destroyers completely burned down into ashes what was once known as the *"garden city"* of the Asante kingdom in today's Ghana, West Afraka. They looted gold swords, helmets, and other massive gold relics that were precious to these kingdoms in Ghana, West Afraka.

The Greeks, Romans, and especially Arab-Muslims, and much later on, the European colonizers used fire to burn down old Ghana empire, Mali Empire, great civilizations of Benin, which housed the longest wall ever built by man in the entire world known as, the *"Great Walls of Benin"*, and literally all kingdoms within the great Afrakan continent.

Everywhere they went to war against the now fallen Gods and Goddesses on the Afrakan continent, they made sure to burn down everything from universities, libraries, technologies, research centers, temples, buildings, to even scrolls. These barbaric destroyers were ruthless, all thanks to the gun powder given to them by China around 9th century CE (Common Era).

They used the same destructive fire burning strategies to completely burn down aboriginal civilizations throughout the Amerikas, and especially in North Amerika as well. There are so many records reflecting these intentional destructive fires, and explosions of great aboriginal civilizations within Amerika.

I cannot emphasize enough that, the Greeks, Romans, so-called Arab-Muslims, and recent European Colonizers teared everything down, brutally looted, and burned down everything built by the aboriginal civilizations into complete ashes. Their nature was complete mayhem around this time. They were blood thirsty rampage destroyers. The records are at their museums, libraries, and Vatican's underground archived library that spans more than 53 miles (85 kilometers) in selective catalogs alone from the time of Pope Innocent III (r. 1198 -1216) to date.

The much recent European colonization was the last straw for Afrakans, especially West Afrakans to entertain. They had to fight to death, or for their freedom/independence. In that, these West Afrakans had nowhere else to move to after losing all their lands, civilizations, and relocating to their current geographical place. Hence, West Afrakans aggressively resisted, fought, and gained their independence with Ghana leading the way.

Another area of importance worth stating, is the reign of the Afrakan Moors. Factual archives unfold that, for more than 800 years, the Afrakan Moors had a massive era of supreme rule over Europe, Asia minor, and the Amerikas. These Moors dominated and ruled with great influence around 711 -1492. Do you now see why the Catholic Pope signed the *Doctrine of Discovery* into enforcement in 1493? Two bulls of Nicholas V are documented to have been implemented obviously after the eventual end of the Moors or may I say, when majority of the Moors merged with the Catholic church, and the Pope to suppress, and oppress the original Afrakan royals, *Dum diversas* -1452 and *Romanus Pontifex* -1455; and Alexander VI's bull *Inter caetera* - *1493*.

Have you really thought about how on earth these so-called "white people" (misnomer) colonized the entire aboriginal lands? It was with the help of the sellout Moors. These Moors looked like the chocolate melanated Afrakans. In other words, the phrase *"not all skin folks are kinfolks"* is literal here. Yes, the early eras of the 15th centuries and below were all dark colored people who fought, oppressed, and colonized another dark colored aboriginal people. *It is important to emphasize that, the "power force" behind the success of the so-called "white" colonizers are actually people who look just like the chocolate, and copper colored melanated aboriginal people.* Mind boggling? Hell no.
So then, you come to the realization that, United States of Amerika have pyramids, and one of the oldest obelisks in the world. The obelisk is aboriginal Afrakans' symbolic representation for the *"god within us"*, and the *"sun God"* who sails overhead. *My explanation of the obelisk is that, the obelisk is just like the spine within us, with the tip at the top representing the axis and the atlas.* Our brain is the holly of hollies, most consciously spiritual, as the seat of the God within us. Hence, the *"sun God"* sailing overhead.

The pyramid on the United States of America's dollar bill with an *"all-seeing eye"* is not evil either. Rather, it has similar symbolic representation as the *"third eye"*, our spiritual eye, representing our God-self, all-seeing one eye, a.k.a *"third eye"* within us, and the rest of the pyramid represents our body from the neck down to our feet. We are all electromagnetic beings, we all generate electricity, we are all souls, and spirits. These are all energies. Hence, it is safe to say that, the Almighty Creator, the all powerful energetic vibrating force lives in us. So, we are not just mere mortals, rather, ethereal energetic vibrating frequencies filled with massive supernatural powers lying dormant. Detach yourself from everything, go within to activate your authentic self, and ignite your "avatar".

This innerstanding is very paramount for the redemption of the original global superpowers of civilizations a.k.a the Afrakans, the Gods and Goddesses, who are spread out throughout the face of the entire earth. There is an obelisk in Washington DC, London, and Vatican City. These folks still show the entire world, either directly or indirectly that, the ancient Afrakans' knowledge, sciences, and spirituality are still at play. Although, it has been hijacked, corrupted, and severely watered-down to misinform the masses of its authentic power, and with its meaning almost diminished; the person who decides to humbly seek wisdom, knowledge, and facts, would know where to go to find it. Travel to Afraka, however, especially West Afraka, and reconnect to the true original first people of planet earth.

Back to the Moors, the Moors originally constituted dark chocolate melanated people from Afraka, mainly from the areas of Western Sahara, Tunisia, Morocco, Niger (the Azawagh Arabs), Mali (the Azawagh Arabs), Mauritania and parts of Algeria. This was far before these dark Afrakan Moors took "Caucasians" as their servants, groomed them, and civilized some of these Caucasians as security guards, servants, army fighters, and even had children with the Caucasian women. You shouldn't be surprise as to why Rome, and the Pope at the time had to relocate (resettle) the "mixed breeds" a.k.a light skin Arabs to most of the regions the Moors invaded at North Afraka, and so-called today's "Middle East".

There is a reason why there are so many hijacks of aboriginal Afrakan cultures, and traditions that were twisted, washed down, and flipped inside-out to form both Christian and the new Islamic religions for these modern new breeds of people. There are unspoken historical facts that are in the British museums, that expose exactly how the "light skin Arabs" came about, and as well as how the so-called Caucasians "white people" (caucus mountains) came about. These facts are all there for anyone willing to research, or better yet, travel to the British museum to learn more about these information.

Amexem, according to Moorish science history, and Moorish topological maps, used to be a beautiful ancient name for the land mass that used to stretch, and constitutes North and South Amerika, Afraka, and what is known today as "Middle East". This geographical region on current topological maps has either been renamed, reassigned or completely erased by current folks who control the information, and media houses. You can dig into Moorish maps, Moorish science, and Moorish history to get more facts that has been distorted in modern day society. Yes, prior to the Greeks, and Romans fighting, toppling over aboriginal Afrakans global rule, and dominance, the Afrakans also fought with much older civilizations. The rabbit hole goes deeper, and it goes all the way to the original royals of earth. Majority of these royals, and kingdoms, literally relocated to today's West Afraka. Countries like Ghana, Nigeria, Senegal, Mali, Niger, and the Sahara desert area (as I call it Saara/Sarai/Sarah desert) hold rich ancient knowledge that has been "shadow-banned" from the world, by the "colonizers" who were not able to conquer these people in West Afraka.

Digging deeper into the long reign of the Moors, which in fact, is even lengthier than the "new face, new mask" European colonizers' era, would connect more dots to validate the high factual possible outcome that, the Amerikas was indeed Afraka, or part of Afraka. Spend massive amount of time to get old literature, maps, and books, written by original Moors to see the names, and locations of places that have been renamed, relocated, and flipped upside down to confuse the masses. It is all done to hide what was stolen from the true original Afrakan rulers, and owners, who lost their civilizations, aboriginal home lands, and wealth, to relocate or re-establish themselves at today's West Afraka.

The Greenwich Meridian (longitude 0 degrees), and the Equator (latitude 0 degrees), meet at Ghana's waters in West Afraka. This indicates that, this is the true accurate fact based *center of the entire Earth*. There is a monument unveiled at a specific landmark in a city called Tema, in Ghana, West Afraka that indicates where the Greenwich Meridian travels through southwards into the ocean, meeting the Equator at the factual, and accurate *Center of the Earth's* location. This makes Ghana, West Afraka, the closest nation in the entire world to the center of Earth. This is not publicized, because, those in-charge do not want the world to wake up, and also, they do not want Ghana, West Afraka to gain lot of tourist attractions. In that, it would lead to their economic freedom, and global popularity. The point I want to establish here is that, the high priests who led the royals, Kings, Queens, and their entourage to relocate to these lands in West Afraka, knew the direction to the true central magnetic pull of Earth.

After all, some of their wisdom, knowledge, and spirituality, which were hijacked by the invaders, are still used to rule the world to this day, although, they lost everything to the invaders who looked like them in appearance. The people of West Afraka, and all the chocolate melanated parts of Afraka, are part of the ancient aboriginal people of earth. These ancient people walked, ruled, civilized, and established many kingdoms throughout the Amerikas, and rest of the world, for several uncountable number of years before their downfall. They are the ones who would rule the entire Earth again, at the appointed time. This is the *"Kingdom of heaven (God) on earth"* era that almost everyone is waiting for it to happen.

There is a strong connection between the aboriginal rulers of the royal seat of London, and the Kings and Queens of West Afraka, especially in Ghana, West Afraka. Once again, these West Afrakans lost all their kingdoms, and had to relocate to their current locations. They will re-emerge to rule the entire earth, when the appointed time arrives. No flesh under the sun can stop this fact from happening. When it is time, the *"Kingdom of God"*, would be established on earth once again. This is the answer to all the parables in the so-called Bible, or Sun Book, a.k.a Helios Biblios.

To know, and to be able to identify a terrorist, is to learn, live, and operate like a terrorist. To learn, live, and operate like a terrorist, is to become the terrorist. So, my question to you now is, who is the terrorist? Is it the announcer of terrorism, who when he or she announces that there is a terrorist in town, then, all of a sudden a terrorist problem emerges, or the town that enjoys its peace far away from the global announcer? Who really knows the ways of the terrorist, but the terrorist himself. Who advises the terrorist, but the terrorist himself. Who supplies the weaponry used by the terrorist, but the in-house terrorist himself.

Who lays out the detailed plans of the networking, and strongholds of the terrorist, but the terrorist, and his affiliates. Who is the friend of the terrorist, but he who supplies the needs, and wants to the terrorist. Oh I say to you, follow the model, make, manufactured date, and components of the terrorist's weaponry, and you will know the backbone of the terrorist.

He who supplies the weaponry needs, and wants for the terrorist, is the terrorist. In that, there couldn't be a terrorist without an inside person supplying sensitive details of information to the terrorist to know the blue prints of planned executions. The accomplice is the terrorist, and the terrorist, is the accomplice. This is how you identify a terrorist, and all his or her terrorism.

Withstanding all the points raised in my submission, the theory or concept of Amerika being Afraka, is very plausible, and not far fetched. The Americas is plausibly, the aboriginal Afraka, and aboriginal Afraka, is the aboriginal Amerikas. Names and locations have been switched, and flipped to confuse the masses. Hence, the truth, and facts are scarier than the very fictitious information that the Western invaders have fed you with so far.

WHAT IS LIFE?

What is life?
Life is breath. Without breath, there is absolutely no life.

Breath is the ethereal harmonization of the four key elementals, those are, the element of fire, air, water, and earth. Breath is the core foundation of all lives. The greatest experience one could ever have in life, is his or her ability to properly learn the mechanism of breathing. The ability to master the mechanisms of breathing, the dynamics involved, flexibility to harmonize changing situations, or circumstances with your breathing, and ability to consciously feel the unseen art of breathing through your cells, and organs, would be key to unlocking life's secrets.

Characteristics of life come into light after the presence of life itself. Hence, the current data of knowledge available to man's kind to describing life, is basically just sharing the properties, or behaviors of life forms, however, none of them clearly defines life itself. This is why, I decided to give a next level innerstanding, a definitive definition of what life truly is.

Biological perspective stipulates that, life is a "characteristic property" of all living things that shows homeostasis, stimuli (response to stimuli), reproduction, growth, evolves, organization, energy processing, respiration, and dependent on their environment.

Scientifically, there is the view that life is about the interactions of matter and energy. The scientific lens sees this property as super complex mechanisms or systems of operational interactions that emerges from not-yet fully comprehensible complex interaction between matter and energy.

Existential and experiential view of life stem from the world of "mysteries", unpredictability, uncertainty, personal, subjective encounters, and perceptions, married with a dose of responsibility, accountability, freedom, relationships, authenticity, thoughts, emotions, and "endless" navigation.

Philosophically and culturally, life is seen as a journey that reflects how you live, love, believe, practice, values, ritual, grow, experience, explore, and learn through discovering yourself through individual meaning, and purpose.

The General Spiritual view on life unfolds from a state of a "sacred gift" from a supernatural creator, that grants grace, and opportunities to explore. This is a start to comprehending life, however, the missing secret fact is that, life itself is the overall *breath* of the *Almighty Creator*, the *Energetic Source of everything*, the *Formless and Shapeless Unseen Force of all forces*. The souls of the soul people are the hidden duplicated parts of the *Almighty Creator*, the *Energetic Source of everything's* existence, and validation of that is the ethereal spiritual essence, known as *Breath*. The Soul, a.k.a "authentic self", taking a material form (*Earth*, physical), lives (breath, breathe, breathing *Air*), through manifestation of its powerful presence (Word, *Fire*) traveling through the ethereal medium (*Water*, Moisture, Moist) to experience itself.

Despite all the Western colonizer's controlled media and distorted information propaganda purported onto the global masses, especially on the continent of Afraka, the fiery wave of spiritual and conscious awakening cannot be quenched. It is time and season for wisdom and knowledge to rise through us all like the golden phoenix rising from the ashes.

For well over six centuries and two decades, since the introduction of the heinous and barbaric *Doctrine of Discovery* by the Catholic church and its Pope, our world has been ruled by thieves, robbers, scammers, bullies, deceivers, murderers, grave ambushes, rapers of aboriginal lands, resources and artifacts, who continuously seek to intimidate those who stand for pure justice, fairness and balance without any fear or favor through non-violent emancipation. Within their own bible, there is a call for restitution from the so-called old testaments (Tanak) and the new testaments. The restitution references from their own bible states that: *"A thief must certainly make restitution, but if he has nothing, he must be sold to pay for his theft."-**Exodus 22:3** NIV/KJV.* Also, restitution from Zacchaeus in Luke 19:8 *"Zacchaeus stood up and said to the Lord, "Look, Lord! Here and now I give half of my possessions to the poor, and if I have cheated anybody out of anything, I will pay back four times the amount."*

Both the Catholic church at Vatican, and all Western colonizers, still have at their possession, the gold, artifacts, books, scrolls, lands, and resources stolen from Afrakans and global chocolate aboriginal first nation people of earth. Restitution must be enforced for the Pope and all Western colonizers to return, or give back in double all the stolen items in their vaults, museums, banks, and lands.

For far too long, false information has been pushed about Afrakans and all chocolate aboriginal first nation people for being lazy, primitive, and uncivilized. Meanwhile, the fact is that, these Afrakans are the most civilized groups of Gods and Goddesses on earth. By now, you should know that Afrakans civilized the entire planet.

By now, you should know that, the Torah was plagiarized from the ancient Kamitic/Kemetic/Egyptian word "Tua Ra". Tua Ra means "the worship of Ra". Let's look at Quran which was also plagiarized and stolen from the ancient Egyptian/Kamitic/Kemetic word "Khu RA". Khu Ra means "the worship of Ra". Now, let us look at the so-called Holly Bible, this book is plagiarized from "Helios Byblos/Bilios" which means "Sun Book or Sun Papers". This is also plagiarized from the RA "Sun worship" in ancient Egypt/Kamit/Kemet.

Ancient Kamit/Egypt/Kemet and other terrifically great Afrakan civilizations like Summer, Old Ghana Empire, Dogons, Göbekli Tepe (a.k.a Ewes/Eves of West Afraka), Mali Empire, Songhai Empire, Kushite Kingdom (Kingdom of Kush), Carthage/Karthage, Punt land (Land and kingdom of Punt), Aksum Empire, Great Zimbabwe, and today's traditional Afrakan cultures are well aware of the facts and paths to connect us to the true Almighty Creator.

Ancient samurais, monks, Buddha, great Gods and Goddesses of India, and all aboriginal people throughout Asia (a.k.a Ephesus or Anatolia far before Herodotus) were all Afrakans, or as I call them, chocolate melanated aboriginal first nations of earth. Withstanding aboriginal people of the continent of Oceania, constituting Australasia, Melanesia, Micronesia, and Polynesia were all Afrakans, chocolate melanated first nation people. Any untouched or "virgin" Islands either inhabited by known men and women, or unknown to the rest of the world, are home to yet-to-be-in-contact Afrakan ancestors living their best lives, disconnected from this colonized world. The true founders of Medicine, Engineering, Mathematics, Astronomy, Metallurgy, Architecture, Navigation, Aerospace, and all inventions under the sun have been revealed to you in this book.

The more and deeper into the earth archaeologists dig, the more dark chocolate melanated Afrakans they find. Be it so-called extraterrestrials, aliens or UFOs, you will always find dark melanated Afrakans a.k.a dark matter, a.k.a the "God particles", a.k.a melanin, a.k.a the Gods and Goddesses of earth who came from infinite into material existence. It comes with no surprise that Afrakans are naturally and biologically spiritual.

All Afrakans, chocolate melanated aboriginal first people of earth naturally have rhythm. They naturally move to the tune of any sound or musical tunes no matter where this sound may come from within the continents of earth, and the universe. The core foundational spark of all creations began with a sound. Sound is coded within the melanin of all Afrakans. They move effortlessly to the tune of all sounds. The connection to the Almighty Creator, moves in rhythmic sound waves. This is the spark of what I call, life. Sound ignites all vibrations, in turn, vibrations ignite what we call life. Air moves in rhythmic vibrations. Everything alive moves within the energetic forces of sound waves. Breathing is movement, breathing in and out is a vibrational movement of spiritual energy sustained by the power of rhythmic sound waves.

So, Afrakans, all chocolate and copper melanated aboriginal first nation people must keep on dancing, and move to every rhythm of music, and sound waves. In that, this is the blue print to awakening the "resting deactivated" God and Goddesses melanated DNA coded within your soul. Meditation is directly connected to the faintest rhythmic sound waves unheard within our noisy, and distracted material realm. The quieter and calmer you become through meditations, the closer you are to tapping into this faint sound wave rhythm. There is a reason why some of the people who meditate, chant at times to resonate the rhythmic sound-waves within their internal universe, to connect to their external cosmos. The key to awakening or reactivating your dormant God and Goddess DNA, is directly linked to your inner soul. It is all found within you.

Permit me to conclude this book by restating a pivotal statement I stated in chapter 1, it goes like this:
One of the most powerful weapons effective to destabilize the strength, power, intellectual agility, and the union of any friendship, relationship, family, community, institutions, municipality, a state, region or a nation is *the seed of discord*.

Once effectively sowed, you can easily control, manipulate and destroy such people's identity, confidence, knowledge and their very worth. Such distorted people will believe anything outside of themselves.

The countries that were involved in the Berlin Conference, a.k.a *"Scramble for Afraka"* included Austria-Hungary, Belgium, Denmark, France, Germany, Great Britain, Italy, the Netherlands, Portugal, Russia, Spain, Sweden-Norway (unified for the span of almost four months of deliberations, from 11/15/1884 – 02/26/1885), Turkey, and the United States of America. This greedy and violently aggressive inhumane decision taken by these European "terribles" divided Afraka among themselves into the current boundaries that we have within Afraka. These European "terribles" used murder, wars, rape, enslavement, inhumane consumption of some Afrakans, their bible, Catholicism, and Christianity to achieve their wickedly demonic goals.

The world is fucked up today because of these European "terribles". Never forget that the Pope's *Doctrine of Discovery* was the European "terribles" root cause of empowerment to carry this demonic act. The devil came to steal, kill and destroy.

The European "terribles" are the devil that everyone is looking for. The European "terribles" are the anti-Christs that everyone wants to be saved from. Who have been tormenting the world from mid 1400 to date? Exactly, that's the devil's work. This is definitely not the work of the *Almighty Creator*. Look no further for the devil, for the devil a.k.a the European "terribles" are right in your faces.

Their museums are filled with Afrakan civilization artifacts and relics. How pathetic is that? They have zero civilization or history to display. If they did, then none of their museums would be filled with 99% of Afrakan civilization artifacts and relics. The evidence is there for all to see. Who are the intelligent and civilized ones in this situation? Is it the Afrakans or the European "terribles"?

With wisdom, knowledge and common sense, we all know that, Afrakans are the civilized and intelligent ones. Look at all the supporting evidences displayed in all the museums of the European "terribles". So, I call on all humanitarian organizations, as well as global institutions to demand for Afraka's immediate restitution of all stolen stuff, and reparations with 45% interest.

Criminals, murderers, and inhumane European "terribles" have no right to tell the world what civility looks like, or how to be a humanitarian.

Whenever you hear of the Anunaki, Akaddians, Mesopotamia, ancient Sumerians (originally El-Zuma/Zuma in today's Sudan), Yoruba/Oruba/Euroba/Europa/Europe, Asia, North and South Amerika/Tameri, Dogons, Göbekli Tepe (Ewes), Afraka/Aeothiopia/Alkebullan/Kemet, Oceania, Antarctica, Atlantis, Pangea, first ever greatest civilizations, royals, the Gods and Goddesses, advanced technologies, and all so-called super heroes, know that they are talking about Afrakans. The true all powerful source of everything lives for eons in time, the first manifestations of physical creations (earth, water, trees, man, woman, animals, etc) were all chocolate melanated beings and entities. The core of all these creations contains dark matter a.k.a melanin in animals, humans, and what is known as chlorophyll in plants. This dark matter is directly from the *divine source of all powerful creative energetic vibrating living frequency.*

Currently, 99% of the world's media both printing and digital is controlled by colonizers. Hence, it is obvious that these colonizers would only place themselves in the mix as the original people, meanwhile, everything in nature, especially the sun, rejects these colonizers.

Yes, the Gods and the Goddess have fallen from their grace and unfathomable spiritual prowess to the extent that, now they die like men and women. There has been a catastrophic disconnect between these fallen Gods and Goddesses, and their true source to the original divine of *all powerful energetic vibrating creator of all frequencies*.

A huge spell of forgetfulness and self-loathing has been cast upon these Gods and Goddesses. However, they are gradually remembering who they are. They're realizing how important dark matter a.k.a melanin is to them and the importance for them to reconnect to the great black sun, in order to reactivate their God and Goddesses self-hood.

The entire world's religions rest on the shoulders of the original authentic Afrakan spirituality, and Afrakan Gods and Goddesses. Majority of these world religions are synthetic, quack, fraud, plagiarized, and baloney lullabies impregnated with lies, deception and forgeries. The synthetic can never replace the authentic original Afrakan spirituality.

Colonizers would never give those whom they colonized accurate information to know who they truly are. So, be extremely mindful of the references and sources of information sourced from all the colonizer's institutions and platforms. To know yourself is to source information directly from your ancestors, inner-self, elders in your ethnic groups, writers and researchers.

This book has come at the age of Aquarius, whereby you have the inalienable power to question everything, and seek divine guidance. Never accept information from any colonizer about who you are, or who your ancestors were at face value. Never accept their so-called "approved" references, and sources of information as the ultimate. It is time for you to know your roots. Know thyself, re-member who you are, reconnect with your true divine ancestors, reconnect with your soul, and to spiritually and psychologically redeem your likeness of the true *Almighty energetic vibrating frequency power of all creations.*

You must decolonize your mind from all the religious indoctrination. You are encouraged to make sure that you become emancipated, and truly independent.

By independence, I mean politically independent, economically independent, socially independent, psychologically independent, spiritually independent, religiously independent, and culturally independent. Connect to your inner-self, know yourself, connect to your roots, embrace your cultural identity, and embrace your original language. Take action now.

Etymology of Compendiums of all Gods and The Almighty Creator

THE END

The greatest war, is the war of disunity among global "black people" under the disguise of manipulative man-made religious books (Bible and Quran) pushed by the Arab infiltrators, and the Catholic-Roman-Christian invaders. To date, "black people" would fight over these "fake religions" instead of choosing the bond that should unite them; which is the ethereal supernatural melanated "dark matter" God-coded genetic force embedded at the bedrock of our DNA. -Samuel K. Anderson

Thank you for Reading and Studying

ETYMOLOGY of COMPENDIUMS of all GODS and The ALMIGHTY CREATOR

by

Samuel K. Anderson

Website: SamuelAnderson777.com
Linktree: https://linktr.ee/officialsamuelanderson777
Tiktok: SamuelAnderson777
Instagram: @real_officialsamuelanderson777
Email: SamuelAnderson777@yahoo.com

ABOUT THE AUTHOR:

Samuel K. Anderson (BSBA-Accounting, MBA-Asset Management, University of The Incarnate Word) is a Ghanaian American citizen. He has served as an astute leader, motivator, philanthropist, father, entrepreneur, mentor, educator, researcher, author, and an avid continuous learner of wisdom, philosophy and spirituality.

His preferred areas of speaking and expertise cover but not limited to Consciousness and Self-Awareness, Emotional Intelligence and Empathy, Ethics and Moral Frameworks, Creativity and Imagination, Human Connection and Community, Personal Growth and Transformation, Spirituality and Transcendence, Philosophical Inquiry and Critical Thinking, Embracing Uncertainty and Paradox, and Holistic Understanding and Integration. He loves sharing his ethereal wisdom and knowledge.

Samuel K. Anderson is a visionary thinker, and ethereal wisdom keeper, ready to collaborate with any innovative future forward focused team! His expertise in intuitive technological advancements can elevate AI developments, infusing them with deeper comprehension, empathy, and human-centric approaches. He seeks to someday be in a position to guide AI development with philosophical and spiritual insights, enhance emotional intelligence and empathy in AI interactions, foster creative and imaginative AI solutions, integrate holistic understanding and human connection into AI design, and explore the frontiers of consciousness and self-awareness in AI.

A motivational and life coach speaker. He served in his early formal education years as the Regional Trustee for the Eastern Regional Students' Representative Council, with the Council's aim to Emancipate Students through Dialogue and a Philosophy of Non-Violence, President of an NGO that aimed at educating the youths on drug abuse, Counselor, and Teacher. He completed formal bible training education, studied Theology at Central University College, before transitioning to San Antonio College, TX USA, then transferred to University of The Incarnate Word, TX USA to pursue bachelor's degree in Accounting, and an MBA with concentration in Asset Management (Real Estate & Finance).

Etymology of Compendiums of all Gods and The Almighty Creator

www.ingramcontent.com/pod-product-compliance
Lightning Source LLC
LaVergne TN
LVHW021754060526
838201LV00058B/3085